The Advertising Concept Book

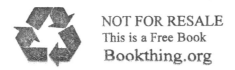

NOT FOR RESALE
This is a Free Book
Bookthing.org

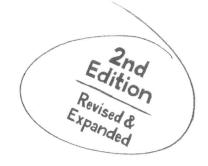

2nd Edition

Revised & Expanded

The Advertising Concept Book

Think Now, Design Later

A
complete
guide to
creative ideas,
strategies
and campaigns

Pete Barry

with over 450 illustrations

Thames & Hudson

Copyright © 2008 and 2012 Pete Barry

All Rights Reserved. No part of this publication may be reproduced or transmitted in any form or by any means, electronic or mechanical, including photocopy, recording or any other information storage and retrieval system, without prior permission in writing from the publisher.

First published in 2008 in paperback in the United States of America by Thames & Hudson Inc., 500 Fifth Avenue, New York, New York 10110

thamesandhudsonusa.com

Revised and expanded second edition 2012

Library of Congress Catalog Card Number 2011937503

ISBN 978-0-500-29031-6

Printed and bound in China by Toppan Printing

Unless otherwise stated, the illustrations in this book are the Author's interpretations of the concepts that were presented to the client.

Every effort has been made to trace the copyright owners of the advertisements used in this book. The Author and Publisher apologize for any unintentional omissions. We would be pleased to insert an appropriate acknowledgment in any reprint of this publication.

For Dad

Special thanks to Jean Koeppel, Steve Montgomery, Tony Cullingham, Nik Roope, Kev Palmer, Justin Kramm, Seb Royce, James Leigh, Darren Giles, Sarah Cooper, John Rodrigues, Joel Bronzeman, and, of course, everyone at Thames & Hudson.

Thanks also to the creative people responsible for the ideas displayed throughout this book. Without them it could not exist.

On the back cover, above, left: *Client: Mattel, Chile. Agency: JWT, Chile. Creatives: Matias Lecaros, Tomas Vidal, Sergio Rosati.*

Below, left: *Client: The Economist. Agency: Abbott Mead Vickers BBDO, London. Creatives: Matt Doman, Ian Heartfield.*

Right: *Client: Playground Outdoor Equipment Stores. Agency: Åkestam Holst, Stockholm. Creatives: Andreas Ullenius, Paul Collins, Adam Reuterskiold, Ellinor Bjarnolf.*

Contents

Welcome to the Second Edition

It took me four years to complete the first edition of The Advertising Concept Book. *Since its publication in 2008, the ad industry has continued to evolve with some truly inspiring work, driven by improved technology and more sophisticated implementations of new media. Socially, Facebook and Twitter are the undisputed Siamese twins; staples for any brand that wants to be liked and followed.*

While engaging, two-way brand conversations have continued to join or replace one-way, interruptive work, we have continued to witness, enjoy, and debate some traditional breakthrough campaigns—for famous, fledgling, and fading brands. In TV alone we've welcomed some legendary characters, including a musky hunk on a horse, the world's most interesting man, and a gifted gorilla performing a Phil Collins' drum fill.

Wherever possible, I've strived to improve this edition of the book— while remaining loyal to its premise: concept comes first. As for new content, I've included a much-expanded Interactive chapter, plus additional exercises and recent award-winning campaigns sprinkled throughout the book.

Much like the American bachelor's degree or Presidential term, four years seems like the ideal period of time to reflect, acknowledge, and celebrate the latest round of timeless advertising.

Thank you for reading, and I hope to see you all again after my next campaign trail.

Pete Barry
Brooklyn, 2012

Gold
Silver
Bronze
Lead

 Great ads start with great ideas. **AdvertisingConceptBook.com**

50 years of timeless, award-winning ad campaigns – in the form of over 400 'roughs' – to help you think now, design later.

Introduction

Concept Over Execution, Substance Over Style

There have been hundreds of great ad campaigns over the years, but there are surprisingly few great books on how to create this level of work. (By "create," I mean those books that focus on concepts and ideas, rather than on the look or final execution of an ad.)

Since the emergence of so-called "Concept Advertising"* in the 1950s and 1960s (the basis of Larry Dobrow's rare, timeless book *When Advertising Tried Harder* [1984]) sadly only a handful of genuine ad titans (of which I'm certainly not one) have shared their words of wisdom on paper. Although insightful, many of these "ad man texts"—waxing lyrical about business-winning philosophies and set-in-concrete creative dos and don'ts—are starting to show their age.

There are also plenty of terrific graphic design books out there, written by much more worthy design folk than myself. Plus every year there's a new batch of award books which will hopefully inspire. Oh, and don't forget those coffee table ad books that look just like cut-and-pasted awards books. And if it's the latest computer software skills you're after, the choice of manuals and how-to guides is expanding by the day.

This book, however, deals solely with the first and most important step toward creating great, timeless advertising: *concept.*

Without a great concept you have nothing but mutton dressed as lamb. The best choice of type or color palette or photography or illustration can't save a bad idea. (Or as someone once crudely put it: "You can't polish a turd.") Concept is to advertising what the little black dress is to fashion: it will always be in demand.

(Most) Great Ideas are Timeless

Art direction, more so than copy, can really date an ad. Trendy art direction techniques in print and TV advertising are coming and going more quickly than ever. But if you take these elements away, one can judge the concept *behind* the advertising, rather than the execution in *front* of it.

Or as Stavros Cosmopulos once wrote:

> *"I've seen stick figures scribbled on wet lunchroom napkins so blurred you could barely discern what was represented. But an idea was there, and it had a life of its own. The words and pictures spring to life in your mind, stimulated and inspired by the basic strength and dynamism of the idea.… Make the layouts rough and the ideas fancy."*

As part of *The Advertising Concept Book*'s determined focus on simplicity and concept, I have chosen to use only hand-drawn versions of appropriate work (also known as art director's thumbnails, roughs, comps, scamps, or tissues). This way, the work is judged by its content, not by its cover. And in terms of my own work, I'd rather have a portfolio of brilliant-thinking roughs than brilliant-looking duffs. Showing fifty years' worth of rough comps not only helps teachers to explain why an "old" ad is still a great ad, but it also forces students to think now and design later, hence reversing their initial temptation to grab a computer instead of a pencil.

But before some of you ad folk say, "I've seen that idea of using thumbnails before"—*so have I.* Rough layouts have been used in pitches, presentations, portfolios, and brainstorming sessions for many years. The fact is, I could have easily presented all the ads in finished form with the same thoughts and words and the book would still have worked. But I soon realized that hand-drawn roughs are definitely the most appropriate solution for a textbook focusing on the topic of concepts and ideas—something that, as far as I know, has never been done.

---

*Note: some designers and advertising creatives, including the ingenious Bob Gill, prefer the term "ideas" rather than "concept," believing the latter should be reserved for Einstein-sized thinking only. One could easily argue that advertising "ideas" sounds too lightweight and general. Depending on their background, some people will use "concept" to mean a big campaign idea that came out of the strategy, into which smaller ideas (executions) are injected. The US tends to use "concept," whereas the UK prefers "idea." It really doesn't matter. I believe that "concept" and "idea" are the same thing: it's what comes after the strategy, and before the executions. I will therefore use the two definitions interchangeably throughout the book. As for its title, *The Advertising Concept Book* simply sounded better to me than *The Advertising Idea Book.*

Well into writing this book, I came across an interesting quote that further convinced me to use thumbnail sketches rather than final artwork. After judging piles of highly finished student campaigns for a CMYK competition, executive creative director Tom Hudder made this fitting remark:

"I still wish that students didn't feel so enslaved to Photoshop. It's a shame that I wasn't sent one pencil drawing. It would be interesting to see how much better these folks might work without the handcuffs (at the concept stage) of technology."

Although this book makes a solid attempt to highlight some timeless ad concepts, not *every* great ad concept is timeless. After all, things do change: people, society, fashion, technology, etc. In some ways the world today is more liberal and carefree than ever. In other ways it's more dictatorial and politically correct. We as consumers are becoming more and more conceptually sophisticated, visually literate and tech-savvy, and yet as a consequence, increasingly wary and intolerant of both the hard and soft sell advertising approach (see Hard Sell vs. Soft Sell, page 13).

Learn to Draw

If the reason for this is still unclear, here's an explanation from famed art director Ron Brown:

"It is an advantage to be able to draw, as it enables you to put down an idea on paper. If you understand perspective, know how light behaves, how anatomy works and how to make use of white space, it will help you do a layout. I use a Pentel to draft an ad and a computer to craft it."

Why Advertise?

This question comes up in the classes I teach every year (usually from the S.S.S., or "single skeptical student").

You'd think the basic answer is obvious, right? That advertising is a tried and tested way to get a product or service noticed in a highly competitive world, etc., etc…

But then the S.S.S. invariably quips: "Yeah, but why bother to do anything creative? Why not just say what the product is?"

"What?!" I'm stunned.

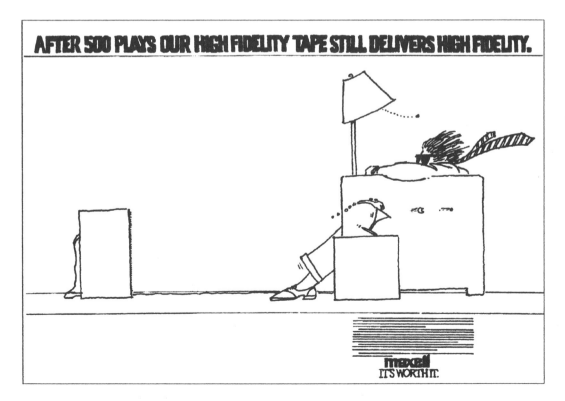

It all began with a pen: Lars Anderson's original art director's rough of the iconic "Man in the Chair" ad. **Client:** *Maxell.* **Agency:** *Scali, McCabe, Sloves.* **Creatives:** *Lars Anderson, Peter Levathes.*

How refreshing: a computer company reminds us that the computer is merely a tool. *Client: Microsoft.* *Agency: Euro RSCG Wnek Gosper, London.* *Creatives: Tim Garth, Steve Eltringham.*

The man that invented the computer didn't come up with the idea sitting in front of a computer.

Your PC is a waste of time. There, we've said it. Never thought you'd hear that from Microsoft, did you? But yes. You see we've come to realise that irrelevant e-mail, meaningless admin, endless charts, the bywords of the modern office, are chewing away at your most valuable resource. Good old fashioned thinking time.

In Office 2000 you'll find a range of tips, tricks and new technology that will dramatically reduce the amount of your day you're spending mindlessly at work. Step back from your PC and rediscover some mental breathing space. Never know, might come up with an idea that puts us out of business. Microsoft. Like your thinking.

Microsoft

The student continues: "Why not just do what our local car dealer does. He has the worst TV ads in the world. He's on all the time, a different ad each week. Everyone finds him annoying, and yet he's made a million from it."

At which point I usually say something along these lines: "The only reason why he's making so much money is because his ads *are* on all the time. He's boring people into submission. They get brainwashed. They forget whether they even like the ad. Plus, it's a regional ad, so the media is relatively cheap, and he won't have as much competition as a national brand. But most importantly, I guarantee he'd be *even richer* in the long run if he did one great ad, rather than a hundred terrible ones."

I continue my point: "It's like a male identical twin chatting to a woman in a bar. He communicates with a string of bad pick-up lines. She can't get away. Then the second identical twin walks in. She wants to die. Twin #2 walks up to her, *but instead* whispers one simple, natural, original line into her ear. She is immediately disarmed. Then they get married and have lots of children. Twin #1? He's probably still at the bar."

That usually convinces the class S.S.S. or at the very least disarms them.

Yet such misconceptions aren't just common amongst first-time ad students. Business people can have the same idea. I was in a meeting once at an architectural firm and the Gap ads came up in conversation. Knowing that I worked in advertising, one slightly conceited architect said to me, "Gap is losing money. They're going down the drain. Their famous ads are not working."

Then I looked at him, and politely said, "How do you know it's because of their ads, and not another problem within the company? Like their brand, their stores, or even their product. Perhaps their advertising is the only thing that's stopping them from losing a lot more money."

At which point he went very quiet.

The Power of Advertising

We all know about advertising's potential to change the way people think, enough to sell a product into the billions. But advertising is powerful even at a very local level, as well as on a national or global one. For example, three years ago I was disgusted with the amount of dog poop along the tree-lined sidewalk outside my apartment. (Poop and flip-

flops don't mix.) The guilty dog owners were clearly ignoring the many residents' signs, most of which were either witty or insulting, but unsuccessful nonetheless. So then I decided to have a stab. In the worst hit area I placed a temporary sign on a tree, which simply read: "This is a sidewalk, not a toilet," followed by the standard "please clean up after your dog." I wanted the tone to be direct, yet slightly condescending. As I left for work the next day I noticed that my sign had disappeared—I assumed an angry dog owner had removed it. But when I returned later that day it was back. Not only that, but every tree on the block had a photocopied version of the sign stapled to it. Within a day the poop had gone, and has yet to return. My "ad" was far from a One Show Gold, but it did do its job.

"Good is the Enemy of Great"

The French writer and philosopher Voltaire penned this famous line (later adopted and applied to advertising by the great Bill Bernbach). As a result, this book attempts to focus on producing great ideas, rather than just good ones, and to help you land a job at a great agency rather than a good one (let's not even entertain the idea of working at one of the many bad "ad agencies" out there).

Put simply, the aim of any creative advertising person is to produce a TV or radio commercial so great that people will want to record it, or a poster so great that people will want to tear it from the wall and take it home.

In his book, *The Do-It-Yourself Lobotomy* (2002), Tom Monahan makes this observation:

"A big part of being a highly realized creative person is having an open mind and being able to recognize great ideas even when you aren't looking for them, perhaps even when they are the last thing you are looking for."

You're a Market Stall Holder

Some people hate the advertising industry. An old neighbor of mine (now a retired bank manager) recently said to me: "Your Dad tells me you're in Advertising. So in other words, you make people buy things that they don't need?"

I was taken aback. True, many products are what people want rather than need. But he would never have said that to me if I worked in, say, a village market selling goods like dish cloths or kitchen knives. It's okay for those people to shout out

We've all advertised something.

adindustry.org

Another argument to justify advertising. Poster to promote the ad industry, and improve its image. Other executions: wedding ring, sports fan with painted face, anti-war sign. *Client: adindustry.org. **Students:** Jamie Gaul, Roussina Valkova.*

product names and prices, or come up with witty one-liners to draw people in. (I once heard an East London salesman shout out, "'Ere luv, if you want to finish your husband off tonight, I've got just the knife for it.") If it means selling more goods, why not? He knows that the other market stall holders will be doing the same. Everyone has to pay the bills. The point is, no one is being forced to buy the goods. They're simply being advertised to.

I wish I'd thought of saying that to my neighbor.

The Role of Advertising
Stephen Leacock wrote: "Advertising may be described as the science of arresting the human

intelligence long enough to get money from it." Although my neighbor may be unusual in his hatred of advertising, it is true to say that the general public don't care about advertising. That's understandable. People have far more important things to watch or read or worry about than an ad.

My Uncle Bob once said, "Commercial breaks on TV are like a clown knocking on your door every 15 minutes. The first time he asks to come into your lounge and do a little performance, you say 'no!' But what's really annoying is, he keeps trying—every 15 minutes! Do you answer the door again? Of course not. And that's why I turn off the TV when the commercials come on."

That's where the challenge lies. To stand a chance of getting an ad noticed (and remembered) it has to be great. Like you've only got one chance to knock on that door. And great ads come from great strategic thinking. The actual ad itself is just one brick in a large wall. It's the final, top-most piece of a giant pyramid, which looks roughly like the diagram opposite, above.

There are three main sections in this list. To make it easier to understand, think of it instead as an iceberg. Between the Business Plan/Idea and the Campaign/Advertising Idea and Executions is the Advertising Strategy. But the only part of the iceberg consumers ever get to see is Executions (with or without a tagline).

Why So Many Bad Ads?
Depending on which country you're in, between approximately 90 and 99% of ads suck. That's because great work scares people. Especially clients. They spend a lot of money at the risk of losing a lot if the advertising fails. And most agencies are scared of losing clients. This largely explains why so much advertising is safe, copycat work. Plus clients have their own people to keep happy: their own boxes to tick. But when a client is educated by the agency about the mutual goals that only creative advertising can bring (to build brands, make money, and win awards), the more they understand and appreciate groundbreaking work. In fact, it was a client who once said it best: "Whenever there is great work, there's always a great client." (See also Critiques and Subjectivity, page 39.)

Remember, as a student your work is purely spec (short for "speculative"). The concept and execution should be great, but the bigger challenge exists in the real world—selling the work and

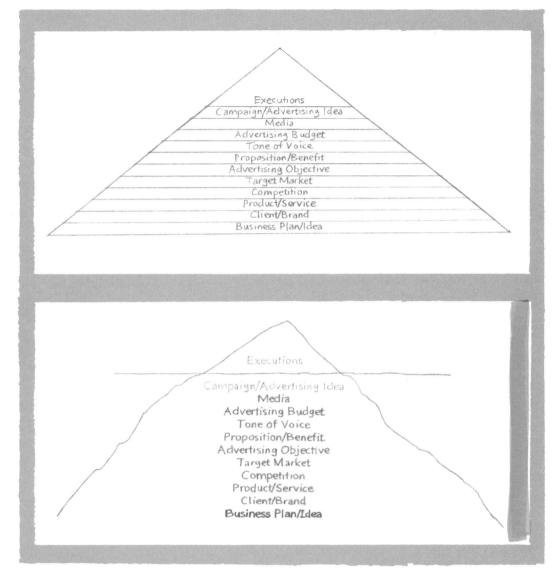

The pyramid shows the layers of thinking that go into a final ad, or execution.

The iceberg illustrates how the only thing the consumer gets to see is the execution. The bigger thinking lies below the surface.

getting it produced. (The Presenting and Selling Your Work chapter explores this topic in detail.) Good or bad, ads are an intrusion into people's lives. The average person in an average city on an average day is exposed to a staggering 5,000 ads. At best, we only remember the great ones, and, perhaps, the really bad ones. The rest are invisible, like wallpaper. So ask yourself: will your ad be remembered? And if so, is it for being great?

Hard Sell vs. Soft Sell

You can argue that over the years the "hard sell" approach to advertising has proven to be financially successful. These type of ads occur across all media, typically shoving the product or special offer down your throat, leaving little space for anything creative or conceptual. This approach might work for certain consumers at certain times, but imagine if all ads were like this. It would drive people crazy. Research shows that today's consumer is becoming more and more sensitive, skeptical, and complex. They need more of a "soft sell" (selling without the obvious sales pitch). This approach, due to its relative subtlety, is a lot tougher to pull off than a hard sell. So for the purposes of this book (and your future challenging-yet-glamorous ad career) start thinking in terms of creating soft sell ads. But make sure you don't think so soft that it's unclear

Think different.

www.apple.com

Dr. Martin Luther King, Jr. One of the many famous mavericks used in Apple's "Think Different" campaign. *Client: Apple. Agency: TBWA/Chiat/ Day. Creatives: Craig Tanimoto, Jessica Schulman, Eric Grunbaum, Margret Midgett, Susan Alinsangham, Bob Kuperman, Ken Youngleib, Amy Moorman, Ken Segall, Rob Siltanen.*

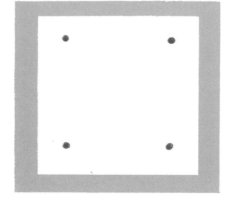

The Four-Dot Test (follow the instructions given in the exercise).

what you're trying to sell. In other words: think hard, sell soft.

Note: "soft sell" is also a term used to describe grassroots marketing and advertising.

....

Exercise: **take a hard sell ad (a basic price-led ad, for example) and "soften" it. Keep the offer in the ad, but create an idea that works as an integral part of the offer, not something that looks stuck onto it.**

....

Be a Thinker

The creative team is usually made up of a copywriter (words) and an art director (pictures). Don't worry if you're still unsure which role fits you best. They overlap. More often than not, a great art director has the potential to be a great copywriter, and vice versa. The copywriter can have a brilliant idea about the art direction; the art director could come up with a great tagline.

Anyhow, you will have plenty of time to be pigeonholed as soon as you start your career. For now, just concentrate on being an art director/ copywriter. Or a copywriter/art director. Better yet, a thinker. And as the famous Apple tagline requests, think different.

What helps you think? Simply absorb yourself in anything and everything: movies, poetry, photography, art, novels, newspapers, current events, sport, etc. Without question, the best advertising people are renaissance people.

....

Exercise: **one of the most clichéd, overused phrases within business as a whole is "think outside the box." It basically means think beyond the usual ways of doing things. This expression is also a clue to solving the problem in (see left): "The Four-Dot Test." Using only three straight lines, connect all four dots without ever taking your pen off the paper. (Answer on page 284.)**

....

Part Logic, Part Creative

The human brain is essentially two interconnected brains, right and left. Until 1962, it was thought that the two hemispheres performed roughly the

Strategic/Creative Team (or Individual)

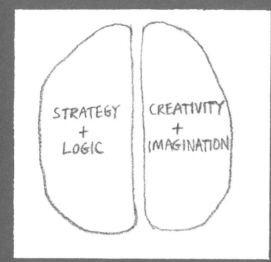

Left Brain/Right Brain

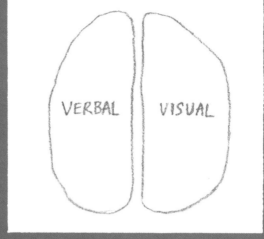

Left Brain/Right Brain

Consumer response

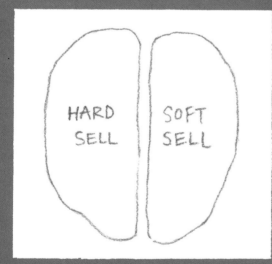

Left Brain/Right Brain

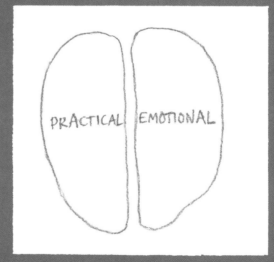

Left Brain/Right Brain

Top left The ideal team/individual possesses a combination of "left brain" strategy and logic, plus "right brain" creativity and imagination.

Top right "Left brain" verbal skills combine with "right brain" visual skills.

Above, left The ideal ad is some combination of hard and soft sell.

Above, right An ad should try to talk to people's logical, practical side (their heads), as well as the emotional, creative side (their hearts).

same functions. Roger Sperry finally proved that some functions are located predominantly in one or other side of the brain. It seems we have two minds. For example, the left brain specializes in verbal and language understanding, and the right is for visual and mathematical problems.

So in terms of producing successful ads, the best strategic, creative team (or individual) is one that/who possesses a balance of logic and imagination, verbal and visual skills, etc. (Many creative teams resemble the classic funny guy/straight guy comedy team, where each member is almost totally reliant on the other in order for their act to succeed.) At the other end of this equation is another human being: the consumer. As readers and viewers of ads, we respond best to *ads* that possess a similar balance. In turn, we make purchases for inner logical, practical, and rational reasons, as well as for emotional and creative ones. Whether you like or dislike an ad is determined by one side of the brain, whereas the other side decides whether or not the ad has convinced you that the product is worth buying/using.

In other words, too much logic will most likely produce a boring, factual, "hard sell" ad, and too much creativity and emotional pull may lack substance or a selling idea. Therefore, the goal for any agency is to ensure that every ad appeals to *both* sides of a consumer's brain/mind.

Work Methods

You have two choices. You can learn to build a portfolio on your own, or work in a pair (a "creative team").

The *good* things about working on your own are:

- Sole ownership of the ideas (you don't have to share the glory)
- Sole choice in terms of when and where you want to work
- Not dealing with each other's egos and habits
- Not having to look at someone for weeks or months (or sometimes years) on end

The *bad* things about working on your own are:

- Can't bounce ideas off someone (the "two heads are better than one" theory)
- Can't make 1 + 1 = 3 (the "two heads are better than two" theory, a.k.a. "the whole is greater than the sums of its parts")

- Harder to get motivated (can't push each another if working alone)
- Less employable (countries such as the UK prefer to hire teams)
- Can't share the workload
- Can't share the pressures
- Can be lonely

Based purely on this simple list, it seems that teamwork makes more sense than working on your own.

How a Team Finds an Idea

No two people are the same. So it stands to reason that no two pairs are the same either. As a result, every creative team works differently. They come up with ideas differently, and they divide tasks differently. For instance, let's take a simple example whereby a team has to come up with a new tagline for Nike. The creative team is made up of individual A and individual B. The year is 1980. Here are three basic scenarios:

Scenario #1: A says, "Just try anything." B says, "Just do anything" and A says, "Just do it."

Scenario #2: A says lots of lines until B stops A at "Just do it."

Scenario #3: B thinks of "Just do it" that night in the shower. Tells A the next day. A loves it, and possibly returns the favor on their next project.

Note that the result is the same each time. Rarely will a team arrive at an answer in the exact same way. It's not that kind of work. Each scenario can happen at any time, on any brief. The important thing is that each person is bringing something to the table. So long as the end result is great, it shouldn't matter where or how it came about.

So what you *don't* want is something like this:

Scenario #4: B thinks of "Just do it" that night in the shower, and tells A the next day. A tries to convince B that it's no good, probably because A didn't think of it first.

(If they can't agree, they should let someone like their creative director decide.)

Remember, ideas are rarely created in a vacuum. It's not like being a fine artist. Once you have a job, you will inevitably find yourself working with others, in a pair, or part of a larger team. This isn't always a bad thing, as outlined above. If possible, try to work with as many people as you can, until you find someone that you work really well with.

The Greatest Barriers to Creativity

Whether working alone or in a group, try to overcome the following barriers while coming up with ideas (also known as—I hate this word—"ideation"). These barriers have been adapted from a section in Tom Monahan's book, *The Do-It-Yourself Lobotomy*.

Fear of the unknown
Fear of looking stupid
Premature judgment of ideas
Attachment
  • Attachment to old ideas
  • Attachment to past successes
  • Resistance to change
  • Reluctance to explore better methods
  • Stopping at the first good idea

Ideas Make the World Go Round

When the phrase "money makes the world go round" is used, one key point is forgotten— *someone created "money."* Coins didn't just appear from the sky one day. Money began as a concept, an idea. So whether you work in the world of advertising or not, the ability to come up with ideas is the most important skill in the world.

Advertising is Not Always the Answer

There are some cases when advertising is not the solution, or is not necessary. Here are some examples:

When a country loses countless lives due to war or a natural disaster, the best way to honor and remember those victims is to build a memorial— an idea that has yet to be bettered. An ad might be able to tell people to visit the site, but a well-designed memorial is a far more powerful piece of communication (see The Pentagon New Day Memorial, page 244).

Or perhaps the product is not marketable, and even the best ads won't help. For example, if men are not buying lip salves because they feel like a woman applying lipstick, the answer might be to make a product that's more appealing to them, e.g., a chunky "man-sized" stick in macho-sounding

flavors. (You may laugh, but this kind of thinking worked for tissues!)

And there are also those rare cases when a product is so successful it doesn't need anything to advertise. But even the mighty Marks & Spencer has had to reverse its "word of mouth" philosophy and succumb to the powers of advertising.

Here's to Ad People

If there was ever a TV game show that tested contestants on creative skills and problem solving, I'd put money on the team from an ad agency to win. One thing that creating great ads will teach you is how to come up with original, clever ideas, and communicate these ideas concisely. Most ad people can appreciate and apply many other disciplines into a final creative product. So even if you don't become a copywriter or art director, or even enter the industry, you will always be able to apply these unique skills to any job or pastime. Famous advertising alumni include Ridley Scott (director), Salman Rushdie (author), and Gary Dahl (inventor of the "Pet Rock").

Here's a real example that demonstrates the ability of an advertising creative, compared to people in similar fields. As a kid, I remember watching a TV show that announced the four finalists of a special competition. The brief was to make a short film, in any style, celebrating the work of the 1950s pop singer/songwriter Buddy Holly. Two main requirements were to use one of his songs and to spend a limited budget.

The first finalist was a claymation-style model maker, who painstakingly animated a cartoon figure of Buddy dancing to "Peggy Sue." The second was a graphic designer, who used animated typography moving in time with the song's lyrics. The third was a filmmaker, who shot an arty black-and-white video of a Buddy Holly look-a-like. Then came the last finalist. This team made a pair of huge black-framed glasses out of cardboard (in the style of Buddy's signature specs), and attached them in front of a camera lens. They then went up to all kinds of people in the street, filming each one as they shoved their face onto the glasses, cheerfully singing along to a famous Buddy Holly track.

What a clever, simple, fun idea that was! It really captured the spirit of Buddy Holly's songs. Above all, this particular finalist thought beyond their specialized craft, and deep into Buddy's music, its impact, and its mass appeal. Twenty years later

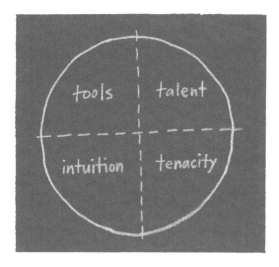

Creativity: a combination of tools, talent, intuition, and tenacity.

and I still remember the idea. And to return to my original point, I also remember that its creator, who deservedly won the competition, worked at an advertising agency.

Tools Not Rules

The Advertising Concept Book attempts to get to the heart of the creative process in ways that other guides haven't. That said, I have made a conscious effort not to produce a book of "rules" on how to create great advertising. As Ed McCabe said, "I have no use for rules. They only rule out the brilliant exception." So please think of them more as *tools* or guidelines. In the same way that a computer is a tool, this book can help you to think of an idea, but it can't supply it.

The tools in the following chapters aren't merely the result of examining ad industry case studies and then post-rationalizing why each one is so creative and successful. I discovered some of the tools through teachers, colleagues, bosses, and ad gurus. But most were developed through actually teaching: the result of personally having critiqued and directed 15,000 student campaigns over a five-year period. It's exhausting work at times, but whenever I see something great, suddenly my weekly 600-mile round trip is worth it.

Teaching. That's been *my* tool. It forces you not only to think, but also to rethink everything you have learnt beforehand. Not just *what* makes great advertising, but *how* to make it great. Again, producing a great, creative ad doesn't just come

down to using certain tools. The rest comes down to a combination of talent*, intuition, and tenacity. And those are things you can't really teach.

As a final note, don't try to memorize the tools word for word. Simply apply them (starting with the exercises included throughout the chapters). This book is as much about practice as it is theory. And as I have discovered, practice can also produce new theories. Or as I prefer to call them, insights.

*Creative "talent" is dependent on the level and number of ideas, imagination, copy/art craft skills, etc.

Finding the Truth

People don't like being lied to, especially by an ad. Take those commercials for hair dye and implants that proclaim, "no one will tell it's not real." But as Jerry Seinfeld once pointed out, "no, *everyone* can tell!"

So if I had to pinpoint one reoccurring theme throughout the majority of the greatest advertising over the last fifty years—aside from simplicity of concept—it would have to be this:

A truth.

It can exist anywhere and everywhere, on many different levels, from concept to execution: be it within the strategy, the idea, the tagline, the headline, the body copy, the visual, the branding, the typography, or the tone. It can be a large or small truth, general or specific, exaggerated, refined, induced, or deduced.

So remember this the next time you come across a particularly profound, insightful tagline, or find yourself reading an Absolut ad and thinking, "Hey, it's true, that does look like the shape of their bottle!"

For as the almighty art director above once said, "truth will out."

Aim High

In terms of the quality of your student work, aim high. In fact, aim higher than high. If you virtually want to guarantee getting a job within the creative department of one of the top agencies, aim to have work that's *even better* than the best award-winning work out there. The fact that you don't have to answer to any clients, or deal with agency politics and egos, gives you the extra advantage you need to pull it off.

01
Basic Tools

What Do You Want to Say?

This is perhaps the most important thing to determine before you start the advertising creative process. Before you start working on any ad, you must ask yourself, "What is this particular company or organization trying to say about their product or service in their current advertising?" If it's unclear, or it's a new product on the market, ask instead: "What could, or what should, they be saying?"

The common term for this is *proposition*. In other words, what is the client proposing that its product or service does? What is the client promising the consumer? An even clearer term for "proposition" and "promise" is perhaps *benefit*. Therefore, what is the benefit of this particular product or service?

Note that I use the word "benefit" rather than "benefits." It is very important that you communicate *one* benefit. In other words, what is the singular most important thing about the product: what could its major strength be, which hopefully sets it apart from its competitors?

This sounds simple, but it's amazing how often clients will try (or want) to say more than one thing: "but our product is fast *and* durable." This may be true—but it doesn't matter. You only have seconds to get your message across. You have to be single-minded. It's hard enough to create something that clearly communicates *one* benefit in a short time, let alone two or three. It's just too much for the reader/viewer/listener to take in. Ultimately, it weakens the advertising message, the client and its brand. To summarize:

single-minded = single-minded = single-minded
  proposition   promise   benefit

Great advertising has stuck to the same single proposition over many years: Volvo is safe, FedEx is fast, Tango is really orangey, Duracell is long lasting, etc. (see Tackling the Double Proposition, page 145, for rare exceptions). There have also been many case studies where as soon as the client has changed its single proposition, it has seriously jeopardized the brand image.

Most importantly, an ad will often be lacking an idea because the proposition is unclear. If you don't know what the proposition is, how can you expect your idea to relate back to what the product does? Therefore, whether explicitly or implicitly, always try to tell the consumer something about the product.

··

Exercise: **rewrite the third proposition in the simplest terms (if possible one word) from the following list. The first two are done for you:**

Place your hands under a Brand X Hand Dryer and it will dry them completely in approximately 15 seconds = Bone-dry hands in 15 seconds

Brand X Hand Dryers have a built-in super-generator engine = Powerful

Brand X Hand Dryers are the only paperless hand dryers to be approved by various environmental and conservational organizations =

Exercise: **turn on the TV, or grab a magazine or paper. Look at each ad and try to work out what each one is trying to say about the product. Is there one benefit being communicated? Are they saying too many things? In other words, identify the proposition.**

··

Who Are You Talking to?

Once you know what you're saying, you have to decide whom you are saying it to. Who is the product (via the ad) talking to? Who you choose to target will determine what you want to say and how you want to say it? It's a great springboard into ideas and concepts.

The final piece of the advertising puzzle: how to make a good ad great. *Client: The Economist. Agency: Abbott Mead Vickers BBDO, London. Creatives: Matthew Abbott, Martin Casson.*

A target audience (also known as "target group" or "target market") is defined by many things, including:

- Age
- Income
- Education
- Marital/Family Status
- Occupation
- Behavior, Tastes, and Attitudes (relating to product and market)
- Hobbies

Target audiences can vary tremendously in size. Broadly speaking, it helps not to be too general. Try to focus on a typical person within that audience. Many ad gurus believe that the best advertising in any medium comes from *understanding people.* To do this, you have to "wear different hats," or imagine you are someone else, just as an actor would. During an average ad career, you will work on many products and markets that you're unfamiliar with, let alone a consumer of. In these cases, try to deduce what the consumer's interests, joys, fears, tastes, and biases are. Think about the audience's relationship with the actual product. Ask why, when, where, and how often they use it. Or if they've yet to use it or stopped using it, find out why (see also Target Market/Group/Audience, page 49).

....

Exercise: **watch TV ads, or look in a magazine or paper and try to work out** *whom* **each ad is directed at, or talking to. Try to be as specific as possible. In other words, identify the target.**

....

And Finally…How Do You Want to Say it?

This is the hardest part of all. You know what you want to say and who to say it to. But *how* you say it is the difference between a good ad and a great ad. (And by "how," I don't mean the tone of voice, or whether to use words, visuals or both.) "How" is the final piece of the puzzle that keeps ambitious creative people up at night (well some of them, anyway). And yet it's much more than overcoming writer's block and "blank canvas," which is why the majority of this book is dedicated to answering this very question.

Another way to explain this fundamental task of creative advertising is:

It's not what you say. It's how you say it.

This line was the message behind a simply perfect campaign for the AAA School of Advertising (see Push It—Visualizing (Literal vs. Lateral), page 146).

KISS: Keep it Simple, Stupid

This is the most common saying in advertising. It relates partly to the number of benefits (i.e., no more than one), and partly to the actual concept or idea you've created to communicate this benefit. "Keeping it simple" is the first step toward creating a successful ad. The word "stupid" is slightly unexpected, but partly refers to the fact that even experienced creatives often forget this golden rule. One could even argue whether you need it; maybe KIS is enough.

The most famous non-advertising example of KISS is probably Shakespeare's "To be or not to be." (Incredible profundity, in six tiny words!) Muhammad Ali was once invited to give a graduation speech at Harvard University. At the end of an inspiring talk, someone shouted, "Give us a poem!" He paused, and then summed up the occasion in two of the shortest words in the English Language: "Me. We."

Another way of looking at simplicity is: get to the point. Remember, an ad is an intrusion into people's lives. In a newspaper, for example, an ad is competing with the reason why people buy it— the news. Likewise, rarely does a person buy a magazine for the ads. Ed McCabe put it this way: imagine your ad is a smoker looking for a light on a Manhattan sidewalk during rush hour. Which of these two approaches will be more successful in getting someone's attention? Asking a passer-by

"Excuse me, Sir, do you have a light on you?" or simply, "Got a light?"

There's Good-Simple…and There's Bad-Simple

Students will often create an ad that is unquestionably simple—but that's all it is. Simple is not enough. Writing a headline like "Starts every time" (next to a visual of a car in freezing weather) communicates the benefit in a straightforward way, but it's boring! I call this "bad-simple." As David Ogilvy once said, "You cannot bore people into buying your product." Ads must have something else that makes them clever, unexpected, and relevant to the product and its target audience. Writing a line like "Have you ever wondered how the man who drives a snow plough drives *to* the snow plough?" is simple yet profound (unlike the first line). So always aim for "good-simple," rather than "bad-simple." John Hegarty put it best:

"Dramatize the Simple."

SLIP IT: Smile, Laugh, Informs, Provokes, Involves, Think

Here is a basic explanation of the difference between a good ad and a great ad (whether it's a poster, a press ad, a TV ad, a radio ad, ambient ad, online ad, or direct mail ad). A good ad communicates its message from a single-minded proposition:

· Clearly
· Quickly
· Simply
· Relevantly

A great ad stops you, hooks you, and hauls you in. (The way an ad looks—the art direction—is only part of the reason.) An ad's original creativity attracts attention by making you react in *at least one* of the following ways:

· *Smile*
  disarms you
· *Laugh*
  really disarms you
· *Informs*
  tells you something you didn't know
· *Provokes*
  there's a reaction, an emotional response
· *Involves*
  there's a connection, an interaction
· (makes you) *Think*

America is a capitalist country

God© Bless™ America®

Two ways of saying the same thing. The first is slow and literal, the second is fast and lateral.

The creators behind this campaign mastered the art of simplicity on two levels. *Client: London Underground. Agency: BMP DDB, London. Creatives: Richard Flintham, Andy McLeod, Nick Gill, Ewan Patterson.*

Making London simple

Or, S L I P I T for short. I know it sounds corny, but this acronym works as a basic, quick, and easy checklist, a useful mnemonic when still learning how to evaluate an ad (a topic that I will be returning to throughout the book).

These are all things that give an ad *impact*. (And there are more you can add.) But of course the final goal for any ad is to *convince* and *persuade* a potential consumer to invest time or money in your product/service…

Near right Western Union's ad (1962) shows us the power of a telegram. It's also a perfect example of what every ad should achieve. Copy begins: Ignore a telegram? You can't. No one ever ignored a telegram. *Agency: Benton and Bowles. Creatives: Dan Cromer, Jay Folb.*

Far right This direct-mail piece for the Alabama Veterans Memorial reminds people of the double power of a war-related telegram (2000). *Agency: Slaughter Hanson Advertising. Creatives: Marion English, Dave Smith.*

Center This is a question you should ask for each ad you write. *Client: The Economist. Agency: Abbott Mead Vickers BBDO, London. Creative: Mark Fairbanks.*

Bottom This ad would make any commuter stop and think. *Client: Time Out. Agency: Gold Greenlees Trott Limited. Creatives: Steve Henry, Axel Chaldecott.*

Ignore it

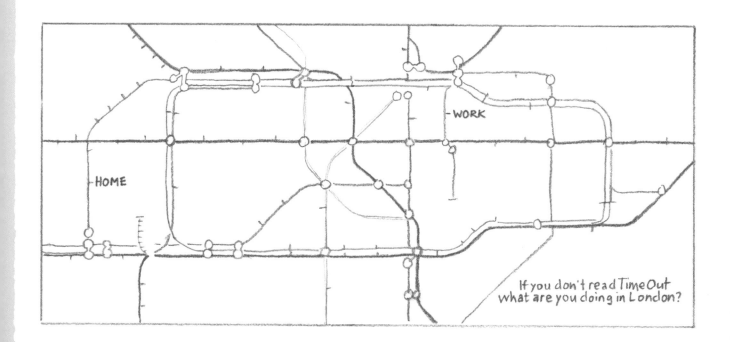

Can you keep people interested or are they easily ooh look, a pigeon.

The Economist

WORK

HOME

If you don't read Time Out what are you doing in London?

(In)effective Creative Advertising: What was the Product?

Many ads are so unoriginal and uncreative, making them instantly forgettable and totally fruitless. These ads have no impact or resonance, invisible in every sense. Neither the ad, the message, nor the product is retained by consumers. There are also many ads that are memorable *as an ad* (concept recall), but the product is forgotten. Whenever anyone makes the all-too-common statement "I don't remember the product," this lack of (product) recall means time and money down the drain.

So just because an ad (for a marketable product) has high impact and retention doesn't mean people will remember which product it is for. That's where branding comes in. And yet even with good branding, it doesn't guarantee the product will sell. That's where relevance and appropriateness comes in: no matter how creative or well branded your idea is, is it right for the product and the target market?

To summarize
Effective, creative advertising is largely:
Impact + Branding + Relevance (= $$$)

Write First, Edit Last

It's highly unrealistic for even the greatest creative person to expect every one of his or her ideas to be an instant award-winner. The higher the level of expectancy, the more pressure you put on yourself, the more frustrating the creative process becomes, and the poorer the results. Coming up with ideas is hard enough as it is, so just get every one down and then decide which ones work later (also known as "brainstorming"). In other words: write first, edit last. As sports fans often point out: the best baseball players, with a batting average of .300, still fail 7 out of 10 times. This brings us neatly onto the next tool.

Note: I'm using the word "write" to mean "create." The phrase "writing an ad" is misleading as it implies only the use of words, whereas an ad can obviously be words and/or pictures. So perhaps imagine this subhead as "write/draw first, edit last" or "create first, edit last."

The 1-in-10 Tool

This simple rule applies to many creative endeavors. It's another way of saying "law of averages." To borrow Thomas Edison's famous line, creativity is 90% perspiration and 10% inspiration. Therefore, if you come up with ten ideas for an ad, it's more likely one of them will be good than if

"I never read
The Economist."

Management trainee. Aged 42.

The pregnant pause.
Make sure
you're not the father.

The Economist

Lose the ability
to slip out of meetings
unnoticed.

The Economist

Client: The Economist. *Agency:* Abbott Mead Vickers/SMS, London. *Creatives:* David Abbott, Ron Brown.

Client: The Economist. *Agency:* Abbott Mead Vickers BBDO, London. *Creatives:* Guy Moore, Tony Malcolm.

Client: The Economist. *Agency:* Abbott Mead Vickers BBDO, London. *Creatives:* Sean Doyle, Dave Dye.

you only came up with five or three or one. This tool works for any part of creative advertising, but especially for headlines, taglines, and visuals. But don't stop at 10 ideas. Do 20, 30, 40 or more. The law of averages will only increase your odds. So don't stop at your first idea, even if you think it's good.

....

Exercise: **write five more headlines in the style of** *The Economist***'s famous print campaign. Then write five more, etc., until you have 20. At the end, show them to a friend in a new, random list. Ask him/her to pick the best three. The best ones should be in the middle to end of your original list.**

Above are a few to start you off.

....

Showing how a window reduces sound is more interesting than telling it with words. *Client: Weru. **Agency:** Scholz & Friends, Berlin. **Creatives:** Kay Luebke, Michael Haeussler. **Creative directors:** Jan Leube, Matthias Spanetgens.*

A visually lateral, less expected way to show the product benefit. *Client: Palladium Fitness Centers. **Agency:** Vitruvio/Leo Burnett, Madrid. **Creative:** Rafa Anton.*

Can You Say Your Idea in One Sentence?

Whether a one-off ad or a campaign idea, and whatever the media, if your idea is truly simple you should be able to describe it in *one sentence*. When screenwriters pitch their 90-page script to busy producers, they do so in one line.

Kill Your Babies

"Babies" refers to those great ideas that we lovingly cling on to, even if we are told they don't work. Applying the 1-in-10 rule is one way to avoid this crazed, precious bond. Why? Because the more ideas you have, the less protective you are of them. (It's much harder to kill an idea if it's the only one you have.)

Give it the "Overnight Test"

Have you ever struggled over a crossword clue, given up and left it, then gone back to it and solved the clue in a split second? Whether you're working on ideas, visuals, or words, use the same approach. Give it the "overnight test" (although it can even work in ten minutes). When you return to the problem, your judgment will be clearer, and your editing skills will be sharper. This is your subconscious at work. Or as art director Steve Montgomery often says to me, "I'm thinking about it even when I'm not thinking about it."

Write Your Ideas Down

It's a fallacy that you always remember a good idea, because how do you know if you've forgotten one? We all forget important stuff from time to time. That's why many great people—from Leonardo da Vinci to contemporary artists, writers, and musicians—write down their ideas. A brief note is usually enough. And even a half idea might become a complete one when you refer back to it later on. Plus, even if you never refer back to it, the mere act of visual, tactile notetaking can help you to remember.

Don't Tell, Show

This is the age-old argument for using pictures instead of words. We all know that a picture is worth a thousand words, and actions speak louder than words. And considering the little amount of time an ad has to communicate, a picture is almost always the quicker option. Plus there's a strong argument to prove that consumers are becoming more and more visual, and less and less literate. In most cases, it's more interesting to show than tell; the visual is more arresting than the headline.

To demonstrate, here are examples of the same idea—one in words, one in pictures.

For *Time Out* (London):
   (Words) Burn the candle at both ends (i.e., work hard, play hard; live life to the full)
   (Picture) A candle, held horizontally, burning at both ends (see page 149)

For Weru Soundproof Windows:
   (Words) Our windows can really reduce the sound of a nearby lawnmower
   (Pictures) Man cutting lawn with a miniature mower (see opposite, above)

For Bic Pens:
   (Words) Our pens last a very long time
   (Pictures) Huge "infinity" sign written in ink (see page 92)

For Palladium Fitness Centers:
   (Words) "I was fat when I joined, and thin when I left."
   (Pictures: literal) Show person before/fat, and person after/thin
   (Pictures: lateral) Entrance = wide door, Exit = narrow door (see opposite, below)

Of course, pictures aren't always more effective than words. There may be times where words are more appropriate and/or more powerful, depending on what you want to say, how you want to say it, and to whom. The "Be Here" campaign for Penguin Books uses the power of pictures to sell, ironically, the power of words (see above, right). And in some cases you might use words to create pictures in the consumer's mind, especially in radio advertising (see Headline Only, Visual Only, or Headline and Visual, page 61; Theater of the Mind, page 230). A print example of this is for Nikon, which is essentially the opposite of the Penguin campaign in that words are used to help create pictures (in this case, famous photographs) in our head.

Imagination: <mark>Don't Reveal, Imply</mark>
People aren't stupid. You don't always need to explain or even show every part of your idea to them. Leaving a bit for the consumer to figure out will engage them with your idea. That's why

Top Ironically, this campaign uses the power of visuals to sell the power of words. Headline: Be here. *Client: Penguin Books.* *Agency: MML, London.* *Creatives: Dean Hunt, Simon Hipwell.*

Above More than words: this ad creates powerful pictures in the consumer's mind. *Client: Nikon.* *Agency: Scali, McCabe, Sloves.* *Creatives: Richard Kelley, Ron Rosen.*

Don't reveal, imply. This ad allows just enough time for the reader to "get it." *Client: Fisher-Price.* **Agency:** *Boase Massimi Pollitt Partnership.* **Creatives:** *Frank Budgen, Bill Gallacher.*

This campaign demonstrates the power of imagination, no matter what springs to mind. **Client:** *ASPCA.* **Agency:** *Saatchi & Saatchi, New York.* **Creatives:** *Jake Benjamin, Mark Voehringer.*

Which of these three kids is wearing Fisher-Price anti-slip roller skates?

Fisher-Price

WHATEVER YOU CAN IMAGINE, WE'VE SEEN WORSE.

Last year, the ASPCA handled over 65,000 cruelty complaints, 6,000 in New York City alone. To learn how you can help prevent cases like this, visit ASPCAspeak.org

ASPCA

imagination is perhaps the most powerful tool of all. So try not to show all your cards. Give them just enough information to be able to "fill in the gaps." Or put another way: *don't reveal, imply.* This is the same principle behind the popular expression "TMI" (too much information) when someone gives an unsubtle or over-detailed explanation. It's the same in advertising. Unless there's a reason for it, subtlety usually prevails over slapstick (see College Humor, page 153).

Remember also that people allow themselves only a few seconds to "get" an ad, especially a print ad. So don't make it too obscure or too hard to fill in the gaps either—people don't have time. Start with the most obvious execution of your idea, and keep making subtle changes until you get the right balance. If in doubt, test each version on a different person (the same person might "get it" based on knowing the previous version, which is misleading and inaccurate).

In other words: *start literal, finish lateral.*

As an example, look at the press ad for Fisher-Price's non-slip roller skates (see opposite, above). This ad could have easily shown the two other kids on the floor, or in mid-fall. But it's funnier imagining them falling on the floor. It's the same idea, just executed slightly differently. The technique of "leaving something to the imagination" applies to other mediums, including TV and radio (see the TV chapter and the Radio chapter).

Compare the two headlines/ads. The first reveals, while the second (the real ad) implies. *Client:* Brown-Forman Corporation. *Agency:* Court, Burkett and Company, London.

The Opposite Tool:
Turn Everything on its Head

Doing the opposite is an exercise worth trying. At worst you'll produce something different and unexpected but useless. At best, it can be brilliant, inspiring, and even revolutionary. The opposite tool applies to strategies, ideas, headlines, taglines, art direction, and visuals. If there's a method to the madness so much the better.

Strategies and Ideas

If you are working on a product that usually has serious advertising, do something humorous (or vice versa). It might work, it might not.

Find a negative about the product (a unique characteristic), and turn it into a positive, e.g., Guinness turned waiting much longer for a pint to be served into a positive, with "Good things come to those who wait."

Find a negative about the product (that everyone else has avoided), and turn it into a positive.

Accentuate a positive by exaggerating and having fun with a possible negative, e.g., Benson & Hedges 100s cigarettes (right).

Make the customer more important than the client, e.g., Headline: The patient will see you now Doctor.

If a product is usually sold to old men, try creating an idea that would appeal to young women.

If sun cream is usually aimed at holidaymakers, persuade people to use it every day.

If small cars are perceived as more vulnerable than big cars, create a convincing argument that says otherwise. (VW Polo managed to do this by observing that to increase their protection, humans and animals make themselves smaller.) In other words, turning a negative into a positive.

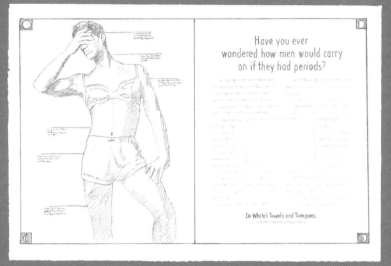

The opposite tool: ideas. BUPA, a UK private health company, makes the customer more important than the client. *Client: BUPA. Agency: WCRS, London. Creatives: Andy Dibb, Steve Little.*

Make women feel better by poking fun at the opposite sex having periods. *Client: Dr. White's Towels & Tampons. Agency: Bartle Bogle Hegarty, London. Creatives: Barbara Nokes, John Hegarty, Chris Palmer.*

Accentuate a positive by exaggerating and having fun with a possible negative. *Client: Benson & Hedges. Agency: Wells Rich Greene. Creatives: George D'Amato, Herb Green.*

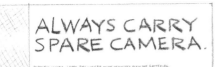

ALWAYS CARRY
SPARE CAMERA.

DURACELL ULTRA. LASTS 50% LONGER THAN ORDINARY ALKALINE BATTERIES.

FOR BETTER PERFORMANCE
CHANGE TOY FREQUENTLY.

Both the idea (Duracell lasts longer than other products) and the headlines (swapping the word "battery" with product names) use the opposite tool. *Client: Gillette Management (SEA). **Product:** Duracell. **Agency:** Ogilvy & Mather, Malaysia. **Creatives:** Donevan Chew, Tan Chee Keong, Gavin Simpson. **Creative director:** Sonal Dabral. **Photographer:** K. H. Mak, Barney Studio.*

Turning a negative into a positive. ***Client:** Volkswagen. **Agency:** BMP DDB, London. **Creatives:** Joanna Wenley, Jeremy Craigen.*

PROTECTIVE BEHAVIOUR

Fig 1

Fig 2

Fig 3

Fig 4

Polo

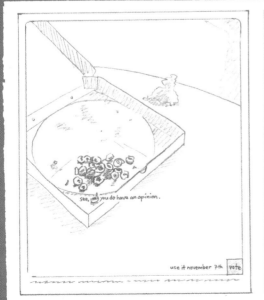

See, you do have an opinion.

use it november 7th   vote

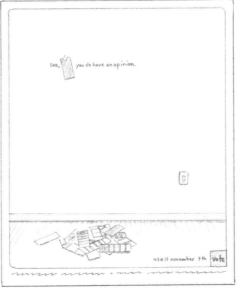

See, you do have an opinion.

use it november 7th   vote

People think they don't have a voice. Show them they do. Headline: See, you do have an opinion. ***Client:** Minneapolis League of Women Voters. **Agency:** Colle + McVoy, Minneapolis. **Creatives:** Liz Otremba, Eric Husband, Dave Keepper.*

Basic Tools • 29

Headlines

"Drink is the curse of the working classes" *becomes* "Work is the curse of the drinking classes" (Oscar Wilde, writer)

"The useless piece of flesh at the end of a man is called a penis" *becomes* "The useless piece of flesh at the end of a penis is called a man" (Jo Brand, comedian)

It can also work in two or more sentence headlines, e.g., "Annoy the neighbours. Turn it down" (Client: Jazz FM)

"You are the weakest link. Goodbye" *becomes* "You are the strongest link. Hello" (*The Economist*) [This is a twist on general knowledge TV quiz show catchphrase, "You are the weakest link. Goodbye."]

Naturally, the opposite tool can be applied to media other than print. A TV spot for Cingular Wireless's Go Phone (BBDO, New York) dramatizes the product benefits by turning a typical mother vs. daughter argument on its head:

Cingular "Wireless" Go Phone

Mother	I have not had it up to here with you, young lady!
Daughter	Why do you insist on treating me like an adult?
Mother	Because you insist on acting like one! Now you're getting this new phone.
Daughter	But it's so small! I really like it! Why is it always what I want?
Mother	Well, do you have any idea how much money this is not going to cost me?
Daughter	I love you!
Mother	I know you really mean that.
Daughter	You never hated me and you never will!
Mother	You are the most grateful little...
MVO	Cingular is changing the conversation about cell phones...

"Toys 'R' Us" becomes "Toys Aren't Us." **Client:** *National Canine Defence League.* **Agency:** *TBWA, London.* **Creatives:** *Trevor Beattie, Steve Chetham.*

Two or more sentence headlines are perfectly structured for the opposite tool. **Client:** *Jazz FM.* **Agency:** *Leagas Delaney, London.* **Creatives:** *David Hieatt, Roger Pearce.*

You are
the strongest link.
Hello.

The Economist

Tock. Tick.

Great minds
like a think.

The Economist

Thank you
for smoking.

Smiden & Son. Undertakers.

In the real world,
the tortoise loses.

The Economist

"You are the weakest link. Goodbye" becomes "You are the strongest link. Hello." **Client:** *The Economist.* **Agency:** *Abbott Mead Vickers BBDO, London.* **Creative:** *Jeremy Carr.*

"Great minds think alike" becomes "Great minds like a think." **Client:** *The Economist.* **Agency:** *Abbott Mead Vickers BBDO, London.* **Creatives:** *Tony Strong, Mike Durban.*

The hare and the tortoise fable becomes "In the real world, the tortoise loses." **Client:** *The Economist.* **Agency:** *Abbott Mead Vickers BBDO, London.* **Creatives:** *David Abbott, Ron Brown.*

"Tick. Tock." becomes "Tock. Tick." **Client:** *Oil of Olay Special Care Wrinkle Smoothing Cream.* **Agency:** *Saatchi & Saatchi, Cape Town.* **Creatives:** *Slade Gill, Mark Mason.*

"Thank you for not smoking" *becomes* "Thank you for smoking." **Client:** *North West ASH.* **Agency:** *Smith-Dennison.* **Creatives:** *Richard Dennison, Markham Smith.*

Visuals

A cheetah chasing a zebra *becomes* a zebra chasing a cheetah. A plate with a steak and some ketchup on the side *becomes* a plate of ketchup with a steak on the side. With the "Big Tags" campaign for Ikea (an innovative use of outdoor media), the impressively low price of Ikea's products is dramatized by attaching an actual chair, cabinet, and other products to a billboard-sized price tag.

Turning the expected (a written note on a Post-It) on its head produces a witty, visual way to dramatize the need for the product. **Client:** *Post-It Notes®.* **Agency:** *Grey, Brazil.* **Creatives:** *Ulisses Agneli, Fulvio Oriola.*

A pregnant woman becomes a pregnant man. British advertising's most famous use of the opposite tool with a visual. **Client:** *UK Health Education Council.* **Agency:** *Cramer Saatchi, London.* **Creatives:** *Bill Atherton, Jeremy Sinclair.*

Literally how to turn a joke on its head. **Client:** *Heineken.* **Agency:** *Lowe Howard-Spink, London.* **Creatives:** *Simon Butler, Gethin Stout.*

Headline and Visual

Visual: VW Beetle. Headline: Think small. (Perhaps the most famous example in advertising, this ad turned *two* things on its head: the common phrase "think big"; plus, the previous consumer trend for big, expensive, gas-guzzling automobiles.) **Visual:** wheelchair-bound man examining a broken television. (Headline: What you see here is a TV set repairing a man.) *Client:* Goodwill Industries.

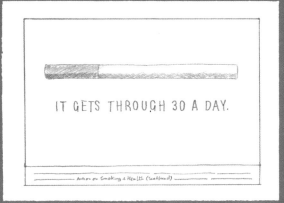

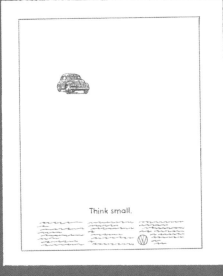

A clever twist on the classic "new" starburst, for the original, unchanged, dishwashing liquid of generations. *Client:* Fairy. *Agency:* Grey, London. *Creatives:* Ken Sara, Dave Henderson.

A common smoker's phrase is inverted into a powerful ad. *Client:* Action on Smoking and Health, Scotland. *Agency:* Marr Associates. *Creatives:* Will Taylor, Tim Robertson.

Turn it on its head: the opposite tool. Headline: If your Harvey Probber chair wobbles, straighten your floor. *Client:* Harvey Probber. *Agency:* Papert, Koenig, Lois. *Creatives:* George Lois, Julian Koenig.

The opposite tool: headline and visual. Plus *Advertising Age's* greatest ad of the twentieth century. *Client:* Volkswagen. *Agency:* DDB, New York. *Creatives:* Julian Koenig, Helmut Krone.

Try to visualize things differently. This is not a typical way to show a shark and a swimmer, but it's arguably the most dramatic.
Client: Universal Studios.
Designer: Tony Seiniger.
Illustrator: Roger Kastell.

Taglines

"Everything you always wanted in a beer. And more" *becomes* "Everything you always wanted in a beer. And less" (Miller Lite). (Alluding to a positive: fewer calories.) "For people with more money than sense" *becomes* "For people with more sense than money." "Nothing is impossible" *becomes* "Impossible is nothing" (Adidas) Although grammatically incorrect, nonsensical, and arguably a rewording of Nike's "Just do it," sounds more intriguing than "Nothing is impossible."

Art Direction

The opposite tool can also be applied to art direction. The result can be subtle or dramatic; both can help to make an ad look more interesting. As famed Art Director Steve Dunn explains:

"At some point you should turn everything on its head. Logos usually go lower right, so put them top left. Product shots are usually small, make them big. Instead of headlines being more prominent than body copy, do the opposite. It's perverse, but I'm constantly surprised how many times it works."

(See the Execution chapter for more art direction tools.)

···

Exercise: **think of something, anything, and do the opposite. Start with visuals, e.g., an egg. It's usually round, so make it square instead. Then turn it into an ad. Maybe a line for this example could be: Have genetically modified foods gone too far? (Not great. Think of some better examples…)**

···

No "Best"

Saying a product is "the best" is too easy and too generic. Think of all the products that would like to say "best" if they could. Using the English language's ultimate superlative destroys all product differentiation. Unless you can back it up (as in the case of Grey Goose, the "World's best tasting vodka," because of its number one ranking by the Beverage Testing Institute), avoid using this word. Instead, be more specific about why a product is good, or better than others. Even Grey Goose attributed being best to something by focusing on taste.

Unfortunately, and usually it's unfounded, "best" still creeps into advertising once in a while, especially in the US (the UK advertising governing body rarely allows its use, if at all). Who can forget Gillette's cheesy line: The best a man can get. But perhaps the worst use of "best" was the dull 1985 tagline for Coke that was killed off the same year: "The best just got better."

The term "best" is often used by people who think they can write copy (like the owners of American diners and pizzerias). The example I always cite is the scene in the movie "Elf," starring

Will Ferrell, when the naïve, childlike hero congratulates a diner that, according to its neon sign, has the "World's best cup of coffee."

Of course the term "best" is not to be confused with "better" or "good." Philips' "Let's make things better" is a big, strong message; the word "better" just happens to be part of it. As is David Abbott's simple tagline for British Telecom, "It's good to talk." Or "Good food costs less at Sainsbury's." Plus, phrases like "there is a better way to…" are often used in TV commercials, albeit with varying degrees of success. An example of the word "good" is Guinness's "Good things come to those who wait" (a concept originally based on the 119 seconds it takes to pour a perfect pint), lavishly executed in commercials such as "Surfer" and "noitulovE." Again, the word "good" is part of a bigger idea—patience in all things is a virtue.

Visualization

It has been said that being a good art director is simply about looking at things differently from everyone else. If you were asked to draw a dramatic picture of a shark and a swimmer, there are many ways to visualize it. The most obvious image is perhaps a side angle of a tiny swimmer, underwater, being followed by a giant shark, mouth open (inspired by the popular childhood drawing of a big fish about to swallow a smaller fish). Another image could be a swimmer on the water's surface, being followed by a shark's fin. Both are simple, and communicate what we want to say. But now compare those with a sketch of the famous poster for the original "Jaws" movie, designed by Tony Seiniger. Look at the unusual way the shark is positioned. Firstly, its teeth are now in full view. The cropping of its head quickly communicates the huge contrast in scale. We are left only to imagine

how long it must be. The shape of its head looks like a speeding bullet. The depth and angle from which it approaches makes the victim even more unaware, and the image more horrifying. The type is big, bold, and blood red, and balances out the shark perfectly. Every time I see this poster I want to shout, "swim faster!" As Tony once said, "[a poster] should be something nobody has seen before—that'll get it attention."

Symbols

A symbol is a type of visual metaphor, whereby one thing represents another (basic examples include red = anger, dog = loyal, cheetah = speed). Symbols are a form of shorthand—a good, graphic way to simplify an idea, especially in print. Symbols can be literal, like a soccer ball to symbolize the entire sport. But even more original is when you take a literal symbol and give it a twist. For example, imagine a woman's foundation/make-up kit with a large decorator's paintbrush next to it (as a symbolic image of the Miss World contests). The kit on its own would still work, but giving it a twist (e.g., swapping a regular foundation brush for a huge paintbrush or a bricklayer's trowel) is what makes the idea lateral. (Pushing literal ideas into lateral ones are examined further in Push It— Visualizing (Literal vs. Lateral), page 146.)

Lateral symbols are very effective. A symbol can be lateral from the start, working on its own without the need for a twist. Below is a spec ad for The Biography Channel which is a perfect example of an obvious thought (yes, we all know Michael Jackson's skin has gotten lighter over the years) executed in a simple, lateral way. One obvious, literal execution of this idea would be to show photos of him over time. But this graphic, symbolic solution is much cleverer.

Symbols are a good, graphic way to simplify an idea. *Client: The Biography Channel. Student: Jenny Drucker.*

A TV spot for Madame Tussauds waxwork museum in London used simple wax candles to represent various models/celebrities on display (e.g., a white candle with a fluttering flame = Marilyn Monroe). This idea was also clever because it involved the viewer in two ways: you had to guess who each person was, and it didn't reveal the actual "lifelike" waxwork figures, which would have spoilt the surprise.

But no matter how literal or lateral a symbol is, or how much of a twist you give it, it's a really useful shorthand tool.

....

Exercise: **create some concepts for six famous people, dead or alive, whom you'd expect to see a biography/life story of on TV. (Client: The Biography Channel.) Start with obvious names and examples (which may turn out to be the best), but also try to give it a twist: be lateral, base it on a truth, exaggerate, but don't contrive, be irreverent, avoid clichés, etc.**

....

Note: for some reason, the one idea that crops up every single time I give out this exercise is a bat with its head bitten off—for Ozzy Osbourne. That makes it an obvious idea without a twist. Some better examples are given below:

Symbol/visual	Famous person
A pair of handcuffs covered in flowery wallpaper	Martha Stewart
(A billboard) riddled with bullet holes	Al Capone
A pea in the middle of a dinner plate	Any supermodel

Students: *Jenny Drucker, Kristin Sorrentino*

Avoid Clichéd Imagery

A cliché is a "hackneyed phrase or idea." There are many clichéd images out there. As Luke Sullivan points out:

> *"Every category has its own version. In insurance, it's grandfathers flying kites with grandchildren. In the tech industries, it's earnest people looking at computer screens. And in beer, it's boobs."*

Below are just a few of my personal "favorites" that should be avoided at all costs. (Or as someone once quipped: "Avoid clichés like the plague.") One exception is when you use clichéd images in the form of a send-up or parody.

Some visual clichés to start you off (new ones should be added over time):

Any Media
- Dracula
- Hell's Angel holding a baby (and other greetings card imagery)
- Man playing saxophone from New York apartment window
- Famous people Photoshop-ed to smoke joints, stick out tongues, etc.
- Nike-style ads (sporty people with attitude)
- Human silhouettes (Apple iPod-style)
- Token minorities
- Andy Warhol-style graphics
- Woman skydiving, etc., during her period
- Car driving along winding, mountain roads
- Animals accidentally having sex with similar-looking objects or products

TV Specific
- Computer-aided talking animals or babies
- Doorstep/housewife testimonials
- Headshots of "everyday actors" repeating the same line (US only)
- Cars and other products turning into transformer-like robots

(For copy-related cliché, see Clichés, page 226.)

Learn from the Best Work...and the Worst

This follows on neatly from the topic of clichéd images, which is only one example of what makes a bad ad, well, bad. Be aware of all the advertising around you, start to assess and analyse each ad. Determine whether it's "good" or "bad." If it's bad, or even okay, make sure you don't fall into the same habits.

At the same time, expose yourself to great work. Seek out the awards annuals and apply the same critique. Again, make sure you don't copy the great work either. Be original.

Even though advertising is very subjective, the trick is to learn how to identify:

- The great from the good
- The good from the okay
- The okay from the bad
- And the bad from the terrible

Over time you will become critical of many ads, even award winners. Learning from the best and the worst is all part of the learning process. Once you start to look at ads properly, it won't be long before you'll be wincing with embarrassment as you look back at the ads that you thought were good.

Don't Do "Ads"

Too often we are influenced by what's already out there, whether consciously or subconsciously. The tendency is to think that because so many ads have similar qualities and techniques, that it must be a good thing. But eventually it just makes them clichéd, bland, forgetful, and above all, "addy." Just because most radio commercials you hear sound alike doesn't mean you have to follow suit. So try not to do "ads."

Do I Have to Use People?

There's no reason why an ad shouldn't have people in it. Likewise, there's no reason why it should. But by using people, you are forfeiting a number of useful tools, such as visual simile, symbols, and other analogies/visual metaphors that often produce a quicker, more creative solution than an ad with people in it. It's simply a form of reductionism. Usually the first thoughts that begin the creative process involve showing people using the product. The result is often "addy." *Try pushing the same idea, but without showing people.* This reductionism may prove that you don't need to show them. For example, imagine an ad for Dr Scholl's that shows a visual of a person pounding sidewalks of Manhattan in their Dr Scholl-lined shoes. Now look at the ad (above, right), a more lateral version of the same concept, produced by a former student. Similarly, imagine an ad for a hair restorer. A boring (and not particularly attractive) ad is to show a man's head before using the restorer, and then show his head after. Now, compare this execution to this ad (right). The Palladium Fitness Centers ad on page 24 is an example where you don't need to show people, but you can imply their presence (see also Push It— Visualizing (Literal vs. Lateral), page 146).

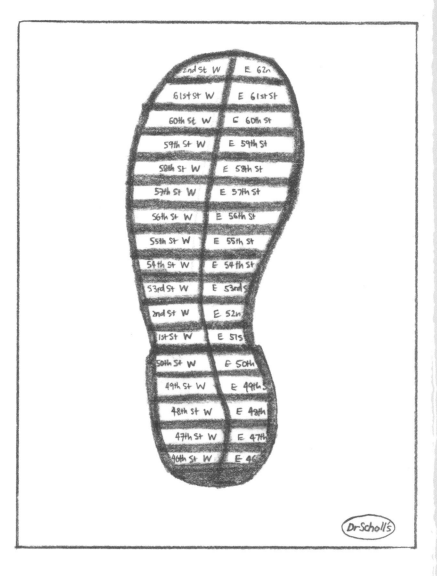

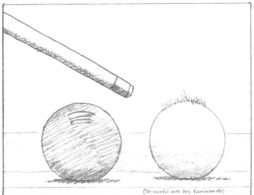

Why show a person pounding the streets of Manhattan? *Client:* Dr. Scholl's. **Student:** Jasmina Meheljic.

Why do you need to use a person in a hair restorer ad? Tagline: (Be careful with the Kaminomoto). **Client:** Kaminomoto. **Agency:** Euro RSCG Partnership (The Ball Partnership), Singapore. **Creative:** Neil French.

Do I Have to Show the Product?

Despite what most clients believe, an ad doesn't always have to show the product/service. There may be times when it's suicidal not to do so (e.g., new products to the market are more likely to be shown in an ad for obvious reasons). Or you might have a visual idea to rival the product-centric Absolut vodka campaign. But otherwise if the ad is interesting and memorable enough (and you know what it's for), its job is done. For the average client, this is still a huge gamble: "At least by showing the product, people will always know what the ad is for, right?" Well, not if the ad's so boring they don't even notice it. Of all the product-shot ads we're exposed to every day, how many of those do you honestly remember?

Another good argument for a "productless" ad is if the product is too generic, boring, or ugly looking that even the client would rather not show it. Or the product might be so well known that showing the brand name creates a strong image of the actual product, e.g., a mainstream European lager. See, for instance, "Pigeon": Tag: How Refreshing. How Heineken (page 32) and Volvo's "Cage" (page 39).

But what if the client *loves* product shots (sometimes known as "pack shots," depending on the type of product)? One compromise that has been used to great effect is to create the type of idea whereby you can gradually phase out the pack shot as consumers become able to fill in the missing product themselves. This may take weeks, months, or years, depending on the exposure/media spend. Similarly, a multimedia campaign may only need to show the product in some of its executions. Consistency in visual branding, voice over, tone of voice, tagline, or other mnemonics help to fill in the product-shot gaps and hold the campaign together. In the executions without a product, the consumer will see it without "seeing it."

....

Exercise: **find a couple of top awards books—one from 20 years ago, and one from the last two years. Firstly, see if there is a big difference between the number of times the product is featured in the ad, and the times it's not. Secondly, see if you believe the ads would have worked better with/without a product shot, or not.**

....

Exaggeration vs. Contrivance

A lot of great ads have managed to exaggerate things in order to get the idea across to the consumer. However, very few great ads successfully contrive things. *The reason why exaggeration is better than contrivance is because exaggeration begins as a truth, whereas contrivance begins as an untruth.* And truth, believe it or not, is a very important factor in the advertising idea.

Determining whether an idea is contrived or exaggerated can be subjective, and is often the subject of much classroom debate. The (italicized) definition above helps with most examples. For the remaining examples, it comes down to *what* is being contrived or exaggerated. There are two main subject matters: people (plus other living things) and objects.

As human beings, we have a fairly good understanding of human behavior. An exaggerated or over-the-top person can still be funny and believable, whereas contrived behavior is by definition forced and unnatural. So in the case of people's actions, the same definition applies. The quickest way is simply to ask yourself: "Would anyone really do that?"

Let's examine this with a case study—the Castlemaine XXXX ads. You could argue that each execution is contrived ("no-one would really do that"). But notice that the overriding campaign idea (Australians wouldn't give a XXXX for anything else) is actually an exaggeration, not a contrivance. I truly believe that some Australian men love drinking beer more than most other things. With a bit of exaggeration, the idea states that they prefer XXXX to *everything* else in the world.

But what if something is happening *to* the person, rather than the person doing something? Again, it all depends on the example. Take the poster on page 40: the top part of a woman's brown hair has been severely bleached in the sun from driving around in her convertible car all summer long. Is this contrived or exaggerated? I'd say it's more of an exaggeration that the sun would bleach someone's hair to this extent, but it's still funny and believable because it's a *truth* that the sun lightens hair. Remember, exaggeration starts with a truth.

Imagine the same starting point as the idea above ("a result of spending a long time in a convertible car"), but in *contrived* form. You should find it easy to come up with examples of these. Perhaps our woman has had all the hair on the top of her hair pulled out because of the constant wind rushing through it. Not only is this idea fairly negative, it's also contrived because it does not begin as a truth: wind doesn't do that to people's hair. Does it dry hair? Yes. Tangle hair? Yes. Pull out hair? No. (If, however, the ad was for shampoo instead of a car, and the idea was an exaggeration of the amount of hairs that sometimes end up on top of the shower drain, it's no longer contrived because that does happen to some people's hair.)

When it comes to trying to define whether something is exaggerated or contrived if the idea focuses on *objects* rather than people, the same rule applies: does the idea start with a truth or not? Another example is the "Unexpected" commercial for Dunlop tires. The simple idea is defined by the tagline: Tested for the unexpected. Allegedly, the script began with the standard series of unexpected events that one might face when driving along a road: sudden turns, children running into the road, things falling off the back of delivery trucks, etc. Just some of the many unexpected things that drivers have to be prepared for every day. However, Director Tony Kaye used the exaggeration tool to great effect, swapping the real for the surreal, school kids for fairy-like beings, and bails of hay for plummeting grand pianos. It still worked with the idea because it was based on a truth: tires go through many tests to help deal with the unexpected and avoid accidents (see page 40).

Another example is the famous 1960s Benson & Hedges 100s campaign, which exaggerates the "negative" of having a new, longer cigarette. A humorous TV spot showed people misjudging the length, like a man who stands too close to a shop window, squashing the tip as a result.

If there is still a debate about whether the ad under question is exaggerated or contrived (or simply, "is the ad believable?"), it's time either to trust your own opinion, agree to disagree, or take a vote on it (see The Exaggeration Tool, page 138).

Safe vs. Irreverent

I sincerely hope the day that we are no longer allowed to laugh at anything never comes. Imagine how terrible it would be if every ad was legally forced to patronize its consumers (which is more offensive than anything in my view). The line

CAGES SAVE LIVES
VOLVO

AUSTRALIANS WOULDN'T GIVE A XXXX FOR ANYTHING ELSE.

between being PC and un-PC is getting finer all the time. Looking at the positive, it should make it more challenging. But there is still plenty of fodder for great ideas and irreverent humor. (Do not confuse irreverence with toilet/college humor, page 153.)

Critiques and Subjectivity

Critiquing, or "critting" any creative idea will often produce a variety of conflicting opinions. Ads are no different: it's a very subjective, rather than objective, art form. In fact, you can criticize anything creative if you really want to. Nothing is universally perfect. (As Philippe Destouches said in 1732, "Criticism is easy; art is difficult.") That said, generally speaking, if most people in the advertising field like your ad, it probably means that it's good. However, there are sometimes very conflicting views about student and industry work, among professionals and consumers. This

No product required. This brand of car (and its safety benefit) is so well known that a simple logo will suffice. *Client: Volvo.* **Agency:** *Abbott Mead Vickers, London.* **Creatives:** *Mark Roalfe, Robert Campbell.*

The overriding campaign idea (Australians wouldn't give a XXXX for anything else) is an exaggeration, not a contrivance. *Client: Castlemaine XXXX.* **Agency:** *Saatchi & Saatchi, London.* **Creatives:** *Peter Barry, Zelda Malan, Peter Gibb.*

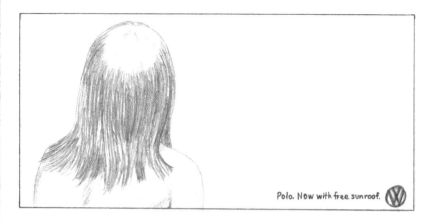

Exaggeration starts with a truth (sun does bleach hair). **Client:** *Volkswagen.* **Agency:** *BMP DDB, London.* **Creatives:** *Nick Allsop, Simon Veskner.*

A surreal ad, but with an underlying truth (car tires are designed to deal with various road conditions and unlikely obstacles). Tagline: Tested for the unexpected. **Client:** *Dunlop.* **Agency:** *Abbott Mead Vickers BBDO, London.* **Creatives:** *Tom Carty, Walter Campbell.*

isn't always a bad thing. At least it's creating a strong reaction. It's usually better to hear "I love it" or "I hate it" than everyone being indifferent.

On the subject of asking the opinions of others, be warned. If you are asking someone who is not a professional ad person, be sure to ask: "Do you get this ad?" and *not*, "Do you like it?" The reason is that most people (especially friends or relatives) are reluctant to offend, even if you ask them to be honest. So if it's a print ad, just hold it up in front of them, as if it were a real ad (which means you don't have the luxury of explaining your idea to each reader). If the reply to "Do you get it?" is negative or lukewarm, try to find out why. Ask them, "What do you think this ad is trying to say?" or "What's the idea?" Listen. Depending on the answers, either destroy it or try to correct it. Even if there's a slight rewrite (or redraw), don't ask them to imagine they haven't seen the original ad, simply test it on someone new instead. It's better that people don't "like" your ad, than they don't "get" it, since an ad should at the very least be able to communicate immediately. If they don't like it, you may still want to show others, to see if the feeling is mutual. Again, if most people "get" and "like" your ad, it's probably a keeper.

However, when you come to show your idea either internally (within the agency) or externally (to the client), you will invariably find yourself up against a committee of people, all desperate to give their two cents' worth. Without proper leadership and general decision-making skills, you invariably end up with a complete conceptual mess. If you try to please everyone (by applying all their thoughts), the purity of your original idea will suffer, which is so often the fate of many potentially great ads. To cheer yourself up, think of this wonderful line someone once told me:

"A zebra is a horse designed by committee."

(See also Why So Many Bad Ads?, page 12.)

Which Media?

The choice of which media to use is usually determined by the strategy people (account planners) and/or the client's marketing people, based on their consumer research into which type of media the target audience most commonly use and respond to. This decision is a key part of the strategy, and therefore the creative brief, which in turn affects the final creative work. In some cases, an unsolicited *media-specific* concept might be presented and sold to the client (e.g., an idea that only works in radio). In this case, the choice of media comes second, not first.

The amount of money spent on media space (the "media spend") is determined by the overall budget, often the cause of much debate between agency and client. Agencies will always claim cost-effectiveness on behalf of their client, when in reality it's usually the client who's always looking to cut costs, whereas agencies are looking to raise them in order to increase their commission, based on a fixed percentage of the client's budget. Having said that, the price of traditional media space (e.g., print ads, TV airing, etc.) is often negotiated between a media buyer (on behalf of the agency and the client) and the media seller (at, or on behalf of the publication, TV station, etc.)

The specific forms of advertising media include traditional (e.g., print, TV, radio), non-traditional (e.g., ambient, guerrilla), direct marketing (e.g., direct mail), interactive (i.e., web related), and integrated (i.e., single concept, in multimedia). With the exception of direct, all of the above forms of media will be examined throughout this book.

Plagiarism

Plagiarism is "taking and using another person's ideas as one's own." There are two types of plagiarism in advertising: (i) from other advertising (despised the most within the industry), and (ii) from non-advertising (despised the most outside the industry). In other words, ad people have a greater tendency to accept mutual "borrowing" between the Arts, yet are very upset (and rightly so) when one agency "re-creates" another agency's ad concept or execution. Conversely, many non-ad people think of advertisers as copycats and don't care if agencies steal from one another.

The key is to try to understand and acknowledge the difference between plagiarism and non-plagiarism. In other words, what would Ron Brown allow (or not allow) when he said, "Don't imitate, originate"? Some cases of plagiarism are clear cut, unquestionable rip-offs, but others are arguable (the Honda "Cog" debate is set to continue ad infinitum).

Plagiarism is either perfectly innocent (e.g., the coincidence is due to working on two similar, narrow briefs), subconscious (your mind somehow recorded the original idea subconsciously), or

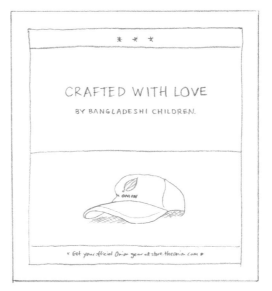

Be irreverent, but be right. This ad never ran because, ultimately, the client didn't believe it accurately exemplified *The Onion*'s voice. *Client: The Onion.* *Agency: The Martin Agency, Richmond.* *Creatives: Sara Grunden, Mike Lear, Kevin Thoem.*

Be shocking, but not gratuitous. This ad is just as powerful with "*"s as it is without. Headline: He told his parents to f**k off. He told his foster parents to f**k off. He told fourteen social workers to f**k off. He told us to f**k off. But we didn't. And we still haven't. *Client: Barnardo's.* *Agency: BBH, London.* *Creatives: Nick Gill, Mark Reddy.*

Reoccurring brief, reoccurring ad. The "blood is running out" concept has coincidentally resurfaced for various Red Cross chapters around the world.

intentional (the culprit is hoping desperately that no one will discover the original).

Equally (and naturally), ideas can keep reoccurring when a specific brief is given to a large number of students. But one recent (and frightening) trend among ad students is to confuse researching a product with blatantly taking predefined strategies, ideas, taglines, copy, or imagery from the client's own website. This is not the same as simply finding a nugget of information from which to create something bigger and better (or as someone once said, it's not where you get an idea from, it's where you take it that counts).

But taking other people's *creations* is not only lazy, it's cheating. Anyone can do that. And eventually someone will pick up on it, whether it's a teacher, creative, or fellow student. Some agencies or clients might request or accept it, but no respectable teacher would. Another scary phenomenon within the ad industry itself is the agency "hack" blatantly flicking through his collection of awards annuals as a way to crack a brief. (As someone once joked about this breed of ad man: "He's not creative…he's *re*-creative.")

To help sum up the anti-plagiarism argument, consider these two quotes:

> *It's better to fail in originality, than succeed in imitation*—Herman Melville, novelist

> *Imitation is NOT the highest form of flattery*—Steve Montgomery, art director

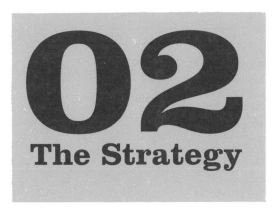

02
The Strategy

Despite the subtitle of this book, the correct "order" in terms of the advertising creative process is:

Strategy *first*
Concept/idea *second*
Campaign *third*

In other words, each campaign comes from a concept, which comes from a strategy.

In advertising, "strategy" refers to the overall marketing or selling approach. It is the thinking behind the concept/idea. (The thinking behind the thinking, if you like.) The strategy (or strategic thought) can come from a proposition/benefit of the product, how it is used, the market background, the choice of target audience, or any combination thereof. Every strategy should have an element of distinction (small or large) from the competition's strategies, as should the proceeding concept and campaign.

All strategies should be written in the form of a *strategy statement*, also known as a "creative brief." In simple terms, the strategy statement outlines the way a product is to be positioned (or repositioned) within the marketplace. (Also known as "product positioning.") Most agencies, especially the larger ones, have account planners, brand managers, marketing executives or strategists to develop, write, and present each "brief" to the creative team(s). Although for this book, I will be concentrating more on the ad agency approach to strategy rather than the marketing firm approach (the latter tends to be a much deeper statistical and analytical study of product, price, place, distribution, and promotion). (See What is Marketing?, page 248.)

The Important Difference between Strategy, Concept, and Campaign

The terms strategy, concept, and campaign often get mixed up. The best way to understand and outline the differences is by using case studies:

Flowers & Plants Association

For many years, flowers were sold primarily for special occasions such as Valentine's Day, weddings, and funerals. The question was, how do you get people to buy more flowers, more often, and not just at these particular times, but all year round? (The product is certainly perfect for this strategy, due to the fact that flowers only last a few days and need replacing.) Various agencies attempted to expand the market by positioning flowers as an alternative to apology/"thank you" products such as cards and chocolates.

But then a UK agency created the perfect strategic solution for the Flowers & Plants Association ("the Cheese Board of flora"). Cleverly, they persuaded women to buy flowers not as gifts for others, but for *themselves*. Suddenly, flowers were being strategically positioned in the same way as products like clothes or chocolates. Moreover, it's a believable strategy (flowers are beautiful things; they look and smell great; they make the owner feel special, etc.)

From this strategy came the campaign idea, based on the general truth that the average male is averse to buying flowers for themselves, their homes, or their significant others. This idea was then expressed in the blunt tagline: Flowers. Why wait? Buy your own. The ads presented their argument in a series of oh-so-true ads about men, and their flowerless wives/girlfriends. What's also clever about this approach is that it reassures single women that when it comes to getting flowers regularly, they're better off without a man.

The strategy proved expandable in terms of campaign ideas and subsequent executions (see overleaf).

BUPA Healthcare

In the mid-1990s, BUPA, the UK's leading private health care provider, needed a new campaign. A "big idea." But in order to do this, they needed to start with a big strategy. BUPA's main competition was the government-owned National Health Service, funded through taxation and available to all. The NHS has always been criticized for not

HUGH NEVER GIVES VANESSA FLOWERS. HE'S WORRIED SHE MIGHT THINK HE'S UP TO SOMETHING.
WHY WAIT? BUY YOUR OWN.

www.flowers.org.uk

FRANK HASN'T GIVEN HIS WIFE FLOWERS SINCE BUILDERS WOLF-WHISTLED AT HIM ON THE WAY BACK FROM THE FLORISTS.
WAIT WAIT? BUY YOUR OWN.

www.flowers.org.uk

Top left Headline: Hugh never gives Vanessa flowers. He's worried she might think he's up to something. Tagline: Why wait? Buy your own. *Client: Flowers & Plants Association.*

Above, left Headline: Frank hasn't given his wife flowers since builders wolf-whistled at him on the way back from the florists. *Client: Flowers & Plants Association.*

Top right and above Same strategy, same tagline, different campaign. The first Flowers & Plants Association campaign gave reasons why men don't like to give flowers, this campaign simply reminds women that men don't give them. *Client: Flowers & Plants Association.*

being able to pay each patient enough attention and each procedure was decided on a economical cost-benefit analysis. (If you are over a certain age and in need of a hip-replacement, you're out of luck.) BUPA, by contrast, could offer a higher quality service, shorter waiting times, etc. But this cost the consumer a lot more money. So what strategy would convince a stoic, long-suffering nation of individuals to go private and cough up the extra cash? The key, as in all great advertising, would be to tell people something that they hadn't thought of before. Simply saying, "We care about you more than the NHS," or "We provide better service," or "If you get ill, we'll take care of you" was too obvious, too literal. Everyone knew this already. And at most the response would be "Well, I hope you care, I'm paying for it!" Instead, the strategy took a lateral approach, and explained *why* BUPA cared, by telling people that they deserved to stay healthy. Suddenly BUPA "owned" preventative medicine, not we'll-try-to-save-your-life-at-the-last-minute medicine. (I'm sure there's a proper name for this!)

From that came the concept, reflected in the tagline: You're amazing. We want you to stay that way. Then came the campaign, which outlined all the amazing everyday processes that the body goes through to keep us alive; incredible facts that we take for granted. The executions were beautifully written, art directed, and filmed. More importantly, this was clearly a big enough idea to expand across all media.

It all started with the strategy, which was inspired by the target market's relationship with both the competition and BUPA. The result of having such a great strategy to work with made the concept and campaign that much easier to create.

Product/Service: Apple

Strategy: Create the perception that Apple is as big and important as IBM. (In 1981, Apple was a tiny company in a marketplace of 20+ key competitors.)

Idea: Recognize IBM's entry into the personal computer marketplace.

Execution: Welcome, IBM. Seriously.

Tone: Sincere, confident, down to earth, and humorous.

Proposition: Apple is as progressive as IBM.

Welcome, IBM.
Seriously.

Welcome to the most exciting and important marketplace since the computer revolution began 35 years ago.

And congratulations on your first personal computer.

Putting real computer power in the hands of the individual is already improving the way people work, think, learn, communicate and spend their leisure hours.

Computer literacy is fast becoming as fundamental a skill as reading or writing.

When we invented the first personal computer system, we estimated that over 140,000,000 people worldwide could justify the purchase of one, if only they understood its benefits.

Next year alone, we project that well over 1,000,000 will come to that understanding. Over the next decade, the growth of the personal computer will continue in logarithmic leaps.

We look forward to responsible competition in the massive effort to distribute this American technology to the world. And we appreciate the magnitude of your commitment.

Because what we are doing is increasing social capital by enhancing individual productivity.

Welcome to the task 🍎 apple

Strategy: create the perception that Apple is as big and important as IBM. Idea: recognize IBM's entry into the personal computer marketplace. *Client:* *Apple.* *Agency:* *TBWA/Chiat/Day.* *Creative:* *Steve Hayden.*

Strategy: target car drivers instead of bikers looking for a better bike. Idea: a moped might be a better option than a car. **Client:** *Vescony, Inc.* **Product:** *Vespa.* **Agency:** *Carl Ally.* **Creative:** *Ed McCabe.*

Strategy: target drivers who don't want a "type" of car, who want to be different. Idea: the Mini can't be categorized with any other car. It's its own thing. **Client:** *Mini.* **Agency:** *Crispin Porter + Bogusky.* **Creatives:** *Ari Merkin, Mark Taylor.*

Product/Service: Vespa

Strategy: Target car drivers instead of bikers looking for a better bike.

Idea: A moped might be a better option than a car.

Execution: Maybe your second car shouldn't be a second car.

Proposition: Vespa is better than a second car.

Product/Service: Mini

Strategy: Target drivers who don't want a "type" of car, who want to be different.

Idea: The Mini can't be categorized with any other car. It's its own thing.

Execution: …Other.

Proposition: Mini is fun because it's so unique.

Note: the Jazz FM Strategy Statement Case Study on page 52 helps to illustrate further the difference between strategy, concept/idea, and campaign.

Exercise: **look inside an awards annual. For each print or TV campaign, define: (i) the strategy, and (ii) the idea/concept. (One sentence for the strategy, and one for the idea.)**

The Strategy Statement (or "Creative Brief")

When forming a strategy from which to create ideas, it needs to be written down in black and white. This helps to focus and steer the formation of ideas from the onset. When people suggest that an idea is "off strategy," they mean that it doesn't relate back to the defined strategy, and will therefore be much harder to sell the idea to the client. (There are sometimes ways around this, which I explain in more detail in the Presenting and Selling Your Work chapter.)

By having a strategy statement at hand, you can keep referring back to it whilst generating ideas from that strategy. It is very hard, even if you are an experienced creative, to produce a great campaign idea (or even a single one-shot) without a solid, tight strategy. It's the same with great movies—they always start with a solid script. Think of the strategy statement as the creative script or story. The extent to which you improvise around it is then up to you.

In short, the better you are briefed, the easier your job will be. A poorly defined, vague, "woolly" brief is no use to a creative person, nor is a highly specific one that restricts the number of ideas.

A basic example of the headings in a strategy statement are listed below. It may look intimidating at first but it's quite straightforward (there are many briefs out there that are unnecessarily detailed). Each element helps to create the basis of a strategy. Each agency tends to have its own equivalent template with slightly different headings and terminology. (I have given some commonly used variations below.) The meanings are still fairly generic, however.

- Client
- Product/Service
- Product and Market Background (Supposition)
- Competition
- Business/Advertising Objective (Problem To Solve)
- Media
- Target Market/Group/Audience
- Proposition/Promise/Benefit
- Proposition Support Points
- Tone of Voice
- "Mandatories" (Inclusions/Exclusions)

Let us examine each section of the strategy statement. Think of it as a more detailed version of the first two subheads in the Basic Tools chapter: "What Do You Want To Say?" and "Who Are You Talking To?"

Client
This is the name of the company or organization responsible for the product or service, e.g., The Ford Motor Company, Eastman Kodak Ltd, Anheuser-Busch.

Product/Service
This is the name of the product or service that you're advertising. Perhaps it's a specific model of a product (for example, the Jeep Wrangler Diesel XL), or the range of Jeep Wrangler Diesels, or the entire range of Jeep Wranglers, or the entire range of Jeep cars, or another Jeep product entirely, or the entire Jeep brand. Each example creates a different

strategy, which then produces different concepts and campaigns.

Product and Market Background (Supposition)
This section lists any relevant product and market information. Background is important for the positioning of a product (i.e., what you want to say about the product, how you want to say it, and to whom you want to say it), relative to what may or may not have been done in past advertising for the same product, or a market competitor. Armed with current and historical information, including successes or failures, plus any product or market changes, one can assess whether to continue along the same strategy, a similar strategy, or whether it's time to adopt a totally new one. In a brief often an agency will simply use the phrase: what do they (consumers) currently think or feel about us (the product/service/client)?

Competition
This section is a list of the product's competitors, in order of relevance, and high-end to low-end. It's a useful reminder during the strategy, concept, and execution stages to originate, not imitate. As a certain Levi's ad written by John Hegarty states: "When the world zigs, *zag.*"

Business/Advertising Objective (Problem to Solve)
Often the objective of an advertising campaign is to solve a marketing problem (large or small), described in the "supposition" section of a strategy. This problem stems from consumers' misconception or ignorance about either the product or the service itself, or the entire product category/market that it is in. This is not necessarily the consumers' fault. It could be a problem with the way the product is being used, targeted, packaged, distributed, or even advertised. Or simply that the competition is seen as being better. The role of the new advertising is to solve the problem by addressing and even reversing these misunderstandings. In turn, this creates greater product and/or market awareness. In simple business terms, this results in selling more units to more people to make more money. (And if you are marketing and advertising a new product instead of a current one, as outlined above, there will be specific problems to solve too, including the basic need to get noticed and make money.) In a brief, often an agency will simply use the phrase (following-up on the question in the Supposition):

what do we want them (consumers) to think, feel (and therefore do)?

A client can calculate how to maximize product revenue through strategic advertising by applying a method called *Binary briefing*. "Binary" is where something is defined as either a 0 or a 1 (or rather, one thing or the other). "Binary briefing" helps to define the creative brief (strategy) of a particular product/service by answering four key "binary" questions. In other words, each question has two possible answers, whereby you can only choose ONE, and never both. Armed with these answers, a client can better assess the strategy that will produce the greatest number of sales.

The questions are:

Are we going for brand share OR are we expanding the market?

If I have a 75% share of the market, it's probably better to spend money getting more people *into* the market, rather than going after the 25% you don't have. (Having a 75% share means that for every 20 people I can talk into coming into the market, 15 of them will *automatically* buy my product. I can therefore benefit threefold by expanding the market, rather than trying to grab the remaining 25% from whomever has got it.) And if I've only got 25%, it isn't going to make much sense spending money trying to *grow* the market. (For every 20 people I can talk into coming into the market, 15 of them will be buying a product that *isn't* mine. But if I spend my money just talking to people who are already in the market, and tell them why they should *switch* brands to mine, I won't lose those sales.)

Are we going for trial by non-users OR are we going to get existing users to use more?

Will increased sales come from getting people who *aren't* using the product/service, to use it? Or will sales come from getting people who *are* using it, to use more? This depends on whether the market is saturated or not. So if everyone already does whatever it is you're trying to sell, then there's not much point in telling them to try it. This "market saturation" means you have to get existing users to use more.

Do we have a USP OR are we going to do branding?

If you have a Unique Selling Proposition (USP), then this is clearly the best benefit to go on. Note the two important words here—"unique" and "selling." You have to have something that people want, not just something that makes you different. If you do have a definite benefit, then advertise it. If you don't, then do "branding-advertising" instead (e.g., what most bottled water campaigns do). (See also The Brand and Branding, page 244.)

Should we be using a logical argument OR a mnemonic, to be remembered?

This continues from the last question. If you have a great USP, logic says you should use it. If you don't have a strong reason for buying your product, you will probably want to do the branding using a mnemonic (a device to aid memory). This can be a gimmick, like "the Pepsi Challenge," which in turn created its own USP (Pepsi tastes better than Coke). There are also smaller mnemonic devices such as the Intel® Pentium® Processor jingle.

To put all this simply, you always have to decide between:

- Brand share vs. market growth
- Trial vs. existing users
- USP vs. branding
- Logic vs. mnemonic

Note: the more clearly you can answer each binary question (based largely on how you interpret the product and market supposition), the better your strategy will be. You can change your mind as often as you like (right up to actually doing the ads).

Of course, advertising objectives and the associated problem(s) that need to be solved are not exclusive to cans of soda and other consumer goods. The same strategic thinking applies to anything that may need advertising. For example, imagine the client/product is a blood drive for the Red Cross. The advertising objective = encourage more adults to donate blood. The problem to solve is ultimately the fact that not enough people give blood (and that blood supplies are therefore too low). But probe a little deeper and you will find other problems associated with giving blood that the advertising could solve, like: people's general apathy about saving lives, the time and hassle involved, the fear of needles, the fear of fainting, etc., etc. Addressing and overturning one or more of these concerns is the key to solving the advertising objective, and therefore creating a successful ad campaign. (For example, one student campaign tackled needle phobia by simply equating the actual pain level of a needle with other everyday "pricks" that we haven't built the same fear around (e.g., a mosquito bite, a rose thorn, a push pin, etc.)

On a final note, creativity coach Tom Monahan believes that it's "virtually impossible to be creative without a problem…. You are at your best creatively when you are solving problems, because problems cause you to stretch."

Media

The choice of media depends upon the type of product or service being advertised, the target market, and the client's budget. Each campaign can be in one form of media, or multiple forms. Traditional advertising media includes print, TV, and radio. Non-traditional includes ambient and guerrilla concepts. In addition, there is direct media, and interactive media. In the UK, each type of media is defined by its relation to a hypothetical "line" that divides the two. Traditional media is "above the line," whereas direct marketing and interactive advertising is "below the line." Companies that produce work in all the forms are referred to as "through the line" agencies, or "full service." (See the Integrated chapter.)

Other divisions within advertising include sales promotion, and business-to-business. The main focus of this book is on traditional, "above the line," business-to-consumer advertising. Once these skills have been developed, the same creative process can easily be applied to these other forms of media and advertising also covered in this book.

Target Market/Group/Audience

The more you *understand* the people you are talking to, the more relevant and persuasive the advertising will be. In the industry, the target group is defined through extensive market research. The audience can be general or specific. But remember, an ad is a conversation between two people (client and consumer), so the more specific the target group, the easier it is to know exactly who you are talking to, and the easier it is to generate ideas.

Once this target group has been established, look at it closely. But don't think of them as a "group." A good strategist/account planner should be able to narrow the field down to a typical *individual* within the group.

Rarely will you be targeting someone exactly like yourself. A strategy or concept that might not appeal to you could really appeal to your target market, and vice versa. You must therefore learn

to "wear different hats," to step outside your world, and get into the different mindset and character of the person(s) you are talking to.

Definitions of target groups use a lot of marketing speak, e.g., "trendsetters," "followers," "cash rich, time poor," etc. Marketing people, account planners, brand managers, and strategists are keen to invent new terms and nicknames, partly to sound professional and partly for simplicity. (Funny as these words and phrases can sound, it's a lot easier to say "sad dads" than "fathers, aged 35–55, who are sadly past buying an expensive two-seater sports car, and are now in the market for a family five-door, but willing to compromise with a powerful engine.")

When writing their own strategy statements, many students tend to put down too broad an age range. For example, imagine you are targeting female teens. Can you be more specific? After all, an early teen has very different tastes and opinions from a mid teen or a late teen, and will therefore respond to the advertising differently. (The ad on page 222 is a perfect example of an ad that talks to a particular type of young "woman.")

Often half the battle of creating a new strategy is finding a new target audience for the product. For example, to sell flowers all year round (rather than Valentine's Day, birthdays, funerals, "get well soons," apologies, etc.), the UK's Flowers & Plants Association targeted disappointed wives and girlfriends. Their tag summed up the idea: Flowers. Why wait? Buy your own. After all, men are often rubbish at giving flowers, and flowers are nice to have around the house, they make you feel good, etc. (This case study is explained in further detail on page 43.)

Take the same approach to promoting non-alcohol beer and think of all the potential target audiences there must be, many yet to be advertised to: recovering alcoholics, designated drivers, pregnant women, diabetics (all of whom still like the taste of beer), or perhaps it's more behavior/situation driven, like targeting business executives who prefer to stay sober at work lunches and events. Suddenly the potential for subsequent interesting ads is starting to take shape in our minds, simply by finding a new, interesting audience to target.

There are *four* areas of target audience information/data that agencies can purchase from "list sellers," some of which are more important to certain products and services than others. These lists are typically a combination of:

- **Demographic**: age (e.g., 18–24, 25–34, 35–44), gender [male or female (Mrs., Ms., or Miss)], marital status, race, family situation, household income, occupation, and education.
- **Lifestyles**: affluent leisure activities (e.g., travel, cooking, arts, charities, investments, etc.), community and civic activities, domestic activities, entertainment, and high-tech purchases, hobbies, self-improvement activities, and sporting activities.
- **Behavioral**: past or new, potential experiences with the product category and/or specific products.
- **Psychographic and attitudinal:** beliefs and attitudes toward the product category, advertisers within the category and/or specific products.

Proposition/Promise/Benefit

This is the single benefit that the product or service is promising the consumer: what it's *proposing*. Again, it's crucial that the proposition is a singular promise or benefit, and not multiple.

The proposition is the most important part of the strategy statement (based often on a product, market or consumer *insight*). Creatively speaking, it's the starting point, or catalyst, for creating concepts. From a client's standpoint, it's the one thing the product or service stands for. For both of these reasons, each idea must at the very least communicate the defined proposition.

Two benefits (fuel efficient and boot/trunk space) expressed in four words. Not easy to do. **Client:** *Volkswagen.* **Agency:** *DDB, London.* **Creatives:** *Peter Harold, Barry Smith.*

The term "proposition" is sometimes referred to as advertising promise, or selling proposition, or abbreviated to single-minded benefit, or single-minded proposition (SMP).

The key is to say one thing that's different about your product (of genuine interest to the consumer), or be the *first* to say something that the competition could say, but has yet to realize it through its advertising. An example of the latter is Citibank's identity theft campaign, which "owned" and advertised credit card security service so well, it made it virtually pointless for other banks to use the same benefit.

The benefit that a product is "the best" is usually too general. It's a lazy, corny approach, and unfortunately appears in a lot of bad advertising. (In fact, in the UK you can't legally say that your product is "the best.") Don't just say that a product's the best (unless it's believable). Instead, tell the consumer *why* it's the best (see No "Best," page 34).

A unique selling proposition, or USP[*], is the ultimate proposition because it's one that *no other* competitor can claim. Of course it has to be something that you could also sell from. Most products are equal, generic, parity products and therefore do not have an obvious USP. But as demonstrated in the Generating Strategies and Ideas chapter there are various methods that can be used to *find* a USP.

Note: there are rare exceptions to the single-minded benefit. One example is the long-running Miller Lite campaign. Its creators found a novel (yet arguably contrived) way to communicate the *two* propositions of "great taste" and "less filling," by creating an argument between two people over which was the most important benefit. Another example that broke the "one benefit only" rule was the Classic FM poster campaign (opposite). However, one could argue that the benefit is single minded: "classical music has many forms." This type of proposition is known as a "variety proposition," and is examined further in the Generating Strategies and Ideas chapter. But generally speaking, unless the executions work as well as Classic FM's, one benefit *per ad* looks unfocused and "addy."

[*]The term "USP" was invented by Rosser Reeves.

Proposition Support Points

These are concrete reasons or facts that allow the proposition to exist. It supports its claim, giving the consumer permission to accept the product benefit. Each list contains between one and five points, placed in order of importance or relevance to the chosen proposition. Support points vary according to the product and are usually a result of research and market positioning. From a creative point of

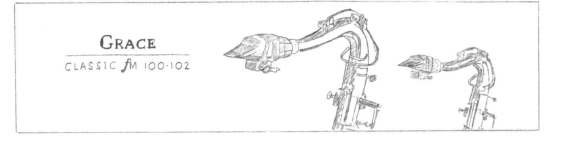

GRACE

CLASSIC *f*M 100-102

This campaign appears to break the "one benefit only" rule, although one could argue that it's a single-minded "variety proposition." The third ad/benefit: Power. **Client:** *Classic FM.* **Agency:** *BST BDDP, London.* **Creatives:** *Steve Hough, Oliver Devaris, Brian Connelly.*

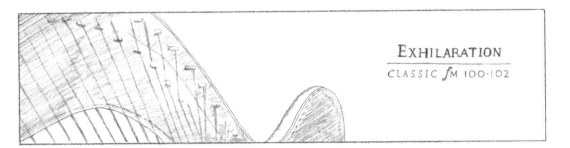

EXHILARATION

CLASSIC *f*M 100-102

view, the support points can often contain an inspiring fact or nugget of information that can launch an execution, or even an entire campaign thought.

Again, try to avoid concluding and claiming that a product's proposition = "the best" simply because it has lots of benefits listed in the support points. Be more specific and pick *one* point or area—it will help you stay focused, thereby creating better ads.

Tone of Voice

The "tone" of an ad is often dictated by the product's target group, and/or by the product/brand itself. Usually described in one adjective or more, the tone of voice should be an extension of the values of the brand itself, and should therefore not contradict these values too much. (Of course, some products may lack brand values, in which case you must try to create some through the tone of the advertising.)

But whether your idea is expressed as a headline only, visual only, or headline and visual (in the case of print), the tone should be evident. In fact, it's really important that each execution within a campaign has the *same tone of voice throughout.* If not, it creates a lack of brand integrity, and the consumer will be left feeling confused, even cheated.

Note: it's also possible to continue this tone through the art direction, which we will come onto in the Execution chapter.

Most tones are obvious. For example:

VW (especially early work)	self-deprecating
Axe/Lynx	fun, sexual
BT ("It's good to talk")	personal, warm
Barnardo's	serious, shocking, informative
Johnson & Johnson	empathetic
Got Milk?	direct, straightforward
Pepperami	edgy, in your face
Fox Sports (various)	slapstick/quirky/irreverent, etc.
The Economist	intelligent, elitist
(Don't) Vote Campaign	sarcastic

Note: tone of voice can be general (e.g., humorous), or specific (think of all the types/brands of humor there are). However, you may only have a rough idea of tone before your initial thinking starts. Don't worry. If it frees you up, use a general term (e.g., for a kid's candy bar, put "fun"). And if that's still too limiting, just put "any" for tone. You can always change it or refine it later. But once it is defined, you mustn't stray from it. (An example of this was when I worked on a TV campaign for the UK charity Guide Dogs for the Blind, pages 175–76. We had a dozen scripts to choose from, of which three were chosen for shooting. After production, and upon reviewing each ad, one of the commercials didn't feel right. It was then clear that the *tone* was slightly more slapstick than the first two. To run all three ads would weaken the entire campaign. Temptation was resisted and the third ad was never used [I don't even own a copy]. This waste could have been prevented with closer inspection at the script stage.)

···

Exercise: **turn on the TV, or grab a magazine or paper. Better yet, use an awards annual. Look at each ad, and try to identify the tone of voice. Write down a few adjectives for each.**

···

"Mandatories" (Inclusions/Exclusions)

These are defined by the client and/or the agency. "Inclusions" might include a simple call to action (e.g., a web address or telephone number), the use of a particular character or personality, a current tagline, a new logo, or a visual branding technique (Kodak ads, for example, must include their famous yellow). "Exclusions" could be any particular client prejudice, a cliché, or a tried-and-failed idea for the same product or within the same market.

Writing a solid strategy statement, like anything else, comes with practice. Each section should be kept as short as possible, a line for each at most (with the exception of Support Points). Once you work in the creative department of an agency, it will be (or should be) written for you. But even then you may have to question it. A poor, "woolly" strategy is virtually impossible to work from. It's a total waste of time. The three biggest culprits in a poorly devised strategy statement tend to be: the non-single-minded proposition, the lack of credible support points, and the undefined target audience.

···

Exercise: **repeat the same tone of voice exercise above, but instead write out a simple strategy statement for each ad, including Client/Product, Background, Problem To Solve, Target Audience, Proposition, Support Points, Tone, Mandatories (have a guess!)**

···

Strategy Statement Case Study: Jazz FM

To understand further the difference between strategy, concept/idea, proposition, and execution, consider this strategy statement for a local jazz radio station:

Product/Service
WBGO Jazz FM 88.3

Product and Market Background (Supposition)
WBGO is a non-profit, public organization in the US. It does not use any advertising during its broadcast of Jazz 88.3. It does not traditionally have a budget/media-spend to advertise itself either. Production costs must therefore be minimal, for local exposure in New Jersey and surrounding areas only.

Competition
Other national/local radio stations and web stations (jazz and non-jazz). Plus other formats of music, including CDs, vinyl, downloads, etc.

Business/Advertising Objective (Problem to Solve)
The ad objective is to increase awareness of the station (and jazz itself) to new and lapsed listeners. (Increase market share with trial users.) The problem with new listeners is that they think jazz fans are pretentious or nerdy, and that the music is hard to listen to.

Media
Black-and-white print.

Target Market/Group/Audience
Adults, 18+ (core group is male 30–65); music fans who are primarily new listeners of jazz and jazz radio, plus any lapsed listeners of both.

Proposition/Promise/Benefit
The jazz we play is performed by the most gifted, creative musicians in the world.

Proposition Support Points

1) They create sounds that other musicians cannot produce.
2) Jazz is the only true form of musical improvisation.
3) Many of the top jazz musicians are household names.

Tone of Voice
Slightly surreal and quirky.

"Mandatories" (Inclusions/Exclusions)

Do not focus on jazz fans, or try to sell the perceived "elitist" jazz sound.

Therefore, the *strategy* is to get new listeners to appreciate the artists first, as a way of encouraging them to listen to the music.

The *proposition* is that jazz musicians have to be incredibly talented to create those amazing sounds.

One *idea* that leads directly from this strategy is that jazz musicians are so talented that they are "beyond human"; it's as if they have some physical advantage that helps them to create those amazing sounds. This thought can be summed up by the tagline: A different breed.

    The campaign *executions* from this idea (see right) show freakish body parts: to play the piano (as fast as Jimmy McGriff) you'd need an extra set of fingers; to blow the trumpet (as powerfully as Dizzy Gillespie) you'd need iron lungs; to improvise on the sax (as well as Charlie Parker) you'd need an enlarged creative side in your brain.

The Importance of Research

The strategy statement contains only the first stage of research. Once the creative team has a creative brief in hand, it is their job to: consider, question, and delve deeper into the facts and insights laid out in the brief, and to continue researching any other useful, related information that may spark off a big campaign idea, a headline/visual concept, or even a persuasive line of body copy. The key is to know which piece(s) of information to focus on, and which to trash (although you'd be amazed what ideas can come from a seemingly dull or irrelevant fact, depending on how you use or interpret it).

    To reiterate, research more than you could possibly need on each particular subject. Why? Because if you research only according to your first impressions on a project, or according to preconceived ideas about what you will finish up with, your end product will be constrained by the limits of your own conformity.

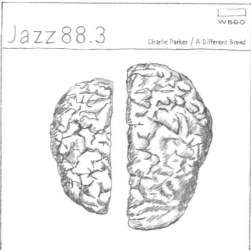

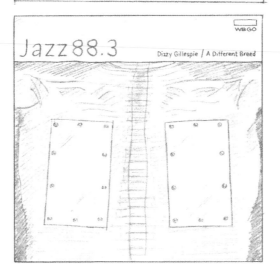

Execution 1: Jimmy McGriff's "extra set of fingers." Execution 2: Charlie Parker's "enlarged creative side of the brain." Execution 3: Dizzy Gillespie "iron lungs." *Client: WBGO Jazz FM 88.3. Agency: ATM Design & Architecture. Creative: Pete Barry.*

Lego: Four Possible Strategies

For any particular product (in this case, Lego), there can be multiple strategies to choose from. The key differences between each strategy are in bold text in each column.

Strategy Statement	1: Growth	2: Durability
Product and Market Background (Supposition)	Lego was invented in Denmark in 1934 and is currently the 6th largest toy company in the world. The Lego brick design was patented in 1958. The word Lego is a contraction of the Danish words "leg" and "godt" meaning "play well." Coincidentally, the word Lego also means "I study" and "I put together" in Latin.	Lego was invented in Denmark in 1934 and is currently the 6th largest toy company in the world. The Lego brick design was patented in 1958. The word Lego is a contraction of the Danish words "leg" and "godt" meaning "play well." Coincidentally, the word Lego also means "I study" and "I put together" in Latin.
Competition	All other toy brands, especially electronic toys, arts and crafts products, and children's books.	All other toy brands, especially electronic toys, arts and crafts products, and children's books.
Business/Advertising Objective (Problem To Solve)	**Lego is losing ground on computer games, electronic toys, and television shows. Parents need to be reminded how much healthier Lego is for a child's mental growth, learning, creativity, imagination, etc.**	**Lego is losing ground on cheaply made computer games and electronic toys. Parents need to be reminded how much better made and more durable (and therefore better value) Lego is.**
Media	Any	Any
Target Market/ Group/Audience	**Primarily parents. Plus grandparents, uncles, aunts, adult friends, etc. (Note: one could argue that children are the actual "consumers" of Lego. However, the following strategies are talking to adults first, rather than "kiddy" advertising.)**	**Primarily parents. Plus grandparents, uncles, aunts, adult friends, etc.**
Proposition/Promise/ Benefit	**Lego is the brain toy for kids.**	**Lego is built to last.**
Proposition Support Points	**Tests have proven that Lego helps to develop a child's basic cognitive skills, creativity, imagination, etc.**	**They are made of specially formulated plastic. Their basic brick design makes them solid, compact, and therefore virtually impossible to break.**
Tone of Voice	Intelligent, authoritative.	Any
"Mandatories" (Inclusions/ Exclusions)	Use the classic Lego bricks only, to represent the Lego brand and its many related products.	Use the classic Lego bricks only, to represent the Lego brand and its many related products.

3: Safety	4: Education
Lego was invented in Denmark in 1934 and is currently the 6th largest toy company in the world. The Lego brick design was patented in 1958. The word Lego is a contraction of the Danish words "leg" and "godt" meaning "play well." Coincidentally, the word Lego also means "I study" and "I put together" in Latin.	Lego was invented in Denmark in 1934 and is currently the 6th largest toy company in the world. The Lego brick design was patented in 1958. The word "Lego" is a contraction of the Danish words "leg" and "godt" meaning "play well." Coincidentally, the word Lego also means "I study" and "I put together" in Latin.
All other toy brands, especially electronic toys, arts and crafts products, and children's books.	Adult education, "creative" computer companies, etc.
Lego is losing ground on the #1 "babysitter"—the television. Parents need to be reminded how much safer and healthier a toy like Lego is, whether you play with your child or not (both are beneficial). Lego is a big enough brand to make this stand.	Lego is losing ground as a brand. It needs to "own" something bigger than "a toy for kids." Lego is synonymous with learning, creativity, and imagination. It needs to own this so everyone feels good about the brand, not just kids. (Products/programs could be developed later in conjunction with this strategy.)
Any	Any
Primarily parents. Plus grandparents, uncles, aunts, adult friends, etc.	Adults, with or without children.
Lego is strongly against children watching/listening to sex, violence, and bad language on TV.	Never stop learning, creating, and using your imagination.
Studies show that by the time a child reaches college, he/she will have witnessed 8,000 murders on TV, plus 4,000 sex scenes, and 250,000 swear words.	Our rate of learning, creativity, and use of imagination drops once we reach adult age (except for those few who have creative careers). Today's average adult performs a repetitive, unchallenging job during a longer working week, and has fewer creative hobbies.
Serious.	Empathetic and empowering.
Use the classic Lego bricks only, to represent the Lego brand and its many related products.	May not need to show any Lego product.

Lego Strategy 2: Durability

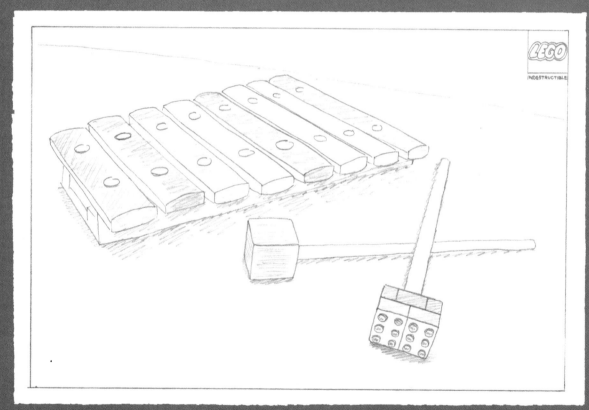

Strategy: unlike other new toys, Lego is built to last. Tag: Indestructible. *Client: Lego. Student: Mariana Black.*

Lego Strategy 3: Safety

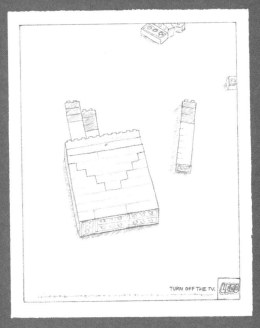

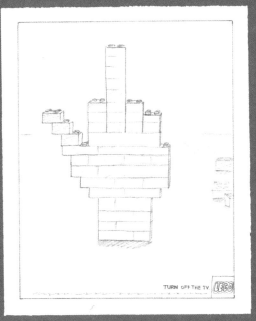

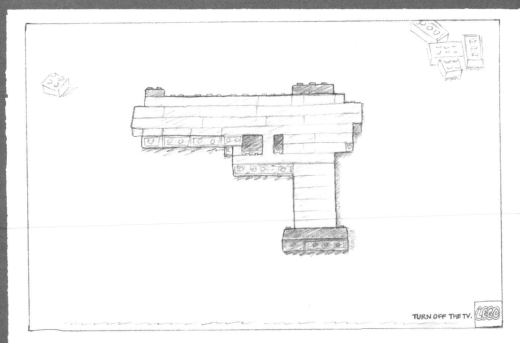

Strategy: safe and socially responsible, Lego is
against kids watching inappropriate television.
Worse than that, kids learn from it. Tag: Turn off
the TV. **Client:** *Lego.* **Student:** *Elizabeth Alexander.*

Print First, TV Second

Traditional, "above the line" *print* ads include:
Posters (or Out of Home/OOH): billboards and other outdoor posters (shapes and sizes shown below), transport posters (bus/train shelter ads, exterior bus-side ads, interior posters/subway cards, platform/cross-track posters), scrolling/changing posters (triptych billboards/posters, illuminated sites), vehicle wraps, giant/supersize posters, building posters, and other special builds.
Press: magazine, newspaper ads (note: in design, the term "print" can also include collateral material, direct mail, brochures, annual reports, etc.)

Print advertising is considered to be advertising's hardest creative discipline, especially compared to broadcast (TV and radio). Think about it, a print ad has to communicate an idea in a few seconds rather than thirty, the images can't "move" or use sound like in TV, and it has to compete with the interesting newspaper and magazine articles right alongside it.

This is precisely why you need to learn to produce print ads before you tackle any other media. The consensus is, if you can do print, you can do anything.

To make a comparison, print is to advertising what figure drawing is to fine art: it provides a creative foundation.

Note: although posters are typically printed on something before they are displayed, the term "print" is sometimes only used to describe press ads. In this case, a "print campaign" = a press campaign (magazine and/or newspaper), and an outdoor/poster campaign is defined separately and not under "print."

Posters: 3 Seconds / 8 Words Maximum

The poster is the quickest form of print advertising and the billboard the quickest form of poster.*
The average time it takes a person to pass a billboard is around 3 seconds. In terms of the number of words, this roughly translates to a maximum of 8 words. The theory is that any longer than this and you may start to lose the reader.

So is this 8-word maximum, 3-second rule set in stone? No. Have there been any great billboards that use lots of words? A few. One example is *The Economist* poster (opposite), which cleverly uses multiple words to dramatize the product benefit.

Therefore the key to creating posters (and arguably press ads, too) is to use the *least number of words necessary* without compromising your idea or affecting the communication. Simply reduce it down to the bare minimum, with an eye on the 3 second/8 words or less "rule." The fewer words you use, the less time it will take to grab someone's attention.

Posters are either "landscape" (their width is greater than their height) or "portrait" (their height is greater than their width), and come in various ratios and dimensions. For now, let's compare the UK and the US (see opposite).

Billboards and other posters are printed and mounted in a number of sections, or "sheets," depending on the final size. In the UK, the "unit" sheet for large posters is a 4-sheet, a poster itself, measuring 40 × 60" (101.6 × 152.4 cm). For example, a 48-sheet is made up of twelve four-sheets, two vertical and six across. In the US, the standard poster size is a one sheet, measuring approximately 27 × 41" (68.6 × 104 cm).

*Billboards are usually alongside roads, where cars move fast and drivers can't be distracted for long. Other posters like bus shelter ads and "cross-tracks" (the ones you read from across the track as you wait for a train) are probably the next fastest to read. Interior bus and subway/underground ads allow for the most time/copy length because the captivity time is longer.

Press (Magazine and Newspaper Ads)

Press ads come in various dimensions, the most common being the single/full page (portrait), and the spread (landscape), also known as a double-page spread, or DPS. Smaller ads include the half page (portrait), half page (vertical), and quarter page.

Note: size isn't everything, as you can see overleaf. The 2.5 × 3.5" press ad on page 60 is part of the long-running multimedia MasterCard campaign.

A poster should contain no more than eight words, which is the maximum the average reader can take in at a single glance. This, however, is a poster for Economist readers.

This poster is a rare exception to the "8 words or less" rule. *Client:* The Economist. *Agency: Abbott Mead Vickers BBDO, London. Creatives:* Tony Strong, Mike Durban.

Common Poster Ratios (width × height)

US	ratio	UK	ratio
		Billboard (48 sheet)	2 × 1
Billboard 1	5 × 2 (approx)		
Billboard 2	3 × 1 (approx)		
Billboard 3	7 × 2 (approx)		
Billboard 4	4 × 1 (approx)	Billboard (96 sheet)	4 × 1
Billboard 5	5 × 1 (approx)		

Transport / Other Posters

Subway card	11 × 1 square		
Poster (Portrait)	2 × 3	Poster (6 sheet)	2 × 3
		Commuter/tube/bus card	3 × 1 (approx)
Subway card 2	6 × 1		

Common Press Dimensions (width × height)

	US	UK
Single/full page	8.5 × 11" (*letter*)	210 × 297 mm (*A4*)
Double page/spread	17 × 11" (*tabloid/ledger*)	420 × 297 mm (*A3*)

Posters vs. Press

Generally speaking, a poster is quicker to absorb than a press ad: people tend to spend more time with a magazine or a paper than they would stare at the average poster, so press ads have the capacity and potential to contain much more copy. (One possible exception is a poster inside a commuter train or bus.) However, you could argue that the 3-second rule for posters should apply to press ads too, in order to grab someone who may be flicking through a magazine or newspaper instead of properly reading it. But with either publication, not only are you competing with other ads, you are competing with the reason why most people buy a magazine or a newspaper—the articles. And surely most of these "competitive" articles take more than 3 seconds to read? The simple answer is that both arguments are valid; both "lengths" of press ad can be effective, depending on what you need to say, how good the idea is, and to whom you are talking. Jim Aitchison differentiates the quick, visually dominant print ad from the longer, copy-driven print ad by asking this simple question: "Do I want to write a letter or send a postcard?" And of the

Polo Crossword

ACROSS

2 Measure for comparing intensity of electric currents (3)

DOWN

1 Common name for Melophagus ovinus, a wingless fly that infests sheep (3)

Small but tough. VW

Last Tuesday's solutions: 2 Across: Vas. 1 Down: Yak.

Small but clever. One of the award-winning print campaigns for the VW Polo. *Client: Volkswagen. Agency: DDB, London. Creatives: Steve Jones, Martin Loraine.*

A small space ad (shown actual size) can still communicate a big idea. *Client: MasterCard. Agency: McCann Erickson.*

grill brush, propane refill and ground beef: $30

(first burger of the season: priceless)

Mastercard

there are some things money can't buy, for everything else there's MasterCard.

two, generally speaking the "postcard" ad could more easily be a poster or a press ad than a "letter." This poster/press ad combination is otherwise known as a "proster" (see below).

Creatively, newspaper and magazine ads tend to be lumped together. But they are clearly not the same. For a start, newspapers are more topical and have a broader audience, so it stands to reason that the ads inside should also be different. Some argue that the ad industry has forgotten this, underestimating the power and potential of the newspaper print ad, which is often seen as a not-so-glossy version of a magazine ad.

"Prosters"

Proster is a relatively new term that neatly defines the hybrid of a press/poster ad. This term reflects the recent trend in visual-led press ads with little or no copy. As a result, these simple press ads can double up as posters, which in some cases has meant a doubling up at awards shows with effectively the same ad (be it in a slightly different format).

The existence of the term "proster" fuels the debate about whether people read copy anymore. The word "copy" once referred to body copy (or long-form copy). Now the concern is whether or not people, in this visually dominant culture, can be bothered to read *any* words on an ad, including headlines and even taglines. It's also a concern that press advertising, the perfect medium for copy, is being grossly under utilized when it is replaced by a proster. There are certainly fewer and fewer copy-dominant press ads appearing in the awards books. Perhaps it's the advertising judges who don't like reading? Although many industry professionals still argue that if something is well written, even body copy, people will read it.

There are a number of recent award-winning ads that prove this point. Interestingly, most have moved away from the traditional "headline followed by body copy" (see opposite). Perhaps presenting and communicating copy in a fresh, new way would "bring copy back" (see also Is Copy Dead?, page 228).

In terms of student portfolios, there does seem to be a concern amongst agencies and headhunters that fewer and fewer books are demonstrating copywriting skills (opting for visual-only campaigns with a logo and tag in the corner)

http://www.landrover.ac.ad.ae.af.ag.ai.al.am.an.ao.aq.ar.as.at.au.aw.az.ba.bb.bd.be.bf.bg.bh.bi.bj.bm.bn.bo.br.bs.bt.bv.bw.by.bz.ca.cc.cf.cg.ch.ci.ck.cl.cm.cn.co.com.cr.cs.cu.cv.cx.cy.cz.de.dj.dk.
dm.do.dz.ec.edu.ee.eg.eh.er.es.et.fi.fj.fk.fm.fo.fr.fx.ga.gb.gd.ge.gf.gh.gi.gl.gm.gn.gov.gp.gq.gr.gs.gt.gu.gw.gy.hk.hm.hn.hr.ht.hu.id.ie.il.in.io.iq.ir.is.it.jm.jo.jp.ke.kg.kh.ki.km.kn.kp.kr.ku.ky.kz.la.lb.lc.li.lk.
lr.ls.lt.lu.lv.ly.ma.mc.md.mg.mh.mil.mk.ml.mm.mn.mo.mp.mq.mr.ms.mt.mu.mv.mw.mx.my.mz.na.nt.ne.net.nf.ng.ni.nl.no.np.nr.nt.nu.nz.om.org.pa.pe.pf.pg.ph.pk.pl.pm.pn.pr.pt.pw.py.qa.
re.ro.ru.rw.sa.sb.sc.sd.se.sg.sh.si.sj.sk.sl.sm.sn.so.sr.st.su.sv.sy.sz.tc.td.tf.tg.th.tj.tk.tm.tn.to.tp.tr.tt.tv.tw.tz.ua.ug.uk.um.us.uy.uz.va.vc.ve.vg.vi.vn.vu.wf.ws.ye.yt.yu.za.zm.zn.zw

LAND-ROVER
GO BEYOND

Reading such a wordy advert is not easy, especially if the person writing it finds it very difficult to put into words exactly what they really sort of mean and they keep using far more words than are absolutely necessary to get the point across quickly and go on and on and on and on about things that are only really interesting to themselves.

And what if the writer starts rambling and ambling with woolly words and nothing he says sense to make seems or maybe he just goes

silent for a few paragraphs. Would you read on, or tell him he's so incredibly funny and take him to the pub where everyone can laugh at him.

Let's be honest, reading takes a little bit of concentration, a smidgen of intelligence and, heaven forbid, time. A telly ad on the other hand is easy to watch and tells you exactly what it means instantly. Why do people like charities write pages and pages of weenie little words about really nasty things when they could just get Tom Cruise saying "Show me the money" – naked. We'd get the point wouldn't we? And it would be a lot less work for us. It's only an advert after all. It's not life and death is it? – well not ours anyway. We don't want to do all that reading, all that hard work, just get to the point.

OK suicide, I want to talk about suicide, now are you going to carry on reading?

(A lot of people just stopped.) But you're prepared to read on and listen. Let's see, yeah I've thought about it, who hasn't? I once thought a great suicide note would be "Things to do today" – be more successful, become a parent, be nicer, get fit, get a conservatory, go on holiday, go mend the tap etc. etc. etc. etc., of course - I knew I couldn't, well wouldn't do any of them, any day – no way José.

So finally I've told you what I want to talk about, sort of. Taken me long enough hasn't it? Why didn't I just put it up front, then you wouldn't have had to listen to all this drivelling on.

But there lies the point and why people like yourselves make good listeners, because they are prepared to put in the effort to "listen".

See, listening properly is just like reading properly, pretending to do them or half doing them doesn't work. If you're thinking about something else you can't read properly, if you take the book down the pub and get pissed you can't read properly, or if you burst into tears and get upset you can't read properly.

Of course you can appear to be reading and listening but in reality it's you that's lost the plot (cracking jokes while someone's trying to confide in you doesn't work either).

No, the ability to listen, like reading has no short cut. It takes effort. It takes patience, and it takes perception, to read between the lines of what's being said. It also takes the brains to know that what's not being said is as important as what is being said, and most of all it takes time.

By now, you've proved you're a good listener. You may be interested to know 16% of men would have told me to snap out of it at paragraph five. 10% of men and women would have simply panicked at paragraph two and 7% of men would have told me to keep my problems to myself.

Statistically speaking, you're also more likely to be a woman (now I know why my wife is so much better at reading books than me) as women find it much easier to talk about their problems because they find it more likely other women will listen to them. Men on the other hand don't expect to be listened to and understood, but joked about, and taken down the pub to forget and fall over. We all know this doesn't help. Neither does being told about all the positive things in your life.

What does help is to really listen, to set aside time to listen, to allow friends to tell you the truth and not play down their problems.

The ability to listen to people in trouble can be the difference between life and death. The Samaritans know this from years and years of experience, but they also know you don't have to be a Samaritan to be a good listener. That's why this year Samaritans Week, which runs from 15th-23rd May, is dedicated to the importance of listening throughout society.

One person in Britain dies by suicide about every 90 minutes. 75% are men. Every 7 seconds someone contacts The Samaritans and every year they receive over 1.5 million silent calls. 55% of young women and 32% of young men have felt that life is not worth living at some stage.

These people are all someone's colleague, neighbour, brother, sister, mother, father or friend. Please take the time to listen to them, use your instinct, if you think someone you know needs help they probably do. Finding that someone actually cares enough to really listen to them really can make the difference between someone choosing life rather than suicide.

Thank you for taking the time to listen.

The Samaritans

---

despite clients still requiring skilled short and long-form writers. So why limit your chances of landing a copywriting job? (See also Chapter 15, The Student Book.)

Consecutive (Sequential) Ads

Such ads work as a set, and can be any identical size, but are usually quarter page or half page ads. Not just "a campaign in a row/in one go," the idea only works if two (or more) ads are read consecutively, one after the other in sequence, often with a twist or product reveal on the final ad.

Headline Only, Visual Only, or Headline and Visual

In terms of print ads (e.g., press ads, posters, billboards, etc.), there are three basic types:

- Headline only
- Visual only
- Headline and visual (or "visual-verbal")

The other components might include the product shot/logo, sub-headline, body copy, and tagline.

Covering planet Earth in a small space print ad (which also became a banner ad). *Client: Land Rover. Agency: Y&R, South Africa. Creatives: Kevin Portellas, Werner Marais.*

If something is well written, people will read it. There's also a conceptual reason for using a single, fully justified paragraph instead of the reader friendly "multiple paragraphs" approach outlined in the Copy chapter. *Client: The Samaritans. Agency: Ogilvy, London. Creatives: Alun Howell, Marcus Vinton.*

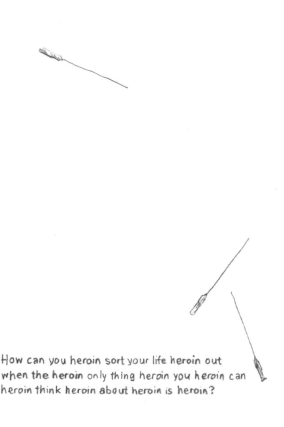

You're freezing your arse off in some doorway every night, you've got no job, no money, and sod all chance of any of it changing. You haven't got any answers but someone's got heroin. There's always someone who's got heroin. Risks? You haven't got anything to lose, remember. So you get off your face and you feel great. You don't have to think when you're wasted. It's a holiday for your brain. But it's only a short trip. It wears off and your life is still crap. If anything, it seems worse. But at least you've got something to look forward to now. The more you use it, the harder it gets to find the money for it, the more you value it, the more you want it, the harder it is to find the money that you owe for it, the more you need it, the harder it is to think about anything else. Alcohol's kind of the same. Give it up? Oh yeah, right. Why? Just because some dickhead in a duffel coat who's read a couple of Irvine Welsh books is telling you that they understand? Words are cheap. Nothing else is. Selling The Big Issue magazine is a way to earn a bit of cash. No strings. No self-righteousness. No law against it. When the vendors come to collect their magazines each week, they get to know about The Big Issue Foundation, that we offer support to help break addictions. We also offer help with mental illnesses, advice and training for jobs, and, of course, assistance with accommodation. It's there if they want it. But there's absolutely no pressure to take it. And that's why hundreds do, every year. The Foundation exists because we believe that homeless people all have the potential to change their lives. Think about it.

How can you heroin sort your life heroin out when the heroin only thing heroin you heroin can heroin think heroin about heroin is heroin?

The use of a consistent type size gives the body copy the same importance (if not more) as the headline. This also encourages you to read the whole ad. *Client: The Big Issue. **Agency:** TBWA, London. **Creatives:** Nigel Roberts, Paul Belford.*

A consecutive (sequential) campaign. (Week 1: red car. Week 2: red and silver. Week 3: red, silver and black. Plus a genie lamp.) **Client:** *Ferrari.* **Creative:** *Pete Barry.*

The executions that make up any campaign should look and feel consistent. That's what makes a campaign stand out. Therefore, a single print campaign should *not* be a mixture of headline only, visual only, or headline and visual.

That said, never approach a project thinking, "I'm going to do a headline-only campaign" (or visual only, or headline and visual, etc.) Think in terms of ideas first, and then try executing your ideas using each variation. One type of print ad will usually help you execute your idea more than another. So once you start, it should be fairly obvious which method creates the greatest ads (in terms of quantity and quality).

Headlines

Punctuation Marks

Let's get this out of the way first. With print advertising, long form copy (or body copy) can accommodate the occasional use of an exclamation mark, italics, or even an underline, to add color to the piece of communication. The same very *rarely* applies to headlines and taglines. In fact, it cheapens them.

Here's why. Take Nike's famous line: Just do it.

This line shouts in a subtle way. The message is so clear and strong that it doesn't need anything else. But imagine if we added some extra punctuation (you know, to really make it shout). The result would be: *Just <u>do</u> it!*

Say this version out loud. Suddenly you can hear the shout of a bad car salesman or an over enthusiastic aerobics instructor. (And that's without even using quotation marks.) *Just do it!* is simply trying too hard to get noticed: trying to dazzle rather than illuminate. In fact, this "approach" goes beyond writing taglines. Neither a headline nor a layout nor an ad in general should have to try this hard to get noticed. If it helps to understand this argument, think of an ad as a person at a singles party. All other things remaining equal, the person who is desperately trying to impress is usually seen as cocky, embarrassing and pitiful, whereas the cool, modest, understated person is invariably more attractive.

So if your headline or tagline needs any of these punctuation marks to help it, chances are it's not a very good line. Only use them if there's a reason for it (i.e., it relates to your idea somehow). A rare example of this was George Lois's rallying cry of a new generation, "I want my MTV!" (1982), reminiscent of James Montgomery Flagg's famous Uncle Sam poster, "I want you for U.S. Army" (1917). The use of an exclamation mark at the end of the MTV slogan helped to emphasize the tongue-in-cheek tone.

The Headline Twist

This is a common technique used by comedians and screenwriters, but can be applied to ads—humorous or serious. It basically starts off by leading the reader's/listener's brain in one direction, and then suddenly pulls it back with an unexpected ending, or "twist." The reason we are misled is because the first half of the line often sounds familiar, even clichéd.

For example, Gomez's line in the "Addams Family Values" movie:

> *You'll meet someone special. Someone who won't press charges.*

Or a one liner, like Dorothy Parker's:

> *One more drink and I'll be under the host.*

Or even Woody Allen's:

> *Life is divided up into the horrible and the miserable.*

Notice that all of these one liners leave the joke until the very last word. It doesn't always have to come in that late, but if you reveal the punch line too early, it will spoil the joke and create an anti-climax for the reader. The key is to keep them guessing for as long as possible. For example, from the movie "Wyatt Earp":

> *My mama always told me never put off 'til tomorrow people you can kill today.*

is funnier than:

> *Never put off 'til tomorrow people you can kill today, is something my mama always told me.*

This ambient ad has a two-part headline (the second part is a good use of parentheses). **Headline:** Keep our beaches beautiful (and pick up the trash, too). *Client: Gold's Gym. Agency: Jack, Los Angeles. Creative: Jack Fund.*

Even a single misplaced word at the end can weaken the delivery of a line. For example:

Men. Can't live with them, can't shoot them.

is better than:

Men. Can't live with them, can't shoot them, either.

because it makes sense to end both of the subclauses with "them."

David Abbott left one famous twist until the last word (or rather, number) in this classic *Economist* ad:

"I never read The Economist." Management trainee. Aged 42.

The second sentence in a headline twist might read better in parenthesis. It tends to make it sound more like a side remark. For example, a sign on the side of a large trashcan reads: keep our beaches beautiful (and pick up the trash, too.) Then we read the logo, for Gold's Gym.

The headline twist can also work off a visual, e.g., the famous Nike poster (opposite, above) shows the French-born Manchester United soccer player, Eric Cantona. The headline begins, "'66 was a great year for English football" (for those

of you who don't know, it was the only year that England has won the World Cup). Then comes the twist: "Eric was born." Ignore the fact that I had to explain the ad—in reality it's a perfect demonstration of the "headline twist" technique.

The contrasting pair is also a type of headline twist, and is explained on page 225.

Headlines (and Taglines) as Questions

The first rule when teaching conversational English is always to structure a question in a way that prevents the student answering with a simple "yes" or "no."

For example: "Do you like football?" is too easy to answer, and requires little English. Whereas: "Why do you like football?" forces more of a reaction; it involves the person.

This is exactly what an ad should do. Suppose for simplicity, the product that you're advertising is football, and headline is as pedestrian as, "Do you like football?" If the reader answers "yes," great, you've found a potential customer. And if they said "no" then that means they're not interested, right? But what if the ad was rewritten to make the reader question his or her lack of interest? Or perhaps get rid of the question and present a good reason for liking football: an example of *why* football is great which could actually help to change someone's point of view.

Remember, an ad is a client's chance to grab someone and get him/her to buy their product. A line that requires a yes/no answer is always a gamble, because the wrong answer is immediately a lost sale. In this case, the ad has categorically failed to do its job.

So if you want to write a line in the form of a question, try to deliver and structure it in a way that prevents the reader from answering "yes" or "no," without weakening your idea. Of course, if it still works better the original way, keep it. However, there are some situations when a question that requires a "yes/no" answer does work.

The first situation is if the reader has already been asking him/herself the same question, or a similar one. For example, someone who has considered joining the army *might* respond well to a boring line such as, "Do you like the idea of jumping out of helicopters?" But in advertising, "might" is not ideal. You want the ad to be the final persuasive argument: the line that clinches the deal and makes the sale. Better yet, try to rewrite the

The pace of this headline twist is helped by the extra line space (beat) between the first and second sentence. *Client:* *Nike.* *Agency:* *Simons Palmer Denton Clemmow and Johnson.* *Creatives:* *Andy McKay, Giles Montgomery.*

This yes/no question makes it virtually impossible to give the wrong answer: "no." *Client:* *Oviatt Hearing & Balance.* ***Students:*** *Kate Ambis, Michael Boyce, Cassandra DiCesare, Anna Bratslavskaya, J. D. Proulx.*

line into something that provokes or encourages all those other individuals who might be army material but haven't realized it yet. This is more likely to achieve the advertising objective—in this case, to maximize the number of new recruits.

The second yes/no exception is if you make it virtually impossible to give the wrong answer. In fact, the reader would have to be a complete idiot to give the wrong answer: either that or a liar. A good example is shown to the right in a student-produced ad for the Oviatt Hearing & Balance audiology center: "If this is how you saw the world, wouldn't you see your optometrist?" This question is very hard to answer incorrectly (i.e., with a "no"). Conversely, a headline for a product that promotes walking as a healthier form of exercise than running: "Has your doctor ever recommended a marathon?" is difficult to answer incorrectly with a "yes."

The fact that these last two headlines also require some *thought* before giving a yes/no response leads us onto the third exception. If there really is no way you can restructure the question to avoid a "yes/no" answer (without weakening your idea), then at least make sure the question forces the consumer to stop and *think* before immediately answering, i.e., come up with an interesting or intriguing question that starts a conversation in one's mind. Perhaps something that gets under the reader's skin and touches a nerve, like this *Economist* headline:

Would you like to sit next to you at dinner?

If this is how you

saw the world, wouldn't you

see your optometrist?

Your hearing is no different. Without it, the quality of your life isn't the same. At Oviatt, our qualified audiologists can accurately diagnose your hearing problem and treat it accordingly.

Oviatt Hearing & Balance
How well do you hear the world?

1001 James Street   315 923 0016

Would you like to sit next to you at dinner?

The Economist

A question that forces the reader to stop and think before answering. *Client: The Economist. Agency: Abbott Mead Vickers BBDO, London. Creatives: David Abbott, Ron Brown.*

The above question is not something one gets asked every day. It's actually a deceptively profound, personal question, forcing the reader to answer with further self-examining questions like: "Am I smart? Am I stupid? Am I interesting? Am I charismatic? Am I funny?"

Similarly, a recruitment ad for the UK's Metropolitan Police force that shows a thug spitting into an officer's face:

Could you turn the other cheek?

This type of direct questioning applies to taglines, too. For example, *The Independent* newspaper's tag:

The Independent. It is. Are you?

In addition, let's not forget those question taglines that are structured to require more than a quick yes/no answer, again making the reader *think*, thereby involving them for a longer period:

Who would you most like to have a One 2 One with? (One 2 One mobile phone company)

What's the worst that can happen? (Dr. Pepper)

Where do you want to go today? (Microsoft)

Conversely, a question may be posed whereby the answer is obvious; the question is merely being used to get the consumer to think about the point that is being raised. In other words, it's to make the consumer think *afterwards* rather than beforehand, as in some of the above cases. This is known as a rhetorical question, i.e., one that is making an obvious point rather than requiring an answer. For example, this ad for Atlanta Ballet's "Romeo and Juliet":

Two dancers die. What better reason to attend?

Here the question is really the answer, i.e., there is no better reason to attend. (Similarly, a question like "who cares?" actually means, "nobody cares.")

Another example is in a Christmas ad for The Episcopal Church. The visual shows two portraits, one of Santa and one of Jesus. The question above reads:

Whose birthday is it, anyway?

Likewise, this question is really saying, "it's Jesus's birthday." Similarly, a headline for the same client, next to a visual of a bible, reads:

What are you waiting for, the movie to come out?

The UK's Flowers & Plants Association tagline was a message to empty-handed women:

Flowers. Why wait? Buy your own.

This question is also rhetorical. It is really saying, "don't wait."

A hypothetical question is also meant to make you think, but in a different way. It's one of those "it would probably never happen but what if…?" type of questions. A famous ad example is the Health Education Council ad portraying a pregnant man:

Would you be more careful if it was you that got pregnant?

Again, the answer should be obvious: "yes."

Some questions that demand a yes/no answer may also have a double meaning, or rather, two questions in one. For example, Gatorade's tagline:

Is it in you?

The first meaning questions whether you drink the product, i.e., "is Gatorade inside your body?" The second asks the target consumer a deeper question: "Is the desire to do well at sport, in you?"

Another (and possibly the last) exception for using a question with a yes/no answer is an extension of the second reason above (when the question is virtually impossible to answer). It's when the ad assumes the consumer will answer correctly and then provide a follow-up response. For example, the Nike poster (opposite):

Ever heard the Algerian national anthem? You will.

(Unless the reader was Algerian, the answer to Nike's question will most likely be the anticipated, "no," which is what makes the punchline work.) Alternatively, the answer could be hidden in the body copy of the ad.

So to summarize, seven possible exceptions for using a question with a yes/no answer:

- It's a question the consumer has already been seriously asking him/herself
- It's virtually impossible for anyone to answer incorrectly (i.e., "no" instead of "yes," "yes" instead of "no")
- It's a question that really makes the consumer *think* before answering
- It's a rhetorical question, i.e., one that is making a point and is not meant to be answered
- It's a hypothetical, "what if?" question

- It has a double meaning: two questions in one
- The ad provides the correct answer with the use of a follow-up line or body copy

TV is an ideal medium for asking direct questions. With TV, you have the option to present the question either visually (text) or verbally (voice over). Plus, you have more time to set up the idea, or ask more than one question if necessary. The extended build-up that TV provides can make the humorous/serious pay-off that much more powerful and surprising.

Got Ideas?
The "Got Milk?" campaign is another good example of making the consumer think before

ATLANTA BALLET'S
Romeo & Juliet

An amusing, self-deprecating rhetorical question: the answer is meant to be obvious. *Client: Atlanta Ballet.* **Agency:** *Sawyer Riley Compton, Atlanta.* **Creatives:** *Kevin Thoem, Ari Weiss.*

This rhetorical question is more interesting than saying, "It's Jesus's birthday." **Client:** *Church Ad Project (church.com).* **Agency:** *Fallon McElligott Rice.* **Creatives:** *Tom McElligott, Nancy Rice.*

 EVER HEARD THE ALGERIAN NATIONAL ANTHEM? YOU WILL.

Another good use of a yes/no question: before you have a chance to answer, the ad gives its response. *Client: Nike.* **Agency:** *Simons Palmer Denton Clemmow and Johnson.* **Creatives:** *Andy McKay, Tony Barry, Chris Palmer, Tim Riley.*

Perhaps the most famous question in advertising. And as a result, painfully plagiarized ever since. **Client:** *California Fluid Milk Processor Advisory Board.* **Agency:** *Goodby Silverstein & Partners, San Francisco.* **Creatives:** *Sean Ehringer. Rich Silverstein, Peter di Grazia, Mike Mazza, Chuck McBride, Jeff Goodby.*

A possible exception to making sure you avoid the ever-tempting rhyming pun. **Client:** *Apple.* **Agency:** *TBWA/Chiat/Day.*

answering with a quick "yes" or "no." This simple, clever idea is based on a problem/solution strategy. The headline/tagline question "Got Milk?" is a friendly reminder on the one hand, and yet demands some thought too. Because the truth is, it's hard to remember whether or not there's enough milk in the fridge. You have to think about it. Part of the idea also plays off the fact that it's a real pain when you've run out of it, with mouth-drying executions to help dramatize this slightly unpleasant feeling (yet another example of John Hegarty's pithy mantra: "dramatize the simple").

But one final comment on this campaign: *the parodying needs to stop.* No more "Got (insert word/product here)?" slogans. T-shirts, mugs, and bumper stickers are one thing, but ads? All these really say to people is: got any new ideas?

Word Puns vs. Visual Puns

Most puns are a silly, contrived "play on words," and therefore give the rich area of wordplay a bad name. Two of the worst habits to pick up from bad advertising are these two types of pun: the rhyming pun, where one word is replaced by a rhyming

word (e.g., pranks for the memories: to pee or not to pee, Hippy Birthday) and the sound-alike pun, where one word is replaced by a word that sounds phonetically the same (e.g., Czech it out, bored of education, let's talk about secs). As you can see, these are not hard to write. Bad puns may work fine for greetings cards, tabloid newspapers, car stickers, hair salons, and goofy t-shirts, but they are largely considered to be the lowest form of advertising. (There's even a word to describe the fear of puns: "paronomasiaphobia.")

Everyone does the occasional pun when starting out, and the rare pun has even made its way into an awards book. Puns that use the same spelling of a word that has a double meaning are much more accepted (see Double Meaning, below).

But keep puns at arm's length. As someone once said, "Puns are like candy—nice and sweet at first, but eventually they'll rot your teeth." So the quicker you get puns out of your system, the better. (If it helps, dig out a copy of *My First Joke Book* from when you were about five!) Of course, there are always exceptions. The headline, "Mental floss" for the Apple G3 is perhaps one. It played off the

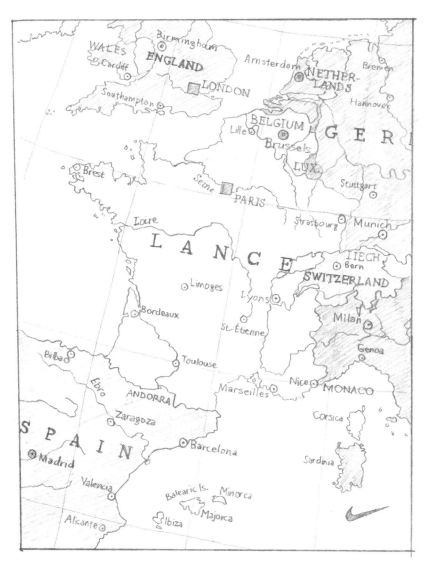

"Think different" tagline well, and implied the machine's "clean," efficient running. The famous Perrier "Eau" campaign ran for more than a decade, with a plethora of "identical rhyming" puns for the sound "o" (as in eau, the French for "water"). Examples included the introductory "H$_2$Eau" and the festive Santa ad, "Heau, heau, heau."

That said, here's one of the best (or should I say worst) examples of a rhyming pun in an ad. It's from a poster for a famous zoo (I won't say which one), nicely art directed, with a cute photo of a little Marmoset monkey. The headline was (brace yourself…): "Marmoset there'd be days like this."

Get it? Marmoset, instead of "Momma said."

Perhaps there's a clever double meaning. Let's see: Momma said there'd be days like this. Days like what? What the hell has this got to do with getting people to go to a zoo? It's nothing more than a lame joke. (Sorry, creative team.)

For some reason, the other type of puns, *visual* puns are less despised than word puns, perhaps because they tend to be simpler, cleverer, based on a truth, or are a little more intriguing and lateral. Being wordless, visuals are by definition less "punny." That's not to say that there aren't any bad visual only ads. (Nike's terrific "Lance" ad could be described as part-word pun, part-visual pun.) (See Avoid Clichéd Imagery, page 36.)

Double Meaning

Lines or phrases that have a double meaning are technically puns in that they're a "play on words." But as discussed above, the puns to avoid the most are the rhyming pun and sound-alike pun. By contrast, double meanings can be used in headlines and taglines to great effect. They are significantly

A more acceptable "identical rhyming pun" campaign, the "o" sound was matched with the French word for water, eau. A festive Santa ad ran with the headline, "Heau, heau, heau." *Client:* Perrier. *Agency:* Leo Burnett. *Creatives:* Mike Trumble, Colin Campbell.

Part-word pun, part-visual pun: the "headline" is a rhyming pun, but done in a visually compelling way. *Client:* Nike. *Agency:* Publicis Mojo, Australia. *Creatives:* Tim Forte, Paul Bootlis. *Creative director:* Dave Spiller.

The best type of double meaning: both meanings relate back to the product, not just one. *Client: The Conservative Political Party. Agency: Saatchi & Saatchi, London. Creatives: Martyn Walsh, Andrew Rutherford.*

Product personification, with a simple double meaning of the word "rich." *Client: Cityscape Deli, Atlanta.*

The headline technique used here is double meaning (constable as in "police officer," and as in "the landscape painter") and the strategy is competitive advertising. (If you can, say something positive about your product before putting down the competition.) *Client: Intercity. Agency: Saatchi & Saatchi, London. Creatives: Alexandra Taylor, James Lowther.*

cleverer and less contrived than rhyming and sound-alike puns because they find and use words that have the *same spelling* for both meanings.

The best examples of a double meaning are those in which *both* meanings (or levels) clearly relate back to the message/product, not just one. Take the UK's most famous poster for The Conservative Party (The Labour Party's opposition):

Labour isn't working.

For a Conservative, both the meanings are correct and "positive": the current Labour Party (both in general and what it stands for) isn't working; and labour (as in the workforce) isn't working because of the high unemployment rate.

Across the Atlantic, a headline for Cityscape Deli personifies a product to create a double meaning with the word "rich":

If our coffee were any richer it would vote Republican.

While Intercity uses the double meaning of the word "constable":

At 100mph, this is the only Constable you'll find alongside you.

Taglines also count:

The car in front is a Toyota.

And for Nissan, one word:

Driven.

For a double meaning to work effectively, *at least one* of the meanings has to be a truly positive reason for buying the product. For example, let's pretend "richness" is actually a negative quality in coffee. The above headline, "If our coffee were any richer it would vote Republican" still has a double meaning with the word "rich," but neither one is a positive reason for buying the product. If there's no obvious product benefit, why buy the product? A coffee company's ability to tell Republican jokes is (in this altered scenario) forced, and says nothing positive about their coffee. Only if the product were more relevant to politics (e.g., The Democratic Party) would the ad work.

Therefore, one of the two meanings can even be a negative or an absurdity. Clearly not applying to the product, this negative meaning only works if the other, intended meaning is equally positive.

One cancels out the other. Here are three humorous examples:

- *My wife doesn't stop moaning* (male "performance" pill)
- *Our product really sucks* (vacuum cleaner)
- *Gets drunk and collapses* (mineral water in a new, collapsible plastic bottle)

Some double meanings have more than two meanings. The earlier Conservative Party example actually works on three levels (the first has two parts to it). This can apply to taglines, too:

> **Client:** Slimfast
> **Idea:** Show fat people laughing about their weight.
> **Tagline:** *If you can't laugh it off, Slimfast.*
> **Triple Meaning:** Laugh it off (i.e., ignore/don't be affected by the fat jokes); laugh off the fact that you are actually overweight; laugh it off (i.e., burn/get rid of) the weight.

Of course, a double meaning can exist visually as well as verbally. Visual-only examples include visual simile, which are examined on page 122.

The Sub-headline ("Subhead")

The use of a single, additional sub-headline creates a slightly different type of ad (with or without a visual). The subhead works directly from or follows the headline, either to complete or explain the idea, or to add some other useful information (in the same way that the first line of body copy might do). This creates a different rhythm, flow or "read" than in a headline-only ad, e.g., a headline/sub-headline only ad.

Note: if your idea requires a subhead, so be it. But if a headline needs one, the headline *usually* needs more work.

Headline and Visual (or Visual-Verbal)

This is the relationship between the visual and the verbal: in other words, how the visual part of an ad relates to the verbal (written) part. This section specifically covers the headline-visual relationship. The tagline-visual relationship is examined in The Tagline chapter.

Direct and Indirect Visuals

When you have an ad with a headline and a visual, the visual is usually a "direct visual," or an "indirect visual." Both have equal merit.

This Boddingtons' campaign has a double meaning in the "Strong Stuff" tagline (strong as in "alcoholic" plus strong as in "hard hitting"). *Client: Boddingtons.* **Agency:** *Bartle Bogle Hegarty, London.* **Creatives:** *John Gorse, Nick Worthington.*

If you can't laugh it off, Slimfast. A tagline with a triple meaning: laugh off the fat jokes, laugh off the fact that you are actually overweight and laugh it off (i.e., burn/get rid of) the weight. *Client: Slimfast.* **Creatives:** *Pete Barry, Sally Evans.*

Headline introducing (cute) visual. *Client:* Volkswagen. *Agency:* BMP DDB, London. *Creatives:* Tony Cox, Mark Reddy.

You can't beat this type of ad: four simple words and a surprising visual. *Client: Horn & Hardart. Agency:* Carl Ally. *Creatives: Ed McCabe, Ron Barrett.*

Headline introducing visual. *Client: The Children's Defense Fund. Agency:* Fallon McElligott. *Creatives: Tom McElligott, Dean Hanson.*

Headline introducing visual, with a thought-provoking twist. *Client: The Health Education Council. Agency:* Saatchi & Saatchi. *Creatives: Fergus Fleming, Simon Dicketts.*

An indirect visual relates indirectly to the headline in some way, but is often just an art direction piece or a background visual(s) that helps to give the ad a certain look, mood or feeling. A common example is the holiday resort ad that contains a compelling headline (and body copy), with a beautiful photograph(s) of the destination. Although not as interesting to look at, an ad like this would probably still work in a headline-only format.

Most of the headline and visual ads that have been produced over the last fifty years use a direct visual, as evident in this book. In other words, the visual relates *directly* to the headline in some way. Direct visuals are arguably more important than indirect ones because without either the headline or the direct visual, the ad wouldn't make sense.

Avoid "Headline Repeating Visual" ("See-Say")

This is one of the most common mistakes made by inexperienced advertising students, in which part of the headline (or the entire headline) is repeating what the visual is already communicating. It's what my ad instructor in the UK called, "see Janet running," which refers to the technique in children's early reading books, where a sentence literally repeats the picture. A US equivalent is "see Spot run." Because most consumers are literate adults, it's unnecessary to spell out the visual part of the ad. Remember, you're doing an ad, not a graphic design piece (design often uses words that repeat the visual). So unless there's a reason, avoid "headline repeating visual." It's a trap we all fall into, possibly because of the desperate, conscious need to communicate an idea quickly and clearly. In reality, it's superfluous, and slows down the communication. Instead, the headline and visual should "play off" each other, either using the headline as an introduction to the visual or a contrast/contradiction. Usually a slight rewording avoids the headline repeating the visual. For example, the ad on page 67 (above, right) is leaner (and better) than if the headline read, "Is it Santa's birthday or Jesus's?" Whenever the *entire* headline is repeating the visual, as in the Jeep "Key" ad on page 122, it is possible to run the ad with just a visual, which did actually happen in this case.

As with all "rules," there are rare, brilliant exceptions, like the famous "Mr. Ferrari drives a Fiat" ad (although one could easily argue that the ad could still work minus either the headline

or visual). However, omitting the photo of Mr Ferrari and his Fiat would reduce both the visual interest and the believability of the headline. Leaving out a headline would have perhaps relied too much on the consumer recognizing his face.

Headline Introducing Visual

This common type of headline introduces or "sets up" the visual. Therefore, this kind of ad makes most sense when you read the headline first, and then look at the visual. The idea or punch line of the ad is "revealed" by the visual. The unexpected is what creates the tension between the two elements. The visual is usually "direct" (it directly relates to the visual). Cover up the visual and the ad won't work, or at least not as well.

The best way of explaining a "headline introducing visual" ad is by showing examples:

"If you're embarrassed by a pimple try explaining this."

The level of tension is perhaps not as "in your face" as contrast/contradiction (see below), but it will produce a more lateral, dramatic, and interesting ad than a "headline repeating visual." To illustrate this, simply change a "headline introducing visual" ad into a "headline repeating visual." For example, Horn & Hardart's "You can't eat atmosphere" is infinitely better than "you can't eat candles, carpet, light bulbs and wallpaper" (see opposite, above, right).

However, should you ever find you have a headline that is not repeating the visual but is not adding much to the ad either, try taking one of the elements out. It may produce a simpler, clearer, better ad. This is known as reductionism (see page 77).

In the case where an ad has body copy, but no direct visual (i.e., a headline-only ad, or headline with indirect visual), the headline could introduce the first line of copy instead. In fact, this is the first step of the "invisible thread" technique found in many types of print ad (see the Copy chapter for more details).

Contrast and Contradiction

The opposite of a bad, "see Spot run" ad (where the headline repeats the visual) is the contrasting or contradictory headline. This classic technique has been used for decades. Its success lies in the *tension* created between the headline and the direct visual. When you look at a headline and visual ad, you

The only squeaks and rattles you'll ever hear in a Volkswagen.

Golf VW

You can't eat atmosphere.

Horn & Hardart. It's not fancy. But it's good.

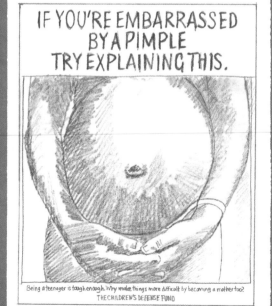

IF YOU'RE EMBARRASSED BY A PIMPLE TRY EXPLAINING THIS.

Being a teenager is tough enough. Why make things more difficult by becoming a mother too?
THE CHILDREN'S DEFENSE FUND

The first time you have sex can be a really unforgettable experience.

Health Education Council

JOHN KENNEDY'S FINGERPRINT.

 John F. Kennedy Library & Museum

Ceci n'est pas une pipe.

Barnardo's

John Donaldson | AGE 23

It killed
Hitler.

ISSUED BY THE CABINET WAR ROOMS

Top This ad communicates to its reader in three steps: visual simile, then headline contradicting visual, and finally the message itself (the first moon landing is part of JFK's résumé too). *Client: John F. Kennedy Presidential Library and Museum.* **Agency:** *The Martin Agency, Minneapolis.* **Creatives:** *Joe Alexander, Cliff Sorah.*

Above, centre, left The line reads, "This is not a pipe." This is not an ad either, but René Magritte's surreal painting (*c.* 1928–29) is an early example of a classic ad technique: contrast and contradiction between line and visual. "This is a pipe" would have been a headline repeating visual ad —boring and redundant.

Above, left Opposites attract: powerful/unusual visual + straight/understated headline. *Client: Barnardo's.* **Agency:** *Bartle Bogle Hegarty, London.* **Creatives:** *Adrian Rossi, Alex Grieve.*

Above, right Opposites attract: straight/understated visual + powerful/unusual headline. (You can't help but want to read the body copy.) *Client: The Imperial War Museum, London.* **Agency:** *Harari Page, London.* **Creatives:** *Stuart Elkins, Graeme Cook.*

How to kill a baby.

It's easy. All you do is walk up to it. It won't run away.

Then, as it looks up at you trustingly, mistaking you for its mother, you smash in its skull with a baseball bat.

That's what happens to baby seals in Canada every year in a bloody ritual that lasts six weeks.

In Japan they do it a different way. They herd dolphins into the shallows, wait for the tide to leave them stranded, then go through the same grisly process.

Then there's the whales. You know what happens to them.

Doing it is dead easy if your mind is warped enough. Stopping it is a whole lot harder, but there is something you can do.

In this week's Woman's Day we're running a thought provoking article on what's happening to these beautiful creatures.

We're also running a simple competition that you and your children can enter. All you have to do is tell us in less than twenty words what the seals, the dolphins or the whales would say to us if they could speak.

There are cash prizes, but far more importantly, for every entry in the competition Woman's Day will donate 10 cents to Greenpeace to help their work in bringing this ghastly business to a halt.

Look for this week's Woman's Day. It's the one with the baby seal on the cover, seconds before it dies.

Woman's Day.

How to kill a baby.

It's easy. All you do is walk up to it. It won't run away.

Then, as it looks up at you trustingly, mistaking you for its mother, you smash in its skull with a baseball bat.

That's what happens to baby seals in Canada every year in a bloody ritual that lasts six weeks.

In Japan they do it a different way. They herd dolphins into the shallows, wait for the tide to leave them stranded, then go through the same grisly process.

Then there's the whales. You know what happens to them.

Doing it is dead easy if your mind is warped enough. Stopping it is a whole lot harder, but there is something you can do.

In this week's Woman's Day we're running a thought provoking article on what's happening to these beautiful creatures.

We're also running a simple competition that you and your children can enter. All you have to do is tell us in less than twenty words what the seals, the dolphins or the whales would say to us if they could speak.

There are cash prizes, but far more importantly, for every entry in the competition Woman's Day will donate 10 cents to Greenpeace to help their work in bringing this ghastly business to a halt.

Look for this week's Woman's Day. It's the one with the baby seal on the cover, seconds before it dies.

Woman's Day.

Again, a straight/understated visual + powerful/unusual headline. *Client:* Sungravure Pty Ltd/Woman's Day. *Agency:* The Campaign Palace, Australia. *Creatives:* Lionel Hunt, Gordon Trembath, Sally Grebe. *Advertising manager*: Fred Brenchley.

Using a shocking visual is arguably less compelling because it's now competing with (canceling out) the shocking headline. Plus the original ad leaves more to the imagination.

tend to read it in a particular order, either headline then visual, or visual then headline. Either way there's a tension.

A non-advertising example (opposite, middle, left) by Surrealist painter René Magritte is possibly the earliest example of a seemingly contradictory headline and visual. With *Ceci n'est pas une pipe* (*c*. 1928–29) which means "this is not a pipe," Magritte is simply saying that this is not actually a real, tangible pipe but an image of an object. Artistic meaning aside, what's important is the tension that provokes an immediate reaction when we look at the painting (compared to the dull "headline repeating visual" version, "this is a pipe").

Similarly, there would be no tension or contradiction if the headline in the John Kennedy's fingerprint ad (opposite, top) read "Neil Armstrong's footprint."

Usually the more a headline and visual can contrast or contradict one another, the better. The general "rule" when it comes to creating the maximum contrast, contradiction, or tension between visual and headline is *opposites attract*. In other words:

Powerful/unusual visual + straight/understated headline = good ad

Straight/understated visual + powerful/unusual headline = good ad

Whereas:

Powerful/unusual headline + powerful/unusual visual = good or bad ad * (can cancel each other out)

Straight/understated headline + straight/understated visual = bad ad (no spark between the two elements). For example, the headline "Learn every little detail about Churchill's war" plays off the same visual (without repeating it), but there's not enough tension, and therefore interest. It doesn't compare to the original version with the "It killed Hitler" headline (opposite, right). This ad is so immediately compelling that it would make anyone want to read all the body copy.

Imagine having your body left to science while you're still in it.

People For The Ethical Treatment Of Animals

A rare example where both the headline and the visual are powerful, but neither cancel each other out. In this case (unlike the baby seal example on the previous page) a cute monkey photo would actually weaken the ad. *Client: PETA.* *Agency: The Martin Agency, Richmond.* *Creatives: Luke Sullivan, Wayne Gibson.*

*There are exceptions to these "rules," particularly in the case of "powerful/unusual headline + powerful/unusual visual." As you can imagine, this example is not easy to pull off (firstly because one powerful/unusual element is usually enough, and secondly two powerful/unusual elements will tend to fight each other). It really all depends on the particular idea. Sometimes this scenario will produce a great ad, such as above (PETA's "Monkey/Body to science" ad). But, by contrast, a cute picture of a monkey (like the seal photo on the previous page) would not work as well as seeing the monkey in pain.

The "hierarchy" of an ad is the order of importance of each element, and therefore the order in which you want the consumer to read the ad. There may be more tension by looking at the headline last—or perhaps the visual last—depending on the idea. Art direction helps to determine the order in which you look at an ad, and therefore the hierarchy (see also Hierarchy, below).

The (Alternative Headline) Headline and Visual Ad

Whether used on its own or with a visual(s), headlines don't have to follow the standard, format of a prose-like sentence. A "headline" can equally be:

- Two or more sentences
- A list of words
- A table of information
- A list of facts and figures
- A series of questions and answers
- A series of letters or numbers

Note: there still has to be an idea to using alternative headlines. See Shopping List Ads and Calendar Ads, and "Dictionary Definition" Ads on pages 87 and 89 for a further explanation.

(See also The Sub-headline, page 71.)

Visuals

Hierarchy (Most-Less-Least)

The maximum number of elements in a single print ad is *six*: headline, sub-headline, visual(s), body copy, tagline, and logo. Again, less usually equals more (see Reductionism, below). So once you have a concept, and know the *minimum* number of elements required, decide on the order of importance (or "hierarchy") of each element. This should reflect the order in which you want the consumer to read your print ad, expressed through the art direction (i.e., the sizing and positioning) of these elements. In other words, the hierarchy dictates where you want the reader to look first, second, third…and last.

A simple way of explaining hierarchy is by applying the most-less-least tool. In other words, think of each layout having the most of one thing, less of another, and the least of another. (Notice that this tool only uses three elements for simplicity, but the principle can be expanded to include a forth, fifth and sixth.)

The main reason for hierarchy is so that each element is not competing or fighting with one another for attention. By art directing the layout, you're basically directing the consumer around the ad. Don't forget, advertising is all about efficient communication.

Some basic layout variations of hierarchy are illustrated on page 78. These thumbnails show different hierarchical choices of the famous "No" Health Education Council press ad. In the first one, you don't know where to look first, second, third, etc. The hierarchy in each layout is arguably "better" than in the one before. The last layout is the one that art director Fergus Fleming used. The hierarchy in his ad makes it very clear where to look first, second, third, and last. (Note how the use of "white space" around the headline makes it tonally less aggressive than in the preceding one, and interestingly, turns the headline into more of a visual.)

There are an infinite number of layout combinations, each with its own hierarchy. The more you experiment with sizing, positioning, and negative space, the more evident these hierarchal possibilities become. A simple demonstration of this can be seen on the right. The press campaign from which this Jamaican Tourist Board ad originated was a radical departure from the standard VW layout that DDB also created. The logo appears large enough to be the "most" element, but its vertical positioning cleverly changes the hierarchy back in favor of the headline and visual.

Reductionism (Fat-Free Advertising)

Reductionism is the practice of reducing the elements of an ad as far as possible, but to the point where the communication still works. But agencies don't always get to cut out all the unnecessary "fat." The conflict lies in the client's dogged desire to tell consumers as much as possible about their product, without realizing that these superfluous elements only serve to overwhelm the consumer and cloud the communication. A famous demonstration of what could be called "anti-additionism" occurred during a presentation by Fred Manley of BBDO in 1963. Ironically titled, "Nine Ways to Improve an Ad" (he chose VW's iconic "Think Small") and demonstrated that the

more you put in an ad, the worse it gets. Today's agencies (and especially clients) can still learn from this lesson in reductionism.

Probably more than any part of creating print ads, students have the most trouble reducing down the elements. Without realizing it, they actually have a leaner, simpler, better ad right in front of them. Sometimes the improvement is the result of omitting just one element, or even part of an element. So when you look at your ad, always ask yourself, "does this need to be in the ad? Will it still work without it?"

Remember, the maximum number of elements is *six* (headline, subhead, visual(s), body copy, tagline, and logo). That's a lot. The chances are you won't need all of them. The number you use depends on a combination of things, namely the brief, the idea, the product, and the audience. But generally speaking, less is more. These terms apply to print and TV visuals in particular.

A headline can be anything (like a list of football results). Here, Arsenal's famous undefeated/no loss season, with a clever piece of observation (namely the letter "L" in the club's name), provides a clever, non-prose ad. *Client: Nike. Agency: Wieden & Kennedy, London. Creatives: Guy Moore, Tony Malcolm.*

A giant logo was (and still is) unusual. But the clever vertical positioning makes it less distracting, therefore restoring the natural hierarchy. Headline: Huntley Levy's ancestors were German, Welsh, African, Portuguese and Jewish. He's pure Jamaican. *Client: The Jamaican Tourist Board. Agency: DDB, New York.*

The Health Education Council
Helping you to better health.

No. Still the most
effective form
of birth control.

No.
Still the most
effective form
of birth control.

The Health Education Council

No.

Still the most
effective form
of birth control.

The Health Education Council

No.

Still the most effective form of birth control.

The Health Education Council

No.

Still the most effective form of birth control.

The Health Education Council

Most-less-least: an exercise in hierarchy. The use of white space in the final (actual) ad is arguably more effective than the bigger headline in the preceding one. The headline may be small, but it's still the "most," i.e., the first thing you look at. **Client:** *The Health Education Council.* **Agency:** *Saatchi & Saatchi, London.* **Creative:** *Fergus Fleming.*

Reductionism: "Skid marks"

To demonstrate the process of reductionism, let's deliberately elaborate on an award-winning print ad for Mercedes adapted from Luke Sullivan's *Hey Whipple, Squeeze This*. E is the final ad that ran, which uses only two elements, visual and logo. But first, let's start backwards, using the maximum six elements (A). (The headline, subhead, copy, and tagline are clearly fake, for the purposes of this exercise.)

The key to reductionism is to *locate and isolate the idea*. Once you find it, you may not need much else. In the above case, the idea is in the title: "Skid marks" (or in a sentence, "When you park your new Mercedes SLK, lots of other car owners will brake to take a look, causing lots of skid marks"). With such a definite, simple idea you don't need anything else. The result is E, the final produced ad. Be careful not to over reduce, as in F. E has two logos (the second "logo" is on the actual car), whereas F may be under-branded without the first logo in the bottom right corner. See also two versions of David Ogilvy's famous "Electric Clock" ad on page 134.

- *Headline:* Ever wondered why skid marks appear in some places more than others?
- *Subhead:* The new SLK starts at £20,000.
- *Visual:* Skid marks next to a parked Mercedes.
- *Body copy:* (Sharp, persuasive copy about why other drivers will be so jealous of your new, amazing-looking Mercedes SLK.)
- *Logo:* Mercedes logo/The new SLK.
- *Tagline:* Building Cars Since 1891.

Ever wondered why skid marks appear in some places more than others?

The new SLK starts at £20,000.

Building Cars Since 1891. The new SLK

(a)

(b)

An exercise in reductionism, beginning with all the possible elements: headline, subhead, visual, body copy, logo, and tagline. E is the final ad that ran, not F, which proves that you can over reduce. *Client: Mercedes. Agency: Leo Burnett, London. Creatives: Mark Tutssel, Nick Bell.*

(c)

(d)

(e)

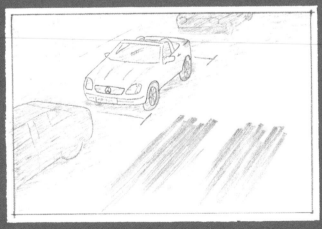
(f)

Reductionism: "Unbreakable"

Reductionism of an individual element is also possible, most often within either a headline or a visual. Typically, beginner students will create ads with either an overwritten headline or an overcomplicated visual. Reductionism not only improves the communication by speeding up and simplifying the ad, it also improves the idea. To illustrate, let's take an initial concept presented by a student. The brief was for Kryptonite bike locks; the proposition was "security." The first layouts were "visual only," and looked like the layouts shown here.

I then asked the student to *locate and isolate the idea*. She said, "Kryptonite locks are as tough as a block of wood that can crack an axe blade...or a railing that can blunt a saw...or a nail that can snap a hammer in two." But what's the *really* clever bit in each ad: the *idea*? She finally answered: "The cracked blade, broken hammer, and blunted saw?" Exactly. I circled these bits (opposite, left column). Put another way, you don't need the block of wood, the railing or the nail! The visual can be reduced down to the individual objects and the ad still works. The original layout used analogy, but was almost too lateral. The final layout is more literal in that it relates the idea back to the product (opposite, right column). Showing only the destroyed object implies that the lock has done it, thereby clearly communicating the product benefit. It's a slightly different ad from the first layout, but a much better one.

Cropping and Framing

Sometimes an element is reduced over a period of time, from campaign to campaign, to form a new version, e.g., the simplification of a tagline or a logo (McDonald's "We love to see you smile" later became "Smile"; the original Nike/tick logo subtracted the word "Nike" to leave just the tick). In both cases, consumers made the connection with the earlier, "fatter" versions, hence the communication still worked (see Tagline Reductionism, page 105).

Conversely, don't overdo the reductionism. Look at the big picture. If your ad's ultimate objective is to encourage children to call an abuse helpline, you should keep the line of copy that includes the telephone number.

Initial Layouts

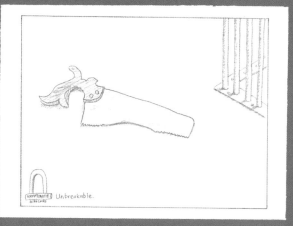

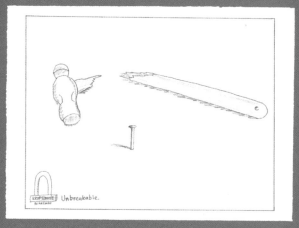

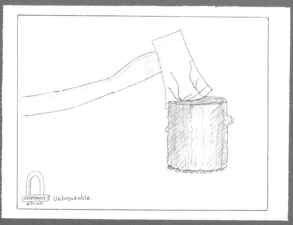

Locating and Isolating the Idea

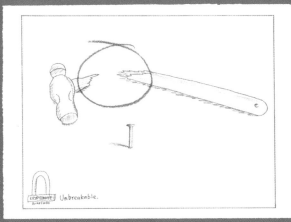

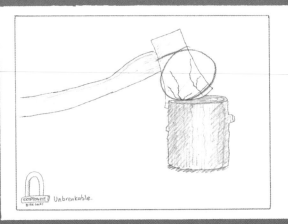

Final Layouts

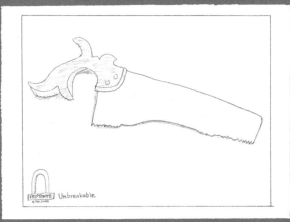

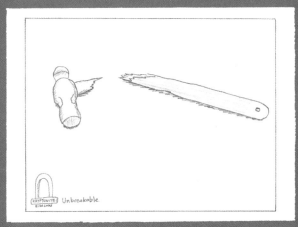

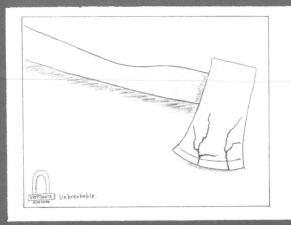

What's the clever bit? A demonstration in reductionism, plus how to isolate and locate the idea. **Student:** *Brittany King.*

Cropping and Framing: "Pick me"

An exercise in cropping and framing. The bottom one is not the final produced ad, the one above is, which proves that the tightest crop/frame isn't always the best option. **Client:** *Pepsi-Cola Company.* **Agency:** *BBDO, Toronto.* **Creatives:** *Scott Dube, Ian MacKellar.*

If, for example, you want to show the drama of a pimple on the end of a teenager's nose, you may already have an idea for a headline, but first decide on the framing (the positioning) of your visual. Is the view of the teenager from above, below, or the side? Sketch out all the possibilities. Then decide where and how far to crop (or zoom). Don't be afraid to *get in there*. Remember, you are "dramatizing the simple." Try lots of versions: head and shoulders, face, nose, pimple, etc. Keep zooming in and out until the cropping and framing of the visual really works well with the headline. There's a tendency to forget that just because you know where the idea is (the pimple), it doesn't mean that the reader does.

Opposite are four cropping and framing examples. Remember, the key is to locate and isolate the idea: ice cubes want to be picked to share and swim in a glass of Pepsi. Therefore, the cropping and framing should include (at the least) the Pepsi can, the glass, and someone reaching for a tray of ice cubes, i.e., opposite, center.

....

Exercise: **take three visually led print ads from a magazine or newspaper. Try to improve them with simple cropping and/ or framing. Hand draw the results.**

....

Dealing with Different Formats
Generally speaking, the less room you have, the harder it is to create an uncluttered, hierarchical layout (another reason for keeping your ads simple). With press ads, a double-page spread will give you more room than a single page (twice the room, to be exact). For posters, a horizontal billboard will obviously give you much more room than a 6-sheet. In reality (other things being equal), the greater the media "surface area," the more it will cost the client. But for a speculative student campaign that's not a concern.

Good Use of White Space vs. Bad Use of White Space
White space (or negative space) can be a good thing or a bad thing. An example of effective white space is the final "No" ad on page 79. Bad use is where there is lots of unnecessary space, usually in relation to the visual. Use logic to decide which size

fits your idea the best: suppose you have a "visual only" ad of a car. If the angle/shot is from the side then to create a natural frame around the car it makes sense to choose "landscape." If it's from the front or back, a "portrait" is probably the best choice. If the car is shot from above, or the classic 3/4 angle, it could work either way. Note: these suggestions are probably redundant once you add a headline, etc., or choose some less conventional cropping and framing, but looking at how to place things within a given space is the backbone of art direction, and therefore always a good place to start. A round (or square) image like an apple *can* work equally well within "landscape" or "portrait."

In reality, a client may buy various media space, which means the idea will have to work in landscape and portrait. The idea may work equally in both formats, but if not, some cropping and framing adjustments to the weaker version may be required.

The Visual Twist
This is different from a visual pun. A visual twist is a clever spin on an idea or an image. It might be a simple case of turning the visual on its head (see the Basic Tools chapter). For example, the ad for Tide, Stain Remover Pen (overleaf, above), in which a leak cleans a dirty shirt, rather than stain a clean one.

Here's an illustration of how a visual twist was created in a class. A student once presented a press campaign for a range of mouthwash. Each ad had an image of a type of food or drink that makes your breath smell: a garlic clove, a tin of sardines, and a cup of black coffee. He had "scratch n' sniff" above each image. Great, an interactive ad. So I asked him, "What happens when you scratch the garlic clove?"

To my disappointment, he replied, "It smells of garlic."

I said, "But that's what you'd expect to smell. There's no twist. What if, instead of smelling of garlic, it smelt of one of the mouthwash flavors? In other words, the mouthwash has killed your bad breath."

With a simple twist, a much-improved campaign was born.

Visual Threes
The "List of Three" tool is used in copy to great effect, e.g., the good, the bad, and the ugly;

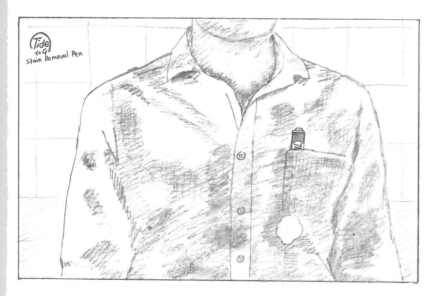

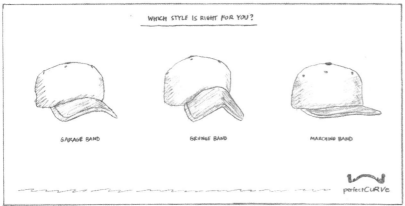

A visual twist (via the opposite tool). *Client: Tide. Agency: Saatchi & Saatchi, New York. Creatives: Menno Kluin, Michael Schachtner, Julia Neumann.*

Visual threes. Three is the classic number for comic punch lines (the joke is too quick with two, and too drawn out with four). Headline: Garage band. Grunge band. Marching band. *Client: Perfect Curve. Agency: Arnold Advertising, Boston. Creatives: David Lowe, Todd Riddle.*

morning, noon, and night; "three men walk into a bar" jokes, etc. Three things give the list a certain rhythm—two is too quick, and four is too long. The same is often true of visuals. If you have an idea that needs to reveal some kind of visual "punch line," three is usually the optimum number. The origins of the "Magic Three" are found in fine art. Note how many classic still-life paintings contain three objects—two or four look too symmetrical and unnatural, and five becomes too much. An example of triple visuals is "bands" for Perfect Curve baseball caps.

Visual Twos (Double Visuals)
Of course your idea may work better with an alternative number of visuals. For example, two visuals always work better in the case of a "before and after" ad (or a "without the product/with the product"). In the Comfort ad on page 110, you

don't need three visuals because the second visual acts as the punch line, e.g., comfort. The ad, opposite, above, is another famous "double visual" example, part of the "perception/reality" campaign for *Rolling Stone* magazine (see "Before and After" Strategy, page 108).

Multiple Visuals
Conversely, you may have an idea that is more interesting with a multitude of visuals, therefore making the punch line less immediate, e.g., VW Polo, "Self-Protection" (opposite, below). Or the idea might work better with a number of similar visuals to help get the point across, e.g., Levi's 501s "Torchure" and "Backside" (overleaf).

Hand-drawn Layouts: Thumbnails, Roughs, and Comps
The difference between thumbnails, roughs, and comps (comprehensives) is shown on pages 90 and 91. Note how each variation has been appropriately used throughout this book. A finished layout is the finished ad, executed on a computer (see the Execution chapter).

Hand-drawn layouts are still the fastest way to get your ideas down in a tangible form. And considering you should be spending most of your time on concept (rather than execution), you need to save as much time as possible.

Tools
- Black "Sharpie" pens (extra fine point to extra thick)
- Pencils
- Eraser
- Color "magic marker" pens (optional)
- Metal non-skid ruler
- Scalpel knife
- Plain white paper (letter [A4] and 11 × 17" [tabloid/A3])

Hand-drawn Type
As with printed type, hand-drawn type should be easy to read. Practise simple, child-like handwriting using simple strokes. Use each thickness of pen appropriately. As a general rule, the shorter the text, the thicker the pen (you wouldn't use the thickest pen for body copy, for example). And before you write the final copy, "tick in" pretend type with either straight or squiggly lines (both examples can be seen throughout this book).

Compare this to Handwritten Type on page 255.

Exercise: **practise hand writing the pangram "The Quick Brown Fox Jumps Over the Lazy Dog" in Roman (regular, condensed, extended), italic/oblique, bold and script handwriting, upper and lower case (five times for each).**

Social Situations

For some reason, many inexperienced students create print ads that involve two or more *people*, in what I call "social situations." These ads are invariably too ambitious, too complicated, or too confusing to work in print. In fact, they sound more like stories: "This person is reacting to this person because this has happened…." Once you start having to explain to someone what's happening in your 3-second ad, you're in trouble.

That's probably why, in reality, very few award-winning print ads show people in these social situations, if they even have people in them at all. Unless it's obvious what these people are doing (e.g., Club 18–30's sexually suggestive poster campaign that showed holiday-goers in various "positions"), it makes it complicated. So why do students do it? I think it probably comes from their over-exposure to TV ads (many of which have time to use the "social situation"), compared to their lack of exposure to good, simple, print advertising. So they think, "I know, I'll do something like in that TV ad for this print assignment," without realizing that it's very hard to convert a 30-second idea into a 3-second one.

Exercise: **write a series of print ads (a "campaign," if you've already read that chapter) for a dating service. Think about the target market and the proposition. But, do NOT show people in your ads. This will force you to create simpler, more lateral ideas.**

"Shopping List" Ads and "Calendar" Ads

At some point, nearly every student will produce the most boring print ad of all: what I call the "shopping list" ad. It's typically a "visual" that consists of a list or table of items, numbers or other similar entries. The most common shopping list

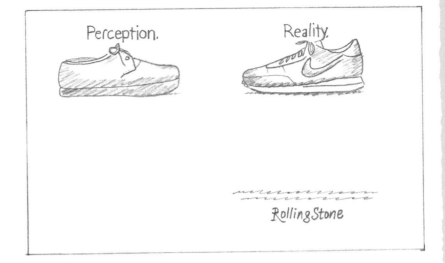

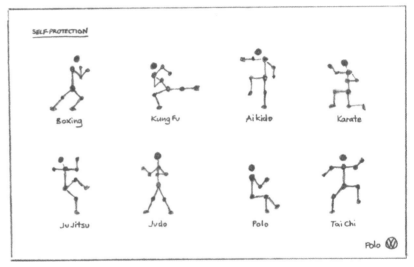

ad is one that compares two price lists: one that refers to the client's product, and one that lists the competition. And look at the money our product will save you! Calculus was bad enough at high school, so don't resurrect it. Unless it's part of a great concept, keep any lists, tables, and charts for annual reports or other brochures, not for ads. (Fallon, London's Timex campaign and Nike's "Agassi vs." ad are notable exceptions.)

Another common (and equally dull) ad is the "page from a calendar or a diary," including various handwritten entries. Again, these are visually boring to look at (they all look the same), and can take time to read. So unless the copy is shocking or funny or has a great twist, avoid the literal approach of using a shopping list or calendar-style

The classic "perception/reality" campaign used the double visual throughout. Perhaps the most famous trade advertising ever created, it targeted business people asking them to advertise their product in *Rolling Stone* magazine. Why? Because as the body copy outlined, the magazine's new readers (during the 1980s) were actually affluent yuppies, not "tree-hugging" hippies. *Client: Rolling Stone. Agency: Fallon McElligott. Creatives: Nancy Rice, Bill Miller.*

Multiple visuals help to reveal the punch line slowly. *Client: Volkswagen. Agency: BMP DDB, London. Creatives: Dave Dye, Sean Doyle.*

Multiple visuals for Levi's 501 jeans. Headline: (washing machines) Torture them; (chairs) Wear the backside out of them. **Client:** *Levi's.* **Agency:** *Bartle Bogle Hegarty, London.* **Creatives:** *John Gorse, Nick Worthington.*

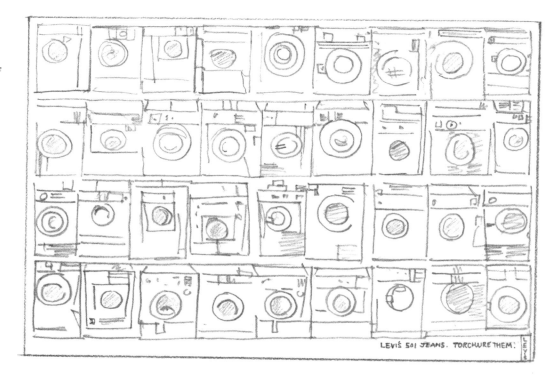

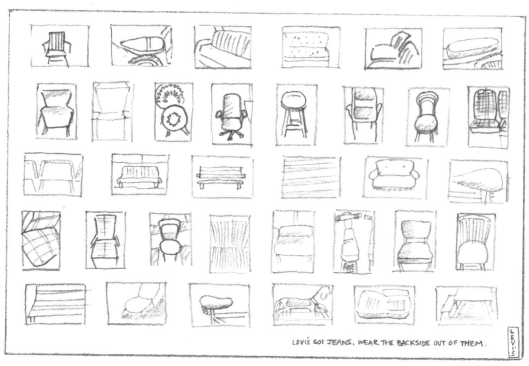

print ad. Instead, think of more lateral ways to dramatize the proposition, whether it's "value for money" or any other benefit.

Fallon cleverly avoided using a written version of a "calendar ad" by employing simple visuals to tell the story instead in their award-winning campaign for London's luxury department store, Harvey Nichols (overleaf).

"Dictionary Definition" Ads

Such ads have become somewhat clichéd within print advertising because this "idea" can be used for literally *any* product or service. (Just grab a dictionary and you've got an ad!) The most common example of a "dictionary" ad is one that spells out the product name and/or benefit, e.g.

smart (smarht) adj.
1. clever, ingenious
2. neat and elegant
3. a brand of small car driven by city dwellers

or

fashionable (fash-o-na-bel) adj.
1. in or adopting a style that is currently popular
2. frequented or used by stylish people
3. Brand X jeans

Stock Imagery: Good vs. Bad

Stock imagery for print is either photography or illustration. For TV and video, stock footage is available. Whether a stock image is royalty free or there is a one-time fee, be careful what you choose (see Stock Imagery vs. DIY, page 259, for more details).

Advertising Design vs. Graphic Design

As the fields of graphic design and advertising design continue to merge, it may be worth mentioning the conceptual and practical differences between the two disciplines.

A primary objective of the *graphic* designer is to organize and present information in a compelling way that will be most easily understood by the viewer/user. To achieve this, a graphic designer is trained to spend much of his or her time figuring out how to: build hierarchy of the information being delivered, establish a visual vocabulary that is most interesting and relevant to the subject, and

Multiple visuals in one: how else do you show the entire contents of a Japanese tourist's digital camera? *Client: Stuffit Deluxe. Agency: Saatchi & Saatchi, New York. Creatives: Menno Kluin, Icaro Doria.*

Opposite Multiple visuals provide a more interesting way to execute a "calendar" ad. Other executions include repeated cat food, and depleted phone book (for toilet paper!) *Client: James Day, Harvey Nichols.* **Agency:** *DDB, London.* **Creatives:** *Justin Tindall, Adam Tucker.*

ensure that the end result is clear, comprehendible and visually appealing. After several studies and experimentation with type, visuals and numerous compositions, a final concept is defined as a potential design *solution.*

Designers as a whole (whether industrial designers, environmental designers, interior designers, multimedia designers or graphic designers), unlike advertising designers, are not concerned with "selling" a product, service, or destination. It doesn't matter if the end solution is for a product, a space, an interior, a website or for print—designers are primarily interested in creating a solution that will benefit the end user. Is the chair comfortable to sit on? Is the exhibit or interior inviting, engaging, and easy to circulate through? Is the website dynamic and "navigatable"? Is *this* book eye catching and comprehendible?

In the case of *advertising* design, its goal is very different. The primary objective for someone in this discipline is to create a strategy and concept that will help *sell* a product or service. Advertising professionals as a whole (i.e., across all media) are not concerned if a product doesn't function well or look good. Their job is to find something (else) to talk about, something that people will hopefully "buy into." (Of course, if the concept is well executed in terms of design, so much the better.)

An interesting case study is Apple, who promote their products both ways. Their iconic "dancing silhouettes" iPod campaign is classed by many as an advertising idea, but is in fact closer to graphic design. By contrast, the "Hello, I'm a Mac. And I am a PC" TV campaign is an advertising concept. Yet most of their other TV spots simply present each new invention in a way that lets the product's design speak for itself. These are like hybrids: TV ads but created, in essence, by a designer. (These points go back to the difference between "hard sell" and "soft sell" discussed in the introduction.)

From left to right
Thumbnail, loose (rough) comp, tight comp, and the final produced ad. *Client: Volvo.* **Agency:** *Scali, McCabe, Sloves.* **Creatives:** *Steve Montgomery, Mike Feinberg.* **Illustrations:** *Steve Montgomery.*

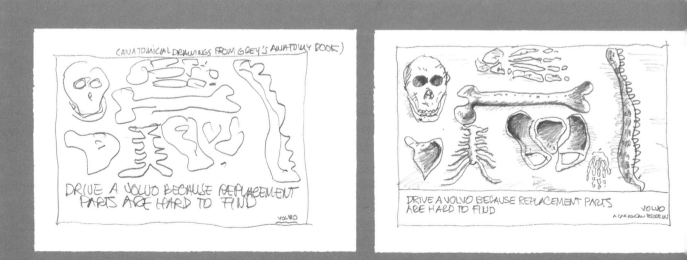

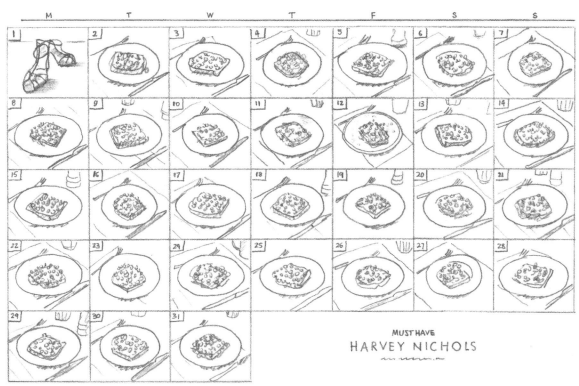

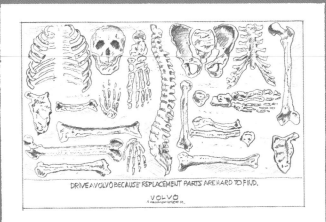

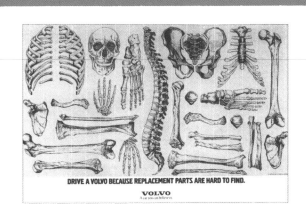

04
The Campaign

What is a Campaign?

A campaign is a series of ads that make up a concept/idea, i.e., an idea that has more than one execution (technically three or more, although sometimes two). Campaigns are therefore considered to be "bigger" ideas than a one-shot, which is why it's often easy to do one or two executions in a campaign, but can be really hard to come up with a good third or fourth one.

The *campaign idea* is the overriding "umbrella" thought that drives and determines each execution. Put another way, the executions are an expression of the campaign thought. This idea is usually expressed in some form of tagline (although sometimes the idea is so clear from the executions that a tagline is not needed: it's superfluous). (See the Tagline chapter.)

Aside from having a consistent strategy and idea, the executions that make up any campaign should look and feel like part of a "family"—in terms of language and art direction. This helps each execution to build on the previous one(s), resulting in a cohesive campaign, rather than a disparate one. Therefore, unless there's a reason for it, three ads in a specific print campaign should not be a mixture of "headline only," "visual only," or "headline and visual" executions.

That said, as with a one-shot ad, never approach a new project thinking, "I'm going to do a 'headline only' campaign" (or "visual only," or "headline and visual," etc.) Think in terms of ideas first, and then try executing your ideas in each form. Once you start, it should be fairly obvious which method creates the best ads (in terms of quantity and quality). The form that creates the most unexpected ads is usually the one to go with. Of course, you may be required to expand the campaign idea into a multimedia campaign. As long as they are conceptually strong and consistent, the posters could, for example, be "visual only," the internet banners "headline only," and the magazine ads might work best as "headline and visual" (see also the Integrated chapter).

Whilst explaining the strategy statement on page 46, I mentioned that the tone of voice in each execution should be consistent. The same is true of the entire campaign: not only should the executions be consistent, so should the ideas behind them. A campaign has the power to reassure its consumers with the same promise over a long period of time. With an inconsistent campaign, the consumer is left feeling (at best) confused, (at worst) cheated. And the time and money spent producing all the work has been wasted.

A final, important point—don't try to think of ideas that naturally come in threes and then try to apply it to your original idea. This doesn't automatically make it a campaign. For example, I remember one student had a print campaign where the first ad was set in the morning, the second in the afternoon, and the third at night. (But then what? The morning ad again?) It's too limiting. Remember, a campaign should have the

A classic one-shot, i.e., one that would be hard to expand into a campaign. *Client: Bic. Agency: TBWA/Hunt/Lascaris, Johannesburg. Creatives: Jan Jacobs, Clare McNally.*

potential to produce more than three executions. Rarely are these triplet ideas any good because it's another idea in itself, leaving you with two ideas instead of one.

The One-Shot vs. the Campaign

Before we start examining the campaign, let's look at the one-shot (a.k.a. one-off, single, or individual ad). A one-shot is a solitary idea with a single execution, usually one that cannot be extended into a campaign of equally good executions.

For example, look at the ad on the opposite page. The Bic ad is a classic one-shot. How many better visuals are there for "incredibly long lasting" than the infinity symbol? There may be alternatives, but the executions would probably lack the simplicity and quality that this one possesses. Adding these executions might weaken the overall idea. Likewise, it would be hard to expand the ad on the right into a campaign because of the nature of the concept (the visual simile of a computer "arrow" = a Christmas tree). It works perfectly off the product name, xmas trees direct; it's a natural one-shot because there are no other visual similes whereby computer screen symbols look like Christmas trees. On page 133 a topical "headline introducing visual" ad for Hertz is a simple message conveyed in the best way possible. To repeat it in one or more slightly different ways (i.e., turning it into a campaign) would be superfluous and redundant.

Note: people often incorrectly refer to an ad "execution" as an ad "campaign." ("Hey, did you see that ad campaign for Nike on TV last night?," when they mean *one ad*.) A campaign is typically made up of three or more ads/executions; it is not a single execution. To confuse matters, the term "execution" also refers to how the ad is produced, its production (see the Execution chapter).

One-shots are smaller, limited ideas compared to a campaign idea. That is not to say a one-shot cannot be conceptually profound. The famous "1984" launch ad for the Apple Macintosh worked best as a one-off. In fact, it was meant to run once (during the 1984 Super Bowl), and yet its impact continued for many years. Some ad professionals have even argued that a great TV one-shot is a platform from which a campaign can develop. Easier said than done. (An attempted follow up to match "1984" proved too hard even for TBWA/Chiat/Day.)

However, the majority of ad pros will argue that "anyone can create a great one-shot," whereas producing a cutting-edge, long-running campaign (which stems from a solid strategy and concept) is much more difficult. This is why there is often a certain level of snobbery surrounding the "easy" one-shot, versus the campaign. But ad guru Ed McCabe saw the power of a one-shot too, often telling his creative teams: "Just show me a great ad!"

But with either a one-shot or a campaign, the same rules of simplicity apply: make sure you can explain the idea in *one* sentence.

Xmastrees**direct**.co.uk

A classic single-only ad (the color version used a green "arrow"). *Client: xmas trees direct. Agency: McCann Erickson, Manchester. Creatives: Dave Price, Neil Lancaster.*

The Apple "1984" commercial: how can you follow an execution this successful? *Client: Apple. Agency: TBWA/Chiat/Day. Creatives: Steve Hayden, Lee Clow, Brent Thomas.*

Opposite A clever, lateral (but ultimately small) idea that uses pictures instead of words to dramatize the game's 7-letter challenge. *Client: Mattel, Chile. Agency: JWT, Chile. Creatives: Matias Lecaros, Tomas Vidal, Sergio Rosati.*

On January 24th,
Apple Computer will introduce
Macintosh.
And you'll see why 1984
won't be like "1984."

Why a Campaign?

You may ask: if campaigns are so hard to create, why bother? Why not do lots of one-shots instead? The main argument is that campaigns are what help to build brands in the long term rather than confuse and dilute them with disparate one-shots in the short term.

In theory (and in practice), a single campaign idea can be executed for decades, whereas a one-shot would lose its appeal fairly quickly. (Of course there are occasions when it would not make sense to keep with the same campaign for a long time: such as an uncontrollable market change that forces a rethink of the current campaign, the brand, and even the product.) However, it is the consistency of a campaign that generally forges and strengthens the long-term relationship between the product/service and the consumer. This creates what's known as "brand loyalty"—a very powerful marketing tool. Brand loyalty is largely why a consumer would rather pay more money for a particular brand of baked beans (for example), compared to purchasing the same product in a "supermarket label/home brand" can. And at the end of the day, that's really what advertising is all about: selling units and making money (see also The Brand and Branding, page 244).

How to Create a Campaign

Arguably the hardest part of advertising is making the move from creating single execution one-shots to ideas that are big enough to work as a campaign, with numerous executions. To help this process, you have to understand two things: (i) the origin of ideas (see the Generating Strategies and Ideas chapter); and (ii) the function of the tagline (see the Tagline chapter). But first, it's important to define and explore the term "campaign."

Small Campaign Ideas vs. Big Campaign Ideas

So even though campaigns are bigger ideas than one-shots, there are two basic size variations within the definition of a campaign: those that start to run out of steam after three executions are "small" campaign ideas while those that can easily exceed three executions are "big." Technically, since both consist of at least three executions, each can be classed as a campaign.

Small campaign idea:
• Scrabble "Elephant," "Guitar," and "Dove"

Big campaign ideas:

- The Economist
- MasterCard's "Priceless"
- John Smith's "No Nonsense"
- Nike's "Just Do It"
- BT's "It's Good To Talk"
- Heineken "Refreshes the Parts Other Beers Cannot Reach"
- Hamlet's "Happiness is a Cigar Called Hamlet"*

*This campaign idea, conceived when Tim Warriner lit up a dry cigarette inside a bus on a rainy English day, lasted 40 years.

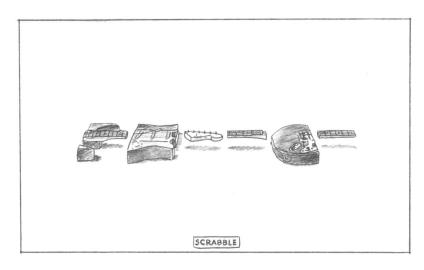

SCRABBLE

Bigger Doesn't Always Mean Better

There are times when you have a campaign idea that produces a seemingly infinite number of executions with ease. It must be a great idea, right? Not necessarily. It could be that the campaign idea is not very creative to begin with and so the executions are too repetitive and boring, as if the campaign "idea" is being spread too thin.

A good example of this is a campaign for Emerald Nuts. The idea is to show the types of people who eat Emerald Nuts and share the same initials as the product, or ENs. So you have an instant series of executions like, "Egyptian Navigators love Emerald Nuts," or "Egotistical Normans love Emerald Nuts." Get it? Clearly you could write an infinite number of these, almost too easy to do, and the "joke" soon wears off. Not only that, this idea is incredibly broad; it could work for literally any product/brand name in the world... Ford Cars ("FCs"), Nike Sneakers ("NSs"), Colgate Toothpaste ("CTs"), etc.

SCRABBLE

The "Same Ad Three Times" (SATT) Syndrome

A balance has to be reached: just as the executions that make up a campaign can't be too dissimilar (for reasons explained above), neither can they be too *similar*. With a campaign, you want people to anticipate the next execution, not expect it.

"It's the same ad three times" is a comment that every creative has heard from someone at some time. It's another way of saying "three ways of doing the same one-shot." Instead, within the overall campaign idea should be three distinct, unexpected, mini ideas that express what you want to say. So the balance to achieve is simply this:

each execution within a campaign should be expressed in the "*same yet different*" way.

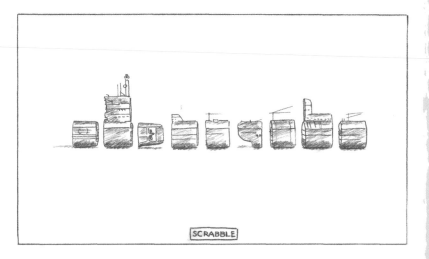

SCRABBLE

BODDINGTONS. THE CREAM OF MANCHESTER.

ARTIFICIAL CREAM.

VANISHING CREAM.

Verdict: clearly *not* the same ad three times. *Client: Boddingtons.* *Agency: Bartle Bogle Hegarty, London.* *Creatives: Mike Wells, Tom Hudson.*

Opposite Verdict: arguably *not* the same ad three times. Tag: Adult only holidays unspoilt by children. *Agency: Ogilvy, London.* *Creatives: Stuart Gill, Di Lowe.*

The executions should be related (the same), but not too closely (different). Think of them as three siblings versus identical triplets. This is probably the *hardest* part of creative advertising to crack (other than having to come up with three executions to start with). And once you've fallen into the SATT trap once, it can be a really hard habit to break out of. The reason it's an easy trap to fall into is purely because of the conscious need to think of campaigns in terms of having "similar" or "related" executions. (Don't panic: it is something you can work out of your system.)

Defining exactly what makes a particular campaign the same ad three times is not always easy. There are grey areas. And by the same token, neither is defining what makes three executions the "same yet different." (In fact, you may well find some famous, award-winning campaigns that could be described as the SATT, as in VW's "Abandoned Left Shoes.") However, the key question is: *how* different, or similar, are the ideas and executions within the campaign, e.g., opposite and overleaf.

- **Boddingtons**
  Verdict: clearly *not* the same ad three times
- **Freespirit holidays**
  Verdict: arguably *not* the same ad three times
- **VW automatic**
  Verdict: arguably the same ad three times*

The fourth (and least desirable) category is a campaign that is clearly the same ad three times. It's the "seen one execution, seen them all" campaign. And it's not worth using up space in this book to show an example. As print ads these can be visual only, headline only, or headline and visual. For example, the visual only "campaign" might show three different kids playing outfield in an adult MLB baseball game (for, say, Big League chewing gum). Same ad three times. The headline only equivalent typically contains three headlines that are worded slightly differently just for the sake of having a campaign. In other words, there's not enough of idea to sustain it beyond a one-shot ad (at best).

Or maybe there could be. Whenever you have the SATT, try to think of executions that will add some variety. Expand them somehow. In the case of the Big League example above, perhaps the kids are playing in different positions (batsman, pitcher, catcher, etc.) Or perhaps show other sports where gum is chewed (maybe one is a kid being

a basketball coach). These thoughts are coming to me as I write, but hopefully you get the point.

*In the cases where one *could* possibly argue that a campaign is the same ad three times, the originality of the idea will overcompensate this fact, such as the VW Polo Automatic "Left Shoes" campaign, of which only two executions are shown overleaf. One could easily argue that both the Coco de Mer "Orgasm" campaigns discussed on page 154 are original enough to fall into this category.

As a general guide, here are the elements of a campaign that should be: (i) the same, (ii) different.

Same	Different
Strategy	Executional ideas (headlines, visuals, etc.)
Campaign Idea	
Tagline	
Proposition	
Tone	
Art Direction	
Branding	

Avoid the "One in a Series of…"

There are various elements that exist within any series of print ads to create a consistent "campaign feel." These include: the campaign idea itself, a single tagline, uniform structure and tone of headlines/body copy, and art direction and visual branding.

Because most consumers know what a campaign is once they've seen or heard a couple of executions, there's no real need to spell it out with an additional "number x, in a series of x." Any campaign could have a line like this on it. It's not unique. It's superfluous, it clutters the ad, and it usually looks contrived, formulaic, and "addy." (Imagine if DDB, Chicago had written, "Bud Light presents Real Men of Genius number 105: Mr…") So unless there's a conceptual reason for adding a line like this, the elements listed above are enough to show consumers that each ad is "one in a series," without having to say it.

Note: this "rule" is very much a personal thing. As with some other "don'ts" highlighted in this book, there are a few exceptions (Fallon McElligott's "The Nikon School: Tip #" campaign is one). However, it is rare to find other campaigns that have used the "numbering" method effectively (e.g., a "collect the set" postcard campaign). (See Bigger Doesn't Always Mean Better, page 95.)

Verdict: arguably the same ad three times (only two of the executions are shown here). The award shows clearly recognized the original "un-addyness" of the work. *Client: VW Polo Automatic. Agency: BMP DDB, London. Creatives: Richard Flintham, Andy McLeod.*

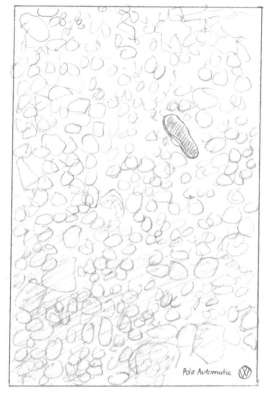

fcuk®

What the fcuk is it for? This edgy, controversial acronym logo began much like a teaser ad. *Client: French Connection, United Kingdom. Agency: GGT, London. Creatives: Trevor Beattie, Jay Pond-Jones, Bill Bungay.*

The Teaser Campaign

A traditional campaign communicates everything the consumer needs to know in each execution (i.e., the idea, the benefit, and what the product is) *immediately*. A teaser campaign—by contrast—takes its time to do this. As its name suggests, the aim is to *tease* the consumer gradually, the intrigue growing with each execution. The final stage is the "big reveal"—the time when the last piece(s) of the "jigsaw" are added. The key to a teaser campaign's success is to know when to reveal; to stop the tease before the consumers' interest drops. Plus the final reveal must be worth the wait (i.e., a clever idea or an exciting message). The Ferrari billboard(s) on page 62 is one example.

If done well, the two or more stages of "teasing then revealing" can be an effective way to launch a new brand or a sub-brand, or revive interest in an old one. (Kmart once announced their first ever Manhattan store with a series of anonymous phrases on posters across the city. Each phrase was related to New York in some way. The intrigue was increased by the exclusion of the letter "K" in each sentence. The final reveal explained both idea and product by adding the famous red "K" of Kmart followed by a line that expressed this thought: the one thing that was missing in New York.)

As with any campaign, a teaser campaign can be either "headline/text only," "headline and visual," or "visual only." In the case of French Connection, United Kingdom, its provocative acronym brand name fcuk began with teaser-like impact when it was launched in the late 1990s.

. . . .

Exercise: pick the product or service that you *love* the most. Create a print campaign for it. Then do the same for the product you *hate* the most.

. . . .

05
The Tagline

Alternative Terms for "Tagline"

- Tag
- Endline (since it is the last line to be read)
- Theme line
- Strapline (UK)
- Payoff
- Slogan (which can also refer to a headline)

Don't worry about the different terminology: they all mean the same thing. For simplicity and continuity, I will use the two most popular US versions only—tagline and tag.

(Then) The Ads Should Write Themselves

The tagline has a very important function within the development of a campaign, and therefore the brand. It helps to harness and support the campaign idea, and generate new executions of that idea. The saying goes that once you have the right tagline for your campaign, "the ads should write themselves." In other words, when you find that the executions are coming easily, it's a good sign that you have a strong campaign idea with an appropriate tagline (a tagline which is also helping to define the brand).

Here's an example:

Product	Vote Campaign
Idea	There are many problems in the world that still need solving.
Tone	Sarcasm.
Tagline	Don't vote. Things are perfect just the way they are.

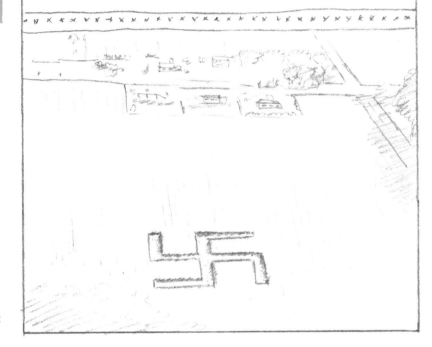

With this tagline (which acts like a headline/tagline) in place, one can easily imagine numerous executions (the sign of a "big idea"). One is illustrated above.

....

Exercise: see how quickly and easily you can come up with more executions. Do the same for the campaigns for the VW Passat and Stella Artois overleaf.

....

This wonderfully sarcastic campaign idea is as big as the world's problems. Headline/Tagline: Don't vote. Things are perfect just the way they are. *Client:* Willamette Week/BPN. *Agency:* Borders Perrin Norrander, Portland. *Creatives:* Ginger Robinson, Kent Suter, Tia Doar.

One look at the tagline and you can see it's a big campaign idea. Tag: The beautifully crafted new Passat. You'll want to keep it that way. *Client: Volkswagen. Agency: BMP DDB, London. Creatives: Rob Jack, Ewan Paterson.*

Three of potentially dozens of executions. Tagline: Reassuringly expensive. *Client: Stella Artois. Agency: Lowe Lintas, London. Creatives: Mick Mahoney, Andy Amadeo.*

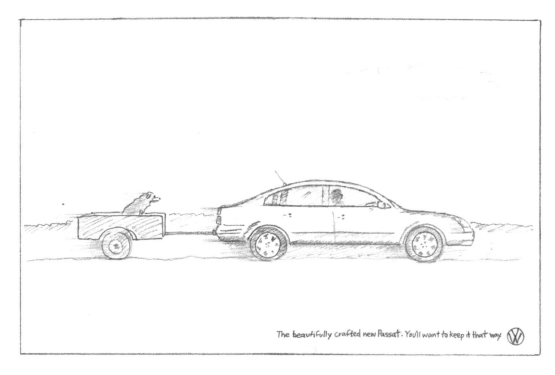

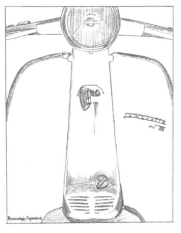 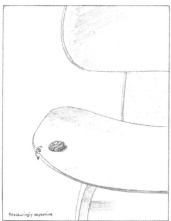 

Product	VW Passat
Execution	"Trailer"
Tagline	The beautifully crafted new Passat. You'll want to keep it that way.

Product	Stella Artois
Executions	"Lambretta," "Chair," "Fender"
Tagline	Reassuringly Expensive.

The Invisible "=" Sign

The tagline is usually the last thing to be communicated in an ad (after the headline, visual, voiceover, etc.) Therefore, a good way to evaluate a tagline is to imagine an *invisible "=" sign* immediately before the tag. In other words, the tagline is a total expression of the campaign idea. It's obvious when a tagline doesn't do this—it will look "stuck on" (or "tacked on") to the end of the ads. In this case, either the ads or the line need to change.

A common mistake is to write catchy, corporate, or attitudinal-sounding taglines that don't actually express the campaign idea. In fact, you'd be better off with a lengthy working tagline (see Working Tagline vs. Final Tagline, page 102). Nor should a tagline repeat the words in a headline.

Another equally unproductive situation is whereby a good tagline exists, but is not expressed in the ads. In other words, having a good tagline that expresses a campaign idea is irrelevant until you do something with it. (Then the tag can stand alone as a powerful, meaningful branding device, e.g., Just do it.) Taco Bell has a clever tagline: Think outside the bun. More than a play on words, this tag openly positions itself away from its competition, the two leading fast food "bun" giants McDonald's and Burger King. But the tag is not being utilized. The actual ads are forgetful, with uninspiring product shots throughout, rather than strong expressions of the tagline.

Tagline master Dave Trott believes that the function of a tagline is "to deliver a USP [Unique Selling Proposition] or branding.* If you love my commercial you shouldn't be able to repeat to anyone else what it's about without mentioning the name of the product and what the ad is saying. It's not there for mood, or tone of voice, or to attract a new generation of users. If you have a five-year idea, that's your [tagline]."

*See also Binary Briefing, page 48.

Types of Taglines

There are five basic types of tagline, with subtle differences:

The "summation" tagline basically "sums up" the campaign idea. It's a natural progression of the message being communicated in the ad.

The "explanation" tagline "explains" the campaign idea. In other words, if you covered up the tagline, you probably wouldn't understand the idea, e.g., The Stella Artois "Bottle Cap" press campaign would not be as conceivable (nor as believable) without the final "Reassuringly expensive" tagline.

The "proposition" tagline is a no frills tagline that is an approximate repetition of the proposition, or product benefit, e.g., fast, long-lasting, juicy. Of course it doesn't have to be a single generic word. Either way, be sure that your product is the first to "own" this benefit. Equally, this type of tagline can include a Unique Selling Proposition, or USP (see page 139).

The "brand" or "umbrella" tagline is often more of a client-driven line that sums up the brand, rather than the campaign idea. It's more of a serious, worthy, corporate positioning statement than a tagline, often used for non-advertising purposes. If applied to an ad campaign, it frequently tries to replace the role of the original tagline, or it's used in addition to the tagline. Either way, it can confuse the consumer (in the first instance), or clutter the message (in the second instance). For a brand tagline to work well, it has to be like an "umbrella"—broad enough to encompass current and future ideas for the brand, but not so broad that it dilutes the brand message.

The "invisible" tagline is literally non-existent. This is more common within one-shot (one-off) ads than an ad campaign. It's for those ads that have such a simple, clear message that the use of a tagline is superfluous. In these cases, a client logo will suffice to understand the idea, effectively replacing the function of the "summation" or "explanation" tagline. The invisible tagline either never existed during the creative process, *or* may have been an extremely reduced version of a pre-existing tagline to the point of eliminating it altogether.

Which Comes First?

Like the old "which came first: the chicken or the egg?" conundrum, there is no right or wrong order in terms of the creative process. Ideas, campaigns, and taglines (even strategies) can, in practice, be thrown into (or out of) the mix at any time. The end result is what matters, providing each element works together as a whole. In fact, some top agencies have proven that a consistent visual solution can work just as well, if not better, than a consistent tagline. Many, like Dave Trott, would agree with this approach up to a point. As he cleverly puts it, "An endline is not the most important part of an ad, but it is the first part."

One alternative "order"—and the way I was taught—lies somewhere between the two. In other words, start with an idea first (whether it's a single execution or a campaign thought) then try to write a "working tagline" that expresses this idea (see overleaf). From there, one starts to brainstorm for more executional ideas that "come off" the working tag. This method adds a bit of "left side of the brain logic" and structure to the typically random collection of "artistic" ideas that arise from the right side during the creative process. At the same time, it's not so rigid that you need a "perfect" tagline first.

Although not every person or project works like this, and not every successful campaign may have followed this particular order or creative process, it's a good habit to get into. It helps you focus, forces you to define your idea (if you can't define it, chances are it's too complicated and "un-tagable"), and can therefore save you a lot of time and effort in the long run. It's also good preparation for the real world of advertising, for two reasons. Firstly, taglines are not always given the time they deserve in the lead up to new creative pitches and presentations. Secondly, the right tagline can continue to be used by a client over many years and many separate campaigns: it's synonymous with the brand. Therefore, any new concepts have to adhere to this tagline. Creatively, this can be highly restrictive (but equally challenging) depending on the idea and how many years the tagline has been worked to. Unfortunately, in some cases the original tagline (and therefore the strategy) has been ignored by the new campaign to the point where the tagline literally looks as if it's been stuck on—or tagged—to the end of the ad.

Working Tagline vs. Final Tagline

Don't worry, a "perfect" final tagline does not have to be written immediately for a campaign to succeed—but a working tagline does. The term "working tagline" is much the same as the "working title" of a book, play, or movie script. It's a temporary tagline that is used until the "final" one is conceived.

The working tagline should still function in the same way as the final tagline, i.e., to express the campaign thought in some way. It can't be any old working line. It can be a long sentence, as long as it's single minded. Once you have an idea for a campaign, write down some working taglines as soon as possible—this will help to define your idea. Pick one that works the best. It doesn't have to be perfect (it can be really long and boring), providing you can work to it and produce a good amount of executions.

Final Tagline

The final tagline is basically a "tweaked" or "reduced" version of the working line. This doesn't always mean fewer words. In some cases, it's virtually impossible to write a better line than the working tagline: It's the best solution, or rather, the line that sums up the campaign thought the best. For example, it's hard to improve on the profundity of the lengthy MasterCard line: There are some things money can't buy. For everything else, there's MasterCard.

Final taglines usually tend to be as short and catchy as possible (as part of the School of Concise Advertising). Note how Nike managed to reduce "Just do it" by one word—to "I can." But the question here, as with all ideas, is which one is better, *not* which one is shorter (see Tagline Reductionism, page 105).

Just as with headlines, visuals, and concepts, you should also avoid clichéd, "addy" taglines as much as possible. As Robert Campbell said, "I don't think they're good if they're just confectionery. They must mean something. They can be a useful centre of gravity for a campaign."

Whether you are trying to write a working line or a tagline, *make a list*. (Remember the 1-in-10 tool on page 23.) Another useful exercise is to approach each line as if it will be translated into dozens of languages. In other words, unless there's a reason, keep to simple, pun-free, and non-colloquial sentences.

Examples of working and final taglines:

Product	Working Tagline	Final Tagline
British Telecom	Talking things over is healthy*	It's good to talk
Guinness	Because thin things suck	Thin sucks**
Tampax Compak	Take them anywhere	Life size

*author's interpretation, for illustration purposes only

**student examples (Philip Galgay; Caitlin McGauley)

Product Name and Tagline in One

The major pharmaceutical company SmithKline Beecham (currently known as GlaxoSmithKline) had their own unusual philosophy on taglines. Once a product had been developed, they would create a product name and tagline *simultaneously* (rather than brand name first, tagline and campaign thought second).

These taglines had to:

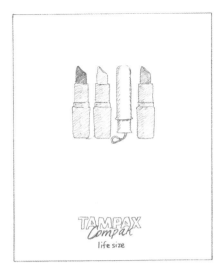

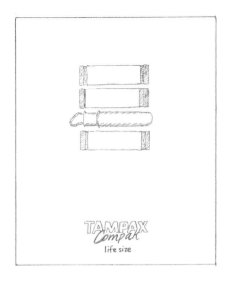

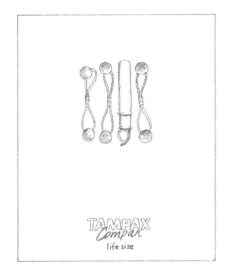

Working tagline: Take them anywhere. Final tagline: Life size. **Client:** *Tampax Compak.* **Student:** *Caitlin McGauley.*

- Include the brand name
- Describe the function of the product
- Be very short and catchy

Two examples that followed this system were "Oxycutem," for Oxy pimple cream (a pun on the phrase "execute them") and "Good Nytol" (as in, "goodnight all" for Nytol sleeping tablets).

At first glance, SmithKline Beecham's successful methodology appears fairly strict. For, in reality, most taglines are created long after the creation of the brand name. However, many tags do include the brand name for the simple reason that it unifies the two elements into an arguably more memorable, "ownable" slogan that helps to drive home the product name. Here are some famous examples, the first of which could almost be a "SmithKline Beecham tagline":

- Australians wouldn't give a XXXX for anything else (*Castlemaine XXXX*)
- Who would you most like to have a One 2 One with? (*One 2 One mobile phones*)
- Happiness is a cigar called Hamlet (*Hamlet*)
- Heineken refreshes the parts other beers cannot reach (*Heineken*)
- This Bud's for you (*Budweiser*)
- Have you met life today? (*MetLife insurance*)
- The one and only Wonderbra (*Wonderbra*)
- The future's bright, the future's Orange (*Orange telecommunications*)
- The Sunday Times is the Sunday papers (*The Sunday Times*)

- These times demand The Times (*The New York Times*)
- You can be sure of Shell (*Shell Oil*)
- You know when you've been Tango'd (*Tango*)
- Have a break, have a KitKat (*KitKat*)
- No F.T. No Comment (*The Financial Times*)
- Whatever it is, you can get it on eBay (*eBay*)
- Pure Genius (*sounds like Guinness*)

A tagline like these will give your student portfolio tremendous clout. One particular student wrote a sublime "SmithKline Beecham" tagline. The brief was to advertise the re-introduction of the classic Triumph Bonneville 750cc motorcycle. The concept was targeting nostalgic, middle-aged men (including ex-motorcyclists), desperate to regain a sense of youthful adventure. The tagline was simply this: Triumph Again. It's particularly clever because it works on two levels: the bike is available again, plus you can feel alive and triumphant again.

Hey, Schmuck

Advertising ideas are essentially *arguments* presented to the consumer, stating why he or she should choose a particular product. Taglines are a condensed expression of this argument. Ed McCabe was a master of presenting and communicating a USP as pure matter of fact. He was affectionately known as the "'hey, schmuck' Guy" because his arguments made so much common sense that it was as if each tagline/ headline had the preceding/proceeding words

"Hey, schmuck…" or "…you schmuck." In other words, the consumer would be an idiot not to buy the company's product or service. Aggressive as it may seem, it worked, and is still a great tool for writing taglines, headlines, and ads in general. Ask yourself: does the tagline I've written still work with a "Hey, schmuck" next to it? Or in other words: have I presented a strong enough argument?

If it helps, imagine that your consumer is the toughest critic out there: an obnoxious, cynical, drunk guy in a bar. A Mr. Know It All (we've all met one of those). If he were to say, "Hell, why would I want to buy that product?" think to yourself: what would be a perfect reason or response. And say it simply and quickly (he's drunk, after all). For example, suppose he rudely says to you "Where did you get that old watch?" Perhaps a factual line like: "This is the same military watch that Steve McQueen wore in 'The Great Escape'" might shut him up. Or better yet, how about: "This precision US military watch helped to defeat the Germans in World War II. If it wasn't for this watch, we might not even be sitting here…. Cheers."

If you can convince an obnoxious, cynical, drunk guy, you can convince anyone (see also Your Idea Should End the Argument, page 155).

Rhyming Taglines
You could argue that a rhyming tagline is more poetic, colloquial or catchy. But such lines only work when they express a relevance to the product and/or what it's trying to say about itself. Some good examples of this include:

- See the USA in your Chevrolet (*Chevrolet*)
- Beanz meanz Heinz (*Heinz baked beans*)
- You can with a Nissan (*Nissan cars*)
- Takes a lickin' and keeps on tickin' (*Timex*)
- Why slow-mow when you can flymo? (*Flymo lawnmowers*)
- A lot less bovver than a hover* (*Qualcast lawnmowers*)
- If anyone can, Canon can (*Canon cameras/ electronics*)

*"Bovver" is London slang for "bother." The tagline refers to the hassle of using a Flymo hovercraft-style lawnmower.

Note: do not confuse these rhyme examples with a rhyming pun, as discussed on page 68.

Question Taglines
The use of headlines as questions is discussed on page 64, but what of "question taglines"? Again, there are no rules. Just because most famous taglines are not questions doesn't mean they are any more valid than those that are. It probably just means that most ideas are better suited to, and expressed with, non questions.

The Advertising Slogan Hall of Fame currently includes only eight "question taglines":

- Where do you want to go today? (*Microsoft, 1995*)
- Got milk? (*California Fluid Milk Processor Advisory Board, 1993*)
- It is. Are you? (*The Independent, UK newspaper, 1987*)
- Are you a Cadbury's fruit and nut case? (*Cadbury's, UK, 1985*)
- Hello Tosh, gotta Toshiba? (*Toshiba, UK, 1984*)
- Where's the beef? (*Wendy's, 1984*)
- Does she or doesn't she? (*Clairol, 1964*)
- Which twin has the Toni? (*Toni, 1946*)

Putting. Periods. In. The. Middle. Of. Taglines.
Taglines that use multiple periods are tried and tested. One notable example: "Marines. The few. The proud." But putting periods where they're not needed, like in the middle of sentences, or between every word? I'm not sure why this "technique" improves a tagline, especially when the individual words don't mean anything on their own (an example of this is Sony's: "Like. No. Other"). I suppose if you're the first to do it then it becomes a technique that you can "own"; something a bit different that makes you stand out. But it's not something worth copying unless you want to be associated with your competitive brand. IBM, for instance, were the first to use colored cinema letterboxing in their TV commercials. Then. Other. Brands. Copied. Them. (Why?)

"Yeah…" Taglines
Such taglines are particularly evident amongst random TV spots, particularly in the US, whereby the "tagline" is more like a chatty end comment on a piece of slapstick humor (like someone having ice poured down their back to show how refreshingly cold a drink is). You may not realize, but you've seen and heard this type of tagline many times.

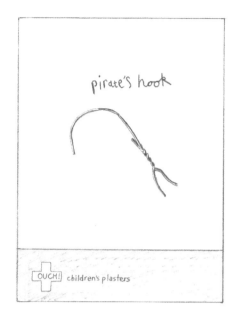

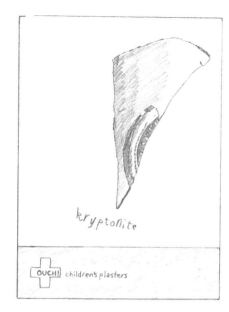

They usually start with the word "yeah." For example, "Yeah, it feels like that," "Yeah, it's kinda like that," "Yeah, it's that (insert benefit here) good/hot/cold/easy/tough."

And *yeah*, it's a trying to be cool, copycat technique that will in fact make your tagline more generic and less memorable. Case in point: which sounds better, "Just do it," or "Yeah, just do it"?

Tagline Reductionism

As I mentioned in the Print chapter, reductionism can apply to the overall ad (broad reductionism), or to any specific element that makes up an ad (narrow reductionism). The latter example includes the reduction of a tagline, perhaps to the point where it's non-existent (see page 101). So if you don't actually need a working or final tagline, don't use one. As Andrew Cracknell said, "People feel naked without it [but it's] just using up screen time, or another blob at the bottom of the page."

Sometimes even a famous, long-running tagline has come under the reductionist's knife. The belief here is that the message, idea, and brand are so powerful in the minds of the consumer that nothing is actually lost by reducing the number of words; the gain is therefore a pithier, spring-cleaned version of the previous tagline. After all, why say something in ten words when you can say it in five? Or even three? Or two? Or one?

Was	Became	Client
Just do it	I can*	Nike
The genuine article	True	Budweiser
We love to see you smile	Smile	McDonald's
Heineken refreshes the parts other beers cannot reach	Only Heineken can do this	Heineken

You'll see from most of the random examples below that tagline reductionism is easier with taglines that do not incorporate the name of the product, since this gives you more editing freedom.

*This line, although shorter and possibly not as strong as its predecessor, was quickly dropped when Champion Products (which had run its own "I can" ads and trademarked "You know you can" in Canada) filed suit against Nike for using the phrase. Arguably a blessing in disguise for Nike, who continue to use "Just do it."

....

Exercise: **create 10 more executions for the simple, tag-free Ouch! children's plasters campaign above.**

....

Sometimes the best tagline is no tagline. This simple campaign idea (for a UK children's plaster) is clear enough without one. *Client: Ouch! Children's Plasters.* *Agency: SHOP. Creatives: Tom Ewart, Dave Sullivan.*

Taglines Don't Have to Be At the End

Rules, they say, are meant to be broken. But they can also be unbroken. Here's an example: at the time, the now famous Avis campaign was very innovative. The press campaign was unusually minimal, with no apparent tagline, and no logo (see opposite). What and where was the campaign idea? The answer lay in the body copy in the first ad. The copy began with "We try harder." This was in a sense the tagline: the campaign idea. (Like this sentence here—buried in the copy.) Over time, Avis's market positioning has become so well known and understood by every consumer in the US that it's been reduced down to this very line, in the form of a traditional tagline below the logo. You could almost call it "reverse reductionism."

Headlines into Taglines

It's not only a line of body copy that can be used as a tagline. In the past (though less common in recent years), the tagline for a new campaign has been used in the form of a *headline* first, as part of its launch. For example, Perdue's "It takes a tough man to make a tender chicken" began as a headline, then switched to a tagline as the campaign's success continued. And interestingly, even though Wendy's line "Where's the beef?" was buried in the original script, it was not used as the tagline until later.

When working on headlines, you may write a line that is perhaps too broad and general for a headline, but works perfectly for a tagline. If so, switch it. I remember one student during a class exercise (to come up with potential headlines for Leagas Delaney's famous Timberland press ads, which described the care and attention that goes into the making of each sturdy work boot) presented this simple line as a headline: Tough love. As a headline it was too general. However, it would have tremendous potential as a *tagline* for an entirely new Timberland campaign.

The World's Favorite Tagline?

British Airways' tagline, "The world's favourite airline'" is a perfect example of how to take a simple, dry fact (BA lands in more international locations per day than any other airline), and turn it into something reassuring, compelling, and aspiring.

Probably the Worst Tagline in the World

I heard a radio commercial recently for Pepperidge Farm cookies. The ad involved a lot of talking about nothing in particular. I just couldn't figure out the idea. Then came the tagline: (spoken in a soppy, cutesy voice) Pepperidge farm. Never have an ordinary day!

Never *what?!* Not only did this line have nothing to do with the initial talking bit, I don't even know what it means. What does it have to do with chocolate chip cookies? *Perhaps* it worked really well for a previous campaign idea, or maybe it was just a badly placed "brand tagline" (see page 101).

The Dying Tagline?

Aside from the continual debate over the "death" of body copy (and whether or not anyone reads anymore), there's a similar concern over the recent decline of remarkable, memorable, and sustainable taglines. The concern is not just because tags help to create a campaign, but because they are an important part of brand definition. (Advertising is, after all, in the business of building and sustaining brands.)

The theories behind this decline are numerous. These include the increase in:

- Mergers and takeovers, resulting in greater campaign "reappraisals"
- Industry politics, causing a rise in account power over creative power (and therefore an undermining of copywriters and their craft)
- Demand from clients for concepts that look like finished ads (the contradictory "finished roughs"), leaving less time to spend on the initial idea
- Young teams who are more concerned with winning awards in the short term than selling brands in the long term

As we have seen, there are many successful visual campaigns that do not require a tagline. But the question is: how far are we prepared to go down the visual route? Let's hope that despite the ever-increasing globalization of markets and brands, advertising doesn't end up looking like one big "mood board," typically designed by account planners for research and focus groups (i.e., no campaign idea, let alone no tagline). Let's hope, too, that history repeats itself, so that clients and agencies will appreciate the importance of taglines once more.

....

Exercise: **start looking at (and listening to) taglines. Ask yourself what type of tagline is it? Does it work? If not, try to think of new ones. If you do find a campaign with a good tag (hint: look in an awards book), write down the tagline, and then try to create some new ads in the series. If the tag is a good summation or explanation of the campaign, you should be able to write many more ads.**

....

Exercise: **below are some classic taglines. Identify each one with its respective client.**

- Just do it
- A diamond is forever
- We try harder
- Think different
- Where do you want to go today?
- Good to the last drop
- Takes a lickin' and keeps on tickin'
- It's the real thing
- See America at see level
- The un-cola
- It takes a tough man to make a tender chicken
- We'll leave a light on for you
- Some of our best men are women
- The ultimate driving machine
- When it absolutely, positively has to get there overnight
- Let your fingers do the walking
- Hey, you never know
- What happens here, stays here

Las Vegas

Army, BMW, FedEx, Yellow Pages, NY Lotto,

Cola, Amtrak, 7-Up, Perdue, Motel 6, US

Microsoft, Maxwell House, Timex, Coca

- **Answers:** Nike, De Beers, Avis, Apple,

....

Avis is only No.2 in rent a cars. So why go with us?

We try harder.
(When you're not the biggest, you have to.)

We just can't afford dirty ash-trays. Or half-empty gas tanks. Or worn wipers. Or unwashed cars. Or low tires. Or anything less than seat-adjusters that adjust. Heaters that heat. Defrosters that defrost.

Obviously, the thing we try hardest for is just to be nice. To start you out right with a new car, like a lively, super-torque Ford, and a pleasant smile. To know, say, where you get a good pastrami sandwich in Duluth. Why?

Because we can't afford to take you for granted.

Go with us next time.

The line at our counter is shorter.

The still-running "We try harder" tagline began life as a first line of body copy. Similarly, a number of other famous taglines began as headlines. *Client:* Avis. *Agency: DDB. Creatives:* Paula Green, Helmut Krone.

06 Generating Strategies and Ideas

This chapter sets out to explore the origins of strategies and ideas, which will in turn help you to create campaigns (now that you have an understanding of the function of both campaigns and taglines).

Remember the conventional order of the creative process: each campaign comes from a concept/idea, which comes from a strategy. Conversely:

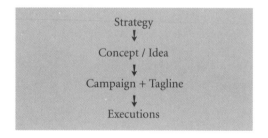

Strategy
↓
Concept / Idea
↓
Campaign + Tagline
↓
Executions

To summarize from the beginning of the Strategy chapter, the "strategy" is a summation, progression, reflection, and expression of the strategy statement. The strategy (or strategic thought) is a magical combination of elements extracted from the strategy statement, although often one element is the driving force behind the entire creative process, above (either the proposition, target audience or tone of voice).

In other words, the strategy is an *approach*, based on market research and insights, as to how a product or service will be positioned/repositioned. It's the thinking that comes before the idea/ concept. The thinking behind the thinking.

The specific advertising *idea* (whether it's a one-shot or a campaign) also has to be created by you, based on the strategy laid out in the strategy statement. The idea has to communicate the proposition to the right audience, all in a consistent tone. This is not as easy as it sounds, and is virtually impossible to do without a relevant, coherent, well-defined strategy to work from.

Every strategy should have an element of distinction (small or large) from the competition's strategies, as should the subsequent concept and campaign.

Note: if you are still unclear about the difference between strategies and ideas, re-read the Flowers & Plants Association and BUPA case studies in The Strategy chapter. Note also that some strategies are more closely linked to the campaign idea than others.

Types of Strategies

Here are some common types of creative *strategy* in the broadest sense of the word (rather than, for example, a simple "strategy = proposition" sense) from which ideas can be created. Some of these ideas might be closely tied to a particular strategy, and some might not. Some ideas might combine two or more strategic approaches, but, as always, communicating one proposition.

The strategies and ideas listed throughout this chapter are meant to serve as a source of inspiration. For a topic that has rarely been explored in such detail, I have tried to categorize both lists to the best of my abilities. Neither are definitive, and nor can they be. For a start, strategies and ideas can combine or overlap, making it very difficult to say which is which. What's most important is that the final ad is a combination of logical and creative thinking that is relevant enough to persuade the target consumer to buy the product.

"Before and After" Strategy

This common strategy is basically: "show life *without* the product, show life *with* the product." It's a simple way to understand the product benefit.

The subsequent *idea* and execution that comes from this strategy is usually a negative visual (without the product) followed by a positive one (with the product). This is not to be confused with the "negative to positive" strategy below. Within this idea there could be other types of ideas, like visual simile or visual metaphor. The famous Comfort campaign manages to combine both of these (see overleaf).

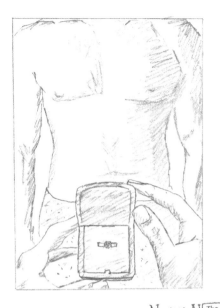

Strategy: before and after (without the product, with the product). *Client:* Natan Jewelry. *Agency:* F/Nazca Saatchi & Saatchi, Brazil. *Creatives:* Eduardo Lima, Luciano Lincoln, Fabio Fernandes.

"Before Only" Strategy

This approach is similar to "before and after," except the "after" is simply the product name/logo and tagline (if applicable). In other words, the consumer can figure out the "after" stage themselves, without having to see it.

"After Only" Strategy

This is a simple demonstration of the benefit. Or in other words, "life *with* the product." A large majority of advertising ideas fall into this category, whether explicitly, or more implicitly (see page 111, below).

"Advice" Strategy

This is a lateral, "we can help you" approach, usually expressed through the benefit. From this, various ideas can grow. For example, for an ad campaign announcing Macy's biggest sale, one student devised a series of ads that provide tips on how to "jump" the line (queue) of people. Another student team devised a campaign for U-Haul removal van hire. The word "haul" in the name "U-Haul" sounded like hard work until the team discovered various safety and time-saving techniques used by professional movers (i.e., U-Haul's competition) on how to pack fragile items, load a van efficiently, move a piano correctly, etc. Add a perfect tagline—We'll Help U-Haul—and a great campaign was created.

The advice strategy creates a positive image in the mind of the consumer. Note also how both of the above examples turn a negative into a positive: waiting in line won't be as long; moving house on your own won't be as tough.

"Knowledge" Strategy

This is similar to the "advice" strategy. This approach demonstrates how knowledgeable the client is about either (a) their own product, (b) a subject related to the product, or (c) the market in which the product exists, including the consumers themselves. For example, a vineyard could show how much knowledge, skill, and care goes into its wine making, or wine making in general, or perhaps something related like food. These demonstrations of knowledge communicate to the consumer that this is a *quality* product or service.

Right Strategy: before and after. Idea: visual simile. *Client: Lever Bros/Comfort fabric softener. Agency: Ogilvy & Mather, London. Creatives: Nick Parton, John Bayley.*

Below Before only strategy (without the product). The "after" is the product name/packshot. Tag: Don't let your eyes give it away. *Client: EJ's sunglasses. Agency: Carmichael Lynch, Minneapolis. Creatives: James Clunie, Tom Camp.*

Opposite, above Before only strategy (without the product). *Client: Weetabix. Agency: Lowe Lintas, London. Creatives: Gavin McDonald, Ken Taylor.*

Opposite, below After only strategy (life with the product). Most ads fall into this category. *Client: Wonderbra. Agency: TBWA/Hunt/Lascaris.*

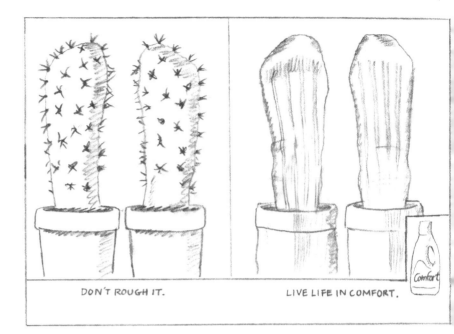

DON'T ROUGH IT.

LIVE LIFE IN COMFORT.

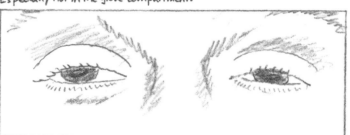

I have no illegal substances in the car officer.
Especially not in the glove compartment.

Don't let your eyes give it away. EJ's sunglasses

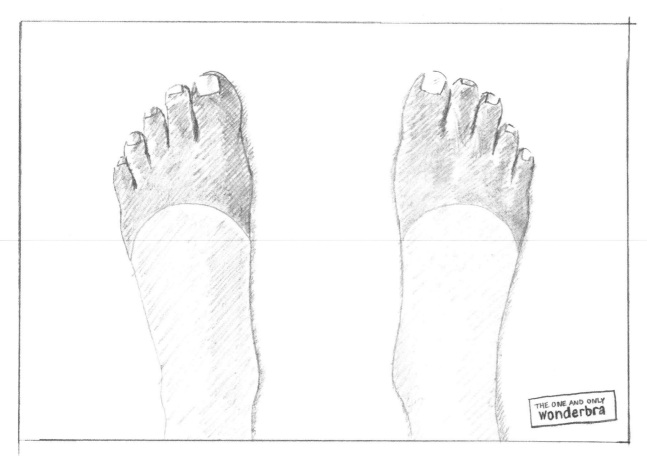

Demonstration strategy. Also ran with an alternative headline "Volvos stand up to heavy traffic" and as a TV commercial. *Client: Volvo. Agency: Scali, McCabe, Sloves. Creatives: Earl Cavanah, Larry Cadman.*

The campaign idea that stems from the "knowledge" strategy can be lateral. For example, a mattress company could perhaps devise a campaign not around the knowledge of mattresses per se, but the knowledge of *dreams*. This idea still communicates that the client understands their own product, but it is via a subject related to the product. The simple tagline, "We understand sleep," underscores this lateral approach (created by Richard Donovan and John Leaney, a former student team at Watford Advertising School).

Understanding the marketplace simply means that if a client produces say, hockey sticks, the campaign demonstrates their knowledge of hockey or players or teams instead.

"Empathy" Strategy

This approach demonstrates how empathetic the client is toward the consumer. It demonstrates to the target audience "We understand and care about you and/or your relationship with the product." In other words, if it does refer to the product, it does so through the consumer rather than the client. Various ideas can come from the "empathy"

strategy, but be careful not to sound patronizing or insincere, which will cause the entire approach to backfire. And for TV concepts, try to avoid the standard clichéd voiceovers: "We understand what it's like to be a woman, which is why we've developed…." In fact, you can be much more subtle about it, as with Johnson & Johnson's insightful campaign which uses the tagline "Having a baby changes everything."

"Demonstration" Strategy

Elsewhere in this section I have used the word "demonstrates" in the *general* sense. Here, in its purest form, this type of strategy focuses solely on ways to show the product benefit explicitly via a "demonstration." A new, clever way to demonstrate the product benefit can actually be the most engaging, direct form of communication. (Note: do not confuse these ads with the cheesy "product demonstration" infomercials that show obscure or useless inventions.) Examples of demonstration ads include American Tourister "Gorilla" (see page 173), Heinz Ketchup "One Reason" (see page 153), and Volvo "Heavy Traffic" (see above). The latter ad also ran with an alternative headline ("Volvos stand up to heavy traffic") and as a TV spot (see also Demonstration Ads, page 172).

"Testimonial" Strategy

Testimonial advertising can exist as early on as the strategy stage, or it can be deduced later, during the concept (ideation) stage. This approach uses a famous or non-famous consumer(s) to report their positive experiences with the product or service. This is a customer and product-based approach (as opposed to demonstration ads, which are purely product focused). Ideas from testimonials range from the sublime (the Tony Kaye-directed "Twister" commercial in which a daring windstorm specialist drives to "work" in a Volvo*) to the ridiculous (most feminine hygiene commercials). In the case of using famous people, the choice of person should be believable: the product should have some logical connection to the person. Also, there should be a relevance to the brand, the benefit, the strategy, and the idea. Otherwise you are guilty of negative "borrowed interest" (i.e., solely exploiting the pre-achieved fame and popularity of that person in order to try to sell a random product). (See also the "borrowed interest" idea, page 129.)

*This ad was also partly a product demonstration.

"Heritage" Strategy

This is an effective strategy because no two company histories or backgrounds are the same: each story is unique. But it must still communicate a Unique Selling Proposition, not just a Unique Proposition. A good example of this is the Jack Daniel's work that combines (depending on the execution) the heritage, knowledge, and staff strategies. Campaign idea: we put a lot of unique care and attention into making Jack Daniel's, which is why it has stayed so good.

"Owner" or "Staff" Strategy

Using the client or owner in the advertising can be hit or miss. The benefit is its down-to-earth integrity, since he or she is the heart and soul of the product. The drawback is that it can often be cheesy or dull. In fact, to paraphrase an old ad joke, "…and only as a last resort, should one show the client's face." Unless, of course, there is a solid, clear strategy and idea supporting the use of a client (the obvious example is Scali, McCabe, Sloves' famous "It takes a tough man to make a tender chicken" campaign for Perdue, starring the lovable owner

himself, Frank Perdue). If done in an original way, using staff members or workers in the actual ads can be an equally useful strategic tool because it gives the product authenticity and humanity.

"Product Positioning" Strategy

In a sense, this is the broadest, most basic type of strategy—simply to position a new or established product in a different way from its competition. Häagen-Dazs (a made-up, sensual-sounding name) positioned itself as an adult ice cream at a time when most ice creams were aimed at children. Also known as "brand positioning," it's the niche in the target market's mind and/or heart that the brand

A JACK DANIEL'S RICKER KNOWS the difference between whiskeywood and firewood.

For the charcoal that mellows our Tennessee Whiskey, we'll only burn hard maple taken from high ground. Anything else is too soft and would just go to ash. (Jack Bateman here is weeding out a stack of creek maple.) A new man in our rickyard must learn many skills before we bring him on. But first is knowing what wood makes the whiskey. And what wood makes the fire you sip the whiskey by.

JACK DANIEL'S TENNESSEE WHISKEY

This ad combines two strategies: heritage and knowledge. Headline: A Jack Daniel's ricker knows the difference between whiskeywood and firewood. *Client:* Jack Daniel's.

aims to "own." One could argue that all good advertising should adopt this strategy, with or without an additional, more specific strategy.

"Product Repositioning" Strategy

If a current product is losing money despite a healthy advertising spend, the product may need to *re*position itself—i.e., switch from the original positioning due to a sudden or prolonged shift in the market. For example, an up-market holiday company could create long weekend packages in response to its over-worked target market taking less vacation time than previously (thereby maximizing their "free" weekend time and minimizing their time away from important weekdays).

Be careful when trying to position or reposition a product. It's not just a question of thinking, "Hey, no one has sold this type of product for this use or to this group before." In order to succeed, it has to be believable, logical, and marketable. For instance, just because it's known that fine artists use cotton swabs doesn't mean that a brand of cotton buds should spend their money cornering that tiny market. They'd probably be much better off finding a new way to encourage a larger audience to increase cotton swab usage in the ways originally intended, such as for personal hygiene. By contrast,

perhaps a better example is selling Nike sneakers to old people. Why not? It's believable that this ever-increasing market could benefit from hipper, cushioned, joint-saving shoes. But again, be careful. This kind of daring repositioning could hurt a brand's image. Volvo suffered when it tried to reposition itself away from a practical, safe, family car, and into the sexy, luxury car market.

"Competitive" or "Comparison" Strategy

All clients compare themselves to their competition to a greater or lesser degree. You should be equally aware of the differences (good and bad) between competitive brands.

This strategic approach can make either an overt or subtle reference to any difference(s) between products in the actual advertising, rather than merely keeping it within the strategy statement. The most famous overt examples are usually between the two market leaders/rivals: Pepsi vs. Coke, Hertz vs. Avis, Budweiser vs. Miller, FedEx vs. UPS vs. DHL, etc. Finding something that the main competitor cannot say (or has failed to say) is key to this type of advertising. This strategy is particularly popular in the US, compared to the UK and other countries, but is used less and less today largely because lawsuits have clamped down on so many "claims" about a product and/or its competitors. Apple signed off on possibly the bravest, funniest competitive advertising of all time: the "I'm a Mac…And I'm a PC" campaign by comparing itself to a market rather than a brand name (see Product and Proposition Personified, page 128, and Competitive Advertising vs. Negative Advertising, page 152).

"Challenge" Strategy

This is the "have you got what it takes?" strategy. Some brands need to persuade people to *do* something, rather than *buy* something. One possible strategic approach is to challenge the consumer, to see if he or she is right for the "product." Typical examples include recruitment advertising (e.g., for the army, police, nursing, etc.) But don't limit yourself to tough jobs. Why not use this strategy to challenge young people to beat the deceptively skilful grannies who play bingo? In 1983, Shredded Wheat famously challenged cereal eaters with "bet you can't eat three!" It was both a clever way to increase sales, and being a particularly

As the differences between competitive products lessen over time, a comparative approach is becoming rarer. In fact, this was the only competitive ad within the campaign. But if you can say it (and it makes a good ad), say it. **Client:** *Tesco.* **Agency:** *Lowe & Partners, London.* **Creatives:** *Jason Cartmell, Jason Lawes.*

Granny Smiths.
What's the difference between ours and our competitors'?
Not much really.
They're the same quality as Waitrose.
And the same price as Asda.

TESCO | Every little helps

healthy product, they probably avoided lawsuits. The "challenge" strategic approach is powerful because it makes people think, and engages them with the product.

"Negative to Positive" Strategy

This strategy turns a boring or negative perception about a product/brand/market into a positive one, usually by adding an extra thought or clever argument. Here some campaign examples that worked off this strategy:

VW's famous "Think small" ad (page 33) turned the common American belief that bigger is better on its head, by showing positive reasons for owning a small car, such as smaller bills and smaller parking spaces.

VW Polo turned the stigma that small cars are unsafe into a positive by citing the natural defense system of human beings and living creatures when faced with danger—they make themselves smaller. Once established, a follow-up campaign simply reiterated this thought with the tagline "Small but tough," no doubt validated by better safety features.

In the 1960s, Hertz were the market leader in car rental business, and Avis were number 2. Avis's genius strategy was to attach the benefit that "We try harder," turning a negative proposition into a positive one. Hertz still owned size, but through logical deduction, by communicating that they were striving to satisfy their customers (and become number 1), Avis now owned something very important: service (see also "Competitive" or "Comparison" Strategy, opposite).

Miller Lite (a name that for the macho beer drinkers of the time sounded like something was missing, or worse, a girly diet product) turned this potential negative around to mean "it won't fill you up" (i.e., you can drink more) which cleverly made Miller more money.

Buitoni also turned a negative fact (the muddy color of their spaghetti was not as attractive as the creamy-looking competition) into a positive, by stating that it doesn't have any whitening starch, and therefore tastes better. Tag: (it tastes good) Because it's so ugly (see the TV chapter).

Ad legend John Webster's famous campaign for Smash effectively turned a positive situation into a negative, and back to a positive. By showing martians laugh at humans' normal approach to making mash potato (digging up a potato, peeling it, boiling it, and then finally mashing it), a natural solution turned into a negative, abnormal, old-fashioned, stupid one. Introducing instant mash in a packet provided a positive solution. And to sum up, his simple yet cunning tagline, "For mash, get Smash" cleverly positioned packet mash potato level alongside the real thing.

"Logic" Strategy

This is the "you wouldn't do that, so why do this?" strategy. Arguably an idea as much as a strategy, this approach can be expressed in various ways, e.g., Oviatt Audiology: Visual: a DIY braces kit (above). Headline: "A hearing aid without an audiologist is like braces without an orthodontist." (See also Hey, Schmuck, page 103.)

"Price" Strategy (Expensive/Cheap)

Overleaf are two examples that turn a boring,

Negative to positive strategy. "Adopt a mutt" is honest but sounds negative, whereas "best of all breeds" is suddenly positive. *Client: Massachusetts Society for the Prevention of Cruelty to Animals, www.mspca.org. Agency: Humphrey Browning MacDougall, Boston. Creative: Katina Mills.*

The logical approach: you wouldn't do that, so why do this? (This campaign added humor to change people's mind about purchasing low-quality, non-prescribed hearing aids from high street stores and coupon ads.) Headline: A hearing aid without an audiologist is like braces without an orthodontist. *Client: Oviatt Hearing & Balance. Students: Alison Venne, Erin Kritzer, Christian Jackson, Matt Silvester.*

Price strategy. While Stella Artois makes expensive sound good, this VW Polo campaign says "cheap" while still saying "quality." Tagline: Surprisingly ordinary prices. Execution: wedding photographer focuses on (literally) an attractive bus ad. *Client: Volkswagen. Agency: BMP DDB, London. Creatives: Neil Dawson, Clive Pickering.*

Surprisingly ordinary prices

Product: Stella Artois
Problem to solve: Stella is more expensive than most popular lagers.
USP: Stella is so desirable and gratifying that it's worth the extra expense.
Idea/executions: People are content to ruin precious objects in order to open a bottle.
Tagline: Reassuringly expensive.

Product: VW Polo L
Problem to solve: The Polo is cheaper in price (but not in design) than most popular small cars, which could be seen as negative for VW's prestigious brand.
USP: The Polo L is the most under-priced small car on the market.
Idea/executions: People are surprised by how affordable a new VW Polo L is.
Tagline: Surprisingly ordinary prices.

common proposition (expensive and cheap, respectively) into a positive strategy/USP. See "Lambretta," "Chair," and "Fender," page 100.

"Honesty" Strategy

Perhaps as much a type of idea as it is a strategy, the honesty approach is one that runs through the strategy, idea, executions, and tone of voice. By "honesty" I mean self-honesty (about the product) rather than honesty about another related or unrelated subject. Done well, the self-honesty approach is refreshing, disarming, down to earth, and often humorous—and therefore appealing to even the most skeptical consumer. This strategy requires a brave client, especially in the heavily self-deprecating examples opposite, each of which has a variation on selling "bad taste." But note how these ads don't simply say, "our product is bad, buy it." Each one actually offers a *reason* why the consumer should do so. In other words, there's a benefit, or resolution being offered. (Even a scandalous, exposed corporation might earn some respect if it ran a full-page ad with a headline like "We screwed up.")

The rationale behind proudly claiming that TCP (antiseptic liquid) "tastes as foul today as it always has" can be supported by the fact that we, the consumer, have had instilled into us from a young age that the worse a medicine tastes, the more powerful (and therefore more effective) it must be. Even the tag tells it like it is.

In the Goebel Beer ad the rationale and benefit is clearly explained in the headline: "One of the best things about new Goebel Beer is that it doesn't taste anything like old Goebel Beer." The message? It's a much better tasting beer.

In the Alka-Seltzer ad the resolution is clearly outlined by the body copy's instructions on how to create an Alka-Seltzer drink that "…doesn't taste like Alka-Seltzer." This idea works for another reason, too, because it uses the opposite tool to give it a twist. At first the drink appears to be an alcoholic one (the culprit) and then we realize it's actually the opposite (the cure).

Written in 1900 by explorer Sir Ernest Shackleton (opposite, bottom), this is arguably the most successful recruitment ad up until that time, receiving 5,000 worthy applications for just 28 positions. It ran in London newspapers, and manages to combine two strategic approaches— "challenge" and "honesty."

TASTES AS FOUL TODAY AS IT ALWAYS HAS.

FOR SORE THROATS DILUTE, WINCE AND GARGLE.

Self-honesty. This ad raises a smile on the face of any Brit who has gargled this unpleasant liquid. But the real truth is, it works. **Client:** *Pfizer.* **Product:** *TCP.* **Agency:** *M&C Saatchi, London.* **Creatives:** *Malcolm Poynton, Paul Hodgkinson.*

One of the best things about new Goebel Beer is that it doesn't taste anything like old Goebel Beer

Alka-Seltzer On The Rocks

More self-honesty. It takes a brave client to admit something like this, especially in public. **Client:** *Pabst Brewing Company.* **Product:** *Goebel Beer.* **Agency:** *Carl Ally.* **Creative:** *Ed McCabe.*

Let's be honest, our product is for hangovers. This ad provides extra relief with instructions to create a drink that "...doesn't taste like Alka-Seltzer." **Client:** *Miles Laboratories.* **Product:** *Alka-Seltzer.* **Agency:** *Jack Tinker & Partners.* **Creatives:** *Mary Wells, George D'Amato.*

Mᴇɴ WANTED for Hazardous Journey. Small wages, bitter cold, long months of complete darkness, constant danger, safe return doubtful. Honor and recognition in case of success — Ernest Shackleton.

Combining the "honesty" and "challenge" strategies. Written in 1900 by the explorer himself, this no-nonsense ad attracted a plethora of willing (and most likely, able) applicants. **Client:** *Sir Ernest Shackleton.* **Creative:** *Sir Ernest Shackleton.*

65th
Art
Directors
Annual

An honest look at advertising's competitive spirit during awards time. **Client:** *Art Directors Club of New York.* **Creative:** *Bob Gill.*

The book cover (left), which was created when all ad folk wore suits, sums up the industry with self-deprecating honesty. In fact, this strategy has been revisited many times since, for various award show "call for entries" ads. "The Most Interesting Man in the World" campaign for Dos Equis is refreshingly honest in its quirky "soft sell" of the product, emphasized by the spokesperson's admission that, "I don't always drink beer. But when I do, I prefer Dos Equis." He's not even saying it's the *only* beer he drinks.

Types of Ideas

Finding new ways to sell a product requires a certain amount of lateral thinking, and a considerable amount of original thinking. Once you have a clear strategy in place, you should be able to create multiple campaign* ideas. Your job is then to pick the best one, or rather, the one that produces the best ads.

If you get stuck at the "ideas stage" (sometimes called "ideation"), here are some common, tried and tested types of ideas to inspire you. These are not necessarily the final, definitive, inspired campaign ideas expressed in a single sentence or tagline with never seen before executions (that's where your creativity really comes in to play). Alternatively, you may have a final campaign idea first, which ends up incorporating one of these types of ideas. The origin and order doesn't matter, only the end result. If you wish, you can always post rationalize.

Of course there may be validity in the first innocent, simple idea(s) you have. This section will hopefully help you to come up with those, too—whether immediately, or after a long, painful, thought process.

Note that in some cases a campaign can possess a combination of ideas or idea tools (e.g., Nintendo Game Boy "Prison" by Lowe Brindfors, Stockholm uses the "product is God" idea plus the exaggeration tool) rather than just one. Equally, any of the general ideas listed below could be part of a bigger campaign idea, defined further by a tagline. As long as the communication isn't being clouded in any way, the ads will be just as effective. Conversely, any of the general ideas could literally be the campaign idea itself, and nothing more. In this case, the ads/executions should be original. This list is comprehensive rather than definitive,

so you may discover a type of idea that has yet to be defined.

* or one-shots, if required

Analogy and Visual Metaphor

Analogy and visual metaphor both use one thing to represent another. An analogy is a partial likeness between two things that are compared often to help explain something, e.g., the human heart and a pump. Similarly, a metaphor is the application of a word or phrase to somebody or something that is not meant literally, but to make a comparison, e.g., "my boss is a snake," "the evening of one's life," etc. In visual terms, analogies and metaphors can include the use of *symbols* to represent something, e.g., red = anger, dog = loyal, cheetah = speed, elephant = gentle, yet strong (the latter was once used for a headache/stomach ache tablet). Symbols can also be given a lateral twist, as examined on page 35.

Simple analogies explain how it feels to go on a ride at Playland (see overleaf, above). Hence, "Fire bell," "Food mixer," and "Catapult."

Pirelli "Carl Lewis" (see overleaf, below) could be described as analogy and visual metaphor. Lewis represents power and speed, i.e., a motorcar. High heels on wet terrain represent control, or rather the need for proper control and grip (i.e., Pirelli tires). The idea is summed up by the line, "Power is nothing without control."

Two types of idea, one simple ad: "product is God" plus "exaggeration." *Client: Nintendo.* *Product: Game Boy.* *Agency: Lowe Brindfors, Stockholm.* *Creatives: Johan Holmström, Richard Villard.*

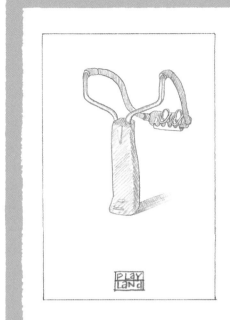

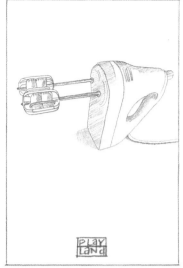

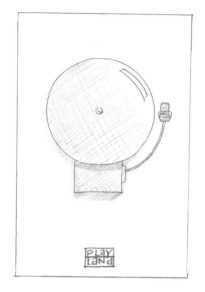

Simple use of analogy explains how it feels to go on a theme park ride. **Client:** *Playland.* **Agency:** *Rethink, Vancouver.* **Creatives:** *Ian Grais, Natee Likit, Jono Holmes.*

Visual metaphor: Lewis represents the power and speed of a motorcar and analogy: the precision and control of a tire is like running in high heels. Tagline: Power is nothing without control. **Client:** *Pirelli.* **Agency:** *Young & Rubicam, London.* **Creatives:** *Graeme Norways, Ewan Patterson.*

Visual metaphor: a tortoise represents slowness. **Client:** *Nike.* **Agency:** *McCann Erickson, Chile.* **Creative directors:** *Guido Puch, Rene Moraga.*

Visual metaphor: the "human camera" represents unfiltered, lifelike coverage and analogy: it's like there's no camera. **Client:** *News Channel 1.* **Agency:** *Euro RSCG Flagship, Thailand.* **Creatives:** *Nucharat Nuntananonchai, Passapol Limpisirisan, Taya Sutthinun, Wiboon Leepakpreeda.*

Visual Simile

Visual simile is when something *looks similar* to something else. This is a common technique, especially in print advertising.* It's basically when a visual/object looks like something related to the proposition or the product itself. The "likeness" is usually a result of the way an object is cleverly cropped, or due to a specific angle or point of view that creates a similar shape or appearance.

Visual simile ads are simple, rarely using more than one visual/object. The challenge is to find a new way to make one object look like two things. Other than being original and clever, the key to visual simile is to make the visual "double meaning" clear (it can't *kind of* look like something), and without the need of heavy manipulation (which will make the whole thing look contrived). Equally, don't make it too easy. For example, a piece of uncooked spaghetti can be twisted to make virtually any letter, number, shape, etc.—not just the one that relates to your product or benefit. Fine as interesting type, but not visual simile. Whereas a handful of spaghetti is more unusual and challenging in terms of visual simile— resulting in a cleverer, more original ad.

Because visual simile is often the result of an inspired observation, it can be hard to expand one execution into a campaign. As a result, visual simile ads are more often clever one-shots than entire campaigns.

* See also the TV chapter.

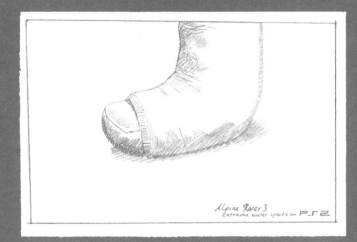

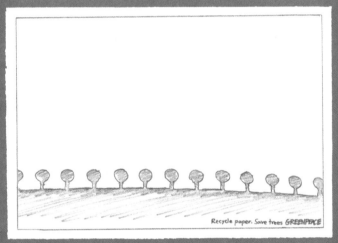

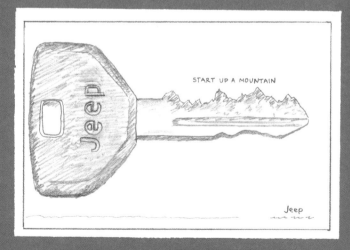

Visual simile: skier's broken foot is actually "gamer's thumb." **Client:** *Sony PlayStation/Alpine Racer III.* **Agency:** *TBWA, Paris.* **Creatives:** *Vincent Lobelle, Jorge Carreno, Stephen Cafiero.*

Visual simile: torn paper looks like trees (the background is green). **Client:** *Greenpeace.* **Agency:** *JWT, Makati City, Manila.* **Creatives:** *Dave Ferrer, Joey Ong.*

Visual simile: key looks like a mountain. Reductionists would argue that the headline is unnecessary (in fact, another version ran without it). **Client:** *Jeep.* **Agency:** *Bozell Worldwide, Southfield, Michigan.* **Creatives:** *Mike Stocker, Robin Chrumka.*

Visual simile: belly button looks like a dot. **Client:** *Vogue.* **Agency:** *M&C Saatchi, London.* **Creatives:** *Tiger Savage, Mark Goodwin.*

Visual simile: kitchen sink drain looks like a plate. (Stylish photography helped reduce the icky factor.) Tagline: Any food tastes supreme with Heinz Salad Cream. **Client:** *Heinz.* **Agency:** *Leo Burnett, London.*

Visual simile: tin looks like ripples. Tagline: Nothing but fish. **Client:** *MV Brands.* **Product:** *John West.* **Agency:** *Leo Burnett, London.* **Creatives:** *Richard Conner, Julie Adams.*

Visual simile: meat looks like two numbers. **Client:** British Pork Executive. **Agency:** DDB, London. **Creatives:** Mike Hannett, Dave Buchanan. **Photographer:** Simon Page-Ritchie.

Visual simile: pin looks like car and visual metaphor: pin represents safety. **Client:** *Volvo.* **Agency:** *Young & Rubicam, Tokyo.* **Creatives:** *Minoru Kawase, Masakazu Sawa.*

Visual simile: car looks like
shark and visual metaphor: shark
represents speed and fear. *Client:*
*BMW. **Agency:** SCPF, Barcelona.*

Visual simile: fish-like logo;
basketball net looks like
McDonald's arches. *Client:*
*McDonald's. **Agency:** Leo Burnett.*

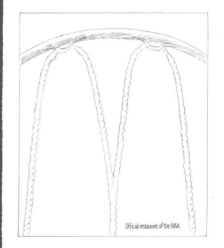

Exercise: **look at the visual simile examples opposite for McDonald's ("Fish," "Net"). Create ten more examples using things that look like the famous McDonald's "arches," either a special offer/menu item or an organization/sponsorship ad that relates back to each visual.**

Interpretation

This is also known as the "you see/we see" idea. It is slightly different from visual simile, in that it's one step removed from looking very similar to something: it requires more imagination and direction to understand the comparison between the two things. Interpretations can be the viewpoint of the client, the consumer, or both (i.e., "we both see the world the same way"). Examples include, Saturn's TV spot, "Sheet Metal," and Microsoft's "We See" campaign.

Two in One

These show the range of products and services (or the benefits and features within a product or service). Works well with a variety or double proposition (see Tackling the Variety Proposition, page 144, and Tackling the Double Proposition, page 145) because it simplifies the range by showing only two things.

Executional Ideas

There are two types of executional idea. The first refers to the individual ideas within each execution that make up a campaign: the campaign executions. Each idea (of which there are at least three per campaign) is an expression of the campaign thought. A successful long-running campaign is one in which the executional ideas can keep being relevant and fresh for the current market place (see the Execution chapter).

The second type of executional ideas are demonstration or ambient ads, etc., that rely on an added "executional" element which takes it beyond a traditional 2-D print ad. In fact, without the element the ad would not work, e.g., the Poster ad "Also stick handles to teapots" for Araldite (page 181), Ikea's "Big Tags" campaign (page 32) and Scratch n' sniff (page 85).

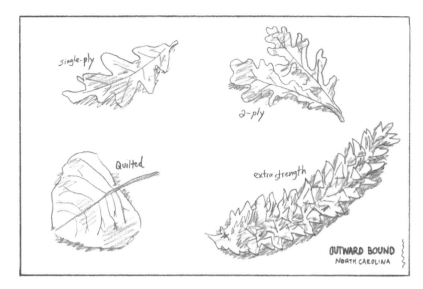

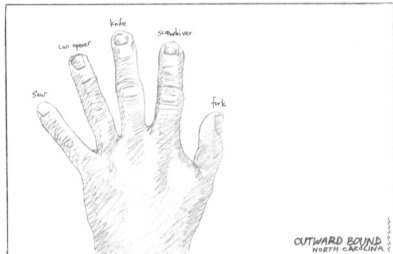

Interpretation. Headline: Single-ply, 2-ply, quilted, extra strength. *Client:* *Outward Bound, North Carolina.* *Agency:* *Loeffler Ketchum Mountjoy (LKM), Charlotte.* *Creatives:* *Doug Pederson, Curtis Smith, Mike Duckworth.*

Interpretation. Headline: Saw, can opener, knife, screwdriver, fork.

Idea: two in one. Proposition: variety. **Client:** *Yellow Pages.* **Agency:** *AMV BBDO, London.* **Creatives:** *Graham Storey, Phil Cockrell.*

Idea: two in one. Proposition: variety. Headline: The lowest call rates to Japan and Scotland. (Imagine bonnie red hair and beard.) **Client:** *Telefonica.* **Agency:** *Y&R, Buenos Aires.* **Creatives:** *Christian Giménez, Sebastián Moltedo.*

Product is God

Such ads have been reinvented many times, and will undoubtedly continue to be. An early example was David Ogilvy's "The man in the Hathaway shirt." Later ones include Castlemaine XXXX beer's "Australians wouldn't give a XXXX for anything else"; Beck's "It's all about the beer" and VW Beetle's "There's a (black/yellow/blue) one" campaign, and Umbro's "Only football": "2. Sex. 3. Money."

Note: this approach is completely different from the safe "product as hero" advertising, in which the ad is basically an image of the product, often seen in print ads for luxury products such as watches, cars, and perfume.

Trends

A trend is a general tendency, movement, or direction. Recognizing trends can produce interesting campaign ideas. An example of a trend is global warming. A student team took this trend and expressed it in the tagline "It's getting warmer." The product they chose was not Greenpeace, but suncream. Rather than the usual strategy of targeting sunbathers and holidaymakers, it focused on everyday use. The idea used facts to show how things have actually begun to change in line with the warming planet, e.g., more outdoor city cafés (see also Truisms: Finding the Truth, page 134).

Obsession

A recurring advertising idea, this focuses on a particular obsession about the product, either from the point of view of the consumer(s), or the client. In the case of the latter, this could stem from strategies like "heritage," "knowledge," and "owner/staff." Similar to Product is God idea.

Exaggeration

Using exaggeration can accentuate a product's benefit (see The Exaggeration Tool, page 138). The Castlemaine XXXX campaign is an example of "exaggeration" and "Product is God." The benefit? It must be really good beer.

Proposition Personified

This is when someone using the product in the ad indirectly becomes the proposition. The characters personify the proposition through their actions or words. The proposition is usually very simple, with the idea playing off a double meaning or equally simple tagline. For example, Bartle Bogle Hegarty, London's Boddingtons Ale "Strong Stuff" (see page

The man in the Hathaway shirt

2. Sex. 3. Money.

"Hey, there's a black one."

Product is God, *c.* 1951. ***Client:*** *Hathaway Shirts.* ***Agency:*** *Hewitt, Ogilvy, Benson & Mather.* ***Creative:*** *David Ogilvy.*

Soccer is God. Tagline: Only Football (double meaning: we only produce football equipment; for people who only care about football). ***Client:*** *Umbro.* ***Agency:*** *DMB&B, London.* ***Creatives:*** *Arthur Hurn, Nick Hastings.*

Product is God, *c.* 2001. ***Client:*** *Volkswagen.* ***Agency:*** *Arnold Worldwide, Boston.* ***Creatives:*** *Don Shelford, David Weist.*

Product personified. **Client:** *Sony.* **Agency:** *DDB.* **Creatives:** *John Caggiano, Marvin Honig.*

I'm a Mac, and I'm a PC: product personification at its simplest. **Client:** *Apple.* **Agency:** *TBWA/Chiat/Day, Los Angeles.* **Creatives:** *Barton Corley, Scott Trattner, Jason Sperling.*

Wonderbra spoofs a classic *Economist* ad (see page 23). **Client:** *Wonderbra.* **Agency:** *DDB Worldwide, Singapore.* **Creatives:** *Khalid Osman, Priti Kapur.*

71) campaign. The beer is strong stuff, plus when you drink it you say "strong" things, e.g., a man says to a woman, "You want equality? It's your round."⁎ Another example is Mad Dogs and Englishmen's campaign for Shelter Clothing. The tagline/idea of "Very, very, very, tough clothing" is reflected through its wearers: a leg tripping up a blind man; a man stealing a child's tricycle.

⁎Coincidentally, a similar idea was used for a difference brand of "extra cold" beer.

Product Personified

Similar to proposition personified (above), this is when the product is clearly compared to a person, or to human behavior. An example of the first: a mini television is compared to a newborn baby in. "Congratulations 'It's a Sony.' 7 lbs. 11oz." An example of the second: Evian mineral water (made of compressible plastic): "Gets drunk and collapses." Alternatively the ad on page 84 for Pepsi shows the personification of a related product (ice cubes).

Note: in this case "product personified" doesn't mean give the product arm and legs and/or make it talk.

Product and Proposition Personified

This is possible to do. For example, Apple's "I'm a Mac. And I'm a PC" campaign cleverly uses two people to personify both the product *and* the contrasting benefits of each product. This campaign is also a great example of competitive advertising.

Spoof Advertising

Spoofs are parodies, satires, send ups, and piss takes. There are two main types of spoof in advertising. The first is the ultimate in self-deprecating humor: parodying other, often clichéd, advertising styles (e.g., weight loss before and after ads, doorstop or taste test challenges), or even specific campaigns, e.g., 118 118 The Number's "Just Works—Cog Spoof" and "Honda Choir Spoof"; Carlton Draught's "Big Ad" that parodies the cast of thousands British Airways ads, and Nissan's spoof of VW's award-winning print ad "Cops."

The UK's most successful spoof advertising in recent years is the Boddingtons' TV campaign, which "sends up" a number of commercials, including Wall's cornetto ice cream ("Gondolas"). In the US, the comedy show "Saturday Night Live" has produced many hilarious TV commercial spoofs over the years, including the wonderful

"Colon Blow," which parodies those annoying " How many bowls of your usual high fiber cereal…" comparison ads.

The second type of spoof is the parodying of everything and anything that isn't advertising, e.g., a TV show, a movie, a play, etc. Former Ogilvy, London creative team John McLaughlin and Mark Orbine produced a series of groundbreaking idents for IBM that parodied the BBC's Children's TV science workshops of the 1970s. For a spoof to work at all, the target consumer has to be familiar with the original in order to get the joke.

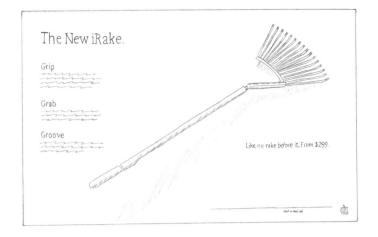

. . . .

Exercise: **think of five types of clichéd advertising styles that have yet to be parodied. Do the same for genres of movies and TV shows. Keep the list for potential future campaign ideas.**

. . . .

"Borrowed Interest"

A category of testimonial advertising (see "Testimonial Strategy," page 113), "borrowed interest" is where a client uses someone or something that is already famous to sell its product or service. Unless there's a *relevant* reason for such an endorsement, the idea will tend to lack substance: it is merely "borrowing the interest" of that someone or something. This is often the case, which is why the term can have negative connotations. But finding good examples is easy: Michael Jordan selling sneakers is relevant and natural, whereas Michael Jordan selling cell phones is irrelevant and forced. Michael selling extra leg room for an airline is fairly relevant, whereas Michael Jordan selling a Hummer is fairly irrelevant. With all these examples, no matter how tenuous the link, the final justification comes down to the quality of the idea and the script. Perhaps there is a great way to use him to sell a bank (perhaps he uses the bank that he can trust with his millions…). Conversely, just because Mr. Jordan is in a sneaker commercial doesn't automatically make it a good ad.

Choosing a *spokesperson* is a less extreme example of borrowed interest. These people are chosen to reflect the brand voice or personality, e.g., voiceovers for TV and radio. Using a famous person may add a bit of kudos. Again, if the choice

Not a real ad, but a spoof on the iPod generation. *Client: Jest Magazine. Creatives: Steven Rosenthal, Frank Vitale.*

Velma, before and after. An example of *good* borrowed interest. *Client: Dove. Agency: Ogilvy & Mather, Chicago. Creatives: Gabe Usadel, Joshua Kemeny.*

is relevant and appropriate (and the ad is good), then you can get away with it.

An example of good borrowed interest includes Ogilvy's "Goodbye Stickiness. Hello Movement" campaign for Dove shampoo. Using a series of famous female cartoon characters, this simple idea applies the before and after strategy in a totally relevant way—because the truth is these "women" do have stiff, sticky hair! This campaign also used the slogan "Unstick your style."

Another clever, relevant use of borrowed interest was casting the one-time World's Fastest Talker,

No wonder our perception
of beauty is distorted

Social commentary: Dove as
spokesperson for real beauty.
Client: Dove. *Agency:* Ogilvy,
Toronto. *Creatives:* Tim Piper,
Mike Kirkland. *Creative directors:*
Janet Kestin, Nancy Vonk.
Producer: Brenda Surminski.
Account lead: Aviva Groll.

John Moschitta, in the classic FedEx commercial, "Fast Paced World" by Ally & Gargano.

Testimonials can be a form of borrowed interest (see "Testimonial Strategy," page 113).

Social Commentary

Don't be afraid to generate ideas that make a social commentary. Make a statement that transcends the benefit of a particular product or service. Let the client be a spokesperson for police brutality, or sexism, or homophobia, or child labor, or the declining bee population. Why not? As long as the strategy and the idea is *relevant* to the brand that you are advertising, this approach can be a very powerful way to win the respect of consumers because of its unexpected attitude and refreshing "non-addyness." But be careful that your brand's message doesn't become too saccharin, worthy or preachy, which can cause the entire thing to backfire. Remember, the whole point is to create something that is not self important or brand centric.

Be Anti Something

Find a topic, activity, behavior, person or group of people that you can take a deserved dig at. Putting your "anti" hat on will create all kinds of edgy ideas that you would not have thought of otherwise. But never be hurtful for the sake of it. You must always have a valid reason to be negative or irreverent; the ads somehow have to relate back to the product. (I'd argue that if everyone did what Kenneth Cole or Benetton does, people would start to get irritated.) And preferably choose something or someone that has never been attacked before. So avoid clichéd targets. The reaction from the consumer should be, "It's about time someone made a (funny/serious) point about that." The three obvious topics that are definite no-go areas (unless it's self-deprecating, e.g., a women's magazine poking fun at themselves) are gender, race, and sexual persuasion (apart from heterosexual activity, which *is* fair game…). Many students are scared to write ads that criticize anything, especially people. Don't be. For example, it's unlikely that teenagers will sue a company that (finally) highlights how loud, rude, and moody they can be. It's real. Just make sure there's a reason for doing it. One student wanted to say that a particular multi-surface household cleaning product is so good you don't need a cleaning

Social commentary: Nike as spokesperson for anti-racism.
Client: Nike. *Agency:* Wieden & Kennedy, Portland.

Hello world.

I shot in the 70s when I was 8.

I shot in the 60s when I was 12.

Hello world.

I won the United States Junior Amateur when I was 15.

I played in the Nissan Los Angeles Open when I was 16.

I won the United States Amateur when I was 18.

Hello world.

I played in the Masters when I was 19.

I played in the United States Open when I was 19.

I played in the British Open when I was 19.

Hello world.

I am the only man to win three consecutive

United States Amateur titles.

Hello world.

There are still courses in the United States that I am

not allowed to play because of the color of my skin.

Hello world.

I've heard I'm not ready for you.

Are you ready for me?

Just do it.

Topical advertising.
Headline: Have a great
Christmas. Leave
the car at home. *Client:*
Carlsberg. *Agency:*
Saatchi & Saatchi, London.
Creatives: David Hillyard,
Ed Robinson.

Have a great Christmas. Leave the car at home.

person. Okay, but what if I don't have a cleaning person? Then *push* the idea further so that no one would want to hire a cleaner. Be…anti cleaning people! Tell everyone why (some) cleaners are creepy: they go through your private stuff, "borrow" your things, etc. It's funny (in a disturbing way) because it's believable. You can also substantiate it because a multi-surface cleaning product is more efficient for a homeowner to use. *And* it makes millions of consumers feel better about not being able to afford a cleaner in the first place.

Topical Advertising

Topical, "opportunistic" advertising takes advantage of either a recent news event (usually well known), a popular TV or movie, or a seasonal activity, and relates it back to the product benefit or to the product's current campaign. Because of its short lifespan (and therefore appeal), topical advertising usually takes the form of a last-minute one-shot, or one execution within a current campaign. The ad might be part of a bigger, current strategy, or a mere brand ad (e.g., there's no connection between Starbucks and America's annual Martin Luther King Jr. Day, but they still spent money on an ad to celebrate it).

Common areas include topical tributes or anniversaries: VW's "Tear" for Jerry Garcia on page 259, holiday messages, e.g., Carlsberg's "No Car," Hertz's "Taxi," or current popular culture, shows, and expressions, e.g., The *Economist* headline: "You are the strongest link. Hello."

Receiving a Fact vs. Finding a Fact vs. Deducing a Fact

In an ideal world, the client and/or account department will unearth an amazing fact or figure into which a great idea for an ad will instantly evolve, like a ready-made headline or visual. For instance, the fact that a particular car undergoes more safety tests than any other. Or perhaps the product is used by astronauts. The most famous Matchbox ad states the fact that "We sell more cars than Ford, Chrysler, Chevrolet and Buick combined." For his 1957 "Clock" ad (overleaf) David Ogilvy used a factual quote from a Rolls-Royce engineer. (Fifty years on, a slightly revised, reduced, re-art directed version of this legendary ad might look something like the one next to it.)

IF YOU PLAN TO DRINK ON NEW YEAR'S EVE, HERTZ WOULD LIKE TO RECOMMEND ANOTHER RENT-A-CAR.

Topical advertising: another way to prevent drinking and driving over the festive season. *Client:* Hertz. *Agency:* Scali, McCabe, Sloves. ***Creatives:*** Steve Montgomery, Earl Carter.

But what happens when you aren't given a fact like this? Or when the fact doesn't spark off any great ideas? Then, you either have to find a new unrelated fact yourself (see The USP and Generic Products, page 139), *or* you have to attach a new *related* fact to the first one through "factual deduction" or "deductive logic." This is the process of taking one fact or figure about the product, and deducing another (more inspiring) fact from it.

For example, imagine the first fact is that a particular car has the longest rust warranty in

"At 60 miles an hour the loudest noise in this new Rolls-Royce comes from the electric clock"

At 60 mph the loudest noise comes from the electric clock.

Facts speak for themselves. David Ogilvy used a direct quote from a Rolls-Royce engineer. *Client: Rolls-Royce.* *Agency: Ogilvy & Mather.* *Creative: David Ogilvy.*

Sacreligiously revised fifty years later, the concept behind the clock ad is still timeless.

the US (five years, compared to the competition's one). This is essentially the proposition. But if few creative thoughts spring to mind, try thinking of another related fact. What if you calculated the average rainfall that this would equate to in five and one year(s)? Imagine a TV commercial whereby the water level surrounding a car is at 18 inches (or one year of rain). Then the level slowly rises until it engulfs the entire car (7½ feet, or five years of rain). Suddenly you have a dramatic yet simple ad, created by a method of factual deduction.

Truisms: Finding the Truth

Truisms are simply *life's truths.* Sometimes called human truths, these are "facts of life," rather than hard, statistical facts and figures (although these can also be useful when writing ads).

Truisms can be blindingly obvious, deep, funny, sad, quirky, general or specific—statements that *most* people would agree with, however meaningless they might appear at first. Observational humor has been the basis of many stand-up comedians' acts. How many times have you thought, "that's so true!" in response to a particular joke? Often the reason why a joke makes us laugh is because it is based on real life: a truth.

Truisms can be (and have been) used many times to advertise successfully and sell a product/service. That's because truisms are (i) simple, and (ii) hard to argue with. Therefore, if you can apply a truism to a strategy or idea for a particular product/service, it will be just as hard to argue with the advertising message. Of course, truisms don't have to be funny.

WE SELL MORE CARS THAN FORD, CHRYSLER, CHEVROLET AND BUICK COMBINED.

MATCHBOX.

Examples of truisms

- Life is too short
- Children can absorb more information than adults
- Doctors have terrible handwriting
- Mondays are officially the longest workday of the week
- You're either a dog person or a cat person
- Money gives you more freedom
- What goes around comes around
- Glasses make a person look more intelligent
- Smile and the world smiles with you
- Over-confident people are usually the most insecure
- You wait hours for a bus and then three arrive at once
- A local resident can make better travel suggestions than a non-local
- Breakfast is the most important meal of the day
- Cheese gives you nightmares

In many cases it's actually possible to take a simple truism and turn it into an award-winning campaign for a global client. Here's one example by a former student team: they began with the truism that "places are often demolished and replaced by modern buildings, etc." From this they devised a strategy that highlighted the importance of keeping a physical record of these things before they disappear for good. (More specifically, to remind people to take photos of everything.) This turned into a perfect idea for a brand such as Kodak, with the simple yet poignant tagline: "Things change." The initial campaign executions contrasted the warm, compelling stories of various people trying to describe how the places looked and felt all those years ago (school yards, dance halls, farms, etc.) with what the locations look like today (supermarkets, strip joints, car parks, etc.) Another example by a student team was a campaign for Goodman's stereos, based on the fact/truism that women hear better than men. I still remember their terrific tag: "Goodman's. Made by good women."

*A great ad, driven by a compelling fact. **Client:** Matchbox. **Agency:** Levine Huntley Schmitt & Beaver. **Creatives:** Allan Beaver, Harold Levine.*

Examples of Truisms

Truism Talking over things with one another is healthy
Client British Telecom (UK phone company)
Strategy BT was virtually a monopoly in the UK. So rather than focus on getting more customers, the strategy was to get people to use their service more often
Tagline It's good to talk

Truism No one likes looking at dirt
Client Flash household cleaner
Strategy Most people are too lazy or busy or cheap to get rid of stains around the house. They assume the only choices are to leave it, cover it or get a professional to remove it
Tagline Don't hide marks. Erase them

Truism The things that really count in life can't be bought: they don't have a monetary value
Client MasterCard
Strategy Tell people not only when they need to use their MasterCard, but also the times they don't. It's a humble, almost anti-monetary approach
Tagline There are some things money can't buy. For everything else, there's MasterCard

Truism A lot of kids' toys have handles
Client Australian lamb
Strategy Because lamb has a natural bone "handle," it's a fun food for kids
Tagline Kids love things with handles

Note: this campaign also combines a USP about lamb, based on its unique shape. (See Physical Characteristics, page 139.)

Truism Patience is a virtue
Client Guinness
Strategy Draught Guinness is a "slow pint," not only in the way it's drunk, but in the way it's served (substantiated by the claim that it takes all of 119 seconds to pour the perfect pint)
Tagline Good things come to those who wait

Truism Dogs often look like their owners
Client Hush Puppies shoes*
Strategy People choose dogs, shoes, clothes, etc., as an extension of their unique personality and character
Tagline Be comfortable with who you are

Exercise: **write a list of ten truisms. Avoid famous quotes or clichés. Think about how each one can be used as a strategy for a particular product or service.**

Note: a Y&R London campaign, the same truism was used for Cesar dog food a decade or so later in "Spaniel" was followed by other executions, including a bulldog and a chihuahua.

Truism: a lot of kids' toys have handles. (A clever way to get parents to cook lamb.) *Client: Meat & Livestock Australia. Product: Australian Lamb. Agency: BMF. Creatives: Andrew Ostrom, Andrew Petch, Warren Brown.*

Truism: no one likes looking at dirt. (Tagline: Don't hide marks. Erase them.) *Client: Flash household cleaner. Agency: Grey, London. Creatives: Ben Stiltz, Colin Booth.*

Truism: dogs often look like their owners. (Hence the use of visual simile.) *Client: Cesar. Agency: Leo Burnett, Lisbon. Creatives: Roão Ribeiro, Leandro Alvarez.*

The Exaggeration Tool

As I mentioned in the Basic Tools chapter, exaggeration is often used in advertising because it usually starts from a *truth* (which is then exaggerated). Contrived ideas, by contrast, tend to begin as an *untruth*, and should therefore be avoided. This will be demonstrated later.

The result of the exaggeration might produce a negative. Often the more negative the situation, the more humorous the idea is, and therefore the more forgiving the consumer becomes about the actual exaggeration. After all, humor disarms people. *However*, there should be a positive reason for buying the product that is equal to or greater than the negative. This will also be demonstrated later.

Whenever you get stuck on campaign ideas, try using the exaggeration tool (which you can easily apply to one-shots, too). The tone is usually funny, absurd, surreal or bizarre, but may be serious too.

Here's how it works:

Imagine you are working on a brand of hiking rucksack (backpack). The chosen proposition is simple: comfort. (Support points include lightweight material, extra padding, ergonomic design, etc.)

Now exaggerate the benefit (comfort) by applying the following sentence:

Brand X backpacks are *so comfortable* that…

Simply complete this sentence in as many ways as you can. Then pick out the ones that have most potential as a big campaign idea. For now, use these sentences as working taglines. (Warning: because you can apply this approach to literally any product or service, you must avoid the temptation of using "*it's so (benefit) that…*" working taglines as final taglines. In most cases you will be able to reduce them into separate final tags, or perhaps the idea can be understood without any tagline.)

Here are some examples:

A brand X backpack is *so comfortable* that…

- you'll enjoy wearing it
- you can keep it on for longer
- you'll want to wear one everywhere
- you won't want to take it off
- you won't realize you're wearing one

The last idea definitely has the potential to be a big campaign idea! Now simply list or draw some executions to this idea, using "So comfortable, you won't know it's there" as a tagline:

- someone wearing one in bed
- someone wearing one in the shower
- someone wearing one in the store (but still trying to buy one) (*good*)
- someone wearing one whilst waiting for it in a luggage claim (*good*)

As with the exaggeration tool sentences, pick out the "best" examples from your list. (The last two ideas from the above list were originally created by a student team from Watford's West Herts College in the UK.)

Note: you may argue that these executions must be contrived because they do not begin as a truth. ("No one would go to a store to buy a backpack forgetting that they are wearing one already!") *But*, the campaign thought behind this execution *does* begin as a truth. (Isn't it true that we've all tried looking for a pair of glasses until finally finding them on our head?) This is why the whole thing still works as a humorous, if exaggerated, campaign. And as mentioned earlier, a negative should be outweighed by a positive. In this example, the negative is looking stupid, but the positive is a very comfortable backpack.

Another example of the exaggeration tool (also by a student team) was a spec campaign for whitening toothpaste. Their tag was "Teeth so white, you can't help smiling." This could have been another safe toothpaste campaign except for the edgy, unexpected executions (one of which used a cheesy photo of one man happily turning to another at the next urinal saying, "I'm pissing blood," another was of a grinning pregnant teenager saying "I've no idea who the father is"). Again, the funny negatives are obvious, but the positive is incredible-looking teeth.

The idea behind Sony's PS2 "Sleeping Beauty" ad (which shows an ancient, still sleeping, cobweb-covered sleeping beauty) is that the PS2 is so addictive that…Prince Charming will forget to wake her.

Note how all four of the last examples show people. This does not have to be the case. The exaggeration tool can be used to create all kinds of ideas and include "people free" ads.

·····································

Exercise: **apply each stage of the exaggeration tool to a brand of really sharp kitchen knives. Start with ten working taglines that begin with "So sharp that…" Pick your favorite line/idea (the one that you can write lots of ads to). Then write a reduced, separate final tagline. Test the idea without a tag.**

·····································

The Unique Selling Proposition (USP) and Generic Products

The Unique Selling Proposition, or USP, is sometimes referred to as "product difference."

In rare cases, some products or services have a unique and impressive proposition/benefit (often a superlative, like the strongest glue or the longest lasting battery). In these cases, you'd be a fool not to write ads based on this USP. However, some ad folk see this as a creative "gift," and think that anyone could come up with good ideas for these benefits. This criticism applies to student portfolios, too (unless your ideas happen to be particularly original or clever).

Therefore, you should try to tackle products that are more group related, or generic, e.g., washing powders, airlines, newspapers, beer, banks, etc., that do not have an immediate or obvious USP. These are sometimes called *parity* products/services.

In these cases, you have to *find* a USP. The product benefit (and even your campaign thought and idea) has to come from one of the following.

Product/Brand Name

Sometimes the name actually comes from the product benefit, or vice versa. For example, the name of the UK vehicle repair company, Kwik-Fit, is clearly positioning itself as "fast." So providing no competitors are already claiming or owning speed, it would be the obvious way to go. What's great about using a proposition from a product name is that each time you see or hear the name, it reinforces the benefit communicated in the advertising. Equally, each time that you see or hear the advertising, it reinforces the name. It's a win-win situation. So when trying to decide on the most appropriate product benefit, don't make it hard for yourself. Try the obvious—there are hundreds of product names that imply a simple, single-minded proposition. Here are just a handful:

- The Comfort Inn (comfortable)
- Easyjet (easy)
- Pete's Wicked Ale (wicked)
- Fresh Direct (two benefits: fresh or direct)
- New School (new, modern, cutting edge)
- Smooth Jazz 98.1 (smooth)
- Payless Shoes (cheap)
- Pepsi One (one calorie)
- Chock Full o'Nuts (nutty)
- FlowersOnly.com (flower-giving experts)

Parking made easy.
The Volkswagen Touran with Park Distance Control.

Exaggeration plus analogy. Idea: It's so easy to park, it feels like the steering wheel is positioned at the rear of the car. *Client: Volkswagen. Agency: DDB, Berlin. Creatives: Gen Sadakane, Tim Stuebane, Jan Hendrik Ott.*

- Concise Oxford Dictionary (concise)
- Clearly Canadian spring water (two benefits: clear or Canadian)
- Reliable Taxi Co. (reliable)
- Kellogg's Variety (variety) (see Tackling the Variety Proposition, page 144)
- Chunky Soups (chunky)
- Greyhound buses* (fast)
- Thrifty Car Rental* (cheap)

*Be careful. Not all benefit-sounding brand names may be valid or supportable. For example, are Greyhound buses really the fastest way to travel across America? And can Thrifty actually claim to be the cheapest car rental company?

One ingenious "name" campaign was for "Patrick Cox *Wannabe*" animal skin shoes, its name inspiring the idea that these are the shoes animals "want to be" made into after they die. (The cartoon-like executions consisted of a suicidal alligator tied to a railway track, a snake pointing a gun to its head, and a cow jumping off a cliff.) Its use of charming illustrations rather than photographs is discussed on page 259.

Physical Characteristics

This means color, shape, design, features, etc. The name of the VW Beetle came from its beetle-like shape. It was the general quirky physical properties that inspired much of the famous advertising that

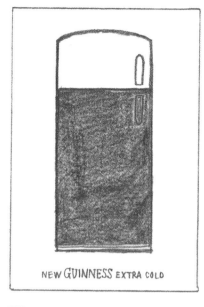

NEW GUINNESS EXTRA COLD

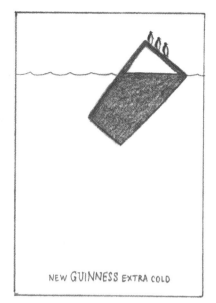

NEW GUINNESS EXTRA COLD

NEW GUINNESS EXTRA COLD

NEW GUINNESS EXTRA COLD

One of many Guinness campaigns inspired by the product's unique physical characteristics. Idea: *visual simile*. *Client:* Guinness Extra Cold. *Agency:* Abbott Mead Vickers BBDO, London. *Creative:* Jeremy Carr.

helped to brand and sell it. (Other benefits communicated included reliability and economy.)

Over the years, the creators of Guinness's advertising have capitalized on the drink's unique physical characteristics. Most notably is perhaps Ogilvy, London's "Not everything in black & white makes sense" multimedia campaign. Later, AMV BBDO's print work on Guinness Extra Cold and Guinness Draught managed to incorporate the color and shape of the distinctive pint glass.

Perhaps a product has a unique *feature* that can be a selling point? Or perhaps it can be a branding device that acts as part of a bigger idea? (A number of PlayStation ads created by agencies around the world have successfully interpreted and reinterpreted the unique "□, ×, ○, △" control buttons, to the point where these symbols could probably replace the PlayStation logo altogether.) This leads us neatly onto the next area.

Logo/Identity
Logo/identity usage is not easy to do without being contrived: there are few examples that compare with Absolut's slick simplicity (see Absolut Inspiration, page 151). So be careful that your concept does not change or cheapen a client's prized logo or design. One example that keeps the brand intact is the print campaign for Mercedes (opposite, above).

Note: do not confuse this technique with campaigns that merely have a consistent "look" or "tone" (as all good campaigns should). Whilst verbal and visual branding is important, it isn't an actual idea, in true advertising terms.

Packaging
Grolsch beer's old-fashioned, hard to open bottles were the inspiration behind the "You can't top a Grolsch" campaign. Altoids mints come in a metal box (the basis of the execution opposite).

Taste/Flavor
"Taste" alone is not a strategic USP. You have to define the taste, e.g., chewy, spicy, cold, refreshing, etc. The most famous taste case study is the Pepsi Challenge, which threatened to hurt Coke's market share considerably. What Coke could have done in response was to point out that "one sip doesn't count," and extend the taste test to a full glass, since it was known that the sweeter Pepsi would always taste nicer at first. Candies and drinks often play off a particular taste or flavor. (Sour Patch Kids bring humor to the change in taste: "They're sour. Then they're sweet.")

Heritage/History/Reputation
e.g., a hotel, a vineyard, a classic sneaker, etc.

Price
e.g., Stella Artois beer is "Reassuringly expensive," and VW Polo has "Surprisingly ordinary prices" (see the explanation on page 116).

How Product is Eaten or Used
e.g., KitKat's famous line "Have a break, have a KitKat" had a clever double meaning in the word "break," and Guinness's "Good things come to those who wait" focused on the time it takes to

pour the perfect pint. And part of the fun of drinking milk is licking the milk "moustache."

Competition
This type of idea leads directly from a "competitive" or "comparison" strategy, outlined on page 114 (see also Competitive Advertising vs. Negative Advertising, page 152).

How Product is Made
e.g., Jack Daniel's distillery.

Ingredients
e.g., caffeine-free, full of nuts, one calorie, etc.

Timing of Use
e.g., seasonal ads on February 14 for Hershey's Kisses.

Product Lifespan
e.g., Elmlea whipping cream "Keeps fresh for up to 8 weeks."

Personality
This is a good starting point when researching any new or established brand. What type of personality could or does the client/product have? Is it appropriate and worth promoting as a USP? Develop one that's radically (or even slightly) different from everyone else's.

Attitude
The more original and unique the attitude, the better, e.g., Nike. Don't create an "attitude" for the sake of it. First decide whether the product needs one. If so, what exactly is it about? Is it directed at the consumer, the competition, or something/someone else? Is it appropriate and worth promoting as a USP? Develop one that's radically (or even slightly) different from everyone else's.

Existing Advertising
e.g., building on/going against a known campaign for the product/competitor.

Consumer
i.e., famous or non-famous people who use the product. Sometimes called "testimonials" or "endorsements." Or is there simply something special or unique about the type of people who buy a particular product, service or brand? Is there a USP or idea about people who don't use the product?

Service

Speed

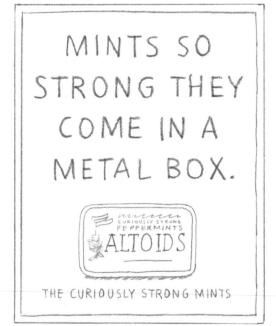

The iconic Mercedes logo, re-created to communicate various benefits including speed, service, and glamor. *Client: Mercedes. Agency: Lowe & Partners. Creatives: Andy Hirsch, Randy Saitta, Marty Zio.*

This idea came from the product's unique packaging. *Client: Altoids. Agency: Leo Burnett, Chicago. Creatives: Steffan Postaer, Mark Faulkner, Noel Haan, G. Andrew Meyer.*

Owner/Staff
This idea leads directly from the "Owner" or "Staff" strategy, page 113. The key is to dig out facts (from the brief or other research) that could lead to interesting, relevant ads. Is there something unique about the staff, employees, etc? Do they have special assets or skills that relate back to a product or service benefit? Are these assets or skills acquired through training, or are they natural? Make it serious and professional, or have fun with it.

The Nauga is ugly, but his vinyl hide is beautiful.

Naugahyde
vinyl fabric

This USP came from the product name and how the product is made, creating a unique character in the process. *Client: Naugahyde vinyl fabric. **Agency:** Papert Koenig Lois. **Creatives:** George Lois, Julian Koenig.*

Character

A unique character can be taken directly from the logo, or packaging. Or it can be an entirely original character creation. (For 30 years, John Webster was the master of developing both for the UK market.) Another possibility is if the product itself is a character, or a group of characters, e.g., Gummi Bears. But whichever route you take, make sure there is still an idea that relates back to a benefit: don't just use a character or group of characters for the sake of it. Even if it's humorous. There has to be some logic.

Generally speaking, the "character" approach produces either good or bad advertising. Award-winning, icon-producing examples include the Pepperami "animal," Levi's Flat Eric, the Hoffmeister bear, the orange Tango man, and the Budweiser frogs. The use of a character can create such a strong branding devise (or mnemonic/memory aid) that even some annoying ones have succeeded commercially (rather than critically). These include the Pillsbury doughboy, the Geico gecko, the Afflack duck, Jeffrey the Toys "R" Us giraffe, and the Snuggle bear.

Outlet

i.e., the particular place or country where a product is sold. Perhaps it's popular in a country other than where it's produced. Both place or country USPs can lead to initial ideas, to which a related fact or observation about the place or country might need

to be attached before creating a final idea. For example, if a tough, off-road vehicle is popular in Russia this may not sound that relevant, until you add that its roads are some of the toughest on the planet.

Note: researching a product may uncover "hard facts," which is great. But sometimes you have to think around the product in order to come up with a unique idea or proposition. (The above list is also a good starting point for this.) And remember, a USP must be unique (unless your brand is the very first to say it) *and* have a viable selling point. There's no point having a unique proposition that serves no interest for the consumer: it needs to have something that would attract the consumers and generate a lot of potential sales. (For example, a brand of car that comes in a unique shade of green is unlikely to be a unique *selling* point.)

Although not easy to pull off, a campaign idea could feasibly come from a combination of the approaches listed above, rather than just one. A perfect example of this is shown left for Naugahyde vinyl fabric. The geniuses behind this ad found a fun way to sell a boring product (and one arguably inferior to its competition—leather). They invented a USP that comes from the product name *and* how the product was made (Naugahyde is named after an ugly "creature" called the Nauga), thereby creating a unique character in the process. It sounds complicated, and yet the ad is so simple to understand (see also Fresh Strategies, page 275, and products to avoid on page 276).

Not a Unique Selling Proposition? Then Be the First to "Own" it

What happens when you only have a (common) selling proposition that's not unique?, e.g., banks have services to prevent and recognize credit card fraud and identity theft. Citibank were the first to make this the focus of one of their campaigns. By doing this, they immediately owned "fraud prevention," even though other banks offer the same or similar services. Not only that, but the concept (and execution) was so good that any subsequent competitive "identity theft" advertising would always be compared to it. Or equally, people might assume it was just another Citibank ad. In short, be the first to own a SP.

So whenever you tackle a generic product, preferably pick a market leader (or joint leader, key player, etc.) and think of an area or subject that has yet to be "owned." The bigger the brand, the more qualified it is to pull off owning something big. In short, if you're big, try owning something bigger. For example:

Before TV, two World Wars.
After TV, zero.

ABC decides to "own" the general benefits of television, rather than saying something unique to them. (Other headlines: "If TV's so bad for you, why is there one in every hospital room?," "Without TV, how would you know where to put the sofa?") *Client:* ABC. *Agency:* TBWA/Chiat/Day, Los Angeles. *Creatives:* Sara Riesgo, John Shirley, Raymond Hwang, Rich Siegel.

Rather than trying to sell its unique TV shows, characters or presenters, ABC's famous ad campaign attempted to own "television" as a whole (i.e., the general power, benefit, and enjoyment of it). Headlines: "If TV's so bad for you, why is there one in every hospital room?," "Before TV, two

Market Leader	"Own"
Watch	Time
Dating Agency	Love
Airline	Earth
Bank	Money
Toy	Education

World Wars. After TV, zero" and "Without a TV, how would you know where to put the sofa?" This kind of approach is clearly risky, since it will encourage many people to watch the competition too. But now imagine a small cable station trying to own television instead of someone like ABC. It just wouldn't be as credible.

ESPN (which originally stood for Entertainment and Sports Programming Network) made an equivalent, obvious choice to own *sports*. The idea was simply to remind people of its impact on their everyday lives, and therefore why we watch ESPN. Each ad begins with the line, "Without sports…" Examples include "…we'd stop believing," "…what would we do over the holidays?" and "…who would cheer for the Nimrods?" Again, the ads were so well executed and tonally defined that it would be hard to own the same topic. One particularly touching TV spot ("Surf Camp") showed a surfing school for autistic children, with the end line: "Without sports, where would we find ourselves?"

Another example of owning a subject is the Waterstone's campaign to be the leading UK bookstore. Talking directly to its audience (book lovers), it simply "owned" books, or rather, the power of books. Instead of talking about specific books, each ad demonstrates why books in general are so special, unique, and joyous (see page 268).

What if you're a smaller brand, i.e., not the market leader? Can you be the first to own something big? You can, but aside from the credibility issue, the other danger is that a bigger brand may come along and steal it. Again, a bigger brand has the clout to own something big: it's a better fit. That said, there are exceptions. Firstly, by owning something big, this may create a perception that you're bigger than you are. Secondly, you may be able to own something big if you put a different spin on it. For example, many sports brands use famous athletes to advertise their products: they own sports professionals. A smaller brand could create a new, unique way to use sports stars that's not been done before. Similarly, perhaps a brand could create a new, unique tone of voice to a tried and tested strategy/idea. Lastly, if the subject you wish to own takes a social, political or moral high ground, often a smaller, braver brand is more appropriate. For example, a student team once used a brand of Jamaican rum to own anti-racism, acting as a spokesperson for current racial issues within the UK's black community. The brand was small yet more relevant to its subject than a big corporate beer company, for example.

Within any competitive market, you don't have to own a generic service (as in the case of Citibank). It can be a much more lateral, indirect property. For example, a large floral company such as 1-800-Flowers or FTD/Interflora may wish to own a related, lateral topic such as color theory (colors are the thing people think of when they imagine flowers). As with any idea, lateral or otherwise, always try to find a way to *tie the product back in*. One student campaign did just that: the ads educate the consumer while also providing floral solutions. For example, one ambient execution has a small sign on a red public bench which said, "Red promotes passion and desire. So send roses to someone you love." (Student: Amy Weber)

Finally, in the cases when the communication aims solely to appeal to consumers on an emotional level (their hearts and not their heads), this is sometimes known as using an ESP, or Emotional Selling Proposition (a term coined by Bartle Bogle Hegarty's co-founder John Bartle). An ESP can also produce an idea that connects consumers with the product through the advertising itself, without offering anything unique other than the ability to trigger an emotional response(s). One could argue that this makes up part of the next approach: advertising *is* the USP.

Advertising *is* the USP: The Last Resort?

What happens when there's no *obvious* USP, you can't *find* a USP, and there's no SP you can *own first*?

At this point, the *advertising* itself becomes the USP. It's the advertising that sets one totally generic product from another, defining the brand while underplaying (and even ignoring) the common generic benefit. Here the advertising needs to break new ground, exhibiting more imagination, flare, and showmanship than its competitors. The more unusual the execution, the greater the impact will be.

You may be questioning this approach, which goes against all the fundamental principles of creative advertising. If people remember your ad more for *how* it looks and sounds and feels than *what* it's saying, that's when style has overtaken substance; execution has overtaken concept; and brand has overtaken benefit. But sometimes you have little or no choice: "advertising *is* the USP" is perhaps a brand's last resort in a sea of parity products. It all depends on how good your ads are. In fact, the Bud Light "Real Men of Genius" radio campaign comes close to being in this final category, along with so much beer advertising. This campaign has a simple, largely ignored idea that

relates back to the beer—toasting and roasting these "great" men. They own toast making. Could any brand of American beer have used this idea? Pretty much. But in my opinion, what consumers really remember is the simple fact that the ads are brilliantly written. These laughs, coupled with strong branding (every commercial begins with "Bud Light presents" and a rock mnemonic), are why people remember the brand, love the brand, and buy a Bud Light. A well-used example of this is the Cadbury's "Gorilla" commercial (shown opposite).

Tackling the Variety Proposition

Occasionally you may be faced with what I call, "the Variety Proposition." These are products or services that have "something for everyone." Examples include things like a department store, a cruise line, and a "listings" magazine (such as *Time Out*).

This type of proposition often confuses the student, since it appears to contradict the strategic "rule" of a single-minded benefit; there are so many beneficial things that this product or service has to offer. Of course in terms of executions, it seems great ("I'll just do one ad for each thing and create a huge campaign!") But be careful. What you often end up with is dull advertising because you have created a campaign idea that is so spread out that the executions start to read like a long, predictable shopping list. Similarly, if you try to cover each part of the variety in one execution, you run the risk of overwhelming or boring the consumer.

One way to tackle the variety proposition— if "variety" really is the most important thing to communicate—is to avoid the trap of thinking about it in terms of each element and approach it in the same way you would a typical single-minded benefit. In other words, instead of trying to advertise each part of the variety, generate ideas that simply say "variety" in a broader sense.

Start by relating variety back to the product. For example, what does the word "variety" mean in terms of *Time Out* magazine? One basic interpretation of this might be that *Time Out* "lists a lot of good things to do." Then try applying the exaggeration tool (above) to create some actual ideas: "*Time Out* lists *so many* good things to do that…" See opposite, above as an example of this. (Idea: "*Time Out* lists so many good things to do that it would make a cloistered monk cry.")

Of course, don't rule out any ideas that might be able to incorporate the "variety shopping list" in one creative execution (without overwhelming or boring the consumer). A wonderful demonstration of this is the Amazon.com TV campaign produced in the late 1990s. Using a cheesy male choir was a perfect vehicle to mention the long list of things you can buy on Amazon's website:

CHORUS: Emahtskcblvdt? Emahtskcblvdt?

Electronics, music, auctions, health and beauty tools, software, kitchen, cameras, books, lawn and patio, video games, dvd, toys.

Put 'em all together you've got emahtskcblvdt and if you say, emahtskcblvdt, boy, you've said a lot

there's nothin' quite like emahtskcblvdt,

only Amazon's got emahtskcblvdt.

Another approach to communicate "range" or "variety" is only to show two extremes or opposites, and merge them into one visual or headline. This immediately simplifies your ad. For example, if a camera or film is designed to take pictures in all weather conditions, don't show all types of weather in each ad (that would get repetitive and complicated), but show two types and then combine them, e.g., a visual of a woollen hat with Aussie-style corks and string attached along the bottom, i.e., summer and winter/sun and snow. That's just one example of many executions from a Kodak campaign. Don't just think of visuals: you apply the same tool to headlines. For example, if The Yellow Pages has many types of business listings, pair two companies that are either opposites, e.g., wealth (Trump Towers and homeless shelters), freedom (vacations and prisons), or connected in some way, e.g., health (dangerous sports and hospitals). You keep going until you have some good ones. If that still seems boring, you play around with visuals as well. Incidentally, Nynex and other Yellow Pages campaigns have used similar approaches (see also Yellow Pages "Dog-leg" ad, page 126).

Tackling the Double Proposition

As you know by now, it's a lot easier to advertise one proposition than two. However, there have been rare cases where a campaign has tackled two benefits in one go, with considerable success. The

Tackling the variety proposition in a broad sense (there's so much listed in *Time Out* magazine…) via the exaggeration tool (…it'd make a cloistered monk cry). **Client:** *Time Out.* **Agency:** *Gold Greenlees Trott Ltd.* **Creatives:** *Steve Henry, Axel Chaldecott.*

A gorilla plays drums to Phil Collins' *In the Air Tonight.* Considered by many to be an example of "advertising is the USP," but you still can't help feeling all chocolatey inside whenever you watch it. (Also a wonderful example of both the Final Twist and the "One Frame" Goal examined in the TV chapter.) **Client:** *Cadbury's.* **Agency:** *Fallon, London.* **Creative:** *Juan Cabral.*

Miller Lite campaign is perhaps the most famous example, although it has divided critics and viewers alike. Its simple premise of two people arguing and fighting over which is the "best" benefit—"great taste" versus "less filling"—has been reused for many years.

Another possibility is applying the two in one tool (page 125). Fallon, London produced a simple yet clever brand campaign whereby each TV execution showed two unusual combinations (e.g., a huge man performing some amazing floor gymnastics, followed by the voiceover, "Big *and* agile. Don't see that very often." The commercial ends with a similar find: a Skoda Octavia 4x4/SUV. Another execution for the Skoda vRS shows a robber being chased by a trouser press for the double benefit of "practical *and* exciting").

You can even apply the two in one tool to the variety proposition, by simply choosing two from the many for each ad (much like the Skoda work does). For example, in the Kodak all-weather film works in all conditions (a classic variety proposition mentioned earlier), the creative team combined two objects that represented two weather conditions, into one image. The result: eye-catching variety made simple.

But unless you have a really original idea, I wouldn't recommend tackling a double proposition for your student book. The same goes for in the real world (unless the client demands it, or it's the only logical strategy).

Push It—Visualizing (Literal vs. Lateral)
The phrase "push it" is popular among creative directors and college instructors. But what exactly does it mean? It basically means "tweak, rework, and improve your idea."

In other words, there's definitely "something" in the original ad or campaign idea, but it's yet to reach its potential. Some combination of the headline, visual, and tagline needs "pushing." Perhaps the ad's just not simple, funny, interesting or powerful enough yet. But often it's 90% of the way there, and a small tweak is all it needs. And if it's still not there after the first attempt, you will undoubtedly hear the other popular phrase: "Keep pushing it."

Pushing any idea (visual, headline or tagline) often results in a more *lateral* way of showing or saying something. Literal ideas are usually straight, boring, and obvious, whereas lateral ideas are more original, unusual, surprising ways of looking at the same thing, and therefore make better ads. The ad opposite is pure lateral thinking: show other types of portable "fuel" to demonstrate how economical the VW Lupo is.

The following push it example is taken from a promotional ad for the AAA School of Advertising, with a second push it "stage" added. The product is Preparation H.

- hemorrhoid cream
- Normal bike seat (*literal but boring*)
- No bike seat (*better but confusing*)
- Saw blade replaces bike seat (*lateral*)

For WWF a student once had a visual simile idea: bar codes look like zebra stripes. It took three attempts to push it visually into the perfect ad. (Tag: Animals are not products)

- Bar code next to zebra, e.g., left side/right side (*longwinded*)
- Rectangular bar code placed on zebra's body (*contrived*)
- Zebra's stripy body is part barcode (*simple, lateral*)

A competitive ad for FedEx:

- DHL box is beaten up. FedEx box is perfect (*literal*)
- DHL box is still. FedEx has already left the ad (*better*)
- DHL box is being delivered inside a FedEx box (*lateral*)

Note: sometimes you can be *too lateral* in the use of analogy (see the Kryptonite example on pages 82–83).

Push It—Copywriting (Literal vs. Lateral)
Headline writing is probably the hardest and most important part of copywriting. Headlines don't just fall out of the sky. In fact, the 1-in-10 tool on page 23 might only produce one half-decent headline. At this point you need to *push it* into a great headline, which can take a few steps. Overleaf are some examples, beginning again with one from a promotional ad for the AAA School of Advertising, this time with *two* additional push it "stages" added:

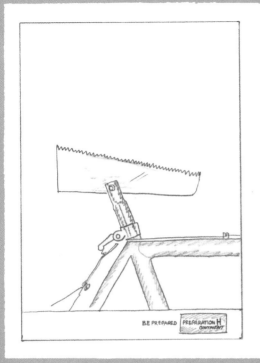

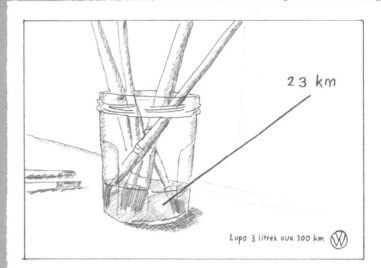

23 km

Lupo 3 litres aux 100 km Ⓥ

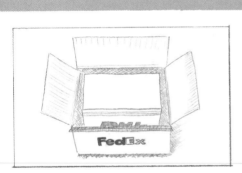

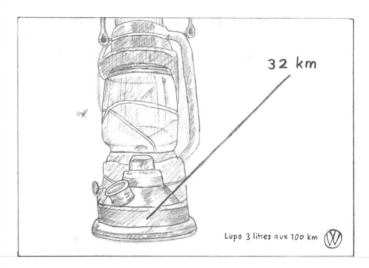

32 km

Lupo 3 litres aux 100 km Ⓥ

The final, lateral ad. This visual is much more dramatic (and less expected) than showing a normal bike seat, or someone's sore behind. **Client:** *Preparation H.* **Agency:** *Bates, Hong Kong.*

Push it: visualizing. A lateral way to communicate how one service is more reliable than another. Strategy: competitive advertising. **Client:** *FedEx.* **Agency:** *BBDO, Bangkok.*

Push it: vizualizing. (Literal = show how fuel efficient a car is. Lateral = without showing a car.) **Client:** *Volkswagen.* **Agency:** *DDB, Paris.* **Creative director:** *Christian Vince.*

Nike

- Our shoes help Michael Jordan jump higher* (*literal, headline repeating visual*)
- Michael Jordan defies gravity (*better*)
- Jordan defeats Newton (*almost there, needs first names, unclear*)
- Michael Jordan 1. Isaac Newton 0 (*lateral*)

The final ad is the same basic idea as the others, but pushed. As are the following:

Mystic Lake Casino

- Walk in poor. Walk out rich (*literal, boring*)
- Walk in a Socialist. Walk out a Capitalist (*better*)
- Walk in a Democrat. Walk out a Republican (*lateral, witty*)

The Economist

- People who don't read *The Economist* sound stupid (*literal, boring*)
- People who don't read *The Economist* sound dumberer (*better*)
- Some people think *The Economist* sounds way dumb (*almost*)
- You can so tell the people who like don't read *The Economist* (*lateral, witty*)

Crest toothpaste (visual = tooth)

- Look after your teeth (*boring, generic*)
- Teeth are a living thing (*a good point, but still boring*)
- Teeth can last as long as you (*thought provoking*)
- Teeth don't die a natural death. You kill them (*a compelling fact*)

Stella Artois

Tagline: Reassuringly expensive.
Headlines:

- "Unfortunately it's my round" (*boring, obvious*)
- "Didn't I buy a round earlier?" (*okay, but could sound like it impairs your memory*)
- "Your round" (next to each empty glass) (*better, still a bit long winded*)
- "Oh, great, it's my round" (*sarcastic tone okay, but not that witty*)
- "My shout," he whispered (*very succinct, with clever use of contrasting words*)

---

*The AAA School of Advertising ad (the Juniper Drawing Room, Johannesburg) used "Our shoes make him jump higher," with copy below that read, "It's not what you say. It's how you say it."

The final, lateral ad. The use of sport scores makes it even more ingenious. **Client:** *Nike.* **Agency:** *Simons Palmer Denton Clemmow and Johnson, London.* **Creatives:** *Tim Riley, Andy McKay.*

A lateral, witty version of "Walk in poor. Walk out rich." **Client:** *Mystic Lake Casino.* **Agency:** *Hunt Adkins, Minneapolis.* **Creatives:** *Bud Atkins, Steve Mitchell.*

Push it: copywriting. This headline is much better than, "People who don't read *The Economist* sound stupid." **Client:** *The Economist.* **Agency:** *Abbott Mead Vickers BBDO, London.* **Creatives:** *Matt Doman, Ian Heartfield.*

This fact is much more compelling than just "Look after your teeth." **Client:** *Crest.* **Agency:** *Benton & Bowles, New York.* **Creatives:** *Sam Cooperstein, Ellen Massoth.*

VW (Visual = VW Beetle body)
- We give each car two layers of paint
  (*literal, boring*)
- We paint it. Then we paint it
  (*better, but still boring*)
- After we paint the car we paint the paint
  (*lateral, interesting*)

Don't just think "headline into better headline," or "visual into better visual": sometimes you can push a headline into a (better) visual, or vice versa. Here are some examples:

Time Out **Magazine**
- Headline: Now you can play hard, too
  (*boring*)
- Headline: Burn the candle at both ends
  (*better*)
- Visual: (Picture of a candle, on its side, lit at both ends) (*best: more immediate and greater impact as an unusual visual*)

Levi's
Two ways of saying that you make a pair of Levi's your own; no two pairs are the same: they are unique. The visual solution is better for each.

- Headline: No two pairs are the same/Every pair is unique.

vs.

- Visual: (A thumbprint, made entirely of the repeated line "No two pairs are the same")

and compare

- Headline: "I make them my own"—Jim

vs.

- Visual: (The famous red tab reads "Jim's" instead of "Levi's")

A visual doesn't have to be a picture, as in the Nikon example on page 25 (see also the Basic Tools chapter).

Here is another example (see page 21) of how there are two ways to say the same thing:

- Headline: America is a capitalist country
  (*slow, literal*)
- Headline: God© Bless™ America®
  (*fast, lateral*)

The red tab, the thumbprint text, and the symbols are all technically type/word ideas, but their use is quite visual.

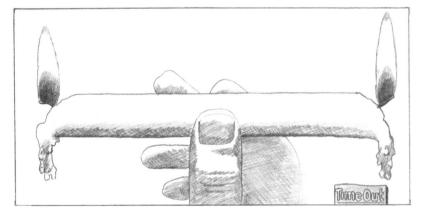

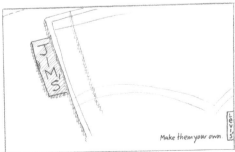

Boil it down. These four contrasting words say so much. Tagline: Reassuringly expensive. *Client: Stella Artois.* **Agency:** *Lowe Howard-Spink, London.* **Creatives:** *Chris O'Shea, Ken Hoggins.*

A lateral, compelling ad is created by taking a common phrase and simply visualizing it. *Client: Time Out.* **Agency:** *Gold Greenlees Trott Ltd.* **Creatives:** *Steve Henry, Axel Chaldecott.*

"No two pairs are the same, no two pairs are the same…" A lateral, graphic way to communicate "unique." *Client: Levi's.* **Agency:** *BBH, London.* **Creatives:** *Graham Watson, Bruce Crouch.*

This Levi's spec ad is much more interesting and lateral than using a headline like: "I make them my own"—Jim. *Client: Levi's.* **Student:** *Maura Florkowski.*

Would you still eat it?

SURGEON GENERAL'S WARNING: Ingestion By Pregnant Women May Result in Fetal Injury, Premature Birth, And Low Birth Weight.

Then why do you still smoke? New York Lung Association.

Literal: health warnings on cigarette packets. Lateral: health warnings on "harmful" food and drink such as bread, bananas, and bottled water. *Client: New York Lung Association. Agency: Goldsmith Jeffrey. Creative: Tracy Wong.*

· ·

Exercise: **create six more execution examples for the O'Doul's campaign. But this time, aim it at female consumers (i.e., poke fun at men's physical features). Hint: think of an attractive physical attribute, using only two words, and add a middle word to give it an unattractive twist.**

· ·

Push It—Campaign Ideas and Taglines (Literal vs. Lateral)

Here are two ways to persuade people to quit smoking (New York Lung Association):

- **Literal**: Why are you still smoking?/Why doesn't this stop you smoking? (Visual: General Surgeon's warning label on a cigarette packet)
- **Lateral**: Would you still eat it? (Visual: banana, water, bread with Surgeon General's warning label) Then why do you still smoke?

Here's another example, created by former student Jen Skelley:

- **Product:** O'Doul's non-alcohol beer
- **Idea:** O'Doul's prevents you from getting "beer boggles"
- **Tagline:** Don't be fooled

Literal:

- **Headline part 1:** Last night
- **Visual(s):** Big boobs, long legs, pretty face
- **Headline part 2:** This morning
- **Visual(s):** Saggy boobs, hairy legs, ugly face

It works, but nothing is left to the imagination: it's very literal. Whereas a simpler, more lateral version is:

Headlines: Big (Saggy) Boobs
Long (Hairy) Legs
Pretty (Ugly) Face

Pushing a campaign idea could involve the exaggeration tool. Again, as long as the thought is based on a truth (e.g., some French words are feminine), the result can be as absurd, surreal or bizarre as you like.

Literal: Females/women are attracted to men who wear Lynx deodorant.
Lateral: Objects that are feminine (in French) are attracted to men who wear Lynx deodorant.

This lateral version, opposite, is truly inspired because it's essentially an idea within the original Lynx campaign idea, but without being complicated.

Push It—Long Term Campaigns

By "pushing a campaign" in the long term, I simply mean creating new *versions* of the campaign. This allows the concept to stay fresh, and therefore extend its run for many more years.

Note: this is not the same as creating an entirely new campaign thought, or working to an alternative proposition.

A good example of this evolution can be seen in the Absolut vodka work, summarized overleaf. The first executional format was to adapt (or add something to) the bottle itself, and then "play off" the headline. (The one on the left is the first ever execution—Absolut Perfection.) Once consumers were familiar with the glass bottle, the second approach was to create visuals that clearly reflected the *shape* of the bottle with the label (Absolut L.A.) and without (Absolut Peak). Finally, the third development was to "hide" the bottle image as a clever way to involve the reader even more (e.g., Absolut Passion, not shown).

Think of each ad as representative of the time period 1, 2, 3, 4. If an agency were to present these ideas to the client, it would be an impressive way of demonstrating the potential longevity of such a campaign. In fact, the only thing that remained constant throughout the campaigns was the use of a two-word headline.

Absolut Inspiration

Although you would usually draw inspiration from only *one* of the areas listed above, Absolut vodka managed to capitalize on three, neatly demonstrating the fine line between proposition, concept, and executions.

The product/brand name Absolut implied absolute, complete, and pure (the proposition); the name also led to the initial campaign concept of adding a word to the logo ("Absolut…") next to an altered image of the bottle; the physical characteristics of the bottle's shape inspired the executions in the next three versions of the campaign.

In Absolut's case, the campaign changes between each time period are not that dramatic. You may find it necessary to push each new "campaign" a lot further. The strategy and tone of voice still stays the same, but the ideas change. But whether subtle or dramatic, if you can build on the knowledge of

PRETTY
~~UGLY~~
FACE

O'Doul's
~~Don't be fooled.~~ NON-ALCOHOL BEER

Push it: campaign ideas. A lateral way to communicate the idea of "beer goggles." Other executions included: "Big (Saggy) Boobs," "Long (Hairy) Legs." Tagline: Don't be fooled. *Client: O'Doul's non-alcohol beer.* *Student: Jen Skelley.*

Lateral thinking: campaign ideas. Rather than showing women (literal), this team used "feminine" objects to communicate the same benefit of attraction through smell. (In the US, the product name was changed to Axe.) *Client: Unilever.* *Product: Lynx.* *Agency: Bartle Bogle Hegarty, London.* *Creatives: Dave Monk, Matt Waller.*

la brouette *(feminine)*
wheelbarrow

THE LYNX EFFECT

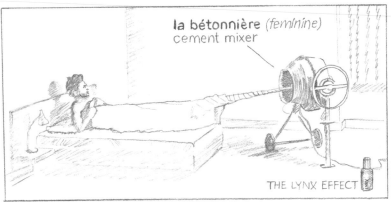

la bétonnière *(feminine)*
cement mixer

THE LYNX EFFECT

ABSOLUT PERFECTION. ABSOLUT L.A. ABSOLUT PEAK.

Absolut First: the ad that launched thousands more. The campaign continued to use the same headline format, but the visuals evolved. The early executions typically used the actual product/bottle. *Client: Absolut. Agency: TBWA/ Chiat/Day. Creatives: Geoff Hayes, Graham Turner, Steve Bronstein.*

The campaign developed into visual simile: "bottle" with label. *Client: Absolut. Agency: TBWA/ Chiat/Day. Creatives: Tom McManus, Dave Warren, Steve Bronstein.*

Then came many "bottle" (without label) executions. *Client: Absolut. Agency: TBWA/Chiat/Day. Creatives: Steve Feldman, Harry Woods, Steve Bronstein.*

Opposite, above, left
Comparative product demonstration can be a powerful way to upstage the competition (whether it's another particular brand, or as in this case, the general competition). *Client: Heinz tomato ketchup. Agency: DDB, New York. Creatives: Bert Steinhauser, Fran Wexler.*

the previous work, you will have a more consistent brand. However, in some cases you may wish not to keep any strategic or conceptual element and start something entirely new. (Perhaps the market for the product has changed.) And if your new approach is stronger than the previous one, so much the better.

Save So Much Time/Money...
When faced with a proposition that either (i) saves more time, or (ii) saves time (compared to the competition), try to avoid these two ideas:

(i) You save so much time with this product/ service that you can spend it doing others things.

(ii) You save so much money with this product/ service that you can buy lots of other things.

Both of these could apply to literally hundreds of products and services. And that's the problem. Even though you could argue that these ideas come straight from the product, it's too general. When it was first done (and done brilliantly) some thirty years ago, it was an original idea (see "The Kremplers" ad, opposite). Now it appears in commercial after commercial, from household cleaners (i), to insurance (ii).

Competitive Advertising vs. Negative Advertising
Competitive advertising (also known as comparative advertising) is more common in some

countries than others, partly because there are differences in the level of restrictions (i.e., what you can and cannot say, legally), and partly because of other cultural differences. However, as Jeremy Bullmore of the WPP Group points out, "Drawing attention to your competitors is a dangerous game," so here are some "tools of thumb" worth considering:

• Don't be negative for the sake of it. If you can, say something good about your product at the same time as putting down the competition. A recent example of this is the Apple "I'm a Mac... And I'm a PC" campaign, which pokes fun at PCs while simultaneously highlighting numerous product benefits of the Mac. The ad on page 70 for Intercity makes it clear why taking the train to work is better than driving. (Headline: "At 100mph, this is the only Constable you'll find alongside you" [the benefit: beautiful, relaxing scenery]). Similarly with taglines, "A lot less bovver than a Hover" explains why a Qualcast is better than a Flymo (benefit: less work).

• Pick on someone subtly. Competition can also be *implied*. The Heinz ketchup "one reason" demonstration ad (opposite, left) uses the fictitious name "Catsup" for weaker, generic brands of tomato sauce.

• Pick on someone with wit and people are more likely to believe you. The FedEx ad on page 147, with DHL "Boxes" is a witty, lateral idea that creates

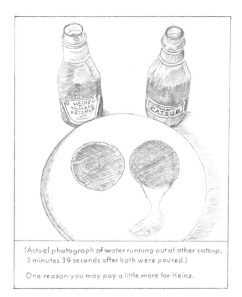

(Actual photograph of water running out of other catsup, 3 minutes 39 seconds after both were poured.)

One reason you may pay a little more for Heinz.

"The Kremplers"

....

MVO: Mr. Jones and Mr. Krempler were neighbors.

They each had three thousand dollars.

With his money Mr. Jones bought himself a three thousand dollar car.

With his money, Mr. Krempler bought himself a new refrigerator, a new range, a new washer, a new dryer, a record player, two new television sets…and a brand new Volkswagen.

Now Mr. Jones is faced with that age-old problem: keeping up with the Kremplers.

a *perception* that FedEx is more reliable, rather than presenting a fact.

• Pick on someone your own size. Pick on someone who is a genuine threat, otherwise you will only bring yourself down to their level. In the Cola wars, Pepsi based some of their ads on taste preference, while Coke (the market leader) was smart not to respond in the same way.

• Pick on someone without sounding defensive. Just think about how the "muck slinging" approach to political advertising has historically turned many voters off.

The print version of the TV ad for Apple's new G3 chip ("Snail") communicates the speed of the new chip by dramatizing the comparative lack of speed of Pentium's (see overleaf).

College Humor

Humor can be an effective way to disarm and attract consumers. Wit, satire, sarcasm, irony, parody, nonsensical, surreal, slapstick, black comedy—the list is endless. And as T. S. Eliot once said, "Humor is also a way of saying something serious."

But be careful about adding bawdy "college humor" to this list (otherwise known as "toilet humor" or "blue jokes"). Creating an ad in this tone may make you laugh, but what about the consumers? Remember, the key to creating original, clever strategies and concepts is the ability to step

Keep up with the Kremplers. The original (and frequently copied) "look what you can save when you buy our product" campaign. *Client:* Volkswagen. **Agency:** DDB.

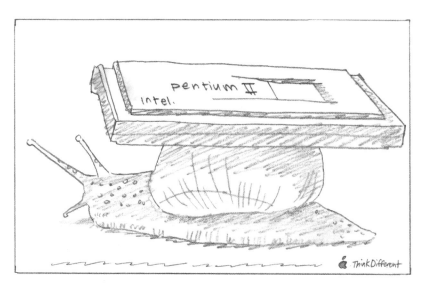

This competitive ad pokes fun at the relative speed of another computer chip. *Client: Apple. Agency: TBWA/Chiat/Day.*

outside your world. Or as stated in the earlier chapter on Strategy, the need to "wear different hats." So if you're a young male ad student, be reminded that most of the world's products are not aimed at you. That's not to say you shouldn't try humor for a funeral home—in fact, it's been done. (How effective it was is another question.) Just try to avoid ribaldry unless the brand and target audience is right, and the humor is implied rather than gratuitous. (Note how the Club 18–30 holiday advertising, aimed at sex-crazed singles, uses *suggestive* rather than explicit humor.)

It's also a personal thing. One example where little was left to the imagination was the multi-award winning print campaign for Coco de Mer, a UK brand of stylish erotic shops and lingerie. The ads showed extreme close-up photos of people's intense (and fairly unattractive) facial expressions during orgasm. Its edginess is perfect for the product (boosting brand awareness) and maybe it worked for the target group, but I'd argue that it probably turned more potential customers off than on. Interestingly, a later campaign by the same agency (Saatchi & Saatchi, London) took a more lateral approach—fractally represented orgasms. In my humble opinion, this stylish, stunning-looking campaign was much more ingenious, powerful, and unexpected than the previous one. These campaigns show two very different ways of saying essentially the same thing, one literal and one lateral. They both won awards, which shows that even if some people hated it, most clearly loved it. And as I mentioned in the Basic Tools chapter it's

always better to have polar reactions to an idea than mutual indifference.

Culturally speaking, the types of acceptable humor vary in each country. When you're working at an agency, you may get lucky (especially if the work raises the advertising bar and wins lots of awards), but that's more to do with the size of the client's balls than yours. Generally when it comes to a student portfolio, as hypocritical as it seems based on some of the advertising out there, most creative directors will frown at repetitious, gratuitous toilet humor.

A Final Word on Humor
Be original with your jokes. Remember, most good creative directors will be aware of every old and new popular one-liner, stand-up comedian, TV/radio sitcom, etc. And so will most of your audience. So unless you are obviously spoofing Monty Python or South Park or whomever, it will just look like a poor reproduction.

Food and Drink Advertising
When it comes to food and drink advertising, make sure that if you're going to show the product, don't make it icky. It seems that some ads have completely forgotten that these products are meant to be *appetizing*. (Why would I want to drink a beer that has a "head" that looks like shaving cream? Why would I want to eat a stick of "long lasting" chewing gum after it's just run a sweaty, puddle-ridden marathon race?) These ideas may have made it past the client, but do they make it past consumers' taste buds? Of course this all depends on the consumer. Within the UK, there have occasionally been cases where relevant humor (and an open-minded, often younger, consumer) has accepted unappetizing ideas: Pepperami's "It's a bit of an animal" campaign, Heinz's "Anything tastes supreme with Heinz salad cream" campaign, Golden Wonder's "Walker" showed crisps down the underpants, and Pot Noodles' laddish TV spots (including boyfriend sneakily giving dog-eaten noodles to girlfriend, and another man licking his plate "clean" before returning it to the cabinet).

Conversely, just because it's a food or a drink, it doesn't mean that all you need to sell it is a mouthwatering shot of the product. A beautiful drop of condensation running down a cold beer may be appetizing, but it's *not* an idea. It's a glorified pack shot that could be for any drink. Part of the reason why "Got Milk?" was so successful is

Good things can happen when your phone's on. Ok, so we're pretty biased here but it's true isn't it? It's just that mobiles are now such an everyday part of life that we take them for granted. We overlook the things they give us. Like the freedom to move about. And organise things on-the-go. And then be really flakey and change our minds at the last minute. Or how they've helped us get better at communicating. Even those of us who are a bit shy. We're all yabbering on more. And texting. And exchanging jokes, and pictures of that dog with the stupid face. Further still, whisper it, but they make us feel a bit more secure. Less isolated. More connected. Like we've got all our friends in our back pocket. Not bad eh? More mobile. More sociable. More secure. Pretty fundamental stuff really. That's why, on the whole, we're feeling pretty up about things.

Good things can happen when your phone's off. We've got to admit, a switched-off mobile can say a lot. It can say to the person next to us "I think you deserve my full attention." Or it can let our kids know, "You're more important than the office." It's a simple gesture but it speaks volumes. Likewise, you can call to say thank you, but if you really mean it, maybe send a letter. A nice hand-written job on fancy paper. And, sure, texting someone a flirty something is all clean fun. But, let's face it, the good stuff doesn't happen until you show up in person. That's the thing about the new gizmos we come up with. They never replace established ways of communicating. They just make them more special. Worth considering. After all, the more special we make each other feel, the better we'll all get on. And that's got to be a good thing.

 the future's bright

due to the simple fact that when you look at those ads, you not only imagine a fresh glass of milk, you can practically *taste* it.

"Tacked On" Products

Always try to create an idea for the product that relates to it in some way. Otherwise you end up with an ad that looks like the product name has literally been "tacked on" at the end. These types of ideas could probably be for any number of products.

A simple way to test these occurrences is to cover the name/logo with your hand, and read the ad again. Then replace the product with another name (firstly, a non-competitor, then a competitor). If the idea still works, then your idea is simply not related enough to the product you are trying to advertise.

Your Idea Should End the Argument

Advertising comes down to creating strategies and ideas that *communicate a strong argument* for buying a product or service. To form the strongest argument, simply think of the strongest counter-

argument(s), and then better it. For example, back to the drunk "wise guy" in a bar (see page 104). Now he's complaining about the Olympics coming to New York City. He hates sport, he thinks it will cost too much money to host, and the subways will be packed, etc., etc. Imagine too that you are working on a campaign to *promote* the Olympics coming to New York. Your campaign idea should be so good that it will shut him up immediately, and hopefully end the argument there and then. Perhaps it is based on a simple fact, like:

The Olympics would raise over *11 billion* dollars for New York (or any other winning city).

If you think that would shut him up (and why wouldn't it?), you should seriously consider working on a campaign based on this argument. After all, if you can silence an angry barfly, you can silence anyone.

The brave client ad ("On/Off"), above, for Orange takes the argument tool to the next level by making an argument for *and* against use of mobile cell phones.

In competition with itself? An idea should end the argument for buying a product. But in this example it's a brave client (and a refreshing idea) to argue equally the cases for *not* using their product. *Client: Orange. Agency: Mother, London.*

Brainstorming Ideas: The Mind Map and Beyond

The very first section in the Basic Tools chapter is "What do you want to say?," i.e., what is the proposition (or benefit)? With a Mind Map diagram you can generate ideas from any proposition, from the scariest thing of all: a blank piece of paper.

The purpose of a Mind Map—as the name suggests—is to capture all your thoughts and ideas as and when you have them. It helps take you (literally and creatively) in lots of different directions, often connecting ideas through multiple "branches." A Mind Map can be produced individually or in a team of two or more people.

Unlike other forms of improvised brainstorming, mind-mapping allows for greater creative freedom, helps you to visualize the overall thinking, and allows you easily to compare, contrast, edit, and focus your thoughts—in real time.

Mind-mapping works for any type of proposition (narrow to broad) and is ideal if you have a big brief to crack in a short time. What's also great is that no two maps will be the same, so it's difficult to find something "wrong" with what's being captured. Creatively, you just need to find at least one "answer" that solves the problem. Some agencies present a completed Mind Map to clients to show all the thinking that went into the final concept (also a useful filler for a business pitch that may not require highly finished work).

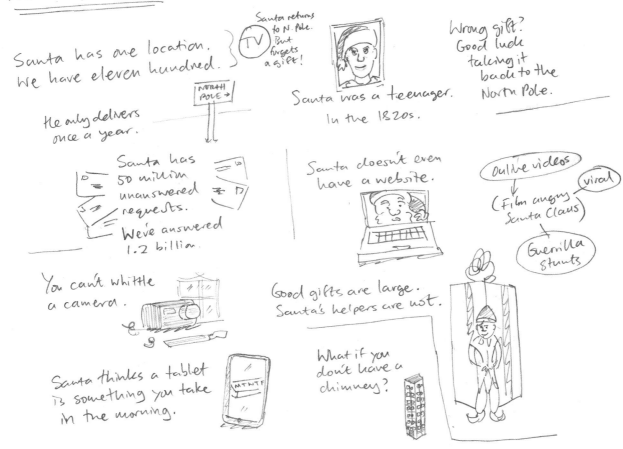

* We out-gift Santa. = IDEA / TAG

Santa has one location. We have eleven hundred.

Santa returns to N. Pole. But forgets a gift! (TV)

He only delivers once a year.

NORTH POLE →

Santa was a teenager. In the 1820s.

Wrong gift? Good luck taking it back to the North Pole.

Santa has 50 million unanswered requests. We've answered 1.2 billion.

Santa doesn't even have a website.

Online videos (Film angry Santa Claus) viral

Guerilla stunts

You can't whittle a camera.

Good gifts are large. Santa's helpers are not.

Santa thinks a tablet is something you take in the morning.

MTNTF

What if you don't have a chimney?

How It Works

Step 1: Write the basic proposition from a strategic brief (word or sentence) in the center of a blank page. (The example opposite is for Best Buy stores/website.)

Step 2: Then begin applying "word association" words and phrases around it. Don't overthink it: it's all stream-of-consciousness thinking at this stage.

Step 3: Create branches that grow linearly and tangentially. When each branch (or "offshoot") ends, explore new ones that begin either from the proposition or a different part of the Mind Map.

Step 4: Once you've completely run out of ideas, go back and circle the ones that have the most potential for a big, simple, and original campaign idea.

Step 5: (above) Start developing executions for all your "circled" campaign ideas. Scribble down headlines, visuals, taglines, and any other related ideas. (If these come easily, you'll know it's probably a good campaign idea.)

TV and cinema advertising is considered to be the most glamorous of all the advertising media (not just within "broadcast," which includes radio and interactive TV). This is presumably because of the level of exposure (more people watch TV than read or listen to the radio), plus the type and scale of production, including the potential to shoot abroad with a top director.

TV or Cinema?

In this chapter, I will refer to "TV and/or cinema advertising" as simply, "TV"—the more common of the two media (think of all those TV channels out there). Sometimes a commercial will be required to run in both media. In these cases, and even if you are required to work on a cinema-only brief, consider some of the subtle differences between TV and cinema commercials.

Some Differences between TV and Cinema

Size of Titles

The difference between the average TV screen and the average cinema screen is still significant. (Sorry, plasma owners.) This has repercussions regarding the size and choice of type. It may be worth considering a typeface that works for both, and/or changing the size accordingly. This is often ignored, which is why you get giant-looking type when applied to a full-size cinema screen (when it was meant to be subtle and understated), or worse—tiny, illegible opening/closing movie titles on a TV screen.

Cropping and Framing

The cropping and framing of shots is less of an issue than the size of type (a good idea will probably work in both media). But it's worth noting this simple logic: a commercial with lots of tight crops will work better on TV (detail too close for cinema), whereas one with lots of wide shots will work better on a cinema screen (detail "lost" on TV).

Be Creative with Cinema

Think about the fact that you are advertising inside a cinema/movie theater, rather than someone's home. By this I don't mean just show an ad for the Indian restaurant next door (that's a media buyer's job). Be more creative about it. One example from 2003 was an interactive commercial for BMW. It opens with a long, dark country road that heads off into the distance. As usual, the theater lights are turned "off" in preparation for the movie. In the darkness, two front lights of a car begin slowly coming down the road toward the screen. Just as the car draws really near, the lights inside the theater are slowly turned up to full blast, to emphasize the power of BMW's Bi-Xenon headlights. As soon as the car lights are switched off the theater becomes dark again (Agency: TBWA/Hunt/Lascaris, Johannesburg).

Note: just because a cinema has a relatively captive audience compared to the multi-channeled TV, don't think it's easy. Treat it, and the audience, with respect (there are still many distractions at a cinema).

Scripts and Storyboards

There are three ways to present a TV concept: script (usually text only, including description), storyboard (text and visuals), and "animatic."

A TV script is always written in the third person. It's a simple, literal description of the action, dialogue, voice overs, and sound effects. (These terms are described in more detail below.) It doesn't need to be flowery or over written. Basic descriptions will do. Opposite is McDonald's "Estate Agent," but it can also be written in a side-by-side format, with "video" on the left, and "audio" (plus minimal description) on the right, as shown opposite, below.

A script is an objective "story" that tells the reader what he or she would *see* if it was actually produced. Equally, the *concept* should be understood without having it explained to them in the script. Nor should the script describe how the people in the commercial feel. It should

Basic Script

We open on a close-up of a juicy McDonald's Quarter Pounder. We then cut to inside an empty living room. It looks newly decorated.

VO: *This is the amount of work an Estate Agent has to do to afford the McDonald's Quarter Pounder.*

A man swings open the door and looks inside the room. A couple is standing close behind him.

SFX: *Door opens.*

The man then simply says:

ESTATE AGENT: *Lounge.*

Then just as quickly he shuts the door.

SFX: *Door shuts.*

We cut back to a close-up of a juicy McDonald's Quarter Pounder. A super appears on the screen:

SUPER: *99p.*

VO: *The McDonald's Quarter Pounder. 99p.*

Storyboard

VO:
This is the amount of work an Estate Agent has to do to afford the McDonald's Quarter Pounder.

SFX:
(Door opens)

ESTATE AGENT: Lounge.

SFX:
(Door shuts)

SUPER: 99p.

VO:
The McDonald's Quarter Pounder. 99p.

Video/Audio Script

Video	Audio
Open on a close-up of a juicy McDonald's Quarter Pounder	**VO:** *This is the amount of work an Estate Agent has to do to afford the McDonald's Quarter Pounder.*
CUT TO inside an empty living room. It looks newly decorated.	
A man swings open the door and looks inside the room. A couple is standing close behind him.	**SFX:** *Door opens.*
	ESTATE AGENT: *Lounge.*
He shuts the door again.	**SFX:** *Door shuts.*
Cut back to a close-up of a juicy McDonald's Quarter Pounder.	**SUPER:** *99p.*
	VO: *The McDonald's Quarter Pounder. 99p.*

Client: McDonald's. Agency: Leo Burnett, London. Creatives: Mark Tutssel, Mark Norcutt, Laurence Quinn, Nick Bell. Note: basic and video/audio scripts are the author's interpretation of the storyboard version; for demonstration purposes only.

GOOD THINGS COME TO THOSE WHO WAIT.

Example of key frames for Guinness's "noitulovE" commercial. *Agency: Abbott Mead Vickers BBDO, London.* *Creatives: Ian Heartfield, Matt Doman.*

only describe the action, not the campaign idea. "Leading the reader" in these ways is especially forbidden at research focus groups because in reality you would not have this help each time you watched a commercial.

As for storyboards, there are two basic types, depending on who is creating them. The first type is produced (usually by hand) in the creative department at the agency. This storyboard is usually a hand-drawn set of "key frames." These are the frames (or shots) that show the *key points of action* within the commercial, including supers (text on the screen). In other words, just enough frames for the story to be clearly understood. Typed next to each frame (usually to the right or below) is any accompanying dialogue, voice over, or sound effect. Key frames vary dramatically from script to script. The first key frame might be a wide, "establishing shot" that sets up the story and/or location. The last key frame (called the "end frame") usually shows the tagline and/or logo.

Key frames for Guinness's Cannes Grand Prix winner "noitulovE" (left) show the key stages of millions of years of devolution until we see a prehistoric fish gagging from some unsavory mud.

Key frames for Honda's award-winning "Cog" commercial (opposite) show a precision led "chain reaction" using various parts of a Honda Accord. The voiceover ends with: "Isn't it nice when things just…work?"

The agency storyboard outlined above is what the client sees at the initial presentation. If the concept is sold—whether in script or storyboard form—the director hired to shoot the commercial will then meet with the creative team to go through his/her storyboard. This version is an extension of the key frames. It will be more detailed in terms of shots and camera angles. This is also produced by hand, with any other material (visual references and stimulus including pictures, film clips, location shots, casting shots, etc.) shown separately. Once agreed upon by the creative team and the client, these frames act as a guide/checklist during the shoot.

An animatic is a basic animation of the script: a mock commercial that simply sequences the key frames of a storyboard, which is then viewed on a ¾" U-matic machine (or equivalent). There may be some documentary-style panning and zooming across the still frames to help create a sense of movement. Voice over, dialogue, and basic sound effects are also added. Animatics are typically used in research to help focus groups understand the commercial. There is much debate over their use because many testers are too influenced by the crude, child-like execution, which can detract from—and weaken—the overall concept.

Time Lengths

In the US, a TV commercial will either air on a major network, an independent station, or cable. Although most last 30 seconds, a single TV commercial (or "spot") can vary in length.

Common time lengths (TV)

- US: 15, 30, 45, 60, 90, 120 seconds
- UK: 10, 20, 30, 40, 50, 60, 90, 120 seconds

Alternative/unusual lengths

- 120 seconds
- 90 seconds
- 1–5 seconds * (also known as an "ident")
- 1 second (also known as a "blipverts") This verges on *subliminal advertising*, which allegedly works on a subconscious level. There is usually a legal limit to the number of frames or milliseconds that an image can stay on screen because it can cause epileptic fits.

  * approximately

Sound Effects (SFX)

The sound effects (SFX) within a commercial refer to any non-speaking sound, including any noises that might add to the comedy or drama. A sound effect might be entirely music based, typically either a continuous segment of original music (or a cover version); or a composed, commissioned track. It could be non-music such as natural sounds that relate to the action or the background/environment. For example, if a balloon pops, simply write "SFX: balloon pops." If the commercial is set in a park, write "SFX: bird singing, children playing, etc." depending on the specific setting. The term "under and throughout" is often used to describe a sound that carries "throughout" the commercial and "under" any voice overs and other sound effects.

Sound is one major advantage of TV over print (aside from moving image and duration). In fact, it

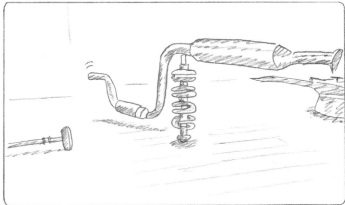

Key frames for Honda's award-winning "Cog" commercial, which shows a precision led "chain reaction" using various parts of a Honda Accord. The voiceover ends with: "Isn't it nice when things just…work?" ***Agency:*** *Wieden & Kennedy, London.* ***Creatives:*** *Matt Gooden, Ben Walker.*

can be the basis of an idea. "Giggle," a commercial for the Skoda Roomster, used only a series of chuckles, chortles, whoopees, hums, sighs, kisses, claps, and whistles. Synchronized to the actions of robots, machines, and workers inside the Skoda factory, the idea is summed up by the super: the Roomster from Skoda. Manufacturer of happy drivers. Conversely, a commercial for Dyson dramatized the inferior suction power of other vacuum cleaners with the sounds of squeaky toys. The Sony Bravia "Paint" commercial ran an alternate version with just the pumping, spraying, and landing sound of the paint.

When choosing an original piece of music, choose a track (or part of a track) that works with the idea, the tone, and the brand. British Airways' operatic choice ("Viens Mallika" from "Lakmé" by Léo Delibes) communicates classy, luxurious relaxation.

Different music can change the mood of an ad entirely (one track could make it humorous, another ironic, or dramatic, etc.) The right track can take a commercial to another level. It can significantly help to communicate your idea, or explain how a character feels without he or she having to say it (one of many movie examples is the opening scene of "Bridget Jones' Diary," when we see our drunken heroine miming to Jamie O'Neal's "All By Myself"). Often a great ad will promote (or re-promote) a song to chart-topping status.

Once you have the script, explore the obvious musical choices first. Then try the opposite with it—it might create something unexpected. Sometimes you won't find the right piece until you have the final edit. (Tony Kaye originally planned to use a classical piece for his famous Dunlop ad, until someone tried Velvet Underground's "Venus in Furs," and with a bit of reediting, the rest is history.)

Don't just choose a current popular track for the sake of it, or because the client can afford it. Even if it's for the ideal brand, it can look like "borrowed interest." Plus the ad can become dated very quickly. As long as the track you pick feels natural, you shouldn't get too many complaints from purist fans claiming that you destroyed "their song."

Of course, for any budding songwriters out there, TV ads create an opportunity to write and record an original track, tailor made to fit your concept. It doesn't have to be a corny kids' jingle, either. If successful, a song can become a selling tool (think of Honda's award-winning "Grrr" song), further promoting the original product.

A final note: whenever you come across an unusual piece of music, *archive it* (just as you would a typeface, or a photograph, etc.) You never know, that organ grinder CD you bought from a street performer might be perfect for a future commercial.

Voice Over (VO or V/O)

Voice over is the "unseen" person's voice that can be heard over the other sound effects, etc. It can be the voice of someone in the commercial, or a third person. It can carry throughout the ad, or just for the tagline and/or product (you may choose just to have text on the screen instead). Note: a VO is different from having a person talking on screen, which would be written as "MAN" or "JOHN," etc. In the case of a VO, you may wish to specify sex:

- **MVO** = male voice over (can use MVO 1, 2, 3, etc., if necessary)
- **FVO** = female voice over (can use FVO 1, 2, 3, etc., if necessary)

You can even include a brief description of the type or style of voice/actor:

- MVO—30s, lively, slight Southern accent
- WOMAN—50s, sincere, Meryl Streep style*

*Or simply use "MERYL" if you can get the real thing (but note that famous actors have been known to turn down millions to appear in an ad).

A voice over is a direct expression of the tone of voice (both use the word "voice," after all). If necessary, include tonal "directions," as you would if someone were speaking on screen (e.g., VO [sarcastically]). Remember, the tone is not an idea, but it should *reflect* your idea.

Avoid writing clichéd, "addy" voice overs unless it relates to your idea. Having been exposed to so many commercials during their lives (and mostly bad ones), many students have a tendency to copy this common, cheesy style of voiceover. They somehow think: "I'm now doing a TV ad, so I have to make the voiceover really, really sincere." Nine times out of ten it will sound insincere, even cheesy. Keep it simple and relevant: write in the tone and spirit of your idea, and of your client.

(Most car commercials in the US look and sound alike. Forget what's gone before, and create something unique. Write voice over that reflects your idea for that specific brand of off-road vehicle, rather than *all* off-road vehicles.)

Super

A super is a piece of text/type that is "superimposed" onto the screen. The super (or series of supers) and the voice over can either replace the need for the other, or be an addition. Understandably, unless very short in length, superimposed text tends to be harder to absorb than spoken text when the sound is on (we hear more quickly than we read), and speech is impossible to understand when the sound is off (a common problem for "muted" ads playing in sports bars). But assuming that the sound is on, if something is spoken *and* superimposed, it's clearly much more likely to be absorbed by the viewer than if it's spoken *or* superimposed. (Therefore the longer the super, the greater the need for an additional voice over.)

The Same Rules Apply

By the age of 35, the average person has seen approximately 150,000 TV commercials (that's two months' worth!) The question, as with any form of advertising, is: "How many were remembered?"

A *good* ad communicates its message (from a single-minded proposition) clearly, quickly, simply, and relevantly. (Admittedly, a TV ad is allowed to take longer than a three-second poster, but compared to a feature film, there's very little time to tell your "story.")

Remember the simple SLIP IT acronym in the Basic Tools chapter. It can be applied to all media, not just print. A *great* ad not only stops you, it may also make you smile, laugh, or think. And it should also either inform, provoke, involve or interact with the reader/viewer/listener.

As explained in the first few pages of this book, whether it's for a 3-second poster or a 60-second TV spot, you should be able to *describe your idea in one sentence* (see also the "one frame" goal, below). This "goal" has been around since great advertising began. To the right is a timeless example for TV.

The "One Frame" Goal

The "one frame[*]" goal is another form of reductionism. The tendency when given the luxury

Agency: DDB
Creatives: Roy Grace, Evan Stark.
Product: Alka-Seltzer
Title: "Mama Mia"
Idea (in one sentence): *A man, advertising a brand of spicy meatballs, needs Alka-Seltzer after failing to do a perfect "take."*

....

JACK: *Mama Mia! That's some special...*
DIRECTOR'S VOICE: *Cut. Spicy meatballs, Jack.*
JACK: *Sorry.*
ASSISTANT'S VOICE: *Take twenty-eight.*
DIRECTOR'S VOICE: *Up Tony. And, action.*
JACK: *Mama Mia! That's a spicy meatball.*
DIRECTOR'S VOICE: *Cut.*
JACK: *What was the matter with that?*
DIRECTOR'S VOICE: *The accent.*
JACK: *(reacting to heat) A-aa-aaaa!!*
DIRECTOR'S VOICE: *Cut.*
JACK: *Meesy, micey, ballsy, balls.*
DIRECTOR'S VOICE: *Cut.*
ASSISTANT'S VOICE: *Take fifty-nine.*
DIRECTOR'S VOICE: *And, action...Jack.*
MVO: *Sometimes you eat more than you should. And when it's spicy besides, mama mia do you need Alka-Seltzer. Alka-Seltzer can help unstuff you, relieve the acid indigestion, and make you your old self again.*
JACK: *Mama Mia! That's a spicy meatball.*
SFX: *(Something falls down in the kitchen) Crash!*
DIRECTOR'S VOICE: *Cut. Okay. Let's break for lunch.*

The same rules for print apply to TV: visual simile. In fact, the final frame also ran as a poster. *Client: Anheuser-Busch.*

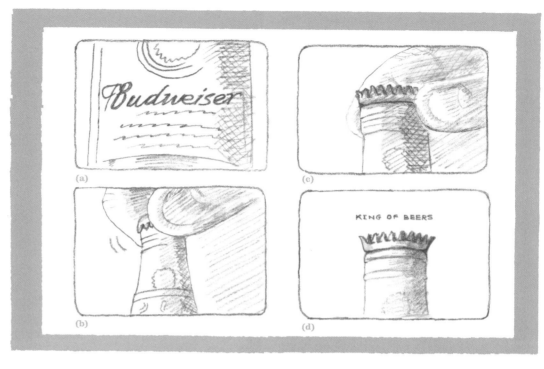

of 30 seconds is to complicate the idea, and use too many cuts, voice overs, etc. If it improves the ad, let the commercial director expand on the basic key frame(s) of your storyboard (see Leave it to a Director to (Not) Understand Your Idea, page 174). By definition, the simplest ad needs only one cut, or camera set-up (not including the end frame). This is not a rule you need to place on every script you write, but it is a useful tool because it forces you to keep it simple. Aim for as close to one frame (two or three is good, too), or at least be in a position to *capture the basic idea in a single frame, as if it were a poster*, even if the final ad uses more frames to improve the story telling. In many cases—although less so in recent years—a simple idea has been translated into both media (print and TV) with little variation or alteration. This "two for the price of one" argument is simple: why come up with a separate idea for each media when you can use one idea in as many forms as you can, thereby increasing the ad's impact?

The ideas opposite (Biography Channel's "Michael Jackson" by student Jenny Drucker, Greenpeace's "Dumb Animals/Fur Coat" ad, Volvo's "Sonogram" ad) are examples of ideas that were translated into print *and* TV, helped by its central, dynamic image. The fact that so many great TV ads can work in print is a sign of their brilliant simplicity. Whether the idea was intended for print or TV is not important: it's as if they were created as one.

Because consumers' attention spans have decreased over recent years (beginning with the so-called "MTV Generation"), many of these simple, "slow" spots have been replaced with fast-cut commercials. This has been the subject of much debate and concern. To touch on this, it is worth pointing out that the human brain has a limit to how much it can consciously absorb. So long as fast-cuts are merely a *stylistic* trend, and *concept* still remains king, the simple will triumph. If anything, simple TV ads will only stand out even more. There are, after all, many more probable reasons as to why advertising has supposedly declined in recent years, than people's reduced attention spans. (For more on this subject, see The Dying Tagline?, page 106.)

*Do not confuse a storyboard "frame" with actual "frames" of film or "frames per second."

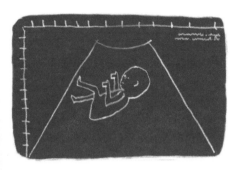

An incredibly simple idea that works in print and TV (see the billboard version on page 35). *Client: The Biography Channel. Student: Jenny Drucker.*

A simple press ad turned commercial. This one simply took the headline: Is something inside telling you to buy a Volvo? and used it as a voice over. *Client: Volvo. Agency: Scali, McCabe, Sloves. Creatives: Steve Montgomery, Joseph Lovering III. Illustration: Steve Montgomery.*

VOLVO
A car you can believe in.

A bloody fashion runway dramatizes the killing of animals for fur. The "super" at the end came directly from the poster headline: It takes up to 40 dumb animals to make a fur coat. But only one to wear it. *Client: Greenpeace. Agency: The Yellow Hammer Company. Creatives: Jeremy Pemberton, Alan Page. Director: David Bailey.*

Michael Jackson

Bio graphy

The "One Frame" Goal

Examples of ads that use one single shot/cut, or could easily be executed in one single shot/cut:

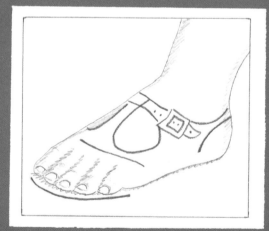

Lost at sea, two men in a boat. Then one. (MVO: "Alka-Seltzer. When you've eaten something you shouldn't have.") *Client: Bayer/Alka-Seltzer. Agency: Abbott Mead Vickers BBDO, London. Creatives: Greg Martin, Patricia Doherty.*

The one-frame goal: from a dog's point of view. (Dog: "I used to like it when she ran. She really didn't go much faster than now when she's walking, but she'd tire out quicker. And then we'd go home and she'd fall asleep in front of the TV…. Now, we go three miles a day, ten miles on the weekends. You know, dogs were meant to sit in the sun and sleep…") *Client: Nike. Agency: Wieden & Kennedy, Portland. Creatives: Mark Fenske, Susan Hoffman.*

An old man shouts at a stationary sports car, "Slow down! This is a neighborhood! Punk!" The super reads: Looks fast. *Client: Toyota Celica. Agency: Saatchi & Saatchi, Los Angeles. Creatives: Verner Soler, Sherry Hawkins.*

A camera, a pen and a child's foot. I remember being mesmerized by this ad when I was a kid. (MVO: "This little foot will get corns and bunions if a shoe is too tight across here.") *Client: Clark's shoes. Agency: Collett Dickenson Pearce, London. Creatives: Neil Godfrey, Tony Brignull.*

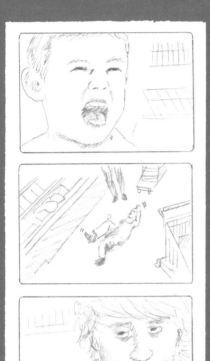

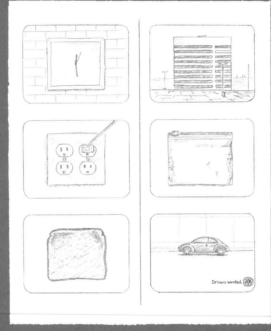

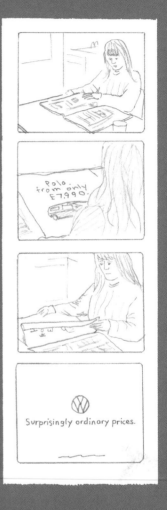

A five-year-old boy throws a major tantrum in public as his father looks helplessly on. (Super: Use condoms.) *Client:* *Zazoo Condoms.* *Agency:* *Duval Guillaume Antwerp, Belgium.* *Creatives:* *Stef Selfslaghs, Stijn Gansemans.*

Print may be quicker, but TV can still be simple. *Client:* *Volkswagen.* *Agency:* *Arnold Worldwide.*

A locked-off camera, a hiccuping woman, and a newspaper. Her hiccups stop when she reads how little a VW Polo costs. (Super: Surprisingly ordinary prices.) *Client:* *Volkswagen.* *Agency:* *BMP DDB, London.* *Creative:* *Andrew Fraser.*

Don't reveal, imply. (Story: a cyclist hears a car playing his favorite song at traffic lights, then keeps following car…along a motorway! But all we see is his front wheel creeping into shot. The humor comes from *imagining* the cyclist peddling frantically, rather than showing it. Super: One love.) **Client:** *BBC Radio 1.* **Agency:** *Fallon, London.* **Creatives:** *Andy McLeod, Richard Flintham.*

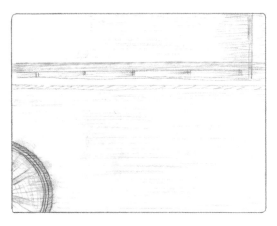

Wrong for Print, Right for TV

As you know by now, it's hard to be simple, especially in print. Sometimes even a good idea can be too complicated or long winded for print. But fear not. With a little tweak, it may be perfect for TV. Here's an example. A student of mine worked on a brief to sell Lego as the fun toy. She had a nice campaign idea that was proving hard to communicate in print: kids deliberately misbehaving at home (graffiti on furniture, running with scissors, etc.) because they want to be sent to their bedroom—where their Lego is kept! It was too much to say in print. But the suggestion to convert this story into a series of vignettes with a final twist produced a really simple, charming TV ad (see also The Final Twist, page 170, and Vignettes, page 172).

Note: even convoluted "social situation" ideas that so many students try in print work a lot better on the TV, purely because you have more time to communicate what's going on.

Don't Reveal, Imply

The "don't reveal, imply" tool outlined in the Basic Tools chapter also works in TV. Again, what we imagine in our heads is often more powerful than anything explicitly shown, whether it's scary, funny, disturbing or otherwise. So ask yourself: "Do I have to show everything?" and if not, "Will it be better?"

A wonderful example of this is in a commercial for Radio One in the UK, created by Fallon, London. The strategy was expressed in their tagline: One love. The campaign was based on the idea that when you hear your favorite song on the radio, you have to listen to the entire track before you can proceed with anything else. In one ad, a cyclist pulls up next to a car at a set of traffic lights. The driver is blaring a sublime track on the radio. The car pulls away. Then we cut to a close-up side view of the same car doing 60 mph along a motorway, with the song still playing. The next thing we see is the front wheel of the bicycle just creep into frame, behind the car.

What makes this ad work so well is *imagining* the effort of the cyclist to keep up with the car. Actually showing the cyclist follow the car to the motorway would have been the obvious way to shoot this commercial. But it would have spoilt it, made it too revealing, too "Benny Hill," and not nearly as funny.

Similarly, the ending of VW Polo's "Lamp Post" is perfectly cut just at the point before a man walks into a "prepped" padded lamp post, the latest victim of a nearby distracting poster.

The Dramatic Medium

As a "moving" medium, TV gives you the freedom to dramatize an idea (even a simple fact) in ways that print cannot. For example, a TV spot for Womankind Worldwide was based around the fact that "1 in 4 women in the UK will suffer violent abuse by men." This fact was expressed in an incredibly realistic, dramatic way by showing a man in a street counting up to, and then punching, every fourth woman he sees. As the man heads home, we realize his next victim is at his house. A female voiceover concludes: "Usually it's hidden behind closed doors." No matter how this idea could be translated into 2D, it would have been flat in print. Instead, TV brilliantly capitalizes on moving action storytelling that the medium brings.

Equally, the Ikea "Freedom" commercial is perfect for TV. Office workers start applauding a man who leaves work at 3pm to meet his wife and presumably spend some quality time with his kids. The music (an added benefit of TV), a fitting chain-gang song by Ervin Webb (chorus: "I'm goin' home…oh yes!"), takes the idea to another level. One could argue that a print version would have been cheesy and soppy by comparison. End frame super/titles: If it costs you less, you can work less…. Welcome to life outside work. Tag: Ikea. Live your life, love your home.

Audio Mnemonics

A mnemonic is a "memory aid" that helps people to remember your product or campaign. These can be visual, audio, or both. TV and radio are ideal for

The dramatic medium of TV combined with the "one frame" goal. This wonderfully scripted, perfectly timed six-minute monologue was filmed in a single take. *Client:* Diageo/Johnnie Walker. *Agency:* BBH, London. *Creative:* Justin Moore. *Illustration:* John Rodrigues.

Johnnie Walker: The Man Who Walked Around the World

....

We see a bagpiper on a dirt path in the hills of Scotland. A man is approaching from behind.

SUPER: The Man Who Walked Around the World. A true story.

MAN: Bagpiper…shut it! Here's a true story about a young lad named John. Just a local farmboy. But there was something special about the lad. A glint in his eye. A fire in his belly. A spring in his step. And one day he went for a walk.

He continues to walk and tell the story of Johnnie Walker. A related object appears along the path at the precise moment the man explains that aspect of the story.

MAN: But by the beginning of the 21st century Johnnie Walker wasn't just the world's biggest whisky brand, but an international symbol of progress, the brand's "Keep Walking" mantra adopted by pro-democracy protestors and parliamentary speechwriters.

What would the farm-born Victorian grocer have thought of all of this? He'd have loved it. A farm-born Victorian grocer he might have been. But he—and the family that followed him—were possessed by a fiery ambition, with the skill and intelligence to match.

Two hundred years later, and Johnnie Walker's still walking. And he's not showing any signs of stopping.

The man continues walking down the path…

The Final Twist

As we have seen in previous chapters, the "give it a twist" works for print headlines, visuals, and body copy. The approach of "sending a person in one way then pulling the rug from under them" is a perfect, popular technique in TV commercials. In fact, it's a tried and tested method.

This Cannes Grand Prix winner positioned the *Independent* as a newspaper for open-minded people who don't like being told what to do or what to think. It does this by depicting how we are constantly bombarded with instructions about things we should not do. The voice over is accompanied by a rapid series of black-and-white reportage images that illustrate each point, e.g., a child holding a pair of scissors, smokers, gay couples, a car engulfed in flames, etc.

The verbal twist comes directly from the product name, with the final shot of a man reading the *Independent* while the voice over ironically concludes, "Don't buy...Don't read."

The Monster.com "Moose" commercial has an amazing visual twist. The spot begins in a large, wood-paneled office where an executive is sitting at his desk beneath a moose head mounted on the wall. The camera pans around until we see that on the other side of the wall there is a plain white office with a man sitting at a small desk. The other side of the moose is protruding out of the wall onto his desk. A super appears: Need a new job? We can help.

Note: the "final twist" is slightly different from the "cut back." The former is usually a key part of the idea, whereas the latter is more of an extra surprise (usually a really quick gag that cuts back to the action) which appears *after* the final voice over/tag/logo has occurred.

....

***Exercise*: watch TV! Count how many commercials per 20 have a twist at the end, and how many have cut backs. Compare the success levels of each.**

....

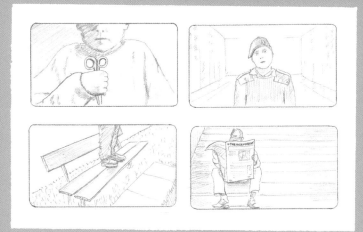

The Independent: Litany

....

MVO: *Don't talk. Don't touch. Don't walk. Don't walk at night. Don't walk on the right. Don't drink. Don't think. Don't smoke. Don't do drugs. Don't do beef. Don't do junk. Don't be fat. Don't be thin. Don't chew. Don't spit. Don't swim. Don't breathe. Don't cry. Don't bleed. Don't kill. Don't experiment. Don't exist. Don't do anything. Don't fry your food. Don't fry your brain. Don't sit too close to the telly. Don't walk on the grass. Don't put your elbows on the table. Don't put your feet on the seat. Don't run with scissors and don't play with fire (pause). Don't rebel. Don't smack. Don't touch. Don't masturbate. Don't be childish. Don't be old. Don't be ordinary. Don't be different. Don't stand out. Don't drop out...*

Don't buy...Don't read.

Federal Express: Spritzer

SFX: Foot steps down the hall.

MAN: Spritzer, that package you sent to Albuquerque last night didn't get there. Spritzer, you're in big trouble Spritzer!

ANNCR: Next time, send it Federal Express.

Opposite Don't do this, don't do that. A litany of orders ends in an ironic verbal twist: "Don't buy…Don't read." *Client: The Independent newspaper. **Agency:** Lowe Howard-Spink, London. **Creative:** Charles Inge.*

Far left Story: businessman is frantically looking for Mr. Spritzer, the man responsible for a lost package. The final twist is a simple pan down of the camera to reveal our guilty man hiding under his desk. *Client: FedEx. **Agency:** Ally & Gargano. **Creatives:** Patrick Kelly, Michael Tesch.*

Near left Two very contrasting offices (and jobs) are dramatized by a clever visual twist that reveals "the wrong end" of a stuffed moose. *Client: Monster.com. **Agency:** BBDO, New York. **Creatives:** Gerard Caputo, Reuben Hower.*

Probably the most famous demonstration ad of all time. (MVO: "Have you ever wondered how the man who drives a snowplow drives *to* the snowplow?") **Client:** *VW Beetle.* **Agency:** *DDB.* **Creative:** *Roy Grace.*

using a memorable voice, or even a simple sound effect or jingle. Although many are cheesy or irritating, the better, subtler ones are highly effective branding devices, generally used at the very end of a commercial, e.g., the Intel® Pentium® Processor four-note jingle, Yahoo's rallying "Ya-hoo-ooo!," and The British Army's triple crunching, stomping sound.

TV Clichés

TV commercials are cliché-ridden, both in terms of concept and execution. Clients and agencies share the blame. Recent "trends" to avoid include:

- Talking animals
- Talking babies
- Products transforming into dancing, running robots (especially cars)
- Cinema-style "letterboxing" (IBM did it first, successfully. They own it, so why copy it?)
- Vintage rock song (car brand, particularly an off-road vehicle)
- Other music groups/tracks (e.g., empowerment = M People, or Des'ree)
- "Flash-bulb" effect at start/end of each shot

Of course, the one exception is when you use clichéd images in the form of a send-up or parody (see Spoof Advertising, page 128).

Demonstration Ads

TV is the perfect medium for "demonstration" ads because you can show a product in action. Here are some classic examples:

VW, "Snowplow"
MVO: *Have you ever wondered how the man who drives a snowplow drives* to *the snowplow? This one drives a Volkswagen. So you can stop wondering.*

American Tourister, "Gorilla"
MVO: *Dear clumsy bellboys, brutal cab drivers, careless doormen, ruthless porters, savage baggage masters, and all butter-fingered luggage handlers all over the world: have we got a suitcase for you.*

Honda C-100 Dream, "Drop"
Rather than demonstrate how far a Honda moped can travel on one tank of petrol/gas (like a typical car ad), we see it run for 30 seconds from a single drop.

Apple MacBook Air, "Envelope"
An orange, "inter-office mail" envelope is placed on a table. The envelope appears to be filled with paper. A hand then removes its actual contents: an ultra-thin laptop computer.

Volvo, "Heavy Traffic" (A print version of the TV ad is on page 112)
MVO: *How well does you car stand up to heavy traffic?*

Exaggeration

The exaggeration tool on page 138 is not just for print. A TV campaign for the French newspaper *L'Equipe* is a perfect example of the "brand X is so good that…" format: a father spends so much time reading the paper that his family doesn't recognize him when his face appears from behind it. After a long scream, calm is restored when his face "disappears" again.

Vignettes

A vignette is a brief scene from a movie or a play. Because a commercial has to tell a "story" in a much shorter space of time than a movie or a play, a vignette (or series of vignettes) is a common and useful technique. Vignettes can cover any period in time—minutes, weeks, years, or centuries that would otherwise take too long to show. They can really help to emphasize your idea. For example, if your idea is about someone who is unlucky in love, you could use a series of vignettes in your commercial that cover different stages of a disastrous blind date. Or alternatively, you could expand the time period, writing each vignette as an entirely separate blind date. Both help to dramatize the idea, and allow us to sympathize with our main character. But remember, vignettes are a technique, not an idea: there has to be a good reason to use them.

Repeat Viewing

It sounds like common sense, but when you create any idea for TV, ask yourself honestly: will this stand up to repeat viewing? In other words, avoid anything that might quickly annoy and irritate (either the entire concept, or part of the idea such as dialogue or sound effects). Remember, TV and radio ads are intrusive at best. (I recently watched an ad showing various individuals with loud, abrasive laughs. Now I scramble to find the mute button every time it comes on!)

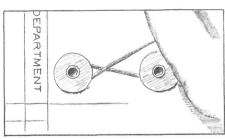

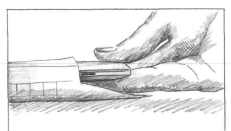

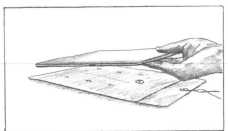

Above TV is an ideal medium for demonstration ads. (Story: Gorilla "plays" with suitcase. MVO: "Dear clumsy bellboys, brutal cab drivers, careless doormen, ruthless porters, savage baggage masters, and all butter-fingered luggage handlers all over the world: have we got a suitcase for you.") *Client: American Tourister. Agency: DDB, New York. Creatives: Roy Grace, Marcia Bell Grace.*

Left A wonderfully simple demonstration ad (with a final twist) to show that a laptop is thin enough to fit inside an office envelope. *Client: Apple. Agency: TBWA/Media Arts Lab, Los Angeles. Creatives: Alain Briere, Demian Oliveira, Krista Wicklund.*

Three Stages of Production

Once the script has been written and approved by the client, there are three main stages of production: pre-production, production (the "shoot"), and post-production.

There are pre-production meetings (PPM): the meetings before a shoot to go over script, director's storyboard, cast, wardrobe, location, etc. The first meeting is usually between the director and producer and the creative team and agency producer. Then the client is informed about the decisions (and may even request another PPM to include themselves and an agency account/project manager).

"Production" is self explanatory. It's the duration of the shoot, be it one day or five, depending on the idea, number of locations, etc. It includes the whole cast and crew, and is a chance for art directors (and hopefully copywriters) to learn. Some even go on to become directors themselves.

Post-production: the period when the director, editor, and creative team sit down at a post-production "house" to watch, discuss, compile, and edit a commercial.

Leave it to a Director to (Not) Understand Your Idea

I've heard creative teams say this many times. A more polite version is "leave it to a director to reinterpret the idea in a way he or she prefers." That's not to say he or she won't be improving your script in the process. Be open minded to suggestions, but remember: *your job is to make the ad communicate*; to make sure the main idea isn't getting "lost." And if it is, you'll be the person doing the explaining to your creative director, not the director!

Most directors are exceptionally creative individuals. Many have worked on features, music videos, and documentaries, which can bring a new flare to the project. However, you usually find that those from an advertising background (especially ex-art directors) are the ones who "get" the script straightaway. And they understand that the primary job of a TV ad is to communicate your idea, rather than make it look good. (If it looks great too, that's a bonus.) And finally, whoever you choose, make sure that they love advertising as much as you do, and that he or she isn't doing ads to fund their next project.

Don't Relieve the Drama (or Comedy)

It's so easy to get caught up in the excitement of finally creating and seeing your own TV ad. Or to spend so long on it that its sparkle has gone. However, suppose you still love the idea, you are confident about the shoot, but then it's time to see the first edited rough cut of the ad…and it's simply not working. It's not the fault of the directing, the acting, the voice over, the location or the music, but suddenly, for some strange reason, what you had in your head (that became the script) seems a lot more powerful than the final product. A common explanation is this. It could be because the drama (or comedy) of the idea is being clouded by extraneous, superfluous shots that were ironically meant to add interest. Remember, this is not a feature film. Instead, these shots should be communicating the drama (or comedy) that your pure, original script had. So try asking yourself: "Is this shot really adding anything, or is it taking something away?"

Get it Covered

If the script seems to be changing during the shoot (even slightly), make sure all the shots agreed to in the pre-production meeting are covered. This is usually the agency producer's job to persuade. If the director wants to try other things (and there's enough time), let them. You can always argue about it in post-production—and you can't argue about footage that's not there!

Great Direction and Production

A commercial with a great, simple script doesn't guarantee a great execution. The success of any commercial relies on a lot of factors: casting, acting, editing, weather. The same is true for bigger, "thematic" scripts, which rely more heavily on the director's vision and production skills to bring it to life. And throwing a lot of money at it is no guarantee of success. Whenever that level of execution is achieved, the director—without question—has taken the entire commercial to another level. Famous examples that raised the production value bar include: Coke's "Teach the world to sing," Apple's "1984," Levi's 501s "Launderette," Electricity Association's "Heat electric"/Creature Comforts, British Airways' "Face," British Rail's "Relax," Dunlop's "Tested for the unexpected," Guinness's "Chain," "Surfer" and "noitulovE," and Honda's "Grrr." This level is set to rise as technology and techniques improve (and to match the increasing level of the audience's visual expectation).

Flogging the Proposition to Death

TV advertising is a luxury. It's lengthy (usually 30 seconds or more), it moves (unlike print), and it has audio (like radio). But this doesn't mean you have to keep repeating the proposition in a lame attempt to drive the message home. You know the kind of ad I mean. It usually involves a series of headshots of actors as "real people." One example was for a high-speed internet service, which went something like this:

> **Woman #1:** *I live in real time.*
> **Man #1:** *I live in real time.*
> **Woman #2:** *In real time.*
> **Man #2:** *In real time.*
> **Woman #3:** *Real time.*
> **Man #3:** *Real time.*
> **Woman #4:** *I live in…real time.*
> **Man #4:** *I want my internet to be in real time.*
> **Woman #4:** *I want my internet to be in real time…*

Okay, okay, we get it! Ads like this are annoying enough the first time you watch it, let alone after repeated viewing.

Note: the same rule applies to over repeating the product name, too.

Topping and Tailing

This is when a TV ad works in two sections or halves (of any length), usually broadcast close together during the same ad break—one toward the beginning (top) and one toward the end (tail). Hence "topping and tailing." The first ad acts like a teaser, which may or may not make much sense until the second half of the ad is shown. Its abrupt, logo-free ending strongly hints at a "to be continued…" (Note: this technique is not the same as ongoing "soap opera-style" campaigns that can extend the storyline over years rather than minutes.)

Sometimes the ad can have more than two parts, like a TV version of consecutive print ads. If there's a strategic or conceptual reason why you want to do this, even better. A perfect execution of this technique was done at Ogilvy, London. One of their media people in charge of buying airtime for Ford noticed that the first television broadcast of "Groundhog Day" was due to air in a few weeks. Rather than just showing their current Ford Mondeo commercial *once* (the ad showed people going on a surfing trip), he had the idea to repeat it intermittently throughout each ad break. Resourcefully, the creative team kept the visual part the same and changed the audio by simply rewriting each character's lines to show their (increasingly amusing) reactions to being stuck in a "Groundhog Day" of their own.

The End Frame

The end frame can be a simple cut away to a blank screen with the tagline and logo neatly centered (voice over optional). But don't stop there. Try being more creative with the end frame. Maybe the tag could be typeset or written on an object that was previously in the script, or something that relates to the idea. Or if the script has oranges in it, perhaps the type can be made out of orange peel. If it doesn't work, don't use it—but at least you tried it.

Art directing the tag/type and logo in an interesting, "relevant to the script" way can put the final touch on your commercial. It's effectively a mini idea within a larger one. One TV campaign that uses this tool is MasterCard. For each and every spot the creators manage to find a simple, clever way to animate two circular objects (that relate to the theme of the each ad) into the orange and yellow MasterCard "circles," e.g., two swinging dog tags. Similarly, director Tony Kaye ended the "Unexpected" Dunlop commercial with close ups of the lettering on the side of the tire—not just the brand name, but the entire tagline ("Tested for the unexpected. Dunlop"). This also helped remind consumers what the ad was for.

When I created a cinema campaign for Guide Dogs for the Blind, I assumed that we'd use the standard charity end frame approach—white type on a black background. Instead, a post-production designer created an end frame that showed a person's hand "reading" braille. As the fingers passed over the letters, the tagline appeared as real type. It was a simple, clever, and relevant way to give the ads some visual branding, which helped to make the campaign more memorable (see overleaf).

Titling Your Script

Avoid the temptation to rush the title of your TV (or radio) script. Titles may seem relatively trivial, but they can be important for various reasons.

The end frame can be more interesting than a blank screen with type. Here, a hand moves across braille to reveal the tagline. (Story: man repeatedly calls out name in a park. Dog is then seen chewing man's white stick.) *Client: The Guide Dogs for the Blind Association. **Agency:** Ogilvy, London. **Creatives:** Pete Barry, Sally Evans.*

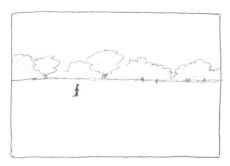

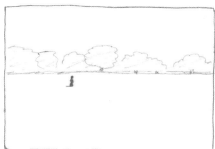

GUIDE DOGS AREN'T BORN.

THEY'RE TRAINED.

Please make a donation

Firstly, it gives the script an identity. Naturally, the title is what everyone will start referring to your idea by (whether it's "Cog" or "Grrr" or whatever), so keep it short and avoid potentially annoying, stupid names. Rarely will you need to be creative with titles, like Guinness's "noitulovE" (Evolution spelt backwards).

Secondly, people usually read or present the title before reading the script, so make sure it doesn't give anything away, especially if there's an unexpected twist at the end of the commercial. (If the key to your idea is a banana in the final frame, don't call the script "Banana." Call it something else. In fact, anything would be better than "Banana.") Thirdly, the title can actually help to sell a script. If the title can refer to the proposition in some way, it cleverly reinforces the fact that the idea is "on strategy." Or, give it a title that will appeal to the client. Something that *elevates* the product. (I once worked on a script about a man confined to a hospital bed. Alone, and with every limb in plaster, we watch him desperately eye up a bowl of delicious strawberries and cream, which have been left in front of him. The idea was for a brand of cream, and the script was quickly titled, "Bed." Weeks of research groups had rejected a dozen previous script ideas and the client was getting anxious. "Bed" was becoming our last hope. Seconds before it went off to the client, my group creative director changed the title from "Bed" to "Torture." It was a stroke of genius. Suddenly the product was the hero; it made the cream really appetizing. The research groups also picked up on this, the script was sold, and the commercial was made.)

TV Guidelines
Every TV script has to be sent to government "authorities" to see if it complies with the current local or national codes and guidelines. (The UK's main ruling body is called the ICC.) Some corporations even have their own personal set of advertising guidelines, and they decide what can or cannot be said or shown. The rules are not universal. What is allowed in one country may or may not be allowed in another, and vice versa. It's not just obvious stuff like swearing and nudity, either. In the US, you can show people toasting with a beer, but not drinking it. Other countries don't allow you to show a child under a certain age eating candy or chocolate. In other markets, teenagers can't be seen eating apart from their

family, for danger of promoting eating disorders. This can be problematic if the ad is planning to air multi nationally, or if your script relies on these situations. These hurdles are something that need not concern you until you're working at an agency. But when you do, such rules and regulations can haunt you, to the point where an entire script can be killed as a result. (And it's always your favorite one in the campaign!) Suddenly scriptwriting becomes a game of how to write in a clever way that keeps the authorities happy, whilst keeping your script alive with the idea intact. A knowledgeable agency producer can advise on any "red flags" early.

Sometimes you can use these rules to your advantage. In the US, it's acceptable to say that your product or service is "the best." But this is not allowed in the UK. Carlsberg beer took a dig at this rule when it created the famous sardonic tagline: Carlsberg. Probably the best lager in the world (see also No "Best," page 34).

Rules change over time, either to reflect the current topics of political correctness, or because of the increasing non-acceptance of product "over claims." The Mars chocolate bar tagline in the UK was for many years: "A Mars a day helps you work, rest and play." This line, which was inspired by the old-fashioned saying, "an apple a day keeps the doctor away," had to be dropped eventually because the product claim could not be proven.

One universal conundrum is this script scenario: when someone in an ad is seen to be hurt (not a paper cut, but enough to cause death), you must somehow show that the person is still alive by the end of the commercial. There are ways around this, like a simple sound effect of the person groaning, or a close-up cut back that shows he or she is clearly moving. One series of ads that ignored this (and got away with it) was the Fox Sports "Local Sports" campaign. These ads had a series of people from other countries performing bizarre yet deadly "local" sports: cliff diving, tree grabbing, blindfold clubbing, etc. As hilarious as these slapstick spots were, the people were clearly left for dead. When I asked one its creators, Taras Wayner, how they got the commercial to run, he said that it only ran on its own channel (Fox) that has its own rules, and thereby avoided anyone else's. (Clever)

The Best Ever Spots

In the UK, the Abbott Mead Vickers BBDO's "Surfer" ad for Guinness was voted as the Best TV Ad of the Millennium. The *Guardian*'s "Points of View" was once voted as the "greatest ad ever." In the US, DDB's "Funeral" spot for the VW Beetle is often considered the #1 TV ad of all time.

And the winner of *Creativity* magazine's Best Spot of the Last 20 Years (1985–2005) was TBWA/Chiat/Day's "Crazy Ones" for Apple. (Note the similarities between these three timeless spots: beautifully crafted voice over combined with simple action and appropriate music to express a clear message, see overleaf.)

The Future of TV Advertising

Because of inventions for DVRs such as TiVo® and other PVRs, it's become a lot easier for consumers to skip the commercials. This has, and will continue to have, a considerable impact on TV advertising, and the industry in general. According to Craig Davis, "We need to stop interrupting what people are interested in and *be* what people are interested in."

The challenge is finding out what that is. Newer media such as Interactive Television certainly has the potential to do this, with the thinking being: great, now we've got your interest, we want to keep you engaged.

Traditionalists still believe in conventional TV advertising, arguing that perhaps what's really needed is better quality, more financially successful commercials. And the notion that the consumer is expected to come to (and sometimes even seek out) the communication is perverted. Futurists would firstly argue that perhaps these critics have yet to be the "victim" of clever new media targeting, and secondly, that today's consumer seems happy to be at the brand helm: not just being entertained, but being part of the entertainment.

Either way, television programs will always exist, and with it some form of viewing device. So in the meantime, shows remain heavily dependent on advertising, and vice versa. (Even the Super Bowl's airtime fees continue to increase each year.) Plus, cinema advertising remains uncut, and since you can't very easily "TiVo" a magazine, print advertising can also breath a sigh of relief.

Things change—including advertising, which will continue to invent, reinvent, and integrate new forms of media (discussed in more detail in the Ambient and Interactive chapters). But if there's one industry that should be able to adjust to any kind of change, it's the ad industry. It just means being a bit more creative....

"Funeral" is considered by many to be America's greatest ever commercial. *Client: Volkswagen.* *Agency: DDB.* *Creatives: Roy Grace, John Noble.*

Including John Lennon, here's to the crazy ones. *Creativity* magazine's best spot of 1985–2005. *Client: Apple.* *Agency: TBWA/Chiat/Day.* *Creatives: Lee Clow, Craig Tanimoto, Ken Segall, Rob Siltanen, Jennifer Golub, Yvonne Smith, Steve Jobs.*

Title: "Funeral"
Client: Volkswagen
Length: 60 seconds

We open on a procession of cars driving to a funeral.

VO: I, Maxwell E. Snaberly, being of sound mind and body, do hereby bequeath the following:

To my wife Rose, who spent money like there was no tomorrow, I leave one hundred dollars and a calendar.

To my sons Rodney and Victor, who spent every dime I gave them on fancy cars and fast women, I leave fifty dollars in dimes.

To my business partner Jules, whose only motto was "spend, spend, spend," I leave nothing, nothing, nothing.

And to my other friends and relatives who also never learned the value of a dollar, I leave a dollar.

We then cut to a man driving a VW Beetle. He is sobbing.

VO: Finally to my nephew Harold, who oft times said, "A penny saved is a penny earned," and who also oft times said, "Gee Uncle Max, it sure pays to own a Volkswagen," I leave my entire fortune of one hundred billion dollars.

Title: "Crazy Ones"
Client: Apple
Length: 60 seconds

We open on slow motion, black-and-white footage of various individuals, including Albert Einstein, Bob Dylan, Dr. Martin Luther King, Jr., John Lennon, Muhammad Ali, Ted Turner, Gandhi, Amelia Earhart, Alfred Hitchcock, Jim Henson, and Pablo Picasso.

MVO: Here's to the crazy ones. The misfits. The rebels. The troublemakers. The round pegs in the square holes. The ones who see things differently.

They're not fond of rules. And they have no respect for the status quo.

You can quote them, disagree with them, glorify or vilify them. About the only thing you can't do is ignore them.

Because they change things. They push the human race forward.

And while some see them as the crazy ones, we see genius. Because the people who are crazy enough to think they can change the world, are the ones who do.

We cut to the face of a young girl as she opens her eyes.

SUPER: Think different.

SUPER: Apple logo.

08 Ambient

The word *ambient* literally means "in the immediately surrounding area." By strict definition, therefore, ambient media ideas appear near or at the point of purchase. But as ambient has evolved, it (less strictly) refers to those ideas that appear in unexpected places—the most aggressive, invasive and elaborate of which is guerrilla advertising (also known as, or part of, guerrilla marketing or guerrilla tactics), which are executed with or without permission.

Forms of ambient and guerrilla are becoming increasingly blurred, even including a PR/creative stunt or a live event. (Guerrilla has been divided into various groups according to their approach: stunts, street propaganda, sneaky tactics, site-specific campaigns and multi-fronted attacks.*)

Therefore, one could easily include "unexpected" online viral marketing that is "spread" (forwarded and shared) among friends, family, colleagues, and even strangers. Viral succeeds in part by appearing closer to those ideal points of purchase that "offline" ambient ads cannot reach. However, because viral has clearly become its own thing, this chapter will focus on the latter, offline forms of ambient media. And as with all forms of media, no matter how it's executed, a good idea is what matters most. (For digital/online advertising, see the Interactive chapter.)

"Under the radar" is another term that is sometimes used for ambient media. Its name refers to its ability to target its message to a relatively wide-reaching, often unsuspecting audience, as a different way to get under their "ad radar." And because of its non-traditional approach, ambient media is sometimes referred to as "alternative, unconventional, or non-traditional media." Ambient and guerrilla concepts also make up what is currently known as "innovative marketing."

Ambient media has grown considerably in recent years. This is due to a number of reasons: the industry's increasing need to find new ways of reaching tough, evasive consumers; the medium's potential to grab these consumers "by surprise" is becoming more realized; and the actual concepts are evolving, becoming more creatively sophisticated as time goes by. As a result, ambient media is now regarded as a legitimate and effective medium—by agencies, clients, and advertising award shows alike.

*Taken from *Guerrilla Advertising* by Gavin Lucas and Michael Dorrian. (Note: Guerrilla can be spelt with one or two r's.)

Effective Ambient Concepts

The most successful ambient concepts are arguably the ones that are:

Simple
Approach an ambient concept like you would any other—keep it simple.

Original
Avoid the tendency to think in terms of what's already been done (in what is still a relatively "immature" medium). Like most traditional print, TV, and radio ads, ambient ideas are rarely great. There are many possibilities for innovative ideas. In fact, the opportunities for creating new ambient concepts are unlimited, so unless your idea for an ad above a men's public urinal is really clever (I've seen dozens of stupid ones), try something fresh instead.

Cost Effective
The cheaper the concept, the more places you can put it, and therefore the greater the audience reach.

Flexible
Is it easy to produce? If your idea can only work within a limited or restricted location, or for a restricted or limited time period or audience, it may not be as effective.

Non-threatening
If the idea scares (or even irritates) people, it could damage your brand (unless perhaps they're not the target audience).

Practical
Some ideas may sound good on paper, but will it work in the real world? Is it logical (e.g., would a pizza delivery company really want to place a Tums antacid ad inside the box?)

Relevant
Like all media, don't just do wacky or shocking stunts unless it's relevant to the idea and the brand.

Interactive

Interactivity is not exclusive to online. Offline ambient ideas are interactive in the truest sense of the word, especially the ones that are hard to ignore. Although one might argue that online guerrilla is better at targeting a consumer, there is a unique physical, mental, and emotional interaction within offline ambient ideas that you don't get with online approaches.

Legal

Remember the age-old warning for fly posters—Bills Will Be Prosecuted.

Always try to push the creative boundaries, but just try not to get sued in the process.

It helps if your idea is temporary or removable (as in the case of *FHM*'s illuminated "billboard," which was briefly projected onto the Houses of Parliament in London to promote their "100 Sexiest Women" election).

Note: ambient media does not include printing out some pretty flyers and handing them out on a street corner. This approach (of basically handing out print ads) may be simple, cost effective, flexible, practical, relevant, mostly non-threatening, and legal, but unless the flyer is highly *original*, it just creates more mess on the ground (by those of you who actually bother to take one in the first place). That's why your ambient ideas should tick off literally all of the above points, without ticking off the consumer.

Using Other Media to Present Ambient Concepts

Guerrilla ads often have a serious message, for a "serious" product or service. The "Truth" anti-smoking work is a good example of this. What makes this work interesting is its decision to film the concepts and "performances" of, and reactions to, the ideas. Broadcasting them across the country creates a much greater, more cost-effective reach, and means that you only have to perform each stunt once. The fly-on-the-wall documentary style helps to give viewers the feeling of being there.

The "Truth" campaign has used traditional print media, as well as TV, to present their ambient ideas (as a way to increase audience reach and awareness even further). But bear in mind that ambient media is most powerful when it's in its *original form*. Think about it: which is more likely to make you notice or think about the homeless problem in your area—seeing a poster of someone looking at a homeless person, or actually seeing a homeless person yourself?

Types of Ambient Media

There are two basic types of non-line ambient media:

1. Using traditional media in an innovative and interesting way

Posters

Using traditional media in an innovative and interesting way. *Client: Wrangler. Product: Camouflage Jeans. Agency: The Martin Agency, Charlotte, NC.*

Using litmus paper immediately communicates the acid rain problem. Note the double meaning in the word "red" (as in "angry"). *Client: Friends of the Earth. Agency: McCann Erickson, London. Creatives: Roger Akerman, John Lewis.*

Rule-breaking teaser campaign for Araldite adhesive. **Client:** *Ciba Ceigy/Araldite.* **Agency:** *FCO.* **Creatives:** *Rob Kitchen, Robert Janowski, Ian Potter.*

Example of a "special build." Person walks underneath, and light bulb goes on. **Client:** *The Economist.* **Agency:** *Abbott Mead Vickers BBDO, London.* **Creatives:** *Paul Belford, Nigel Roberts.*

Clever use of a triptych poster, showing it frozen in one position to communicate "no spin." **Client:** *The Economist.* **Agency:** *Abbott Mead Vickers BBDO, London.* **Creatives:** *Tony Strong, Mike Durban.*

Press

A powerful use of a magazine spread (with the help of glue). Headline: If you have to use force, it's rape. **Client:** *POWA/People Opposing Women Abuse.* **Agency:** *Lowe Bull Calvert Pace, South Africa.* **Creatives:** *Xander Smith, Gareth Lessing.*

Pop-up: student ad for a quick-pitch tent.

Note: one could almost class these as "executional ideas," as outlined in the Generating Strategies and Ideas chapter. Award shows might also choose to categorize these types of ads not under "ambient," but under "innovative use of outdoor/press media," or simply amongst the other "posters" and "press" work.

2. Creating a new medium

As with any great advertising concept, all of these ideas are simple (with a simple line that demonstrate a simple proposition).

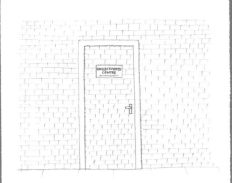

Creating a new medium: a series of strategically placed signs for a local mechanic. Headlines: Dodgy brakes?, Balding tyres?, Dicey steering? **Client:** *Peter Johnson, Station Garage.* **Creatives:** *Julie Hill, Mark Waldron.*

A doorframe and handle is fixed to an exterior brick wall. (I remember the creative team building this in their office.) **Client:** *London Karate Centre.* **Agency:** *Ogilvy, London.* **Creatives:** *Andrew Jolliffe, Paul Best.*

Handwritten (in the snow) guerrilla campaign for a beach vacation website. **Client:** *Sixt AG.* **Agency:** *Jung Von Matt/ Alster.* **Creatives:** *Hans Weishaupl, Peter Kirchhoff, Alexandra Marzoll.*

Two executions from a thought-provoking campaign. (Tagline: When you're homeless the world looks different.) **Client:** *The Miami Rescue Mission.* **Agency:** *Crispin Porter & Bogusky, Miami.* **Creatives:** *Alex Bogusky, Markham Cronin.*

Toilet humor: the entire script from the show is printed on the theater's loo roll. **Client:** *Jerry Springer: The Opera.*

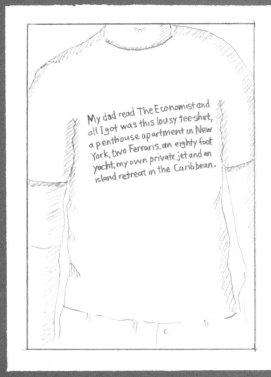

My dad read The Economist and all I got was this lousy tee-shirt, a penthouse apartment in New York, two Ferraris, an eighty foot yacht, my own private jet and an island retreat in the Caribbean.

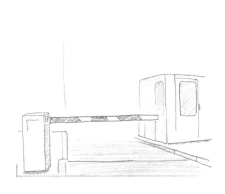

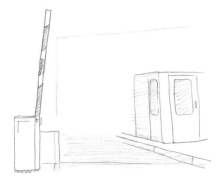

Top left Applying the exaggeration tool to The Economist readers' brainpower. *Client:* The Economist. *Agency:* HarrisonHuman Bates, South Africa. *Creatives:* Pete Englebrecht, Roanna Williams. *Creative director:* Gerry Human.

Top right Human billboard: a wonderful spoof on the cliché vacation gift. *Client: The Economist. Agency: Ogilvy & Mather, Singapore. Creatives: Simon Jenkins, Steve Hough, Kelly Dickenson, Naoki Ga, Richard Johnson, Craig Smith, Andy Greenaway.*

Above, left and above, right Viagra's product logo was placed on a parking lot barrier. *Client: Viagra. Student: Mariana Black.*

Ambient Awards

The Cannes International Advertising Festival awards recognize and accept the following types of ambient:

- Special/one-off build
- 3D
- Petrol pumps
- Washroom
- Floor media
- Ticket barriers
- Miscellaneous (e.g., napkins, coasters, glasses, "free" food packets, matchboxes, etc.)

The British D&AD awards list the following categories under "ambient":

- Live events
- PR and creative stunts
- Direct ambient

Note: some award shows include Ambient within "best use of outdoor media" (or vice versa), whilst others keep them separate.

Which Comes First—Concept or Client?

Ambient advertising, perhaps more than any other medium, allows you to—dare I say it—think outside the box. You are no longer confined to the two dimensions of print, or the time limits of TV.

As a student, you have the added flexibility of creating the idea first, and then finding the perfect client to fit your concept. In the real world, you usually start with the client, and then create the work. That doesn't necessarily mean it's any harder or easier to do; it's just different.

Look around you, and you'll find that there are many (untapped) sources of inspiration for great ambient ideas. A good place to start is with familiar, everyday objects. Simply keep asking yourself, "what could that object advertise?" A yellow taxi cab became a perfect vehicle (no pun intended) for a teeth-whitening product (overleaf).

Another good source of inspiration for ambient ideas is places and locations. A student once sat on some steps and came up with the idea of using them for Alcoholics Anonymous's "12 Step Program" (overleaf). A mirrored changing room in a clothing store became an ideal place to target would-be nudists (overleaf). Another student wondered what would happen if the male and female restroom signs came together.

The result was an award-winning ad for match.com (overleaf).

If you are working with a specific client in mind (i.e., client before concept) and you are finding it hard to generate ideas, it may help to think of a proposition to work from first (as you would any other brief). For example, one student chose to work on Red Bull energy drink (with energy being the clear product benefit). Her ideas began by simply thinking of places and things that have energy or power. The solution: electrical outlets (overleaf).

Again, what makes all these ideas great is the fact that they are simple, original, cost effective, non-threatening, flexible, practical, and relevant.

....

Exercise: pick *any* five products or services and create as many original ambient ideas as you can. Try both types of ambient ideas, outlined above, but try to avoid obvious charity organizations, or condom ads in toilets, etc.

....

Near right A trip to a clothes store was the inspiration behind this ad. (Headline: You're half way there already.) *Client: AANR/American Association for Nude Recreation.* **Student:** *Allison Baker.*

Below A yellow taxi with a white door effectively demonstrates a teeth-whitening product. *Client: Crest Whitestrips.* **Student:** *Jason Ziehm.*

Far right This idea came to a student while sitting on some campus steps. (Headline: The first step is calling 212 870-3400.) *Client: Alcoholics Anonymous.* **Student:** *Mike Pudim.*

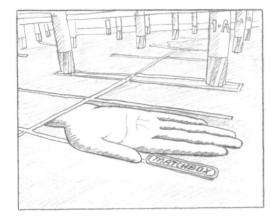

Top Playing with scale. Giant (palm-up) hand stickers were placed in parking spaces at toy stores. *Client: Mattel. **Agency:** Ogilvy & Mather, Mexico.*

Above Ambient ideas often come from looking at common things in a different way. Bringing the symbols for men's and women's toilets together produced this ad for a dating agency. *Client: Match.com. **Student:** Noah Phillips.*

Electrical outlets are the perfect place for an energy drink ad. *Client: Red Bull. **Student:** Lauren Tree.*

Campaign vs. One-Shot

Although many ambient ideas are one-shots, there's no reason why it can't be bigger than that. In fact, the greater the executions, the greater the impact.

Right and below Art as street art. London's National Gallery hung life-sized reproductions of famous paintings on the streets, giving the public a series of hard-to-ignore "tasters" from its permanent collection. *Client: National Gallery, London. Agency: The Partners, London. Creatives: Jim Prior, Greg Quinton, Jim Davis. Photographers: Matt Stuart, Brad Haynes.*

Opposite The "what goes around comes around" message used to describe the spiraling cycle of war is perfectly executed by a series of "pillar" posters. *Client: Global Coalition for Peace. Agency: Big Ant International. Creatives: Frank Anselmo, Alfred S. Park, Jeseok Yi, Francisco Hui, William Tran, Richard Wilde.*

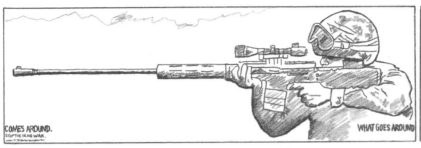

09 Interactive

What is "Interactive"?

Generally speaking, "interactive" media covers any advertising/design that has been created using digital technology (not to be confused with digital radio, digital TV, etc.) in which the communication demands some form of immediate and ongoing response. The term can also include interactive/innovative methods such as ambient media and other guerrilla tactics (for more information on these, see the Ambient chapter).

This chapter will focus on *digital* concepts, and the similarities/differences between digital and analog (or online and offline) based on digital media's current level of technology, and therefore sophistication.

Naturally, the term "digital" becomes interchangeable with terms such as "new media" (see What is New Media?, page 243) and "interactive advertising" is also a common term (see Interactive and Advertising: Two Different Things?, below). And when the focus is specific to websites (and related media), terms like "web," "internet," "online," "desktop," and "mobile" advertising are also used.

Note: one could argue that the term "interactive" is as old as advertising itself. Every ad (whether using traditional or non-traditional media) is on one level "interactive" in that it aims to engage the consumer for long enough to get a response or reaction, eventually leading to a sale. But since the birth of the internet in the late 1980s/early 1990s, the term pertains to non-traditional or digital media.

Interruptive Can Be Interactive

Not every form of traditional media is a purely interruptive, one-way communication. Before people "opened" emails, websites, or expandable banners, they opened envelopes. Or anything else the postal service would deliver. And, of course, people still do (or not, depending on how intriguing the piece of direct mail is). So whether your direct response idea appears in parcel or pixel form, the basic objective is the same: to create something that the receiver feels compelled to "learn more" about; to make the "opening" a worthwhile experience. Concluding, ideally, with a tangible response—whether it's a completed coupon, a subscription, or a product sample—thereby completing the second part of the two-way "conversation."

Interactive and Advertising: Two Different Things?

Many interactive creatives are keen to separate these disciplines, for two main reasons: they don't want to be associated with "old fashioned" traditional advertising and the two disciplines require two different schools of thought.

Some interactive ideas (and therefore executions) are essentially digital ads, e.g., banners. You could also argue that a website (although technically a design piece) is also an ad. So for the purposes of this chapter, I will also be focusing on interactive ideas/executions that take you somewhere further (e.g. a website), or to the final destination itself.

The bottom line is that both disciplines (interactive and advertising) perform the same basic task: to create ideas for brands (executed through various media) that make people like them more. And as the lines between the two continue to blur, the combined term "interactive advertising" will undoubtedly become more acceptable. P. J. Pereira puts it this way: "Online advertising is just the intersection of the interactive and advertising worlds." To avoid this debate altogether, an alternative term, "interactive marketing," can be used.

Currently, the world consumes almost 70% of its information digitally. And according to Teressa Iezzi, author of *The Idea Writers*, "Digital is not just another channel. Digital is how you live your life. If you think of digital as just another kind of advertising, you are missing almost all of its potential."

Online Advertising vs. Online Design

By this I mean the comparison between creating ads (design, copy, etc.) that go on the web vs. pure design/copy that makes up the web. Online (or web) advertising forms the bulk of interactive advertising. However, because of the merging disciplines of advertising and design, "interactive" often implies both forms, i.e., interactive advertising/design.

Interactive: Advantages Over Traditional

To summarize, the advantages are:

- More direct, engaging, and longer lasting than traditional media (a stronger bond between consumer and brand)
- Cost-effective (lower production and media costs; viral provides free advertising)
- Targets the younger, techie generation (and its increasing disposable income)
- Diverse (web can incorporate film, animation, photography, and illustration)
- Fewer legal restrictions than broadcast and print
- Open 24/7

It Starts and Ends with a Concept

As we know, traditional media has been around for many decades, whereas interactive media remains, to a large extent, pioneering territory. Yet the success of both (now and in the future) will depend on one thing: a good idea. The tendency is to fall into the same trap outlined at the very beginning of this book—style over substance, or execution over concept. Visual slickness might draw people in, but it won't keep them there. The key question is more important than ever: will your idea stand out? (See also Entertainment vs. Informational, page 200.)

The Consumer Control Era

Consumers have an unprecedented degree of control over their media environment, i.e., what media they consume, plus how and when they consume it. This consumer-controlled, on-demand, social, conversational world makes every company more transparent. Put simply, brands can't escape the consumer, even when they want to. People have the power to build/promote, demote, and even destroy a brand. As a result, as Kevin Roddy points out, "The age of transparency will keep brands more honest."

The Click Factor

The technology within interactive media creates two simple advantages over traditional: the speed and ease with which a consumer can consume.

It's not just digital that's "interactive." This recent analog example is a box wrapped in a white T-shirt (addressed and stamped in ink, plus heavily handled and dirtied en route) with a free sample of washing powder inside. Hence the concept name, "Torture Test." *Client:* Unilever, Thailand. *Brand:* Breeze Excel. *Agency:* Lowe, Bangkok. *Creatives:* Dominic Stallard, Clinton Manson.

Within seconds, a consumer can react to a communication message and even purchase a product (the advertising objective for the majority of clients, known universally as e-commerce). It might not always be as easy as expecting someone to click on a banner and immediately buy the product, which is why marketers will reach buyers at different stages of the buying cycle, or use online to complement their offline advertising—now and in the future. This is part of what's known as Relationship Marketing, or RM.

Again, websites have also helped to speed up the process for traditional, too: you see an ad with a web address, you go online to find out more, sign up for something, or perhaps complete the sale with a purchase.

Broadcast media (first radio, and then TV) made the world seem smaller. The web, web-based applications, and its related technology, has done the same—and then some. One could say it's a www.evensmallerworld.com. But its real power goes beyond "reach." Its uniqueness lies in its ability to deliver intimate experiences to consumers in a highly targeted and sensitive way. The consumer is much like a hummingbird—a picky, tricky creature who has the ability to except or reject the things that do or do not interest it (the hummingbird will only consume nectar that has the right level

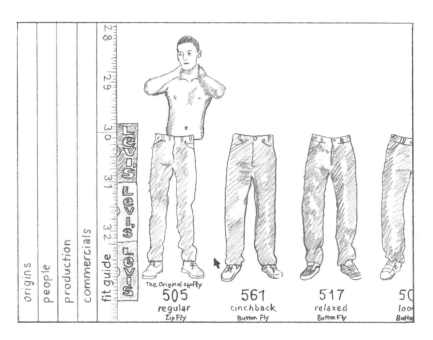

An early, yet ground-breaking example of how interactive can customize online shopping. *Client: Levi's.* *Agency: Antirom.* *Creatives: Nicolas Roope, Tomas Roope, Sophie Pendrell.*

of sweetness). Technology is an integral part of the entire process. It helps to inform a brand about what people are doing and where they are doing it. From this data a key insight into consumer behavior can be extracted and used to create an idea. Technology can (and often will) be incorporated to execute this idea, in the hope that the right consumer will engage with it, and share it with other like-minded "hummingbirds" via their own tech devices.

Customizing the Experience

The key to most of the successful interactive applications is therefore to customize the experience: to make it feel tailor made. The more options a user is given, the more personal and intimate the experience will be. Ultimately this makes the consumer feel like they are in control, rather than being (or at least trying to be) controlled (see The Self Sell, page 194).

A Brand New Relationship

For many, the difference between traditional advertising and interactive lies in the relationship between the consumer and the media itself. Traditionally, people don't *use* an ad, but they do *use* the internet. A traditional ad is usually always an intrusion, e.g., interrupting a TV or radio show, or a newspaper/magazine article. It communicates to the individual consumer but in one direction,

whereas interactive, as its name implies, is designed not only to get a response from the consumer, but also for him/her to become part of the message and experience. It's an invitation rather than an interruption: a two-way relationship. A common phrase that sums up the added value of interactive is: *tell someone and they'll forget, show them and they'll remember, involve someone and they'll understand.*

Therefore, you have to make people *want* to interact. It has to be relevant to them. This is especially true with cases such as banners and pop-ups, which are highly intrusive. Any method (no matter how interruptive) might be able to locate the consumer initially (for example, through research geo-location, or memory-based targeting), but from that point on the consumer is free to choose whether or not to take "the relationship" further. The real test of an idea is to make it consistently engaging, from beginning to end: to create an ongoing dialogue. Once the final connection has been made, businesses can easily keep in touch with customers through newsletters, chat (IM), and promotions on their websites. Because of all these unique relationship properties, one might argue that interactive is more than a type of mass media—it's a culture, made up of many communities.

The "Gray or Gorgeous?" Dove campaign for real beauty is an integrated campaign, but with an interactive piece at its heart. Part of the website asks women for their point of view on different aspects of beauty, thereby debunking any stereotypes in exchange for a wider, more refreshing view. Its creators believe this allows the consumer to "own" the brand as much as Dove does (www.campaignforrealbeauty.com).

Create an Ongoing Experience

Ajaz Ahmed, co-founder of AKQA, believes: "The key word is 'experience'—to engage fully with a brand, consumers today expect a healthy new dialogue that enables them to converse easily with an organization, and the ecosystem that supports it. Social media offers a new level of flexibility, interaction, and engagement."

Tom Himpe, author of *Advertising Next*, makes this keen observation: "While traditional advertising is essentially about buying time, online exposure is about creating it." For Himpe, the marketing end game has transcended reach, or just grabbing eyeballs—it has become a matter of engagement, of inviting a conversation and

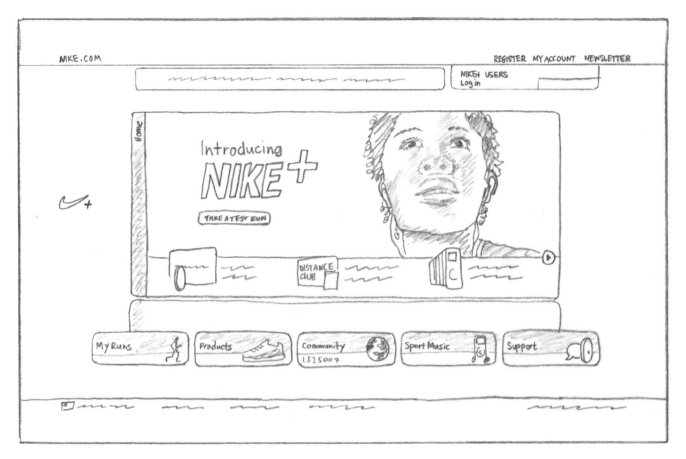

NIKE.COM

REGISTER MY ACCOUNT NEWSLETTER

NIKE+ USERS
Log in

HOME

Introducing
NIKE+

TAKE A TEST RUN

DISTANCE
CLUB

My Runs

Products

Community
1525007

Sport Music

Support

campaignforrealbeauty | Dove

what do you think?

☐ gray?
2752 votes

☑ gorgeous?
10570 votes

› Invite a Friend

www.nikeplus.com. Creativity meets technology in a multi-sensory, intersecting brand experience for Nike and Apple. And it began as a product idea (a piece of kit you put in your shoe to track running data). *Client: Nike. Agency: R/GA.*

www.campaignforrealbeauty.com: this integrated campaign is a perfect fit for interactive, asking women for their point of view on different aspects of beauty. *Client: Dove. Agency: Ogilvy, London. Creatives: Joerg Herzog, Dennis Lewis.*

Interactive • 193

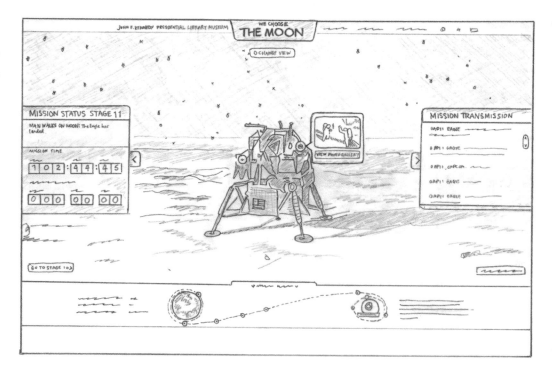

Re-experiencing an experience at wechoosethemoon.com. The agency's assignment: return to the moon and take the world with them. *Client: The John F. Kennedy Presidential Library and Museum. Agency: The Martin Agency, Richmond. Creatives: Wade Alger, Brian Williams.*

making it a meaningful, ongoing connection. Fortunately (or perhaps unfortunately), we're in a world that never sleeps, so it makes sense that people expect brands to be awake 24/7 also. This constantly changing, never-ending communication creates a permanent interactive experience between brand and audience.

There's nothing more ongoing or continuous than time itself, which is part of the idea behind the Uniqlo "Uniqlock" campaign on page 216. Meanwhile, the Martin Agency's "We Choose the Moon" campaign allowed us to re-experience a monumental moment in time, shown above.

The Self Sell

Over time, in response to the increasingly skeptical consumer who "doesn't like being sold to," the traditional hard sell has gradually been joined by the soft sell. And now with interactive, one could almost call the approach a "self sell." Rather than always being told what to buy, consumers are increasingly making their own choices.

Interactive allows the user to play, investigate, navigate, explore, and share as they go. To ensure that consumers are receiving the correct initial "pieces of cheese" (and therefore not always exploring blindly), the targeting technology has had to become more sophisticated. This includes

the introduction of compulsory registration of certain sites (free or otherwise). The information is then used to track and target the consumer for products that are most likely to interest them.

Personalization: Relevant vs. Private

As Himpe explains, "It's as annoying to receive a blunt, anonymous message that does not seem to acknowledge you as an individual as it is to feel a brand is invading your privacy through an overtly personal message that you haven't asked for."

So how do brands that want to be increasingly relevant to each consumer do so without reducing the consumer's privacy?

The right balance is achieved through personalization (i.e., leaving it up to customers to personalize the message or product on their own terms). Message personalization includes: adding a picture, or text, or a spoken message to some online content; or changing the sequence or music of a video. Product personalization includes: adding or changing the functionalities of a core product; or building a custom product from scratch.

According to Himpe, "personalization tactics should either enhance the entertainment value or relevance of the message or increase the usefulness of the product or service."

The Utility Factor. Or is it Useful?

Brand utility is the genuinely useful benefit that someone gets from a product or service, rather than just being told "this brand will make you do or feel or think [blank]." Particularly in the interactive field, the question brand marketers will ask is, "How can I be of use in the everyday life of the group of people I'm aiming at?" i.e., create real things that human beings care about and want to interact with and share with their friends, and therefore the world.

Pereira approaches it this way: "First, we find an idea that is interesting for the consumer where a brand can play some role, then we find the best way to include the product there somehow." The answer could be an app, a widget, an online service, or none of these things. What matters is the brand utility that is being provided.

Some of the best brand ideas are things that make people's lives easier or better. Fiat "eco:Drive" uses a computer application and an in-car USB port to mine driving data and calculate driver efficiency so that the system can recommend ways the owner can reduce fuel costs and carbon emissions.

So always ask yourself: "Is this creation adding something to someone's life? Would he or she enjoy using it?" It doesn't have to be a totally practical solution, either—useful can be entertaining and beautiful too.

Know Your Media, Know Your Audience

It's essential to understand your target market and how they use the web and digital technology. When deciding which media to include/exclude in the mix, according to Darren Giles and James Leigh from Glue, London, "Age is an important factor. Campaigns targeting younger audiences would probably include the use of mobile phone technology, a game, or viral."

Just as an aspiring screenwriter needs to read screenplays, in advertising (especially interactive) you must position yourself as a consumer. What better excuse do you need to go online or play with the latest technology?

Shake Things Up

Social media are not sacred. So have fun with them. Crispin Porter + Bogusky created the perfectly named "Whopper Sacrifice" for Burger King. It was a Facebook app that allowed users of the social network to defriend their "marginal" friends in favor of a coupon for the famous burger.

Facebook quickly shut it down, but by then an estimated 35 million media impressions had been generated.

Virtual Behavior Meets Actual Behavior

Some of the most compelling web campaigns have been rooted in real-life experience. For example, an outdoor interactive guerrilla idea can lead you back to a site to continue the experience. Or vice versa. These real-world gatherings of online groups or communities illustrate the crossover between online and offline socializing.

As Andreas Dahlqvist, Executive Creative Director of DDB, Stockholm, says: "There is a need to add 'realness' in an increasingly digitized world. It's about making digital tangible."

In a way, Augmented Reality is another example of real world meeting digital world (see page 214).

So as the line between digital and traditional, in full-service agencies, continues to fade, the "digital" prefix will soon disappear from most agencies. In the words of Pereira: "Stop thinking about digital as a separate thing. [Don't do] gimmickry. Don't do things because they're new but instead because they are meaningful and interesting."

And due to the reduction in consumers' attention spans and information overload, it's more important than ever to be quick, interesting, and true.

Awards Categories

One Show Interactive, which began in 1998, was the first awards program to recognize creative excellence for advertising in new media, and now includes the following categories:

- Business to consumer (single and campaign)
- Business to business (B2B)
- E-commerce
- Public service/non-profit/educational
- Online
- Mobile
- New/experimental media innovation and development (e.g., installations)
- Other interactive digital media
- Integrated branding campaign*
- Websites (consumer/primary brand, business to business [B2B])

*"Advergames" (games derived from an ad campaign) are included in this category, e.g., Burger King's "Xbox Games" innovative campaign by Crispin Porter + Bogusky and Equity.

Meanwhile, to keep step with changing industries and new technologies, the British D&AD Global Awards divide its digital sector into numerous groups, to include the following categories:

- Online advertising (e.g., banners, interstitials, pop-ups, etc.)
- New uses of online advertising
- Websites and microsites
- CD/DVD-ROM design
- Mobile marketing
- Viral
  – viral films/commercials (webisodes)
  – interactive virals (e.g., viral games)
  – new uses of viral
- Gaming
  – massively multiplayer online games (MMOGs)
  – online games
  – mobile/cell phone games
  – console games
  – handheld games
  – PC games
- Digital advertising campaigns (e.g., a combined microsite, online advertisement, branded online game, and digital kiosk)
- Digital installations

The Interactive Team
Prior to interactive, there was the conventional "creative" copywriter and art director (CW/AD) team working alongside traditional account strategists/planners, account managers, and agency producers. Post interactive-age, copywriters and art directors will also collaborate with a:

- Digital strategist (S&A)
- Media/communications planner
- Creative technologist
- Information architect (IA)
- Interaction designer
- Flash designer
- Motion graphics designer

"The greatest ideas always come not from a single source but from a combination of sources," says Pereira, with a new, key question for the interactive team being: "Can this idea physically be done?"

Jeff Benjamin, former head creative at Crispin Porter + Bogusky believes that, "A technologist is as creative, in a way, as a writer." With "Subservient Chicken," (see page 199) media was part of the idea—an example of how digital campaigns blur the lines between creativity, production, and technology.

Craft Skills
Interactive is not just about technology—the craft skills below should be considered when creating and executing creative interactive work:

- Art direction
- Writing
- Sound design
- Use of music
- Animation and motion graphics
- Interface and navigation
- Illustration
- Typography
- Photography
- Graphic design
- Film direction
- Cinematography
- Special effects

The Interactive Writer
On this subject Iezzi points out: "The web isn't just another channel through which ads can be distributed…writers should think first about ideas, not media-specific ads…digital permeates everything a brand and, by extension, a writer does."

Leo Premutico of agency Johannes Leonardo believes that "the best writing has always been interactive in nature, in the sense that you leave it to the audience to complete the story, and contribute their imagination."

Nowadays we have a chance to react and adjust to a conversation. Ty Montague, Founder and Co CEO at Co Collective, sees it as "a live piece of theater in that if you see the audience is not responding or is getting bored, you have to respond and improvise on the fly…it's a living thing that requires ongoing curation and involvement on the part of storytellers and participants." So keep the intrigue going by making the audience interact with the story while it's being pieced together—and vice versa.

How do you this? Benjamin believes "copywriting in the digital world is not just about beautiful copy, but it's about how people speak; being a master of language."

To this point, Guy Barnett, co-founder of The Brooklyn Brothers adds: "Your choice of phrasing and syntax needs to be that much more nimble and unusual... The role of the writer is more vital than ever because people read more than ever." As advertising legend Howard Luck Gossage once wrote, "Nobody reads ads. People read what interests them, and sometimes it's an ad." Or it's a tweet, a blog, a post, or any other form of social media content.

Roles of a Post-Digital Copywriter

- Collaborator
- Content writer
- Conversation keeper/curator
- Copywriter
- Idea generator
- Inventor
- Social media developer
- Sociologist
- Storyteller
- Tech appreciator
- Utilitarian

Today's copywriter has an incredible opportunity to push brand narrative to interactive, dynamic places.

Social media allows for a two-way conversation, meaning that you can actually converse instead of pitch or "copywrite." Nicke Bergstrom, Co-founder and Creative Director of Farfar, compares it to going on a date: "If all you were doing was talking and not allowing the other person to say anything, [it] wouldn't be very successful."

Copy guru Joel Kaplan gives this advice: "Look around at what's going on in the real world, what conversations are happening, what trends are going on, what people are talking about and where they're talking about it. And try to find a way that [the] product or company can have a voice in that conversation. [That way] people don't feel like you're showing them an ad. They feel like they're having a conversation. And if they like that conversation, they like that brand."

Writing for the Web: Non-Linear

By this I mean writing copy for a website as opposed to writing ads that live on the web. Thanks to the dramatic increase in websites, blogs, and other digital platforms, creative writing (and writers) continue to boom. Although many of the copywriting tools outlined throughout this book (in particular in the Copy chapter)

can be transferred from print to digital form, because of the fundamental difference in the way consumers read web-based copy, there are some new tools to apply. Many copywriters who are new to interactive think that they can simply drop in the same type of body copy created for print. This doesn't always work (except for short-form digital ads such as banners). The reality is that digital copywriters are closer to information architects than masters of the "invisible thread" (see page 219). The main reason for this is that web copy is not linear or sequential, i.e., consumers require more than one path to information during their search. They don't want (or need) to read lots of long, flowing copy. And scrolling loses visitors. Therefore, any body text is generally kept in concise, bulletproof form, depending on where the copy is being read, sometimes resulting in necessary overlap and repetition. Above all, make each site easy to read, navigate, and understand.

The Brand Story's Back Story

Tom Himpe recognizes that "new tools for [brand] storytelling are gaining ground. New, more immersive media are giving brands the opportunity to convey stories with a level of complexity and depth previously unimaginable."

Part of this process is creating a "back story." This behind-the-scenes writing is equivalent to that used in the development of a screenplay, but for a brand campaign instead of a movie. It's the writing people feel, but don't get to see—a set of guidelines or parameters that help the agency and client define the brand story and, for the audience, the rules of engagement.

The Viral Effect: Free Advertising

The web has obviously made it easier to pass on links and files. Therefore, any online advertising can ultimately become viral (contagious) media. Even the spread of a traditional yet popular TV, print, or radio ad acts as free advertising for client and agency alike. Common call-to-actions such as "send to a friend" serve as an additional prod. A viral hit can encourage enormous coverage, exposure, and goodwill. Standard online ads will only ever engage a percentage of visitors who visit the site on which they appear, while virals are not restricted by a website, and have the *potential* to reach millions around the world.

Viral: Questions and Ingredients

Before digital social media, there was a basic analog version (much like my "dog poop" poster example on page 9) which generally involved a lot more work. But the relative ease and popularity of digital social media has created a false sense of security amongst brand builders. They often assume that because an idea is shareable then people will automatically share it. Not so. Each idea should be, as the saying goes, "social by design." To that point, begin by asking yourself these simple questions:

What's the idea?
What is it telling me about the brand?
Why would people engage in, and share it?
What will someone get out of it?

Nick Moore, the head creative at Wunderman, New York, believes the question you should ask yourself isn't, "why would someone share this?," the question should be, "why wouldn't they?" And if there are no or few reasons why they wouldn't, you have a potentially solid social idea.

Therefore, you won't create anything viral unless the following goal is achieved: to have your message proactively talked about and shared by people—a mass recommendation. Just because someone says a concept is viral, it doesn't mean it will be. It's only viral in retrospect. The Viral Factory co-founder Ed Robinson outlines three fundamental questions before a good idea can be a viral idea:

1. Would anyone with no interest in this product care about the idea? It needs to hold a human truth that transcends what the agency or client thinks is good.
2. Is it new? There must be a hook that makes you want to explore and share.
3. Does it help express something on behalf of an audience in a way that they can't? It should help them articulate love, loss, hope, fear, or hope, etc., to their friends and family.

Go Viral, a "seeding" specialist, have identified seven key ingredients that determine whether a message will be passed on by people:

1. An immediately outstanding story
2. Stickiness (to what extent something sticks in people's minds)
3. Relevance

BMW Films "The Hire": a series of short, action-packed films proved that viral isn't limited to 30 seconds. *Client: BMW. Agency: Fallon Worldwide, London. Creatives: Kevin Flatt, Joe Sweet, Chuck Carlson.*

Better than a bottle. This site allows you to send personalized, mission-like messages to friends. Realistic sound effects enhance the virtual experience of being a naval officer. *Client: Royal Navy. Agency: Glue, London. Creatives: James Leigh, Darren Giles.*

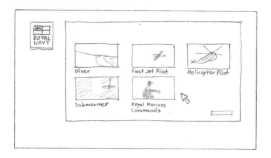

4. Portability (how free the idea is of physical, technical, and human barriers)
5. Shareability (how "network cementing" it is)
6. Timing/actuality
7. The hook (the one-liner that grabs your attention)

"Word of mouth" applications include, but are not limited to, the following three areas:

Viral Films vs. Viral Commercials

The fundamental difference between these alternative webisodes is duration. But with the relaxed variation of time lengths and branding levels (some heavily branded, some lightly) of both forms, and the ability to download bigger videos and audio files to various devices, the two are becoming virtually indistinguishable. Viral videos can be produced by practically anyone. But as an ad student, don't just produce a funny or shocking video for the sake of it. What's the benefit? What's the idea? Would someone really want to share it? At least think about how you can attach a relevant product or piece of branding to your idea so that it becomes something more meaningful and less gratuitous.

Websites vs. Microsites

Websites refer to the main website for a brand. Microsites (or mini-sites) refer to sites that are specific to a single message or campaign and are therefore separate from the main website. However, sometimes successful microsites become the main brand website.

A site can be an ad in itself. So can email. Try to create a website that makes consumers want to enter their email so they can be targeted again via subscription (until they choose to unsubscribe). Better yet, create something on a brand site that encourages a consumer to forward an email to their friends. (See Personalization: Relevant vs. Private, page 194.)

"Creative" Blogs

Whether text only or audio/video blogs (v-blogs), many amateur blogs have blossomed into powerful, highly influential message boards. Along with other phenomena such as YouTube, MySpace, and Wikipedia, the blogging phenomena convinced *Time* magazine to choose *you* as their unusual Person of the Year in 2006. Meanwhile, some awards shows are even open to blog submissions.

One of the biggest questions facing interactive agencies today is how brands can effectively tap into this new era where everyone is a broadcaster.

Types of Website

In terms of *content*, a website can be information/education-based, entertainment-based (e.g., a branded game), or both. In terms of *category*, a site can be one or more of the following:

- Brand awareness site (represents an entire brand or sub-brand)
- Microsite (has a concept-specific theme and "vanity" URL)
- Teaser site (for a teaser campaign, including a "vanity" URL)
- Product/service site (a site that is the product, e.g., Nike+)
- Promotional site (offer-specific)
- Unbranded site (semi-stealthily created by a brand, e.g., a pharmaceutical company's site that provides general awareness and information about a condition and the treatment options, rather than promoting one of their specific drugs)

....

Exercise: pick your five favorite websites and categorize them using the list above. (Note: some may fall into multiple categories.)

....

www.subservientchicken.com: type in a command and the chicken will gladly respond. A simple, fun idea that comes directly from Burger King's "Have It Your Way" product message. *Client: Burger King. Agency: Crispin Porter + Bogusky, The Barbarian Group. Creatives: Mark Taylor, Bob Cianfrone.*

Get chicken the way you like it. Type in your command here.   SUBMIT

Entertainment vs. Informational

Broadly speaking, there are three types of interactive concepts: entertainment-driven, information-driven, and some combination of the two. One might argue that the latter is the most desirable, in the same way that any ad should be both critically and commercially successful. In the latter case, the key is for the entertainment part to have an interesting, relevant concept that draws the consumer in, followed by interesting, relevant product information to keep them interested, and in some cases make a sale. In other words, entertainment is not enough. Just as there is good-simple and bad-simple (see page 19), whereby you shouldn't make an ad so simple that it's boring, you shouldn't make it gratuitously entertaining either: there should always be some sort of interesting message, benefit, or takeout for the consumer.

One might also argue that any successful interactive idea will also become informational in the sense that the "information" will potentially be shared amongst billions of users—colleagues, family members, and friends. This viral work includes a variety of entertainment and/or information-driven communication, either pre-produced by an agency or self-produced in the form of blogs, chat rooms, etc.

In the past, marketers have viewed interactive as entertainment-focused concepts for teenage consumers with shorter attention spans. But as older generations continue to adopt the latest technologies, they too will continue to benefit from the availability of information-driven communication (whether for consumer purchases, general interest and hobbies, or scholarly and educational research purposes), entertainment-driven communication, or some combination of both.

Arguably the most famous example of interactive entertainment is "Subservient Chicken," www.subservientchicken.com, by Crispin Porter + Bogusky and The Barbarian Group (see page 199). Pros: 396 million hits in first year and reached a younger generation. Cons: some people debate its commercial success, while others added that perhaps KFC would have been a more fitting brand (do people think of Burger King for a non-beef/chicken burger?) Perhaps, but the concept comes from Burger King's unique "Have It Your Way" brand message, rephrased in the command: "Get chicken just the way you like it. Type in your command here." It's fair to say that few web applications in the past decade have been as successful in demonstrating the power of viral while helping to boost a brand.

Legitimate vs. Illegitimate

Legitimate forms of online include search-engine advertising, desktop advertising, online advertising directories, advertising networks, and opt-in email advertising. The illegitimate side includes spamming (the digital equivalent of "junk [direct] mail").

Interruptive Methods
Banners

Banner ads are often loathed by consumers, but loved by companies because you can measure in real time just how effective each one is, even down to the choice of visual or copy. A good banner ad has a click-through rate (percentage of times people click on it and then go to the website) of 1%. A great banner ad will have a 2% rate or higher.

An interactive banner, as opposed to a simple "flag waiver." *Client:* Hewlett-Packard. ***Agency:*** *Goodby, Silverstein & Partners, San Francisco.* ***Creatives:*** *Jeff Benjamin, Rick Casteel, Will Elliot, John Matejczyk.*

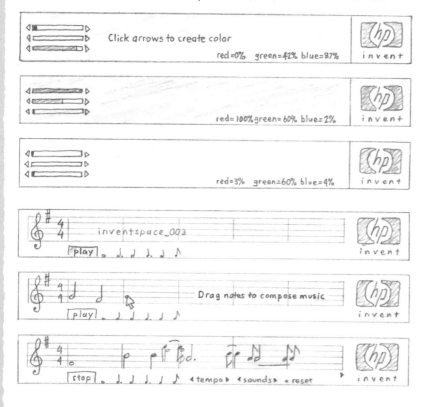

In terms of concept, there are two main types of banners. The first is merely a "flag waiver" that provides a quick link to another "landing" site or application, while the second is more interactive in nature (e.g., Hewlett-Packard "Invent" banner campaign). In both instances, keep it simple. Banners are like billboards in that you don't have time to tell a long story. Fortunately, the tough stuff to communicate can always be done elsewhere (or in deeper applications within the banner) once the user's attention has been attracted. This is also where the copy that you don't have room for in the banner can live.

In terms of the memory (measured in K) and size of banner ads, there are two main types: Standard Banner ads (STDs) and Rich Banner ads. STDs are usually produced in Flash, take up only 30K in memory, and run for up to 15 seconds (although depending on the media buy, it is possible to "loop" any animated banner). Rich banners are usually over 100K/30 seconds, and often squarer in shape. These can be videos, clickable demos, or anything else, provided they don't require the size and space of an actual website.

Memory size is important because K is the measurement in which digital media is bought and sold (just as broadcast is measured in seconds and print media is measured in size and color, amongst other things). Some universal banner sizes (height × length) shown in the boxes to the right.

The banner ad has become the standard unit of the online medium, mostly because it showed the creative possibilities of something (on the surface) so basic. Its usage may have shrunk, but its format has evolved from its 468 × 60 rectangular roots to include the supersized leaderboard (728 × 90), the skyscraper, and the vertical/horizontal tandem (and often synchronized) ads. The latter effect is sometimes called a "roadblock" and should be conceptually more than a wasteful, repeated ad. Plus, with some consumer involvement, banners were soon able to expand and contract. On the whole, the interactive qualities of a banner make up for its size, equivalent to a small-space press ad. That said, it is possible to make an ad that takes up the entire screen, called "page takeovers" (see "Over the Page" Animation, overleaf).

Like many traditional ads, roughly 90% of banner ads are boring and unimaginative, resulting in an equal need for fresh ideas within this media.

Rectangles and Pop-Ups	
300 × 250	*Medium Rectangle*
250 × 250	*Square Pop-Up*
240 × 400	*Vertical Rectangle*
336 × 280	*Large Rectangle*
180 × 150	*Rectangle*
300 × 100	*3:1 Rectangle*
720 × 300	*Pop-Under*

Banners and Buttons	
468 × 60	*Full Banner*
234 × 60	*Half Banner*
88 × 31	*Micro Bar*
120 × 90	*Button 1*
120 × 60	*Button 2*
120 × 240	*Vertical Banner*
125 × 125	*Square Button*
728 × 90	*Leaderboard*

Skyscrapers	
160 × 600	*Wide Skyscraper*
120 × 600	*Skyscraper*
300 × 600	*Half-Page Ad*

Also remember that not every product needs advertising. And if it does, banner advertising (with its typically low click-through rate) might not be the best option.

"Talking Banners"
Multiple banners (usually two) that communicate to each other are called "talking banners." Creatively, any Mother–Daughter banners should be different rather than identical. (See the two "Baby" banners for a UK lung cancer foundation on page 202.)

Have you ever clicked your mouse right HERE? → YOU WILL

Join photopop today

Passive smoking kills 80 babies a year.

THE ROY CASTLE
LUNG CANCER
FOUNDATION

FIGHTING LUNG CANCER

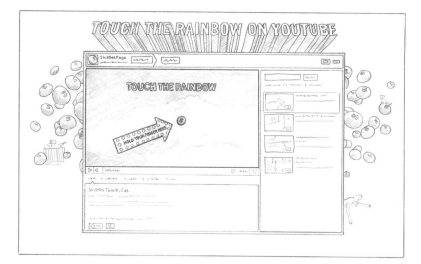

TOUCH THE RAINBOW ON YOUTUBE

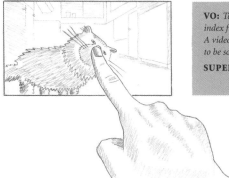

VO: *Touch the rainbow. No, seriously. Put your index finger on your screen where the Skittle is. A video is going to start and your finger is going to be so delicious.*

SUPER: *Lick the rainbow. Taste the rainbow.*

Top The first ever banner ad (*c.* 1994) had a prophetic message. ***Client:*** *AT&T.*

Left Talking Banners: a "mock" banner ad was created to dramatize the effects of secondhand (passive) smoke. ***Client:*** *The Roy Castle Lung Cancer Foundation.* ***Agency:*** *Clemmow Hornby Inge, London.* ***Creatives:*** *Thiago De Moraes, Ewan Paterson.*

Above Poking fun (literally) at interactive. Touch the computer screen and watch your finger play a starring role in a series of bizarre Skittles commercials. ***Client:*** *Wrigley, Canada.* ***Agency:*** *BBDO, Toronto.* ***Creatives:*** *Chris Joakim, Mike Donaghey, Carlos Moreno, Peter Ignazi.*

Small stage, big performance. Axion, Dexia's youth bank, gave bands a little (yet powerful) promotion by hosting a series of 25 banner concerts. An innovative use of an advertising format considered by some to be "dead." *Client: Axion.* **Agency:** *Boondoggle, Leuven.* **Creatives:** *Vanessa Hendrickx, Alexander Cha'ban, Peter Vijgen, Kevin Crepin.*

Pop-Ups

Pop-ups do just that. These are ads that automatically appear as separate windows on your screen and can often be blocked by users via computer settings.

"Over the Page" Animation

Similar to a pop-up except it appears as superimposed imagery rather than within a solid window, and is therefore more visually surprising and interesting. One example is an NSPCC campaign by the UK's Agency.com, which included various children innocently walking "onscreen" to deliver each thought-provoking message. Not dissimilar to page takeovers, this type of ad could be a combination of a roadblock and a takeover, such as Spiderman swinging from one ad to another. Over the page animation is the most expensive media to produce and buy, so the idea has to be strong.

Instant Messaging (IM) and Texting

For many people, these methods have joined (or even replaced) email. The shortest real-time text messages are "texts" of fewer than 160 characters, written on mobile/cell phones, tablets, etc.

Email Marketing

Consumers' general dislike of commercial emails has meant that agencies have had to become more creative, appealing, subtle, and personal when using this approach. While there are slicker interruptive methods, email continues to survive because it's easy, cheap, measurable, effective, and has a broad reach.

Here are the three key best-practice tips for an effective interactive email:

- The "sweet spot" area above the fold (the area visible without scrolling; usually 420 pixels deep) should contain concise copy (headline, subhead) and a primary call-to-action (CTA) button or link.

- Below the fold contains secondary information (more copy, etc.) and a repeated CTA.

- The email subject line should be 50 characters or fewer in length.

Embrace the Space

Just as we examined small space ads in the Print chapter, don't let the area size (real estate) of a banner limit your creativity.

Interaction is Action-Reaction

Interaction starts with an action from the brand toward the consumer: a prompt. Often part of what makes an interactive idea compelling or clever is the way the user then has to interact with it (the "reaction"), and why he/she does so. In traditional media, a concept (big or small) can start from almost anything: a strategic insight, an image, a fact, a headline, a tagline, etc. The end result is more important than the origin of the idea. Therefore, with digital, an idea might arise from a particular action-reaction. In other words, the action (and the consequent reaction) is key to the concept. This is something to think about—rather than religiously stick to—when you're creating an interactive piece, wherever it may live. Have fun with it. Skittles did, with its simple but hilariously silly "Finger" videos that lived on their own YouTube channel, as shown opposite.

Typical "actions-reactions" performed by users

Mouse

Click
Rollover/mouse over
Cursor takeover*
Click and hold
Click and drag

*Cursor changes or disappears; another object/element is controlled in its place

Keyboard

Typing (open field, e.g., letters, numbers)
Other keys (e.g., arrows, spacebar)

Built-in Microphone

In (voice, air)
Out (react to sound)

Built-in/External Camera

Mobile Phone/Tablet

Touch screen
Finger and thumb (expand, pinch)
Finger (tap, swipe/race, etc.)
Photograph (e.g., QR codes)
Video see-through (e.g., Augmented Reality)
Tilt
Bump

Ways We Digitally Interact

A simple click of a mouse can come from the heart as well as the head. Just like the ESP (Emotional Selling Point) outlined on page 144, digital is about building an emotional connection with an audience. Jeff Benjamin advises: "When we say interactive, you think, oh, I got someone to *do* something, but the more basic part of interactive is to make people *feel* something." Left are examples of typical "actions–reactions" that we users perform every day (organized by the device being used).

....

Exercise: choose an everyday object (e.g., a type of drink or an article of clothing) and think of all the ways you interact with it. Go through the five senses. Now apply this to a digital interactive experience (e.g., a website, an app, etc.) and see if any of the first ideas can work for a particular brand. Use the list to the left as a starting point.

....

Time Scale: Static vs. Animation

With the ever-decreasing attention spans of consumers, one can understand the notion that eventually every digital ad will be short and static (the equivalent of a 3-second poster)* rather than longer, animated ads. However, the time people spend in front of the computer is increasing and, with it, the ways in which they absorb information. Sometimes people spend their time switching, and other times they stay in one place. As for the effect of the internet on TV advertising, there will always be a level of demand (just as cinema survived the birth of television). All that will change is the way we engage with its equivalent, what is now called web video content (e.g., "pre-roll"), and the choice of devices with which a "commercial" is viewed (see Interactive: The Ever-Merging, Ever-Changing Media, page 217). In other words, as long as the technology for snappy, static ads and long animations is available, there will always be a need for both forms.

*Note that if a digital ad is 100% static (i.e., no animation or interaction), it is little more than a traditional print ad, and may not therefore be benefiting from any of the additional qualities the media has to offer. That said, some of the best pieces of online advertising to date have been in static gif form.

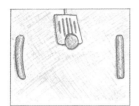

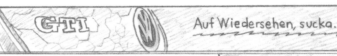

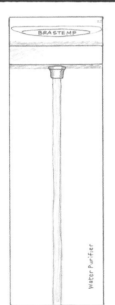

Cursor takeover

Top left *Client: Arno. Agency: F/Nazca Saatchi & Saatchi, São Paulo. Creatives: Vagner Godoi, Cristiane Gribel, William Queen.*

Click

Top right *Client: Remembersegregation.org. Agency: DDB, Seattle. Creatives: Jason Stanfield, Eric Gutierrez, John Livengood, Ray Page, Keith Anderson.*

Rollover/mouse over

Above, left *Client: Brastemp. Agency: AgênciaClick, São Paulo. Creatives: Fabiano de Queiroz, Jones Krahl, Jr.*

Click and hold

Above, right *Client: Volkswagen. Agency: Crispin Porter + Bogusky, Miami. Creatives: James Martis, Mike Howard.*

Microphone (in)

Client: *The Economist.* **Agency:** *OgilvyOne Worldwide, Hong Kong.* **Creatives:** *Thibault Kim, Houston Wong, Carrie Leung.*

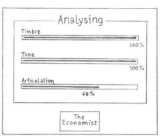

How influential is your voice?

Click here to start The Voice Analyser.

The Economist

Analysing

Timbre — 100%.
Tone — 100%.
Articulation — 68%

The Economist

LIBRARIAN   TARZAN

Read this sentence aloud:

An inability to stay quiet is one of the conspicuous failings of mankind.

Analysis

You speak softly but carry a big stick. There's power in your carefully chosen words. Ensure you always speak with authority, get The Economist online free for 4 weeks.

Try again / More...

The Economist

Click and drag (scrollbar/website)

Near right An ingenious, never-ending, vertical scrollbar dramatizes the product benefit. **Client:** *Orange.* **Agency:** *Poke, London.* **Creatives:** *Julie Barnes, Nicky Gibson, Nicolas Roope.*

Typing (open field)

Far right **Client:** *Playground Outdoor Equipment Stores.* **Agency:** *Åkestam Holst, Stockholm.* **Creatives:** *Andreas Ullenius, Paul Collins, Adam Reuterskiold, Ellinor Bjarnolf.*

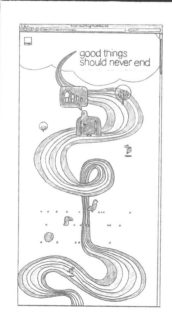

good things should never end

SUGGESTED JACKET FOR TODAY'S WEATHER:

CURRENT TEMPERATURE IN NEW YORK, NY:

7°C 7 m/s

WRITE YOUR DESTINATION

PLAYGROUND

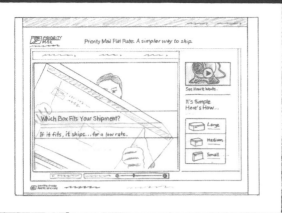

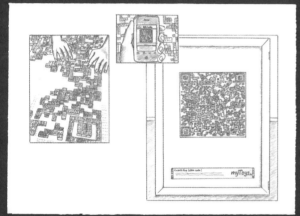

Built-in/external camera

Top Your camera finds the
best/minimum box size to
package and deliver your mail
item. (Copy: "If it fits, it ships.")
*Client: The United States Postal
Service.* **Agency:** *AKQA,
Washington, D.C.* **Creatives:**
*Holly Tegeler, Jason Fuqua,
Rachel Gillett.*

Photograph (QR code)

Above My Toys "Lego" invited
cameraphone users to discover
one of the many imaginative
things that can be built with Lego.
Client: MyToys.de. **Agency:** *Lukas
Lindemann Rosinski, Hamburg.*
Creatives: *Dennis Mensching,
Tom Hauser, Christian Mizutani,
Moritz Schmidt.*

Video see-through (Augmented Reality)

Above *Client: United Nations.*
Agency: *Saatchi & Saatchi, Australia.*
Creatives: *Vince Lagana, Steve Jackson.*

JERRY HERE. I'M THE HP ENGINEER WHO DESIGNED THIS THING.

(hp) HEWLETT PACKARD

JERRY 11

YOU 01

Above The first *interactive* banner ad allowed mouse users to play a 12K version of Pong. *Client: Hewlett-Packard. Designer: Chris Hurwitz.*

TV Overlap

There is often an "overlap" with TV ads (i.e., when a commercial that is broadcast traditionally is also streamed online). Although this can potentially reach a larger audience (especially a viral version), clients often fail to understand that uploading a TV commercial online does not make it a digital concept.

One-Way to Two-Way

Popular TV spots or videos become viral by simply being shared. This makes it social, but not particularly interactive. Wieden & Kennedy capitalized on the success of its Old Spice spot ("The Man Your Man Could Smell Like") with the interactive "Responses" video campaign, the ultimate "two-way" experience that allowed fans to have their ideas produced into dozens of entertaining scenarios. It was a brilliant use of social media: a very simple, entertaining idea that didn't use technology for the sake of it. As Cannes judge Masashi Kawamura points out: "The creative team understood the literacy of the medium to make entertaining content on the right platform."

Exercise: in teams, find a traditional ad campaign and think about how you would extend it out to interactive (if it hasn't already been done). Include ideas for banners, webisodes, games, etc. (Note: this is an exercise, not a suggestion for a final portfolio piece, unless it's part of your own original campaign.)

Exercise: writers: rewrite a long-form copy print ad for a website landing page (for the same brand), e.g., headline, subhead, body copy. (Total copy length: 3–5 sentences.)

Big Ideas vs. Small Ideas

It has been noted in this book that with traditional media, the consensus is that a big campaign idea is harder, more important, and more effective than a "single," one-off idea. But with interactive, Nicolas Roope of Poke points out, "Some of the more pervasive and powerful things possible in interactive media are small, rich ideas that slowly eat their way through the network."

On the other hand, many creative directors take a more "traditional" approach, believing that there is more mileage by creating a big brand campaign idea, either exclusively for the web, or as part of an even bigger integrated campaign.

Many post-digital branding people argue further that a small idea is always best—with execution being more important than the size of the concept. Let's think about that. Firstly, any execution has to be conceived, so you could argue that both are equally important. Secondly, a small idea could be the start of a bigger concept (e.g., changing the Google logo to an addictive Pac-Man game is one of many "morphing" ideas). Lastly, thanks to social media (and the sheer genius of a particular small idea), the potential for it to become huge is, well, huge. (BakerTweet began in a London bakery, but could easily be used in bakeries throughout the world.) Therefore it's fair to say that a big idea doesn't have to mean a big campaign in the traditional sense. As Iezzi states, "Ideas can and often should be iterative, evolving, interactive and nimble."

Build It to Be Big

How social can something be? Answer: global. Social media can have immediate worldwide impact, so create ideas that everyone (or as close to everyone) has an interest in. How do you pay tribute to the King of Pop in a fun, engaging way? Ignore his complicated life and create an ingeniously simple web experience that invites Michael Jackson fans everywhere to submit their own moonwalk.

Integrated Interactive

As the number of interactive formats grows, there are more possibilities to produce all-digital integrated interactive campaigns. "An appreciation for the arc of a longer story [is] becoming more and more important," explains Ty Montague.

Susan Credle, Chief Creative Officer at Leo Burnett USA, asks herself a series of questions: "Am I setting up an idea that will have a life of its own?," "What's the ongoing story?," "Can a social media idea draft off of it?," "Can PR be part of it?"

The Integrated Idea "A" (or Really Big Idea) described on page 238 is one that "has legs." The addition social media (in particular) has brought is that a fully integrated idea has legs of its own.

Games and Gaming

Popular digital games are certainly fun, but there's plenty of scope to think beyond guns and goblins. Games have always been able to sharpen memory and improve hand-eye coordination, too, but as Tom Himpe explains: "Gaming has matured beyond the realm of pure entertainment, and is increasingly used as a learning mechanism in military, medical, educational and political spheres." Ben Sawyer, who runs the Games for Health Project, adds: "They can be used to teach problem-solving skills, increase our awareness of world issues, help with social phobias and can even treat those with serious illnesses." And don't forget the social opportunities of gaming either. Computer-generated, multi-user role-playing has been around since the birth of dial-up

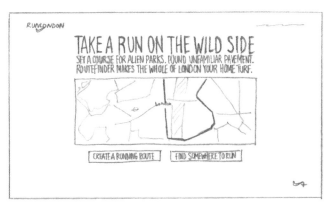

www.runlondon.com: with interactive, a one-shot idea can make a big impact. This example has already motivated tens of thousands of people to run.
Client: *Nike.* **Agency:** *AKQA, London.*

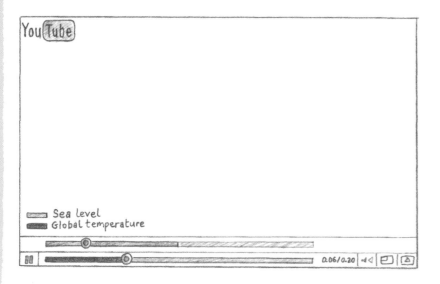

```
You Tube

▭ Sea level
▭ Global temperature

┃┃                    0.06/0.20
```

Build it, and they will blog about it. "GreenTube" shows the impact of global warming with a series of extremely simple (and wonderfully un-YouTube-like) videos that "play out" the facts of our environmental future. *Client: Greenpeace. Agency: AlmapBBDO, Brazil.*

(something I remember with equal fondness and bemusement).

From a creative standpoint, coming up with ideas for interactive (including games) should involve an equal amount of playfulness, inquisitiveness, and irreverence—all qualities that were mentioned at the start of this book.

••••••••••••••••••••••••••••••••••••••

Exercise: **pick a brand (or start with a market, if it's easier) that has yet to produce a gaming experience, and create ideas for one. Maybe produce it too. (Either way, it could become a stand-out piece in your portfolio.)**

••••••••••••••••••••••••••••••••••••••

The Translation Problem

Whenever you're being briefed to create an integrated campaign that includes interactive executions, a question worth asking is: "Does the idea translate equally well into traditional advertising and interactive?" The answer will, of course, depend on the idea itself, plus which types of web applications are being incorporated.

Naturally it helps if at the early conception stage only those ideas that work in *all* media, including interactive, are considered. This should reduce any problems later on, producing a well-integrated campaign. But what often happens is that a separate interactive firm or department is asked to translate an ad agency's original concept over to the web. One of four things can happen: firstly, the client/agency wants the concept to be translated verbatim. Because of the particular concept it proves easy to do and works for the most part, but is not the best use of the new media. Secondly, the concept is translated verbatim, but the idea is lost in the translation (it actually weakens the concept). Thirdly, the client/agency requests an interactive "twist" on the original, but the concept simply doesn't have the legs to work in a non-traditional format. Lastly, the most desirable outcome is when the interactive twist is equally as creative as the original (it actually adds to the whole campaign).

Although most "translation projects" are good business for interactive agencies in the short term, many interactive firms substitute the "polishing" approach for working independently to create the best interactive idea possible, without trying to fit in with other communications. Given their common belief that interactive and advertising are two separate disciplines, in their opinion this is the most desirable outcome of all. The key is to assure clients that their idea is still "on brand," and will not weaken or contradict the bigger strategic thinking.

The Replication Problem

Although not exclusive to online advertising, a common mistake occurs when agencies and clients try to replicate (i.e., plagiarize) previously successful *interactive* ideas. The problem is that these ideas rarely compare with the original, brand-tailored concept. The reason interactive replication happens is partly because the client knows the importance of this media, plus there are relatively fewer online success stories worth "mimicking." As discussed earlier in the book, traditional advertising has produced numerous "re-creative" ads during its relatively long history of "answers," so it's (sadly) expected that the same is happening with interactive. (See Social Re-Networking, overleaf.)

Gettheglass.com gave the benefits of milk an adventurous twist in this beautifully produced game. *Client:* California Fluid Milk Processors Advisory Board. *Agency:* Goodby, Silverstein & Partners, San Francisco. *Creatives:* Jorge Calleja, Jessica Shank, Katie McCarthy, Brian Gunderson, Paul Charney.

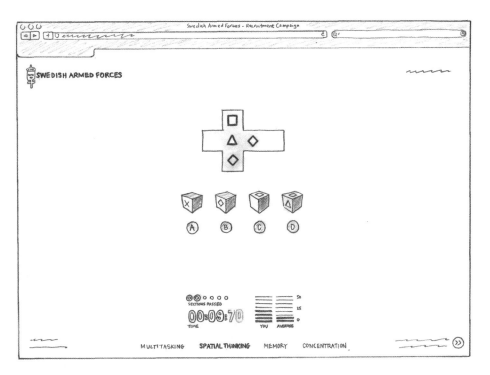

A series of mind-bending exercises creates a fun yet relevant way to recruit future members of the military. To keep things fresh, the site (and games) change periodically. *Client:* Swedish Armed Forces. *Agency:* DDB, Stockholm. *Production:* North Kingdom.

Place your bets, please. To help build a brand (a Swedish gambling site), the agency made two 500-kilo steel dice and dropped them down a mountain from a helicopter. The bidder with the closest start-to-finish time won a holiday to Greenland. *Client: Gnuf.com. Agency: Acne Advertising, Stockholm. Creatives: Adam Springfield, Kalle Gadd.*

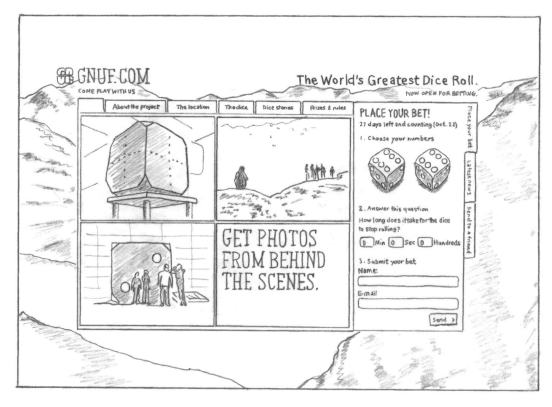

Think Beyond the Visual

As Nicolas Roope states, "The biggest mistake advertisers make is to approach the web as though it was only a visual medium. Too many brands obsess over the way things look and try to make things as impressive looking as possible at the expense of everything else." He believes that even those who approach interactive from an advertising standpoint should learn from the big web success stories such as Google, eBay, YouTube, Twitter, and Facebook by focusing on "all the things that engage people—stories, information, socializing, relationships, etc." And don't forget about sound either.

Social "Knitworking"

All brands want to become part of the social fabric, online and offline. They don't speak to people from afar—they go out of their way to meet their customers. As for online, research has revealed two major reasons why someone would want to socialize with a brand:

1. Social-networking users are simply interested in associating themselves with their favorite brands.

2. They want to hear about free giveaways or exclusive events.

But according to Tom Himpe, brands can do more than try to be the most popular. They can become social facilitators by trying to help others become more popular. For brands to become the social glue, they need to enable conversations amongst people by providing them with content and tools that can stimulate social interaction. This is no easy task, especially because online social networking has blurred the lines between friend, acquaintance, and complete stranger.

Therein lies the challenge. A "social" ball of wool can become an unappealing, tangled mess with knots that stop its connective growth. Or it can knit something attractive, useful, and ever growing.

Social Re-Networking

According to multimedia designer Kevin Palmer, a common problem is clients trying to jump on the bandwagon of the social networking phenomenon by attempting to mimic MySpace, YouTube, Facebook, etc. As he points out, "The beauty of these sites is that they are made by the people for the people. Any big corporations who try to imitate will be sniffed out in a second, ridiculed and ultimately fail. Therefore the challenge is for brands to tap into the entertainment-driven/consumer-driven new media phenomenon, and do it honestly and creatively without trying to hide behind another guise or badly mimic what has gone before."

Facebook and Twitter: Like and Follow

The rise of social media has made the sharing of opinions, creativity (and almost everything) easy and accessible to every demographic. Of all the social media platforms that have sprung up over the years, the hardest-working survivors are Facebook and Twitter (based on the argument that more brands have a FB or Twitter page than a YouTube channel). With this comes a constant challenge for brands in terms of how they can truly utilize these intricate platforms. While many campaigns rely on incorporating two or more platforms for maximum social impact, the success of many concepts is based on the ability to focus on, and fully utilize, only one platform. Concept and platform become inextricably linked—joined at the hip. This is an example of Ajaz Ahmed's conviction that "Simplicity is the ultimate sophistication."

....

Exercise: be like Tony. To help run his company (and put "a face" to the largest online store), Zappos.com CEO Tony Hsieh uses Twitter regularly: http://twitter/zappos. Imagine that you're in charge of a brand (choose one with your classmates) and brainstorm a list of tweets that would attract followers (employees and/or consumers).

....

Exercise: create an "unauthorized" blog for your favorite brand. Compete with a classmate (or entire class) to see who gets the most interest by the end of the semester/term.

....

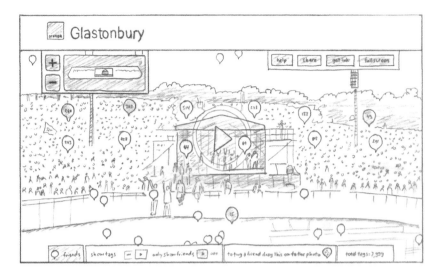

words

photos

videos

music

places

all of the above

Top A bigger (yet still focused) idea: a crowd photograph so huge that everyone at the festival could find and tag themselves, declaring "I was there" to Facebook friends. *Client: Orange. Agency: Poke, London. Creative: Jason Fox.*

Above A small, focused idea: a practical, custom-built box connected to the internet via Twitter is a useful and relevant way to let people know when their freshly baked goods are ready. *Client: Albion Café Bakery, London. Agency: Poke, London. Creatives: Nicolas Roope, Andrew Zolty.*

Right It seems to make sense that the "natural state" of social networking has settled on five core specialties and a one-stop shop. (LinkedIn owns the social space for employment as the world's largest professional network.)

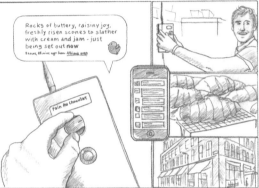

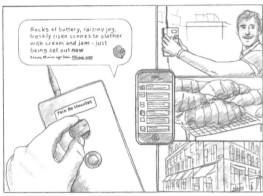

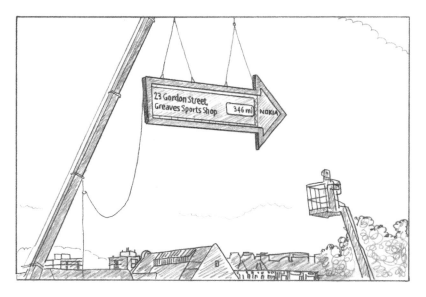

The "World's Biggest Signpost" points the way for disorientated mobile users in this wonderfully cartoon-like approach to the media. *Client: Nokia. Agency: Farfar, Stockholm. Creatives: Tomas Jonsson, Carl Fredrik Jannerfeldt, Jimmy Hay.*

Mobile Marketing

While "There's an app for that!" has become the standard joke to describe the rapid infiltrating growth of this medium, it's relatively hard to find timeless examples for generic, "pre-app" brands. Whether it's a social connector such as Foursquare or a tilt-controlled game, they have typically begun and will probably end as just that: an app.

....

Exercise: create an app for a brand that's never been done before. Really.

....

QR Codes

The ad industry can be its own worst enemy at times. Just when we in the West have finally caught on to QR codes (they've been part of everyday life in Japan for many years), the industry here decides that they're an outdated disaster. However, this failure is largely because the technology has not been fully understood or applied well. As a result, QR code usage has been relatively primitive, redundant, and therefore ineffectual. Hopefully this will change as the number of successful case studies increases.

Creatively, think beyond the design-focused, "executional" use of QR codes (like unusual positioning/placement, or photographic mosaic montages) unless it's relevant to the brand or concept. A notable example of this is the German My Toys campaign that used QR codes made from multicolored Lego bricks, shown on page 207.

....

Exercise: create an original, compelling QR code concept for a brand of your choice.

....

AR (Augmented Reality)

AR apps, implementing standard or more sophisticated technology (such as Aurasma), have the power to turn everyday objects (e.g., any 2-D image) into video content that can be instantly viewed on your phone or tablet. The Museum of London app allows you to hold your phone up in various locations to see what London looked like hundreds of years ago. The United Nations "Listen To Me" on page 207 is one of the more powerful "talking" campaigns that have popped up since AR's inception.

....

Exercise: create a mobile (phone or tablet) Augmented Reality concept for any brand.

....

Widgets

As with websites and other interactive formats, keep a widget engaging so that it's not sitting on someone's desktop, etc.

Call-To-Action (CTA)

Traditional media has used CTAs for almost a century, each with some combination of interruptive and interactive. Therefore, the same principles apply to digital CTAs: keep them short and straightforward. But don't always rely on the "Learn more"s. Perhaps there's a CTA that nicely ties back to the overall idea? That said, if an ad is good enough, consumers will choose to learn more online about almost anything—even a toilet cleaner!

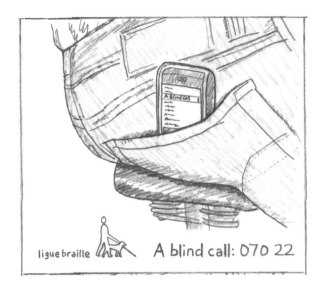

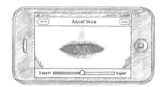

Top left Charitable fun made from a common mistake. Unlocked phones make unintentional "blind calls" to the first number in your contact list (in this case to "A Blind Call") at which point an automatic donation is made. And friends like Abby or Alex will no longer be disturbed. ***Client:*** *Brailleliga.* ***Agency:*** *Duval Guillaume, Brussels.* ***Creatives:*** *Katrien Bottez, Jean-Marc Wachsmann, Peter Ampe, Benoît Menetret.*

Top right The most globally charming travel app. Simply take a photo of your mouth and when it speaks in another language it will look like it's coming from you. ***Client:*** *Emirates.* ***Agency:*** *Lean Mean Fighting Machine, London.* ***Creatives:*** *Alex Shapowal, Alex Buchanan-Dunlop, Anna Charity.*

Above Airwalk meets Augmented Reality. These "Invisible Pop-up Stores" could (and did) appear around the world. ***Client:*** *Airwalk.* ***Agencies:*** *Young & Rubicam, New York and GoldRun.* ***Creatives:*** *Feliks Richter, Alexander Nowak.*

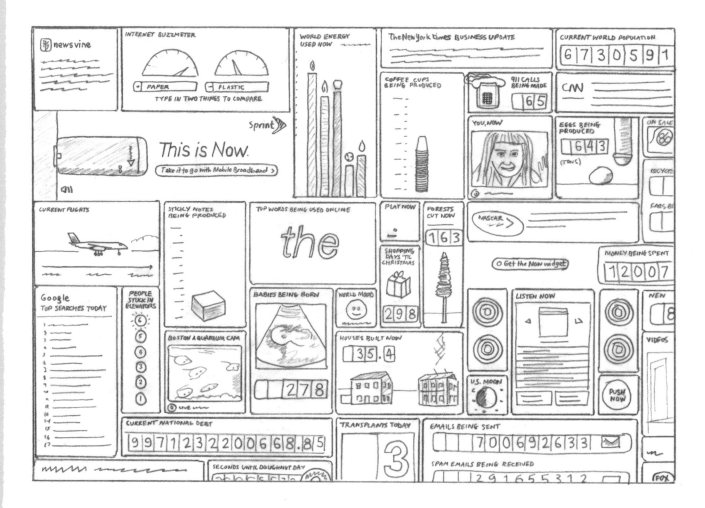

Sprint's "The Now Network" campaign inspired the world's most elaborate widget. Non-stop information and entertainment via a digital curator of live feeds, cams and streaming data. *Client:* Sprint. *Agency:* Goodby, Silverstein & Partners, San Francisco. *Creatives:* Aaron Dietz, Mandy Dietz.

Uniqlo's "Uniqlock" is a 24/7 presentation of Japan's leading fashion brand via time-signal music, dance video routines, and store installations. This branded widget connected Uniqlo with the world's bloggers, recording and mapping the global buzz over time. *Client:* Uniqlo. *Digital Agency:* Projector.

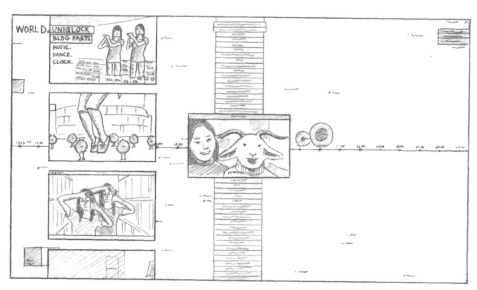

Exercise: instructional copy should be good copy too. Go online or browse an interactive annual. Pick out CTAs: banners and websites are the best bet (most use the standard "learn more.") Now try rewriting each CTA in a way that's more interesting and/or relates to the idea.

Interactive: The Ever-Merging, Ever-Changing Media

Interactive is obviously much younger than traditional advertising, and is therefore pioneering territory. (Most major awards shows only began to recognize new media in the late 1990s, but now every major show has a separate awards annual/event.)

Although technology continues firmly in the direction of multi-functional digital devices (either in mobile form like a smartphone or tablet, or fixed like a web-based home entertainment system), the way in which the communication is received will vary over time. Therefore, the concepts (and content) will often have to adapt to increase its effectiveness. In short, one idea may not translate as successfully to each outlet or device, due largely to the way/speed the information is read (e.g., screen size, download speed, etc.) But as technology improves, issues such as poor download speed will diminish. Also, as Kevin Palmer explains, "The blur between the product, the social network website, the TV show, the movie, the podcast, etc., is becoming indistinguishable. People are interacting with all media without questioning it."

As with fully integrated media solutions, the key for brands using interactive media is to cover all the bases, or, rather, to cover the right bases by understanding the capabilities (and limitations) of each outlet. This will be true whenever a new interactive device is invented, or improved.

The Future of Interactive

Interactive, still in its infancy, is an ever-evolving, experimental media. That's what makes it such an exciting media to work in. The debate about how far it has come in the first 15 or so years is a popular one. One thing is certain, its growth will only continue, taking over from traditional media as the hub (the core idea will be expressed through interactive and everything else will hang from it, rather than the other way around, which has often been the case). Only time will tell to what extent this will occur and it will depend on the campaign itself.

The issue of measurability and the effectiveness of online advertising has already been well addressed, thanks to the technical ability to follow, record, and snag users as they browse in each "environment." In the future, agencies will be constantly looking for new formats, new ways to connect with the consumer, and how to pitch ideas to non-captive audiences. Meanwhile, media buyers will adaptively learn to restructure their buying habits.

Lastly, the growth of 3-D interactive applications will open up many more ways to engage the consumer way beyond the realms of popular 3-D games and cube-shaped web graphics (a "classic," ground-breaking example of the latter was an MTV2 website, shown overleaf). Designers will become more like architects as they experiment with spatial relationships outside the conventional two dimensions to create exciting new experiences and environments (such as live events with a seamless use of online media woven in).

Exercise: with a number of friends or students, each create a video (about anything), and put it on YouTube. The person with the most views after one week is the winner.

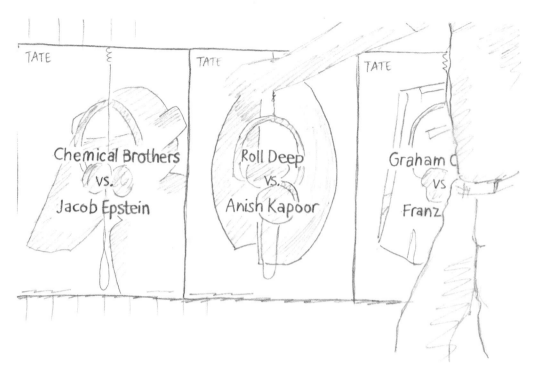

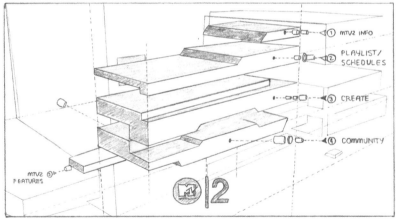

Top Tate tracks: famous musicians were commissioned to create a piece of music for their favorite gallery exhibit. Targeting teens, the visitors could then listen to each track as a new way of experiencing art. *Client:* Tate Modern, London. *Agency:* Fallon, London. *Creative:* Juan Cabral.

Above, left and above, right A groundbreaking example of 3-D web graphics. *Client:* MTV2. *Agency:* Digit, United Kingdom.

10 Copy

Robert Sawyer describes copywriting as "Not exactly prose, not exactly poetry."

Headlines, sub-headlines and taglines (i.e., short copy) were covered in the Print, The Tagline, and Generating Strategies and Ideas chapters. Plus, those copy tools specific to TV, Radio, Interactive, and Integrated campaigns can be found in their respective chapters.

This chapter focuses primarily on *long copy* found predominantly in print, also known as *long form*, *body copy*, or *body text*. (Note: some of the tools mentioned in this chapter can be applied to headlines and taglines, plus TV, radio, print, web, etc.)

As you know, advertising is all about communication. And whether it's with pictures or copy, it's all about simplicity. So despite what you might think, anyone can write decent long copy. Think of your job not as a writer of words, but an *avoider* of words. You're not writing a novel or a poem (although these skills don't hurt). But you rarely need to use long, fancy words. Focus on getting down the important stuff in a pithy, persuasive way.

Start by learning the following tried and tested tools of effective copywriting. Once you start applying these basic tips, your copy skills will improve dramatically.

The examples overleaf use various copywriting techniques and styles to great effect.

Again, good copywriting isn't limited to print. Today's copywriter is expected to master the craft across all media, and beyond. (See The Integrated Writer on page 249.)

The Invisible Thread: Make it Flow

Your primary goal is to make the body copy flow seamlessly, from line to line, paragraph to paragraph, as if an "invisible thread" is joining everything up. The bulk of ads with considerable body copy use this technique (as well as the other tools in this chapter) to a greater or lesser extent. According to instructor Tony Cullingham, once you have found a central thread, it should read like a drip of water slowly sliding down a wall; a light but unstoppable descent toward the final thought.

The first flow is from the headline (if applicable) to the first line of body copy. Then the first line threads into the second, and so on, until the end line, which flows from the penultimate line of copy. (You may wish to complete the circle by relating the end line back to the starting point: the headline. See The Final/End Line, page 222.) Just be careful not to make it sound too mechanical.

Note: there are also headlines that lead the reader into the body copy as a whole, not just the first line. (One might call this "headline introducing body copy.")✱ The structure of the headline in Sainsbury's "Nappies" ad (see page 223) clearly sets up the entire copy. There are more subtle approaches, too, such as the Imperial War Museum's "Hitler" (see page 74) which uses a highly intriguing headline/visual to draw the reader into the copy.

✱ "Headline introducing visual" was discussed in the Print chapter.

Start Out with a Bang

The first line of copy has to grab the reader and pull him/her in; it sets up the rest of the piece. So start with the most surprising, persuasive, or intriguing line first. It could be a fact, a statement, or a comment. Maybe even a question. But as always, keep it simple (which doesn't always mean short). For the ultimate invisible thread, you may want to refer the first line directly back to the headline. However, there is one argument that states a very strong headline doesn't need to be referred back to in the copy.

Sentence Flow: Short-Long-Short-Long-Short-Long

Think of a piece of body copy like a piece of music. A quick, simple note played repeatedly gets boring. Conversely, a long, drawn-out instrumental solo is most effective if it's allowed "space" in which to breath. So to give body copy rhythm, create variety. The most obvious technique is to alternate the length of your sentences. Successive long or short sentences are equally dull. Successive long

You can tell it's a perfect ad just by reading it. *Client:* Jaffa. *Agency:* WCRS/Wight, Collins Rutherford Scott, London. *Creatives:* Andrew Rutherford, Ron Collins.

The clipped, chatty sentences help to make a multiple headlines short and snappy. *Client:* Tesco. *Agency:* Lowe, London. *Creatives:* Jason Lawes, Sam Cartmell.

You can tell a melon's perfect by squeezing it.

You can tell a pear's perfect by sniffing it.

You can tell a banana's perfect by peeling it.

You can tell a plum's perfect by pinching it.

You can tell an apple's perfect by shaking it.

You can tell a grapefruit's perfect just by reading it.

If it doesn't say Jaffa, it's not a Jaffa.

Cheese.
Can cause nightmares.
Like you shopping elsewhere.
Scary.
That's why this piece is only 87p.

TESCO

With good writing skills, nothing is impossible (like starting each sentence with the same word but in way that still makes you want to read it). *Client:* Adidas. *Agency:* TBWA/Chiat/Day, 180 Amsterdam. *Creatives:* Boyd Coynet, Amee Lehto, Kai Zastro, Sean Flores, Brandon Mugar.

IMPOSSIBLE IS JUST A BIG WORD THROWN AROUND BY SMALL MEN WHO FIND IT EASIER TO LIVE IN THE WORLD THEY'VE BEEN GIVEN THAN TO EXPLORE THE POWER THEY HAVE TO CHANGE IT. IMPOSSIBLE IS NOT A FACT. IT'S AN OPINION. IMPOSSIBLE IS NOT A DECLARATION. IT'S A DARE. IMPOSSIBLE IS POTENTIAL. IMPOSSIBLE IS TEMPORARY.

IMPOSSIBLE IS NOTHING.

FOREVER SPORT

We're for dogs.

Some people are for the whales.

Some are for the trees.

We're for dogs.

The big ones and the little ones.
The guardians and the comedians.
The pure breeds and the mutts.

We're for walks, runs and romps.
Digging, scratching, sniffing and fetching.
We're for dog parks, dog doors and dog days.

If there were an international holiday
for dogs, on which all dogs were universally
recognised for their contribution to the quality
of life on earth, we'd be for that too.

Because we're for dogs.

And we've spent the last
60 years working to make them as happy
as they've made us.

Dogs rule.

Pedigree

This copy simultaneously defines the brand's mission statement, campaign strategy, and idea. *Client: Pedigree. Agency: TBWA/Chiat/Day, Los Angeles. Creatives: Chris Adams, Margaret Keene.*

Because I've known you all my life.

Because a red Rudge bicycle once made me the happiest boy on the street.

Because you let me play cricket on the lawn.

Because you used to dance in the kitchen with a tea-towel round your waist.

Because your cheque book was always busy on my behalf.

Because our house was always full of books and laughter.

Because of countless Saturday mornings you gave up to watch a small boy play rugby.

Because you never expected too much of me or let me get away with too little.

Because of all the nights you sat working at your desk while I lay sleeping in my bed.

Because you never embarrassed me by talking about the birds and the bees.

Because I know there's a faded newspaper clipping in your wallet about my scholarship.

Because you always made me polish the heels of my shoes as brightly as the toes.

Because you've remembered my birthday 38 times out of 38.

Because you still hug me when we meet.

Because you still buy my mother flowers.

Because you've more than your fair share of grey hairs and I know who helped put them there.

Because you're a marvellous grandfather.

Because you made my wife feel one of the family.

Because you wanted to go to McDonald's the last time I bought you lunch.

Because you've always been there when I've needed you.

Because you let me make my own mistakes and never once said "I told you so".

Because you still pretend you only need glasses for reading.

Because I don't say thank you as often as I should.

Because it's Father's Day.

Because if you don't deserve Chivas Regal, who does?

No headline required. This idea is all in the body copy. *Client: Chivas Regal. Agency: Abbott Mead Vickers BBDO, London. Creatives: David Abbott, Ron Brown.*

The wonderfully chatty, empathetic tone of this ad allows the writer to talk to (not at) an individual young "woman." **Client:** *Tambrands.* **Product:** *Tampax.* **Agency:** *Abbott Mead Vickers BBDO.* **Creatives:** *Mary Wear, Damon Collins.*

point, be aware that too many short paragraphs can create "widows" in your copy. Look at your layout from a distance to see immediately how inviting and balanced it is.

Although there are exceptions to the reader friendly "multiple paragraphs" approach, (Samaritans' "Reading," page 61, and Reebok "Long Headline," page 224, both have obvious *conceptual* reasons for using a single, fully justified paragraph of text), I would argue that the initial visual impact is usually negative. People are fairly reluctant to read long copy at the best of times, so why make it any harder? (See also Is Copy Dead?, page 228.)

Grammar Perversion

Just as the rules of grammar exist to create reader friendliness, so too can little departures of grammar, like the ad copy favorite, the "verb-less sentence."

Like this one.

Other examples include the "subject-less sentence," and sentences beginning with "and" or "because." You don't have to break any grammatical rules unless it aids comprehension. But if used appropriately, grammar perversion can spice up your copy, sharpen a point, change the rhythm, etc.

The Final/End Line

Here are three common ways to end or "sign off" your body copy:

- A call-to-action (e.g., phone number, website, email or street address, or other prompt)
- A concluding fact that completes the argument
- A line that relates back to the headline*

In traditional advertising terms, the third approach is the most common. It shows the reader that considerable thought has been put into the entire piece, and depending on the tone, the reader is left with a little smile in the mind, almost like a reward for finishing it.

*Note: if the ad does not have a headline, then substitute it with the first line of copy.

Collect Unused Headlines

Gather any unused, alternative headlines. These could be used for the first line of body copy, or perhaps the last, or even somewhere in between.

sentences require prolonged concentration, whereas successive short sentences read more like a list than a piece of prose. Therefore, keep to an *approximate* short-long-short-long sentence flow.

And a quick point about long sentences being the result of embedded clauses (sentences within sentences): although not unacceptable, even a slightly complex piece of embedding is probably better off as two sentences. Therefore, write how it should be said (avoiding unintentional word repetition), then try breaking it up into simpler components. If the result sounds boring, it may be the content that's boring, so say something interesting instead.

Separate Paragraphs

As with long sentence followed by long sentence, big blocks of text are usually off putting to read. Dividing long paragraphs up at appropriate points immediately makes body copy more inviting to read. (Part of what makes David Abbott's flowing copy for Sainsbury's so utterly readable is his use of relatively short paragraphs.)

To help the piece of copy flow as you're writing it (and to avoid producing stodgy, Dickensian-sized paragraphs), break up each sentence into a separate paragraph. This helps to organize your thoughts, structure your argument, and speed up your writing. Then once you're done, connect the sentences into appropriately sized paragraphs— some large, some small. (Remember, even a single word can be a separate paragraph.) From a design

The first part of the headline introduces the (waterfall) visual, the second part introduces the body copy. *Client:* Sainsbury's. *Agency:* Abbott Mead Vickers BBDO, London. *Creatives:* David Abbott, Ron Brown.

Body copy that flows like water: creating many separate paragraphs helps the reader. *Client:* Sainsbury's. *Agency:* Abbott Mead Vickers BBDO, London. *Creatives:* David Abbott, Ron Brown.

This is an unusually long headline for a print ad. With good reason though. By the time you've read from the first word to the last, including all these words you're trying to hurry past right now - you are, aren't you? - anyway, as we were saying, by the time you get to the last word, you'll have an idea of just how much time Elana Meyer carved off a world record - a world record - not just 0,2 seconds or 2,2 seconds - when she competed in a half marathon in Tokyo on Sunday, running in a pair of Reeboks.

A case when the idea works best with a single block of copy.
Client: Reebok. *Agency:* SM Leo Burnett, South Africa. *Creatives:* Mark Vader, Joost Hulbosch.

Linking Words/Phrases

Also known as "transitions," linking words are useful because they bridge thoughts and help to make copy flow from one sentence or paragraph to the next. These words or phrases create the illusion of natural flow, but can irritate if overdone, so only use in moderation. Examples (of which there are dozens more) include:

- So
- However
- Therefore
- First
- Second
- Additionally/In addition
- In fact
- Furthermore
- On the other hand
- But
- Indeed
- Of course
- After all

Punctuation (In Moderation)

Punctuation can add richness and texture to copy. Examples include:

- Colon
- Semi colon
- Brackets (parentheses)
- "Quotes"
- Dot, dot, dot…

De-stress Stresses

If you have to underline, *use italics*, bold letters, exclamation marks (!), "inverted commas," and hyphens—unless demanded by grammar or convention, it's probably just a lazy way to imply tone of voice (see Punctuation Marks, page 63).

The List of Three

The number "three" is not only preferred for some visual solutions, but also in copy. It appears that two words, facts, phrases or sentences are too few, and four too many. The third element can give a sentence *rhythm*, *balance*, and *closure* (comedians describe three people walking into a bar). Also known as "The Magic Three."

Some other well-known (non-advertising) threesomes:

- *Friends, Romans, countrymen, lend me your ears* (Shakespeare's *Julius Caesar*)
- *Government of the people, by the people, for the people* (Abraham Lincoln)

- *Never in the field of conflict was so much owed by so many to so few* (Winston Churchill)
- *Father, Son, and Holy Spirit*
- *Hip, Hip, Hooray*

Note: "threes" are also prevalent in visuals: the origins are in fine art. For example, the standard still-life painting often contains three objects. Two or four look too symmetrical and unnatural, and five becomes too much (see Visual Threes, page 85).

The Contrasting Pair

This tool can be (and has often been) used for headlines, taglines, or body copy. Shakespeare wrote the most famous contrasting pair: "To be, or not to be," closely followed by Neil Armstrong's "That's one small step for man, one giant leap for mankind." In the UK, Argos's tagline used a contrasting pair: famous names at unheard of prices. Equally, the Friends of the Earth tagline: Think globally, act locally.

The contrasting pair is a type of "headline twist" (examined on page 63), in that the first part (word or phrase) sends the reader in one direction, and then suddenly sends him/her the opposite way. It's this disarming nature that gives it power.

Alliteration

Alliteration is another powerful tool. It's the occurrence of the same letter or sound at the beginning of several words in succession, e.g., sing a song of sixpence. Dr. Martin Luther King, Jr.'s "I Have a Dream" speech used one of the most famous alliterations "…will not be judged by the color of their skin, but by the content of their character." This sublime example works on another level because it's symmetrical: there is a balance between the two parts of the sentence, almost including the number of syllables. This gives it extra impact, and makes it even more memorable.

Note that alliteration, the list of three, and the contrasting pair can be combined. Julius Caesar's "Veni, Vedi, Vici" is both alliteration and list of three. Muhammad Ali's famous "Float like a butterfly, sting like a bee" is almost an alliteration plus contrasting pair.

Tone of Voice

Nowhere is tone more evident (and therefore more important) than in long copy. Tone can vary tremendously, but matching the unique personality of the client/product is a good place to start. Two other factors that can determine how you want to talk to your reader are (i) the idea and (ii) the target audience. Research is a good place to start.

Whatever your final tone or attitude, start by thinking in general terms. You might wish to sound like a dignitary making an important speech, or like you're chatting to someone sitting next to you on a bus. (Bill Bernbach once told a young writer to make his copy more conversational by imagining he was writing a letter to an uncle he had met, but rarely saw.) Whatever tone you choose, the more you can make your copy sound like one person talking to another, the better. This helps to disarm and engage the reader. Perhaps pick a friend, neighbor, or relative who might be a typical consumer. This will help you to get under their skin and talk their language.

Once you find the particular tone and attitude, don't stray from it (it will lack brand integrity and confuse the reader). From its launch, Crispin Porter + Bogusky defined Mini's tone of voice so well it was almost as if the ads wrote themselves (see overleaf). Remember, tone can be as general (e.g., humorous) or specific (e.g., a type/brand of humor) as you want to make it. For more details on the subject, see Tone of Voice, page 51.

Write in a Style or Theme

Depending on your idea, you might be able to extend it into your body copy. In other words, take an opening idea right through to the end. But choose carefully: if it seems contrived or tedious to continue a theme throughout an entire ad, drop it.

Although the two are linked, writing in a *style* or *theme* can actually offer up more than one possible *tone*. For example, a radio ad in the style of a Valentine's card can be written in one of a number of serious/humorous tones within that theme, depending on what you want.

....

Exercise: find the classic children's story "Little Red Riding Hood" online. Rewrite a 200 word version in the style of either: 1) a women's fashion magazine; 2) a horror writer; 3) a wannabe, street-talking rapper; or 4) the voice over on a nature show/film.

....

Be a Speechwriter

Famed writer Alfredo Marcantonio believes that copywriting is closer to speechwriting: "It's not simply about informing, entertaining or amusing the audience. It's about winning them over, to a particular product or point of view."

Find a tone of voice or attitude and stick to it: Mini's ads are so well defined it is as if the ads wrote themselves. *Client: Mini. Agency: Crispin Porter + Bogusky, Miami. Creatives: Ari Merkin, Steve O'Connell, Mark Taylor.*

LET'S BURN THE MAPS. Let's get lost. Let's turn right when we should turn left. Let's read fewer car ads and more travel ads. Let's not be back in ten minutes. Let's hold out until the next rest stop. Let's eat when hungry. Let's drink when thirsty. Let's break routines, but not make a routine of it. LET'S MOTOR.

"How to Do a Volkswagen Ad"

The following copy was written under the headline above, and has inspired many a copywriter ever since:

> *Call a spade a spade. And a suspension a suspension. Not something like "orbital cushioning." Talk to the reader, don't shout. He can hear you. Especially if you talk sense. Pencil sharp? You're on your own.*

Facts, Stats, Demonstrations, and Quotes

Using facts, stats, demonstrations, and quotes within an ad help to create a convincing argument for the client. More so than opinion. Whether used within the body copy or elsewhere, these create an important sense of objectivity, as if saying, "don't just take our word for it." Fs, Ss, Ds, and Qs act as part of a "need I say more" tone of voice that has worked well for many famous campaigns. For example, Charles Saatchi's "Fly" poster is made up entirely of facts, without the need for opinion or even persuasion. If you have a list of facts, use the tools in this chapter so they don't read like a *list of facts*.

Don't Write, Borrow

As with radio scripts (see page 229), sometimes borrowing a piece of writing (as long as it's relevant) can be more effective than creating a new, "scripted" piece of body copy. The writer of an award-winning press campaign for Amnesty International simply used a collection of transcripts of the words of torture victims. To use the same example, the "Fly" poster (opposite) uses barely edited text from a government-issued pamphlet on food hygiene. This tip applies to all other media—TV, radio, and online writing.

Clichés

A cliché is a trite word or phrase that lacks originality because of frequent and prolonged use. As with disguised puns, even subverted or cleverly modified clichés are usually just lame jokes. Therefore the general rule is to kill them. Here are a few examples:

- Green with envy
- Cool as a cucumber
- A night to remember
- Family entertainment
- Go for a spin

- Up and down the country at this moment in time the winds of change are blowing

There are some possible reasons for using a cliché. It may be apposite (i.e., it works perfectly with your idea), or part of the deliberate use of sarcasm, or as a revealing commentary through the dialogue of a particular character. It may also be poetic, of special character, a way to introduce a note of familiarity into a difficult subject, or perhaps it has fallen into disuse.

In addition, there is also the inevitable, useful, and therefore overused *mini cliché*. Unlike the larger clichés above, if used sparingly, these can add a comfortable quality to a piece of writing. These include phrases like:

- On my way
- As a matter of fact
- Very occasional
- Here goes

Certain visuals are clichéd too. For examples, see Avoid Clichéd Imagery, page 36.

Puns

Like clichés, only a small fraction of puns work as useful and effective ways to put across information quickly, but preferably as newspaper headlines, rather than ad headlines or copy. The use of puns is discussed in detail on page 68.

Long Words

In general, use plain, simple, familiar spoken English. The only time to include a long or little known word is when absolute precision of meaning is vital. And if the audience doesn't know the word, what's the point of being precise about the meaning?

Long words often spoil the simplicity of a sentence. For example, "the very occasional minor cliché" sounds better as "the odd minor cliché."

Every time you come across a long or fancy word in your writing, spend 15 to 30 seconds to think of a one-syllable version.

Dull Words

The use of active, exciting words is another way of passing more information in a short space. It's not that words like "went" or "cut" are particularly boring, but they do miss the opportunity to describe *how* someone/something went or cut.

This is what happens when a fly lands on your food.
Flies can't eat solid food, so to soften it up they vomit on it. Then they stamp the vomit in until it's a liquid, usually stamping in a few germs for good measure. Then when it's good and runny they suck it all back again, probably dropping some excrement at the same time. And then, when they've finished eating, it's your turn.

Cover food. Cover eating and drinking utensils. Cover dustbins.
The Health Education Council.

Don't write, borrow: these facts speak for themselves, without the need for opinion or persuasion. *Client:* The Health Education Council. *Agency:* Cramer Saatchi, London. *Creatives:* Charles Saatchi, Michael Coughlan, John Hegarty.

For example
went slid, bounced, waddled, jetted…
cut hack, dissect, bite, saw…
Note, too, that verbs like these create faster pictures than adjectives.

Gerunds

The use of too many "-ing" words make sentences sound more complex than they need to.

For example, compare

This is part of the thinking behind avoiding gerunds, and it's surprising how using them can make writing unexciting.

with

This is why you should avoid gerunds. They gum up your sentences.

Selling Point vs. Sales Pitch

You could also call this understating vs. boasting. In terms of copy, this usually comes down to the amount and/or use of particular *adjectives*. For example, compare the understated "smell of pine" to the boastful, hollow "heavenly smell of pine." There's a fine line, especially as the whole point of most copywriting is effectively to boast about a product. As the writer, it's your call. At the least, compare and contrast by taking any words like "great" and "tasty" out before putting them back in. As a definite rule, honest humanity beats phony every time.

Is Copy Dead?

This argument pops its head up every now and then. So *is* copy dead? Luke Sullivan argues that no one reads it. Although he also points out, "Long copy ads can be great. Even if a customer doesn't read every word, it looks like the company has a lot to say." Ken Muir makes a similar point: "It's all there to read if [people] want to, but the first and last lines are really the ones that matter."

Dylan Williams of Mother, London argues, "[with email and text messaging] people are respecting the written word again but also playing with it and coming up with new words. There's a renewed energy and passion for language." The internet (i.e., websites, email, and blogsites, etc.) has also increased the use and interest of the written word.

The reason why copy might continue to "come and go" could simply boil down to the need to create advertising that stands out. Perhaps it will be a never-ending cycle: when image-driven communication reaches saturation point, people will start to ignore the visual sound bite approach. The obvious strategy is to do the opposite, replacing the split-second image with longer, word-driven ads, until the cycle is reversed again.

Summary

Research

Find rational and emotional reasons to purchase the product. (Rational fact-finding: gather previous ads, factory visit notes, annual reports, brochures, articles, and independent test results. Emotional reasons: discover and deduce what the target audience is like. What's important to them, how do they feel about the product/manufacturer/marketplace, and what role does each play in their lives?)

Organize

Review what findings you have; keep and/or rewrite the good points. Put the findings in the correct, logical order.

Shape

Work on the structure (beginning, middle, and end), plus the overall "look" and flow of your argument.

Edit

Cut down the copy by a third.

Rewrite

Try rewriting the whole piece from memory. It might produce a more natural result. Compare with the original version.

Edit

Cut down the copy (if applicable).

Finesse

Work on the details; look for possible use of alliteration, contrasting pair, or list of three. Check spelling, grammar, punctuation, and sloppy layout.

Speak

Read the entire ad out loud, not to oneself. Adopt the appropriate tone or accent. You'll hear immediately if anything sounds strange or doesn't flow.

To remember these stages, use the simple acronym ROSE REFS. (If it helps you further, imagine a group of sweet old ladies judging the roses at a flower contest—the rose referees, or refs. Like writing a piece of copy, the judging process takes time. You have to keep returning to each item, checking, and double checking, until you're happy with your final choice.)

••

Exercise: **write body copy almost like a poem, i.e., one thought or sentence per line on the page. Put a space (hard return) between sentences. This dividing technique will "free up" the page by making it easier to view and organize sentences. When you're happy with the content and flow, arrange the copy into final paragraphs.**

••

11
Radio

Radio is comprised of either network/national radio or local radio (most of which can now be accessed internationally via the web). But despite the vast number of radio spots that have been made over the years, the standard is universally considered to be low. Creatives just don't seem to take the same amount of pride and care with radio. In a traditional ad agency, the relatively "unglamorous" radio briefs are often left to the junior team(s). And surprisingly little has been done to improve the situation. (Compare this to all the graphic design or TV and screenwriting books/classes/awards that exist.)

Easy to Do, But Hard to Do Well

The reality of writing radio ads is this: it's easy to do *something* that will answer the brief (you have at least 30 seconds to talk your way through the idea). But this seems to be a false sense of security. It's actually hard to do something *great* with radio. This could be because visuals are more repeat-friendly than sound; you can't rely on visuals; and there are very few good radio spots to be inspired by. But as with any medium, once you understand its possibilities, it suddenly opens the door to great ideas.

Voice Overs

In radio, a particular voice over (VO, MVO, or FVO) might be better described as an ANNOUNCER (e.g., "Bud Lite presents, 'Real Men of Genius'"), or a NARRATOR (e.g., "This is the story of…")

Sound and SFX

A radio script is basically a TV script without the written description/visual part. (Storyboards are obviously not applicable.) Zero visuals means having one less element to play with—all the action has to be driven by *sound* alone (the human voice, music, and sound effects).

Sound is the biggest single advantage over all silent media (i.e., press and posters). As a result, radio scripts rely more heavily on these three elements. But instead of letting the script breath, the tendency with radio is to use constant sound; to overwrite with wall-to-wall dialogue and voice over as a way of compensating for the lack of visuals (or worse, for the lack of an *idea*).

Sound can be grand, subtle, complex, obscure, comical, spine chilling, or emotive. Think about how a particular sound or an old song can make you feel; how it can transport you to a precise moment in time. If a sound exists, it can be easily recorded, re-created, or imitated in the studio. And don't forget about audio mnemonics (memory aids like voice overs and jingles), which can help to brand a product or campaign (see Audio Mnemonics, page 168).

Note: with radio spots, as opposed to TV, individual sound effects take a bit longer to "work." Allow at least 3.5 seconds for each. As with TV, use "under and throughout" for continual background noises. The volume tends to go up and down, depending on if there is no sound, or conflicting sound like a voice over. This is easy for a sound editor to fix.

The Personal Medium

The radio is more like a friend than a medium. Although all types of ads should be a conversation between two people (client and consumer), the radio possesses a different, strangely intimate relationship. The audience is truly captive, because unlike when watching TV or reading a press ad, people are relatively "free." They are either driving, doing the housework, sunbathing, in the bath, etc.

Research also shows that they are usually alone, which makes the communication more personal and informal, as if whispering into someone's ear. You'll therefore find that simple ideas are more effective than bragging rambles. Short lines also allow for pauses and more scope for character in the intonation, both of which help the actor give the right performance.

The Same Rules Apply

As with creating print and TV ads, the same rules apply to radio. Write a strategy statement and make sure every script communicates and dramatizes the single-minded proposition. As Tony Cullingham once explained, if you have to say that a melamine kitchen table is 100% scratch resistant, why not "have the sound of someone tap-dancing on them in rough boots to prove your point?"

Of course, demonstration is just one possible approach. Look again at the others listed in the Generating Strategies and Ideas chapter. As ever, the final test is: does it stop the listener? Make them think, smile, or laugh? Provoke, intrigue, or inform?

And finally, as with all ad writing, make it seamless so it flows, rather than choppy compartments.

Set the Scene Quickly

Unless there's a reason to keep the listener guessing *where* the commercial is talking place, set the scene as quickly as you can (it will help the listener to imagine the situation straightaway, and therefore understand the ad). The last thing you want is for a listener to think, "Hang on, where am I? What's going on?" Try to set the scene with a combination of voice over, dialogue, and sound effects in the *first line* if possible.

Real Dialogue

Write the way people *speak*: informally, not colloquially, in shorthand, not in sentences; one word instead of ten; in abbreviations (e.g., "n't" instead of "not"). Be clear, direct, and explicit because with radio it's all over in seconds. Listeners cannot look back over the body copy, or take a second look at a visual, so make each radio spot communicate in a succinct and pithy way.

Tony Cullingham adds, "Ever since we started school, we've been writing material that will be *read*, not listened to. Therefore very few people have the gift of writing realistic dialogue. We are not expert at listening accurately to how real people talk, or making our voice overs sound like real people rather than actors in a commercial radio script."

In dialogue, it's hard to avoid clichés because that's the way people talk. However, try to avoid *really* clichéd turns of phrase (e.g., COCKNEY: Alwight guv!, or New Jersey HITMAN: Fuggedaboutit!)

In reality, people don't repeatedly use each other's name during conversation (unless you're writing a soap opera spoof). Dialogue actually sounds more natural when people's names are totally omitted.

Finally, don't give children adult-like words and sentiments to say unless your idea demands it.

Anytime. Anyplace. Anywhere.

The old Martini jingle also applies perfectly to radio ads. You can go anywhere with radio, and it costs *nothing* to get there. Go back in time, into the future, or go "live." Travel anywhere on Earth, or throughout the universe. Maybe create a fantasy location. But whether your ad is set inside a mud hut in Africa, or on a glacier in Greenland, the only limit with radio is your imagination.

Be Anyone or Anything

The list is endless: dead, alive, rich, poor, famous, non-famous, real, fictional, human, or non-human. Create a monologue, a dialogue, or a cast of thousands. And again, it's a lot cheaper than re-creating characters for TV, which would mean buildings sets, hiring crew, paying stars, etc.

In script 1 note how the beginning is written to create just the right amount of intrigue about who is speaking, where he's located, etc.

Theater of the Mind

The "don't show, imply" tool used in print and TV advertising demonstrates just how powerful people's imagination is. In a sense, implication is a given in radio because there are no actual visuals. Radio can use the imagination more than any other medium (both in terms of the writer, and the listener). It creates what's known as a "theater of the mind," or "pictures in the mind." The mind, after all, has no boundaries.

Think of ideas that use the fact that you can hear but not see. Carling Black Label's long-running "I bet he drinks Carling Black Label" campaign included a radio spot set in a police station. A policeman asks a man to empty his pockets. It begins with typical objects like keys and coins being placed on a table. Then follows 20 seconds of increasingly larger, more ridiculous objects, concluding with the SFX of a cruise liner foghorn. After a pause the policeman says, "Come on, and the other one." A far-fetched scene, but the listener has no problem imagining the objects. And a TV version of this idea would be contrived by comparison.

1. **Client/Brand:** RSPCA
Title: "Injection"
Time: 60 secs

....

MVO: *I'm not very well. At least I don't think I am. Actually, I...I feel fine, but I must be ill because I'm here. I'm where you go when you're not very well. I must be really quite bad because I've just had an injection to make me better. My friend brought me here which shows he cares. Didn't think he did at first. But on the way here he was very nice. (Pause) Very nice. (Slow) I feel tired now. Very tired, here on this table where they put me down. Put me down. (Slower) Tired...make better... injection...very tired.*

FVO: *Every Christmas, the RSPCA has to rescue thousands of unwanted animals. If you give a damn, don't give a pet.*

Agency: Abbott Mead Vickers BBDO, London
Creatives: Peter Souter, Paul Brazier

---

2. **Client/Brand:** Hamlet
Title: "Therapy"
Time: 30 secs

....

SFX: *Background chatter.*
FVO: *Welcome to the group. I see we have a new member with us. Would you like to stand up and introduce yourself?*
MVO: *My name is Peter and I'm an alcoholic.*
FVO: *Peter?*
MVO: *Yeah?*
FVO: *This is a yoga class.*
(Pause)
SFX: *Match being struck.*
SFX: *Hamlet theme tune.*
MVO: *Happiness is a cigar called Hamlet. The mild cigar.*

Agency: CDP, London
Creatives: Tad Safran, Tim Brookes, Phil Forster

---

3. **Client/Brand:** Kodacolour Gold
Title: "Colours"
Time: 60 secs

....

MVO: *To prove to you just how clear and vibrant Kodacolour Gold's colours are, I'm going to conduct a little exercise.*
Imagine for a moment that you can actually hear colour. (pause) Now, you'll have to concentrate, mind.
Right. This is the sound for blue.
(long pause)
I said you'll have to concentrate.
SFX: *Harp plays*
MVO: *Thank you. And this is the sound for green.*
SFX: *Wind organ plays part of a tune.*
MVO: *And now let's hear it for yellow.*
SFX: *Flute plays part of same tune.*
MVO: *And finally.*
SFX: *Loud trumpet interrupts.*
MVO: *Er, wait for it lads. Red...*
SFX: *Trumpet plays.*
MVO: *Right. I'm now showing you a photograph of a magnificent sunset over the Grand Canyon, as taken on Kodacolour Gold.*
SFX: *The instruments play simultaneously to reveal theme tune to "Bonanza."*
MVO: *And now I'm gonna show you that very same sunset, taken on ordinary film.*
SFX: *Toy kazoo and cymbals, playing theme tune to "Bonanza."*
MVO: *Well, I suppose it has a certain raw charm...*
MVO: *Kodacolour Gold. For a symphony of colour, we have the clicknology.*

Agency: Y+R, London
Creatives: Paul Burke, Dave Bell

Involve the Listener

Whatever medium you are working in, try to involve the consumer as much as possible. If it's print, get the consumer to look closer; if it's TV, get them to watch closer. For radio, create an idea that makes the listener want to listen and participate.

For example, script 4—part of integrated campaign—had an equivalent approach on TV.

Contrived Situations/Conversations

You've heard these literally hundreds of times: two people talking about a product in a detailed, unnatural manner; a quiz show, where the questions and answers all relate to the product, sounding like a contrived "shopping list" of features. And then there's the unnatural, constant repetition of the product name and telephone number. It all sounds like a bad infomercial.

Don't be influenced by the types of radio shows or commercials that have gone before (unless it's a first-ever parody). In a print ad an unusual visual helps it to stand out, so in radio create something that's unusual to the ear.

The Magic Three

The magic three is a standard structure in comedy, ever since the old "three men walk into a bar" jokes. Two parts is too quick, four is too long: three is just right. The first part gets a smile, the second part another smile, and the third gets a laugh when the punch line is revealed. In other words, save the best bit until last.

Situation Comedy

Situation comedy is a tried and tested platform in radio advertising. Putting characters in an unusual, original, bizarre, or tense situation (and seeing how they react to it, and each other) has tremendous comedic potential. It also creates original material, avoiding the temptation to steal jokes, or copy a style of radio show.

Create colorful characters. A good character is like a well-defined tone of voice—personified. If it helps, base him/her on a particular person you know, or have seen. Exaggeration is okay in the general sense (see below), but unless the idea requires it, don't always go for over the top caricatures (people with exaggerated characteristics).

Note how every character in the Bud Light "Real Men of Genius" ads is original yet believable, without the need to exaggerate or use caricatures.

So whatever characters you're creating, make them fresh. And put them in situations that you've not seen or heard before. Above all, don't copy famous comedic styles or characters (see Real Campaign of Genius, page 236).

Situation Drama

Just because so many radio shows and ads are entertaining, it doesn't mean they all have to be hilariously funny. Drama works just as well. This chapter alone includes some highly effective "serious" ads, some of which apply the sitcom tools mentioned above.

Exaggerate

The exaggeration tool works particularly well in radio because the listener can suspend disbelief using their imagination. And because you are implying rather than showing, you can get away with a lot more in radio, too.

Remember from the Generating Strategies and Ideas chapter that, "exaggeration" is based on a truth, whereas contrivance is not. Try using the exaggeration tool from page 138: "The product is so *(insert benefit)*, that…"

Here's an example: a pizza is so large that you will need a very, very large dinner table. (Read script 5 aloud for maximum comedic effect.)

Listen to the Radio

Listen to plays, remote news reports, and sports commentary. A sports commentator's job is to visualize the game for you. The more description they use, the more you feel like you're watching it. The better ones describe the actions and reactions of the players, the weather, the atmosphere, the sound of a bat hitting a ball (the only real sound effect they can rely on is the crowd). Note: sports commentary is another cliché in radio advertising.

Time Lengths

Radio spots are typically 30 or 60 seconds in length (although 20s, 40s, 50s, 70s, 80s, and 90s do exist). It's hard to communicate an idea on radio in 30 seconds (which is largely why it's becoming less common), whereas something over 60 seconds can get boring, especially after repeated listening. You could argue that a great 30-second spot is the most effective because you don't have to keep the listeners' (ever-shortening) attention for as long. With a 30, you just have less time to be interesting.

4. **Client/Brand:** COI Army
Title: "Tank"
Time: 60 secs

....

MVO: Listen closely. You're about to get a crash course in using the Milan anti-tank missile.
MVO: This is the sound of a British tank.
SFX: (split second) British tank.
MVO: This is an enemy tank.
SFX: (split second) Enemy tank.
MVO: You got that? British Tank.
SFX: (split second) British tank.
MVO: Enemy tank.
SFX: (split second) Enemy tank.
MVO: Enemy tank.
SFX: (split second) Enemy tank.
MVO: British Tank.
SFX: (split second) British tank.
MVO: Now, just imagine that it's night.
SFX: Forest sounds, night creatures.
MVO: You're in a battle and armed with a Milan anti-tank missile. A tank is coming towards you through some trees.
SFX: Muffled tank sounds.
MVO: So which is it? Friend or foe?
MVO: One. Two. Three. Four. Five. In the Army, you may only have seconds to decide. That's why before soldiers are trained to use equipment like Milan, they're trained to use equipment like their ears. If you're between 16 and 26, and you'd like to learn skills like this, phone 0345 300 111. Or visit your local Army careers office or job center.

Army Soldier. Be the Best.

Agency: Saatchi & Saatchi, London
Creatives: Jason Fretwell, Nik Studzinski

5. **Client/Brand:** Little Caesar's
Title: "Family Dinner"
Length: 60 secs

....

DAD: (shouts) So how was your day, Timmy?
SON: (distant shout) What?
DAD: (shouts) I said how was your day?
SON: (distant shout) Oh…pretty good.
ANNOUNCER: Eating a pizza as long as Little Caesar's new Pizza by the Foot has its drawbacks.
DAD: (shouts) Great pizza, huh son?
SON: (distant shout) Sure is. Hey, Dad.
DAD: (shouts) Yeah?
SON: (distant shout) Is that Mom sitting next to you?
MOM: (to Dad) Good eyes on that boy.
DAD: (shouts) Yeah, that's your Mother.
SON: (distant) Say hi for me, will ya?
DAD: (to Mom) Timmy says hi.
MOM: (to Dad) Ask him if he'll pass me a slice with pepperoni.
DAD: (shouts) Hey, son.
SON: (distant shout) Yeah?
DAD: (shouts) It's your dad again.
SON: (distant shout) Oh. Hi, Dad.
DAD: (shouts) Hi, son. Listen. Pass me a slice with pepperoni.
SON: (distant shout) Okay.
SFX: Slice being thrown through the air, and landing nearby.
DAD: Boy, has that kid got an arm.
MOM: (to Dad) I'm so proud. (shouts) Nice throw, son.
ANNOUNCER: Little Caesar's new Pizza by the Foot. Nearly three feet of pizza and free Italian bread. Just ten ninety-nine. Carried out or have it delivered.
SFX: (jingle) Pizza! Pizza!

Agency: Cliff Freeman & Partners, New York
Creatives: Wayne Best, Ian Reichenthal

But whatever length, the tendency is to write way too much voice over or dialogue. To help, here's a "word length" guide:

Length (in seconds)	Words (maximum)
30	80–100
60	160–180
90	240–280

Don't forget, these numbers include product names and contact details (client addresses, web addresses, and/or telephone numbers).

In terms of word count, aim low. If the script is too short in recording, it's a lot easier to slow down the read, or stretch out the sound effects than to cut the script down.

Time It
To check the length, simply read it out loud (you'll read it too quickly in your head) *at normal speed*, accounting for sound effects. If it's too long, cut it down. This is rarely done, which is why so many radio spots characters and voice overs end up talking incomprehensibly fast in order to squeeze in all the information.

Don't Write, Borrow
Sometimes borrowing a piece of writing (as long as it's relevant) can be more effective than creating a new, "scripted" piece. A famous UK radio spot for the Red Cross entitled "Emergency Call" combined 150 harrowing seconds of actual telephone conversation of a Red Cross medical volunteer helping a desperate mother revive her dying baby. No "script" could have bettered it.

Scripts 6 and 7 are two more powerful examples that use the same approach.

Don't forget that you can borrow music and other sounds, too. Two simple radio spots that combine excerpts from famous songs (with just a single payoff line) are: a Heinz "Any food tastes supreme with Heinz salad cream" commercial (using UB40's "Rat in the Kitchen," including the punch line "I'm gonna fix that rat, that's what I'm gonna do"); and a VW Polo "Surprisingly ordinary prices" (using the theme tune to "Tales of the Unexpected").

Don't Do Radio "Ads"
As with any media you are working in, don't do radio "ads."

6. **Client/Brand:** Imperial War Museum
Title: "Letter"
Time: 90 secs

PRIVATE: *To the best Mum in the world…*
Dear Mum. This letter I hoped you'd never receive, because it's just a verification of that terse black-edged card which you received some time ago. Tomorrow we go into action, no doubt lives may be lost. But if this leaves the world a slightly better place, then I am perfectly willing to make that sacrifice. Don't get me wrong though Mum, I'm no flag waving patriot, no my world is centred around you and Dad, you are worth fighting for. And if it strengthens your security in any way, then it's worth dying for too. I want no flowers, no tears, no epitaph, just be proud, then I can rest in peace knowing I've done a good job. Surely there's no better way of dying. I loved you Mum, you were the best Mum in the world. Goodbye, Your Son.
MVO: *This letter was written by a young private the night before he died in battle. At the Imperial War Museum we don't try to glorify the war, we try to give you an idea of what it was like to be part of it.*

We're open 10 until 6 every day. Nearest tube is Lambeth North.

The Imperial War Museum: part of your family's history.

Agency: Ogilvy + Mather, London
Creatives: Alun Howell, Ian Sizer

7. **Client/Brand:** Marie Curie Cancer Care
Title: "Angel"*
Time: 60 secs

MVO: *A man finds himself on a beach with his Guardian Angel. As they walk he notices two sets of footprints.*
"Whose are those?" he asks.
"They are yours," the Angel replies, "this is the path of your life."
"And who do the other footprints belong to?"
"They are mine," the Angel answers, "I was there throughout your life."
As they walk on, the Angel points to a place where one of the footprints begins to limp.
"There," he says, "that is where your wife fell ill. You see, I was there with you even then."
"And what about here?" the man says, indicating a part of the beach where there is only one set of footprints.
"That is where your wife died."
"Well where were you then?" the man asked angrily. "Where were you when I needed you most?"
"At that point," the Angel replied "I was carrying you."
FVO: *Thousands of Marie Curie nurses provide free care and 24 hour support to cancer patients in their homes.*
Marie Curie Cancer Care is a registered charity. Please make a donation to support us on 0800 661199.

* This is based on a story originally entitled "Footprints in the Sand" by an unknown author

Agency: Impact FCA!
Creatives: Shaun McIlrath, Ian Harding

8. **Client/Brand:** Life of Brian
Title: "Mrs. Cleese"
Time: 30 secs

MRS. CLEESE: *I?…into this?…*
SFX: *Noise of microphone.*
MRS. CLEESE: *Hello. My name is Muriel Cleese and I live in a very nice elderly people's home in Weston-super-Mare.*
My son John is in the new Monty Python film "Life of Brian."
I do hope you'll go and see it, because he's on a percentage and he says if it doesn't do well he won't be able to keep me on in the home any longer.
So see "The Life of Brian" now because I'm 102 years old and if I have to leave here it'll kill me.
(Laugh)
MVO: *If you want to help Mrs. Cleese please go and see "Monty Python's Life of Brian."*
(Mrs. Cleese laughs)

Agency: Lonsdale Advertising
Creatives: John Cleese, Terry Gilliam, Michael Palin

The Monty Python team took this approach when they had to produce a radio spot to promote their upcoming feature "Life of Brian." They could easily have played funny excerpts from the movie, or had people coming out of previews saying how great it was. (Borrrrrring!) What John Cleese, Terry Gilliam, and Michael Palin produced instead was fresh and lateral (see script 8).

The Cut Back
Like in TV, radio uses a cut-back technique (after the final voice over). As with any technique, use it sparingly and as necessary.

Call to Action
A "call to action" is sometimes used at the end of an ad, depending on the particular strategy, idea, client, or product. It's simply a line that tells the reader/viewer/listener the action to take to find out more information, make a donation, etc. This usually consists of a simple telephone number and/or a website address. The effectiveness of adding a call to action varies between media. Web banners and print (especially press ads) can rely on continual visual recognition (reducing the need for memorization, or running for a pen and paper). And TV ads can use combined visual and verbal call to action. But radio can only rely on verbal/sound. Aside from repeating a telephone number throughout the commercial, or using a "catchy" info jingle, repeat broadcasting/listening of the spot reduces the need to memorize important response information at the first attempt.

No Pack Shot
Remember, you can't rely on a pack shot in radio, so get the product name across (without repeating it a dozen times).

Over-used Actors
Because so much relies on voice over in a radio spot, it is arguably more important than in TV. Choose a voice that reflects the tone of the idea and the brand. Think about what kind of voice would work (describe them in your script). Give examples of famous people or actors that would fit. It will add to the feel of the commercial—and help sell it (it adds glamour). If you can afford it, and they agree, get someone famous. This type of borrowed interest is subtler than for TV, because you only hear the person. But note that the flavor of the month will date a commercial quickly, and generally over-used actors might not make your commercial sound distinguishable. There are plenty of good actors out there. Use a voice that's memorable (as part of audio mnemonics), but don't just think of the obvious actors: it will help to brand your campaign and make it unique.

As an aside, here's a good way to *critique* your own radio script. Simply ask yourself, "Would I be embarrassed to let my all-time favorite actor read the script?" If you would, you might want to write something better.

Real Campaign of Genius
Bud Light's "Real Men of Genius" campaign (formerly called "Real American Heroes" and later changed after 9/11) is the most awarded radio campaign ever. And deservedly so. It's a big idea that never seems to run out of well-written, well-produced executions. There have been a number of great one-off radio spots, but very few campaigns—especially of this caliber. What's also interesting about "Genius" is how much better it worked on radio than on TV, proving that people's imagination can be replaced, but not necessarily bettered. This campaign also answers those critics who believe that America doesn't understand irony (scripts 9 and 10 are personal favorites).

The Future of Radio Advertising
The future of radio, as with traditional TV advertising, has been subject of much debate in recent years. This is centered around the exact impact that commercial-free satellite radio will have on network and local radio. The prediction is that the former will completely replace the latter, confident that people will pay a fee to be commercial free. But the introduction of a radio category at the 2005 Cannes International Advertising Festival awards implies a revived confidence in this media. Only time will tell whether or not this is naïve optimism.

9. **Client/Brand:** Bud Light
Title: "Mr. Way Too Much Cologne Wearer"
Length: 60 secs

SFX: 1980s power ballad (under and throughout).
ANNOUNCER: Bud Light presents… Real Men of Genius.
SINGER: Real Men of Genius…
ANNOUNCER: Today we salute you… Mr. Way Too Much Cologne Wearer.
SINGER: Mr. Way Too Much Cologne Wearer.
ANNOUNCER: Like a bullhorn, you're cologne announces your every arrival… four blocks before you get there.
SINGER: Here he comes now!
ANNOUNCER: Here a splish, there a splash—everywhere a splish-splash. You don't stop 'til every square inch of manhood is covered.
SINGER: Everywhere a splish-splash!
ANNOUNCER: Overslept and haven't got time to shower? Not to worry, you've got four gallons of cologne….and a plan.
SINGER: Pour it on!
ANNOUNCER: So crack open an ice cold Bud Light, Mr. Way Too Much Cologne Wearer…
SFX: Beer pops open.
ANNOUNCER:…because we think we smell a winner.
SINGER: Mr. Way Too Much Cologne Wearer.
ANNOUNCER: Bud Light Beer. St. Louis, Anheuser-Busch, Missouri.

Agency: DDB, Chicago
Creative: John Immesoete

10. **Client/Brand:** Bud Light
Title: "Mr. Nosebleed Section Ticket Holder Guy"
Length: 60 secs

SFX: 1980s power ballad (under and throughout).
ANNOUNCER: Bud Light presents…Real Men of Genius.
SINGER: Real Men of Genius…
ANNOUNCER: Today we salute you…Mr. Nosebleed Section Ticket Holder Guy.
SINGER: Mr. Nosebleed Section Ticket Holder Guy.
ANNOUNCER: Congratulations. With the help of two sherpas and a mountain goat, you have finally reached your seats.
SINGER: Touch the sky!
ANNOUNCER: Tickets…check. Souvenir…check. Oxygen mask…check.
SINGER: Gettin' dizzy!
ANNOUNCER: From where you sit, you can see your house…and Canada…and Japan.
SINGER: Oseokanowa!
ANNOUNCER: The one thing you can't see? The game.
SFX: Oh no!
ANNOUNCER: So crack open an ice cold Bud Light, oh chairman of the cheap seats…
SFX: Beer pops open.
ANNOUNCER:…because you sir, sit on top of the world…literally.
SINGER: Mr. Nosebleed Section Ticket Holder Guy.
ANNOUNCER: Bud Light Beer. St. Louis, Anheuser-Busch, Missouri.

Agency: DDB, Chicago
Creatives: John Baker, Rob Calabro.

12 Integrated

What is "Integrated"?

When an idea is translated into more than one form of communication or media (be it advertising, design, or both) it's known as "integrated." In other words, it's not just a big idea that translates within one creative area, it's a big idea *realized* across many areas.

Or put simply, a Really Big Idea.

"Integrated" is the current term that is most commonly used, especially at awards shows. Here are some alternatives that mean the same thing:

- Multimedia*
- Multiple media
- Multi-platform
- Mixed media
- Transmedia
- 360º branding+
- Through the line
- Cross channel (or Cross media)

*Confusingly, "multimedia" is also used specifically within design firms that focus primarily on various forms of interactive and digital media.

(+Adapted from Ogilvy's "360º Brand Stewardship")

These days, everyone wants to be seen as providing an "integrated service"—from global marketing companies to the creative freelancer on the street. But exactly what integrated branding solutions are they each providing? Can you compare the two? At this point in time, the definition of integration (and therefore the answers to these two questions) remains fairly broad and ambiguous. However, although integrated seems new, it's fundamentally old—especially within the ad industry. For years, agencies have successfully pitched for accounts by showing how their big idea can translate into every conceivable media. But what has clearly changed since its birth is the *number of applications*. Traditionally, "through the line" (as it was more commonly called) was limited to print, TV, radio, direct marketing, and perhaps PR. Recent additions to the mix include: ambient/guerrilla, social media, viral (e.g., buzz marketing), digital/interactive (i.e., websites, online ads, web videos, mobile apps, etc.)

The appearance and recognition of these newer forms of media has caused an increase in the number of ad agencies/design firms defining themselves as "full service." Again, how each firm defines this term (and "integrated") varies. Here are four possible translations (or levels) from the hardest to pull off (A), to the easiest (D).

A   A big idea for a single client/project with multiple executions (no "repeats"), translated into multiple media.

B   A big idea for a single client/project with multiple executions (some "repeats"), translated into multiple media.

C   A big idea for a single client/project with multiple executions (all "repeats"), translated into multiple media.

D   A series of smaller ideas for various clients/projects, each translated into one or two media, but when combined, the agency's portfolio is multimedia.

Clearly, the key difference between levels A, B, and C is the extent to which the executions from an idea are being repeated (e.g., a print headline becomes a voice over for TV and/or radio, plus a banner ad, etc., etc.) Although approach C has been used to great effect in the past (e.g., "start with a press ad, then blow it up…and it's a poster! Stick it in an envelope…and it's direct mail! Film it…and it's a TV ad! Animate it…and it's interactive!"), the ever-cynical ad industry is beginning to question the credibility of the "matching luggage" approach.

However, one could easily argue that outside industry awards shows (i.e., in the *real world*), it shouldn't matter if the same execution is repeated into various media. Firstly, if an execution can be easily repeated into other media, it's probably a sign that it's a really simple idea. Secondly, with all the communication clutter around, it may be smarter and more effective to drive a message home by simply repeating the executions verbatim. If it ain't broke, why fix it? (Or the "why make more work for yourself?" argument.)

So to conclude, perhaps any agency that calls itself "integrated" should be able to provide *all of these levels* of integration, from A to D, depending on the client, their budget, and their needs.

According to the agency TBWA/Chiat/Day, Pedigree's "Dogs rule" integrated campaign (overleaf) "began by helping Pedigree find their inner dog lover. Dog-friendly offices were created. A new corporate bible, *Dogma*, was written. New business cards featuring employees' dogs were printed. They even created a health plan for their dogs. In twelve countries spanning five continents…we did print. We did outdoor. We sponsored dog adoptions. We drew on sidewalks. We did online. We took the message all the way to the products on the shelf. And, of course, we did TV."

Creative director William Gerner explains "Gamekillers," an integrated campaign, as follows: "In the mating game, there are forces working against young guys. People whose sole mission in life is to cause guys to lose their cool and get the girl. They are called the Gamekillers. We created over a dozen of these cock-blocking characters and taught guys how to beat them: Keep your cool with Axe Dry. Then we launched a one-hour TV show that aired on MTV [and] a highly integrated multimedia campaign."

Youth Vote 2006 (see page 242) is an integrated media campaign that dramatizes the power of voting, as well as a need to have an opinion and "take a side." Targeting young apathetic adults, it provokes spontaneous political debates, assessment of personal beliefs, and ultimately, a higher percentage of youth votes.

The Wales Tourist Board (overleaf) tagline summed up the idea: for many inner-city English people, Wales is only "two hours and a million miles away." The campaign broke with a 60-second TV spot, billboards, tube cards, and cross-track posters. Then it spread to magazines, direct mail, and guerrilla marketing (including ads on dirty vans and road workers' jackets).

The Gamekillers: recognizable characters who prevent guys from scoring. The launch included a one-hour TV show and an integrated multimedia campaign, both aimed at teaching guys how to overcome these human obstacles, and get their girl. Tag: Keep your cool with Axe Dry. ***Client:*** *Axe.* ***Agency:*** *Bartle Bogle Hegarty, New York.* ***Creatives:*** *Jon Randazzo, Amir Farhang, William Gelner, Matt Ian, Kash Sree.*

This integrated campaign
includes product redesign,
a corporate manual, press,
outdoor, online, ambient, and
TV. *Client:* *Pedigree.* *Agency:*
TBWA/Chiat/Day, Los Angeles.
Creatives: *Chris Adams,*
Margaret Keene.

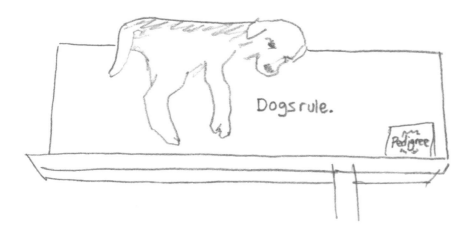

A collection of ways to dramatize the fact that for many English folk, Wales is within a two-hour drive. (Headlines: Peace and quiet/Genuine stress relief/Clean air/Real fresh air/is just two hours away. Tagline: Two hours and a million miles away.) *Client: Wales Tourist Board.* *Agency: FCA!* *Creatives: Justin Tindall, Adam Tucker.*

Integrated campaign uses "opposing outcomes" to encourage apathetic young voters to have an opinion on topics that affect their daily lives. Tag: Take a side. **Client:** *Youth Vote 2006.* **Students:** *Nicholas Panas, Chris Jackson, Anna Bratslavskaya, John Meglino.*

Fully Integrated Brands

Some awards shows like to keep "integrated advertising" and "integrated design" as two separate categories. But as the general disciplines of advertising and design continue to merge—and the number of "other media" increases—all these parameters will eventually disappear. This will result in a fully integrated concept or solution; or the "really, really big idea."

Strictly speaking, an integrated concept should include three or more media applications, not just "more than one," as stated above. A *fully* integrated concept should be able to incorporate multiple creative disciplines and technologies. The purest example of this is what some call "from the ground up" brand integration, beginning with the conception of an actual product (its name, strategy, design, merchandising, etc., etc.) When it comes to integration, this is the most ideal position for a brand to be in. If it's not, it makes full integration very difficult to achieve.

Kevin Palmer of Imagination, London makes this argument: "I think good creative will always be able to live outside of its medium. We are, like many art forms, telling stories, and if that story is a good one then there's no reason why it shouldn't transcend platforms and media. Just as there are many good books that have been turned into great films, video games and even merchandise, so good interactive concepts (for example) should be able to work in other media—as long as the core idea, the core story, is a strong one."

A comprehensive multimedia list (starting with advertising, then design, and finally "other") includes, but is not limited to:

- Print (advertising only)
  - Press (magazine and newspaper—from color spreads to small-space black and white)
  - Posters (billboards, transit, specials/other)
- TV
  - Major network
  - Independent station
  - Cable
- Cinema
- Interactive TV
- Radio
  - Network/National
  - Local
- Ambient/Guerrilla
  - Special/one-off build

- 3D
- Petrol pumps
- Washroom
- Floor media
- Ticket barriers
- Miscellaneous (e.g., napkins, coasters, glasses, "free" food packets, matchboxes)
- Direct ambient (see direct, below)
- Live events
- PR and creative stunts
• Direct
- Direct mail
- Direct TV and cinema commercials
- Direct CD Rom and DVD
- Direct mobile phone advertising
- Direct ambient
• Integrated direct response
• Corporate and brand identity
• Product design
- Home/industrial use products
- Health and leisure products
- Others
• Packaging
• Graphic design
- Brochures and catalogues
- Annual reports
- CDs, DVDs, record sleeves
- Posters
- Book design (covers and complete books)
- Greetings cards, invitations, and stamps
• Environmental design and architecture
• Interactive and digital media
- Consumer/primary brand websites
- Business-to-Business (B2B) websites
- Microsites (mini-sites)
- Installations and experimental media
- Online, console, and portable games
• Environmental design and architecture
- Retail and services
- Leisure and tourism
- Industry, transport, and workplace
- Public environment and community
- Exhibitions, museums, and installations
• Point of purchase/sale displays (POP/POS)
• Online/viral advertising/contagious media ("word of mouth")
- Webisodes/viral films (original and adaptation)
- Webisodes/viral commercials (original and adaptation)
- Banners

- Interstitials
• Public relations (PR) (see Ambient/ Guerrilla, above)
• Buzz marketing
• Grassroots marketing
• Creative blogs
• Text messaging/mobile
• Product placement
- TV shows
- Music videos
- Films
• Sponsorship
- Event
- Exhibit
- Site
• Miscellaneous media
• Beer mats
• Coffee cup sleeves
• Gas pumps
• And so on

(As you can see, advertising is only one piece of the pie.)

What is New Media?

New media was once used to describe interactive and other internet-related media at a time when it *was* new. Now web is old, defined as part of a new tradition, so to speak. Therefore, the term "new media" now often refers to any media that has yet to be defined. It is boundary blurring. One example is the VW Polo Twist "ice car"—a life-size, exact replica of the car was sculpted out of ice and placed on a London street to promote its air conditioning. This could be equally defined as ambient media, alternative media, a PR stunt, street art, or a sculpture. But who cares how it's defined? Whatever it is, it's original in every respect— part new idea and part new media.

In a sense, this example of new media is the opposite of integrated because it's typically a "one-off" creation. Its newness is due to the fact that it's something you've never seen before. Again, the media, execution, and concept are virtually identical (whereas with integrated, the media platform is already defined and the concept is created around it, or vice versa). Desperate to find the "next big thing," the ad industry is notorious for elevating the size and significance of a new media concept. But if a particular "idea" does catch on, then it becomes something bigger, something else, something defined, and no longer new media. (Relating back to the above example, it's unlikely

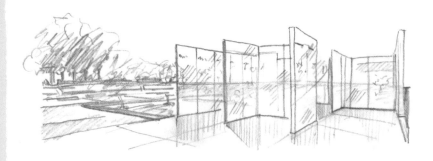

What is "new media"? Something that's never been done before (like this creation for The Pentagon New Day Memorial). *Client:* The United States Pentagon. *Agency:* ATM Design & Architecture. *Designers:* Jean Koeppel, Tom Kowalski.

that "Ice" will become the next recognized form of media, not that it was ever intended to be.) Over time, new media will also include new hybrids of old and new media that create a unique twist on what's been done before.

The genius of the design of The Pentagon New Day Memorial for Washington, DC's 9/11 victims is that it does the opposite of a typical memorial. Rather than being stone, and remaining totally unchanged, it is *interactive*. 183 giant, glass monoliths represent each of the victims. A self-producing layer of condensation allows visitors to pay their respects in writing, and be "at one" with the memorial itself. Overnight the condensation naturally disappears, with the opportunity to continue the healing process again, thereby creating a new, unique memorial each day. (This creation also relates back to the discussion in the introduction that points out examples of when an ad doesn't have to be an "ad.")

(For digital forms of media, see Integrated Interactive, page 209.)

The Brand and Branding

As mentioned in the Generating Strategies and Ideas chapter, you may be required to position a new brand, or reposition a dying one. Both tasks require that you define what the brand is. But first we need to ask, "what is *a* brand?" Strategically, a brand is a general term that tells you a product is not like anyone else's; it has its own identity. This identity goes beyond rational product differentiation (a rare thing these days, anyway) and beyond how a product is advertised or promoted.

Much has been written about the subject of brands. Here are three of the clearer explanations:

"A brand isn't just the name on the box. It isn't the thing inside the box, either. A brand is the sum total of all the emotions, thoughts, images, history, possibilities, and gossip that exist in the marketplace about a certain company."
—Luke Sullivan, *Hey Whipple, Squeeze This*

"A brand is a person's gut feeling about a product, service, or company."
—Marty Neumeier, *The Brand Gap*

"Brands come in all shapes and sizes; they may be specific or general, palpable or impalpable, global or national, expensive or cheap but in

most cases, it's not just what they are, but also what they represent that makes them powerful."
—Wally Olins, *On Brand*

My first US bank was European American Bank (EAB). I was happy enough with them, but when they told me they were being bought out and converted into Citibank, I was secretly excited, *even though* I had never been into a Citibank, seen one of their cards, or spoken to anyone about them. But my gut told me it was a much cooler, more contemporary, efficient, and prestigious bank than EAB. That's the power of a well-defined brand.

A brand is the most important asset any company can have. It's the heart and soul of a product. Its essence. Its personality. An intangible "something" that marketing, advertising, and design professionals are entrusted with. Consumers have a relationship with each brand: a level of trust. This trusting relationship creates *brand loyalty*, which has the potential to last a lifetime, even generations. As Wally Olins states:

> *"The power of a brand derives from a curious mix of how it performs and what it stands for. When a brand gets the mix right it makes us, the people who buy it, feel that it adds something to our idea of ourselves."*

A strong brand can mean the difference between making hundreds of dollars and thousands, or millions versus billions. For example, if you get enough people willing to pay a few pennies more for one particular brand of canned baked beans instead of a cheaper "supermarket label," over time these pennies really add up.

"Branding" is the process of recognizing, building, and executing a particular brand. The key to branding is *consistency*. Each element of the advertising, design, and marketing should own the same brand attributes: the same look, feel, tone, and personality. This is easier said than done, especially when you are dealing with a growing number of media. However, the more media that you successfully integrate into the mix, the greater the brand experience will be. That's the challenge that integrated brings. Without consistency, you'll end up with a "dog's dinner," which weakens the brand and confuses the consumer.

"Visual branding" is only one strand of design advertising, which is only part of brand building.

These techniques include the choice of type, color palette, actor(s), director, and other mnemonics (memory aids like an audio voice over, jingle, etc.) But long before a creative team reaches these decisions, the client, its marketing department, and the agency strategic/planning department should have already been building the brand—from the product up. After that, the visual branding itself can be integrated and translated throughout the product design, packaging, advertising, etc.

"Brand First"
In his insightful article, "Are You Brand-First?" Nick Shore argues that in business, a well-defined brand is everything: "…if you systematically dismantled the entire operation of Coca-Cola Co. and left them with only their brand name, management could rebuild the company within five years. Remove the brand name, and the enterprise would likewise die within five years…. That's the mark of a brand-first enterprise. More than a framework for marketing and communications efforts, the brand is the emotional source of the organization itself…. In the brand-first enterprise, everything about the company is derived from an emotional blueprint, a central organizing principle, a compelling essence…. Virgin calls it Virginity. Disney calls it Magic. Nickelodeon calls it Kid Power." He later points out that if you were to ask 25 employees to articulate their company's brand in five words, and the *total* list is more than 10 words, then the brand's emotional blueprint is not established.

Brand Research
The more you research about a brand and what it means to people (compared to its current or potential competition), the closer you'll be to defining it. The questions listed below are a good starting point. The sum of the answers help to determine the brand's equity, or value. The answers should be honest, whether positive or negative. The advertising (and the marketing and design) should then reflect this equity. In fact, you can have the best idea in the world, but if it isn't right for the brand (let alone the product), it will be a waste of time and money.

Note: brand research could also cover "product research," which focuses more on practical product details, including how the product works, plus any actual or potential benefits that can be used to create a strategy statement. These benefits are boiled down to a single-minded proposition, or "core value," that the brand stands for.

Exercise: pick two well-known brand names from the same market, i.e., they are in competition with one another. Answer the questions below to determine whether or not each product/service (p/s) has a distinct brand identity.

- What is the first thought that comes to mind when you think of the p/s and its brand?
- What other images come to mind? (Be honest and imaginative)
- Would you say that overall the p/s has a strong brand image? If so, what is it? Is it positive or negative?
- What emotions/feelings/memories do you and other people have when you mention the brand? And what about when they think about actually using the p/s?
- Research and outline the p/s's history since it began. Include any interesting facts or insights.
- Where is the p/s sold?
- List as many competitors to your p/s as you can.
- How are their brands different from yours?
- How do you think the people behind the p/s see their brand? In your opinion, does it match how their competitors see them?
- Could (and should) the p/s do more with its current brand image? Should it rethink the brand itself?
- If appropriate, what is the one core value (promise/benefit) that the brand has?
- Is their advertising currently reflecting the one core value accurately? If not, why not, and has it ever done so in the past?
- What is the tone (of voice) of the current advertising? Do you think it's appropriate?
- Who is the target group/market/audience?

Exercise: in 500 words, describe your favorite brand, explaining in detail why you like it.

How to Integrate a Big Idea

On paper, a big idea (that begins with a big strategy) should be easy to integrate. But in reality, it's not so easy. Smaller clients may not have access to an agency qualified enough to integrate every media. Nor do they have the budget. Larger firms often lack the level of communication within its organization to help an agency create the desired level of brand consistency.

There is one success story that stands out: Apple. Few brands of any size are as fully integrated as theirs. Part of their secret is Apple's ability to create virtually everything in-house—from product design to store design to distribution to advertising. This control leads to all-important consistency. The integration process began with a clearly defined mission and strategy: an apple is simple ("a" is for "apple," "b" is for "boy," "c" is for "cat"); Apple makes the computer simple. Apple also has a personality that transcends plastic, glass, and wires. They are (and support) innovative mavericks who "Think different." Lastly, Apple has standards. Their cool, user-friendly, high-quality products stand up to their advertising, and vice versa. Their first famous TV ad for the Mac assured us that 1984 wasn't like "1984." This integrity creates further brand loyalty.

Another brand that has built integrated product and communication is Mini. Crispin Porter + Bogusky's "Let's Motor" campaign has been diligently translated into every conceivable media. [There's even a mini ad (no pun intended) inside the car next to the sun-roof switch which reads, "Ask yourself, is it really necessary to close the top? Be honest."] The tone of voice and visual branding is so well defined the ads can practically write themselves—no matter where they appear (see overleaf).

Other executions of the campaign are found elsewhere within this book: "Checkboxes/Other" (page 46), and "Let's burn the maps" (page 226).

Remember, whatever the type or number of media you are working with, the most important element is, and always will be, *concept*. And the bigger the idea, the more you can do with it. In a pitch situation, it shows any prospective client that "we, the agency, have the ability to help grow your brand."

Brand vs. Sub-Brand

A brand is the main product or service name. A brand can be made up of a series of smaller, sub-brands. For example, Apple is the main brand; iPod, iTunes and PowerBook are examples of its sub-brands. Again, for the main brand to be successful, the branding for each sub-brand should always be consistent. Conversely, each sub-brand should be an offshoot: an expression (rather than a contradiction) of the main "umbrella" brand.

Targeting "Cool" Brands

Brands such as Apple and Mini are the quintessence of cool. But what is "cool"? It's a difficult word to define, and a quality that many brands desire, given the number of potentially competitive "cool" products aimed at the growing youth market. In terms of advertising, the worst thing you can do is *say* that a product is cool. As Luke Sullivan states, "The answer is to *be* cool. Nike never once said, 'Hey, we're cool.' They just were." Cool brands start and end with the product. If the product is cool, it won't have to try hard (a sub-trait of coolness), and therefore the brand can be cool too.

Narrowing the target market to "teenagers" creates further challenges. Teens are historically and biologically moody and stubborn—just ask a parent. They not only hate being told what to do, but they also hate being told what to buy. (Even more so than the average modern day adult-age consumer.) This comes neatly back to cool brands. Much like a rebellious teen, a cool brand doesn't care what people think (or at least that's the impression it gives out), which is why the two are such a formidable pair.

The term "teenager" was coined some fifty years ago. So it stands to reason that today's teen is not the same as the last generation's teen, or the one before that, and so on. And as mentioned in the Strategy chapter, a thirteen year old is a different creature from an eighteen year old. As a result, the youth market is becoming harder to define. And it's growing. For example, the traditional way to target even younger kids (who now make up part of the Generation Y population) was to target their parents instead. However, this is becoming increasingly redundant because many of these

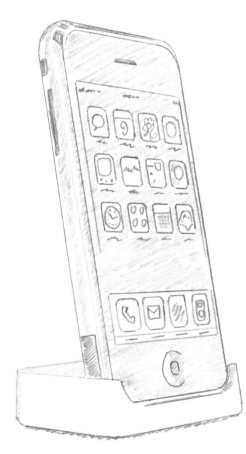

Apple's full brand integration starts from the ground (product) up. *Client: Apple. **Design group:** Apple Industrial Group. **Designers:** Bart Andre, Danny Coster, Richard Howarth, Daniele de Luliis, Jonathon Ive, Steve Jobs, Duncan Kerr, Matthew Rohrbach, Doug Satzger, Cal Seid, Christopher Stringer, Eugene Whang.*

Put very simply, "marketing" is the process involved in putting a product or service on the market. Marketing is sometimes defined by the "marketing mix," which is made up of four components—called the "4 Ps":

- **Product:** packaging, branding, trademarks, warranties, guarantees, product life cycles, and new product development
- **Price:** profitable and justifiable prices
- **Place:** physical distribution of goods
- **Promotion:** personal selling, advertising, and sales promotion

As you can see, marketing is much more than selling or advertising. It encompasses everything from what products or services you sell, to how you get them to the customer.

But suppose a current product needed a sales boost, a marketing solution might be anything from a "2 for the price of 1" promotional offer, to a competition to find "special" packs of colored candy. The point is, whether an agency defines itself as full service, marketing, advertising, or marketing and advertising, it all starts with strategies and ideas.

Successful Brands vs. Unsuccessful Brands

Marketing, strategy, and branding techniques aside, there is something else that determines the success (or lack of) a brand—us. Wally Olins states in *On Brand*, arguably the best book on brands and branding:

> *"We like brands. If we didn't like them, we wouldn't buy them. It is we consumers who decide which brand will succeed and which will fail. Some brands are successful because people love them and can't get enough of them; nobody forces anyone to buy a baseball cap with the Nike logo on it. Other brands fail because people simply don't want them."*

He goes on to argue:

> *"…the brand is not really controlled by marketing people, despite their huge budgets, their research programs and their panoply of branding, advertising and event managing…. The brand is controlled by us—the consumers."*

Above Mini: another brand that has built integrated product and communication. *Client: Mini. Agency: Crispin Porter + Bogusky. Creatives: Ari Merkin, Mark Taylor (top); Ari Merkin, Steve O'Connell, Mark Taylor (above).*

Opposite Gatorade "Replay" incorporated the sports drink brand into an ingenious athletic event: a rematch of a tied championship game between two high school teams played fifteen years after the first match. The nation followed this dramatic, uplifting documentary online and on network TV, and it was well covered in the news media. *Client: Gatorade. Agency: TBWA/Chiat/Day, Los Angeles. Creatives: Brent Anderson, Steve Howard.*

children are being given a disposable income at a younger age. More than ever before, pre-teens are financially able to make purchasing decisions by themselves. This has questioned the appropriateness of using traditional advertising, while the industry searches for new, non-advertising methods to attract this and other markets.

These are all reasons why corporations such as Sony have spent millions researching and comparing this most recent generation, Gen Y, born between 1979 and 1995 (who, numbering 57 million, are the largest consumer group in the US).

What is Marketing?
Marketing is a huge, business-oriented subject. Part science, part arts, some people spend their life gaining degrees, business degrees, and doctorates in marketing.

The Integrated Writer

The ongoing evolution of the interactive, digital copywriter (which is examined fully in the Interactive chapter) has had a knock-on effect on the role of today's integrated, multimedia copywriter.

In short, copywriters now occupy a vast creative territory—from the biggest business-building idea to the word on the screen. As Teressa Iezzi explains, "While any copywriter worthy of the title strives to make better ads, now those 'ads' can be almost anything—a film, a TV show, and mobile app, a blog, a retail experience, a product, a song, a game, a distribution idea, a tweet, a scheme to get people to pay for tap water."

Leo Premutico believes that, "[Writers] need to be flexible, to write for different formats, to be able to react quickly and to create something that people can latch onto." Meanwhile, Rob Reilly, Co-chief Creative Officer at Crispin Porter +Bogusky states: "We're not an advertising agency anymore. We're in the business of invention. Copywriters are inventors."

Relating to this statement, Iezzi makes an interesting point: "The best agencies realize that the value of their offering isn't tied to one medium. Their function is building brands. Always has been. In fact, many would argue that today's new model agency is more similar in terms of the scope of its work to the agencies of yore, which handled everything from package design to point of sale before the TV juggernaut made it profitable to create silos and to place certain tasks 'above the line' and certain tasks 'below the line.'"

....

Exercise: create a unique idea/brand or content/brand "story" that isn't an ad. (Get inspired by HBO's "Voyeur," BMW's "The Hire," and Gatorade's "Replay.")

....

Exercise: try the Crispin Porter + Bogusky approach. Write a press release (a PR article) for your integrated campaign idea as if it was being produced. Is your idea good and big enough for the mainstream press to write about it? Use a catchy "editorial style" headline, etc. If it doesn't sound compelling in this form, it's unlikely to create much buzz if executed.

....

Integrated interactive using a new medium: the "Chalkbot."* This machine was able to chalk the entire Tour de France course with (bright yellow) messages of hope and encouragement in the fight against cancer. The messages were sent by supporters via SMS, web banners, Twitter, or WearYellow.com. Other media included a TV spot, press ads, and OOH (out-of-home advertising).
Client: Nike Livestrong Foundation.
Agency: Wieden & Kennedy, Portland.
Credits: Adam Heathcott, James Moslander, Shannon McGlothlin, Marco Kaye, Tyler Whisnand, Danielle Flagg, Mark Fitzloff, Susan Hoffman, Marcelino J. Alvarez, Jeremy Lind, Sarah Starr, Peter Lindman, Rehanah Spence, Rob Mumford.

*Chalkbot came from the word "Chatbot" (Chat robot)—a computer program designed to simulate an intelligent conversation between one or more people. The "chalk" in Chalkbot refers to a cycling tradition where spectators chalk the streets with positive written messages for their favorite riders to read en route.

13
Execution

In advertising, the word "execution" can mean more than one thing. In previous chapters concerning concept, an execution meant "each separate, individual ad that is derived from a campaign thought." But in the context of this chapter, execution means "the final layout design and production of an ad." Or simply, "how an ad is executed." (Hence, "poor execution" means a bad or sloppy-looking ad.)

The types of layout, in order of "finish" are: thumbnail, loose rough layout/hand comp, tight layout/hand comp, computer comp, and finished ad (including crop marks, etc.) Hand-drawn layouts are sometimes called "tissues," taken from the tissue/tracing paper on which the ads are drawn. Agencies often call the first round of concept critiques a "tissue session." (Note: for the purposes of this book, I have used mostly *tight* hand comps for three simple reasons. Firstly, thumbnails and loose roughs are not always clear unless you know the idea already. Secondly, a tight comp incorporates many of the art director's layout decisions, which is useful for students to see. Lastly, a computer comp is too close to a final ad.)

Once all the conceptual elements of a print ad or campaign are in place (i.e., headline, tagline, basic layout, final body copy, logo, etc.) it's time to art direct and design it into a stylish finished ad, using digital artwork. This is not only to make the ad "work," but also to make it look visually compelling. This is when the craft skills of digital layout, typography, and photography or illustration take over. The key word (that everyone uses) is *craft*. Good art direction creates a good first impression, and helps to brand an ad (see the TV chapter for TV production and execution, including directors, editors, actors, voice overs, location and music, etc.)

In terms of final execution across all creative fields (advertising, design, movies, etc.), the level of *sophistication* is improving all the time. It's a self-perpetuating, upward spiral: technology improves, execution improves, consumer expectations increase, technology improves, execution improves, etc., etc.

Numerous books have been written about each craft skill that is used to execute a visual ad— be it for print, TV, or interactive. These books also include the numerous software application manuals and self-help guides. (A list is included at the end of this chapter.)

But as always, you have to learn to walk before you can run. Being an introductory chapter, I will focus primarily on the basic, practical tools for executing print ads, some of which can also be applied to creating TV storyboards, plus other media.

Agency of One
Until recently, in order to get a good entry level job at a decent agency, the ad student had to create a portfolio of print and TV *concepts* that could win awards in the industry—in the form of *rough* layouts only. But because of the increasing affordability, availability, and advances of computer equipment and software, today's student is also expected to *execute* these potentially award-winning concepts as if they were produced by an agency, especially print (student TV work is typically executed in unfinished, storyboard form, rather than "shot" pieces). To get a job as a junior creative, their ads have to look like they actually ran! This expectation is particularly common in countries such as the US, an early adopter of personal computer technology in the workplace. Combine this fact with the growing number of small, full-service "hybrid" ad agency/graphic design firms, and today's job market expects "entry levelers" to be "all round techno savvy ad concept designer freaks," ready to hit the ground running from day one.

For various reasons, other countries have been slower to adopt these demands (although it is changing, in the UK, a higher percentage of student print/TV portfolios seen by traditional agencies are still hand drawn). In truth, each agency culture is different, too, wherever the location. Some larger agencies opt for a more traditional division of labor approach to producing each piece of work, whilst others rely on an in-house training program, where you start as an assistant art director rather than a junior art director.

But in terms of putting a portfolio together in the *US*, students (along with guidance from their instructors) have to produce everything themselves, essentially becoming a modern-day Renaissance person: an "Agency of One." Before it was all about concept, now it's all about concept *and* execution. This means if you're an ad student, especially an aspiring junior art director, you have to cover all the craft skills that a creative department at an agency would have. In other words, you have to be an art director, a graphic designer, a typographer, a photographer, an illustrator, and a storyboard/director (TV).

Here's how to pull off this seemingly impossible task:

- Learn the computer inside out. (Photoshop, Quark, InDesign, Illustrator, and Flash are a must. Freehand is particularly versatile. These software programs will empower you.) (See Which Software?, page 264.)

- Learn photography and get a digital camera. (4 mega pixels is enough for up to 11 by 17"/A3 prints)

- Learn typography, collect typefaces, and experiment with a handful of popular, well-designed ones (see Typeface and Typography Websites, page 256).

- Be resourceful. Beg and borrow for props, use of locations, etc. (Say it's for a student project instead of professional use, and people are usually very accommodating.)

- Know where to get royalty-free stock imagery (gettyimages.com is one of the largest. For a full list, see page 260).

- Collect interesting visual material (see Keep a Visual Scrapbook, below).

- Borrow fellow students (photography majors, illustrators, models, etc., can help your ads look good. In return, they have something for *their* portfolios.)

Do Whatever it Takes

Do whatever it takes to get your work looking as professional as possible. I had a student who was working on an anti-litter print campaign. He needed a powerful, realistic shot of a wild animal that had died from accidentally trying to swallow a polystyrene coffee cup (a common problem). He found a photo of a dead animal, but he couldn't make the coffee cup in its mouth look real, despite hours in Photoshop. So what did he do? He drove around the countryside until he found a dead raccoon on the side of the road, shoved a cup in its mouth, and took a photo! A bit sick perhaps, but he got exactly what he needed for his book. (The Student Book chapter explores the whole portfolio/job searching process.)

Keep a Visual Scrapbook

Many good art directors are like visual magpies, often keeping a scrapbook-type folder full of various visual materials that happen to catch their eye. These can include photos, paintings, drawings, typefaces, film and TV clips, animation, other ads, design pieces, postcards, magazine and newspaper clippings—antique, retro, kitsch, contemporary or futuristic looking. Basically anything that might be useful one day, as part of your finished ad. You may wish to borrow a tiny element or the entire style. In addition, start building a general library of good visual reference books on art, photography, design, type, stock images, etc.

Searching for imagery is particularly useful at the execution stage because it solves art direction "blank canvas" when you can't think of a way to craft the ad visually. Stimulus material does just that: it stimulates and inspires, triggering off new ideas. These visual references can also be used at a presentation to give the client an idea of the look and feel of the final ad. If presented loosely on large pieces or card (rather than as a close replica of the final layout or commercial), they are known as "mood boards" (see also Search, page 266).

Don't Make it Look Like You've Used a Computer

I mean this in two ways: firstly, unless there's a reason to create surreal "graphic art" visuals, avoid over-designed computer layouts that look like you've used every Photoshop tool in one ad. (If you're not sure what these visuals look like, look inside an old stock image book, usually listed under "concepts"!) Secondly, avoid all pixilated, bitmapped, and blurred type, images and logos, and "cloudy" retouching.

Avoiding Pixilation: Do the Math

Pixilation occurs when the resolution (number of pixels/dots per inch) is not high enough for the size the image is being printed or displayed at, creating a low quality, "blocky" looking image. For the screen (e.g., the internet), 72 dpi is sufficient, whereas any printed work usually requires images to be saved at a minimum of 300 dpi (some print jobs require an even higher dpi).

When the final image size *equals* the original image size, dpi does not change, and quality is unaffected (remaining at 72 dpi for screen, 300 dpi for printed material).

When the final image size *is less than* the original image size, dpi and quality will appear to improve.

But when you want to print an *enlarged* version of the original image, the dpi and quality will decrease. For example, by doubling the size of the original image (twice the height and twice the width, or photocopying it at 200%), you are actually *quadrupling* the surface area. This means the dpi will appear to decrease fourfold.

In other words: 72 dpi becomes the equivalent of 18 dpi (screen), 300 dpi becomes the equivalent of 75 dpi (print).

The key to avoiding this decrease in resolution and quality is to *compensate* for any difference in size between your original image and your final image, by calculating the required dpi in advance. Here are some examples in the table below (see also Common File Types, page 265):

Logos

Logos are sometimes called "identities" or "marks." In a finished layout, the logo should look perfect. Even though logos are small, many students have poor quality printed logos in their books. Part of the reason is that corporate website logos (that you can drag onto your desktop) are low-res 72 dpi GIFF files. Some websites such as brandsoftheworld.com have lots of well-known logos at higher resolution EPS files (see Common File Types, page 265). Another possibility is to re-create the logo in Illustrator. But the best option is to scan in the original logo (from a brochure, packaging, etc.) at 300 dpi. Either ask the company to send you some free printed literature you can scan, visit a participating store for literature, or simply buy the product itself.

. There are three basic types of logo: *letter form*, *word form*, and *picture form*. Some are literal, others are more abstract. The best logos are those that have the most flexibility in terms of size/scale,

Logos: word form, letter form, and picture form. Some are literal, others are more abstract.

Examples of Size Ratios to Avoid Pixilation			
Increase	*Size of Original*	*Division*	*Final Size*
200% (× 2)	288 dpi	÷4	72 dpi
	1200 dpi	÷4	300 dpi
150% (× 1.5)	216 dpi	÷3	72 dpi
	900 dpi	÷3	300 dpi
125% (× 1.25)	180dpi	÷2.5	72 dpi
	750 dpi	÷2.5	300 dpi
100% (× 1)*	72 dpi	÷1	72 dpi
	300 dpi	÷1	300 dpi
50% (× 0.5)	72 dpi	n/a	72 dpi (288 dpi equivalent)
	300dpi	n/a	300 dpi (1200 dpi equivalent)

*No compensation is required for the same or lesser final image size

point size | cap height | ascender | top line | mid line | x-height | baseline | beard line | descender

The anatomy of type.

color, and medium. A logo should be equally legible as a tiny mark on a business card, small space ad, or internet banner, as on the biggest of billboards. In terms of color, keep your options open. A simple, well-designed logo should work in either all-white, all-black, or its original color(s). This gives you the flexibility to use it in a black-and-white ad, or when your choice of color palette clashes with the all-color logo (in which case, to maximize contrast and legibility, you would use the white logo with a darker background, and the black logo with a lighter background).

Again, an excellent resource for famous and lesser-known downloadable logos is brandsoftheworld.com. This can save you time finding hardcopy logos to scan, plus the resolution is higher than simply dragging a 72 dpi logo from a product's website.

Basic Typography

You could probably study typography your entire life and still not know everything. People forget that it's a career in itself. (That's why the smarter agencies hire a typographer as well as an art director to co-produce their award-winning print work.)

Basic terms:

- **Type:** a general term for letters and lettering (letter, word, and sentence displays). From the Greek word "typos," which means "letterform."
- **Typeface:** a specific design of an alphabet (e.g., Baskerville, Bodoni, Futura, Times Roman).
- **Font:** a complete set of *one* size of *one* typeface (e.g., the keyboard of a typewriter).
- **Roman:** the most common typestyle, in which the letterforms are upright.
- **Italic/oblique:** the second most common typestyle, in which the letterforms slant to the right.
- **Script:** a typeface based on handwritten letterforms (e.g., Thomson Quillscript).

- **Serif:** type with short stokes, or "feet," which project from the ends of the main strokes.
- **Sans serif:** a font without short strokes, or "feet," ("sans" is French for "without").
- **Weight:** the thickness of stroke, e.g., black, extra bold, bold, semi bold, medium, regular, light, ultra light, thin.
- **Condensed:** a narrowed, compacted typestyle.
- **Extended:** a widened, expanded typestyle.
- **Family of type:** all the combined styles and sizes of a given typeface.
- **Point size:** the standard measurement of type, measured between the top of the ascender to the bottom of the descender.
- **Pica:** a unit of measurement that calculates the horizontal space/length of a line of type.
- **Justification:** the way in which the text flows from left to right. Text can be left, right, center, or fully justified. Other terms include "flush left," "flush right."
- **Lead(ing):** the spacing between the baselines of text. (Originally from the strip of soft metal separating lines of type.)
- **Kern(ing):** the overhang of one letter to another, which affects the spacing of pairs of characters. Kerned text is altered to make it clearer, e.g., T o (un-kerned); To (kerned).

The standard typewriter is a one-unit system, meaning that each character and mark occupies the same amount of space. Typesetting effectively "pre-kerns" the characters to occupy varying amounts of space, although further kerning may be required.

- **Letterspacing:** the spacing between the (typically capital) letters of a word, sometimes varied to improve legibility. (This is not the same as kerning, which deals with "problem pairs" of letters.)
- **Wordspacing:** the spacing between words. This is reduced or increased to make type fully justified, or to change the overall read of "ragged" (unjustified) text.

- **Gutter:** the space between a number of columns, or between the text and the spine or edge.

There are hundreds of books on type and the use of type. A list is included at the end of this chapter. (An excellent, highly recommended reference book is *Basic Typography: A Design Manual* by James Craig.)

Type = Brand, Message + Tone

The choice of type can help to define the brand, communicate the right message, target the right audience, and emphasize the chosen written/visual tone of voice. In short, it can make or break an ad.

The following is the most basic demonstration that I've seen of how important the choice of type is:

For example: "Fresh Eggs" (what says "fresh"? Freshly hand-painted sign outside a farm) and "John Smith. Brain Surgeon" (what says "qualified, professional"? Times New Roman, on a gold, mounted plaque).

Now suppose we switch it: "Fresh Eggs" (Times New Roman, on a gold, mounted plaque) = clinical, artificial, preserved, and unappetizing. "John Smith. Brain Surgeon" (freshly hand-painted sign outside a farm) = I would never go to this man for brain surgery!

Handwritten Type*

Just as illustration may be more appropriate than photography for your campaign, handwritten type offers something that digital typography lacks: character. *Handwritten: Expressive Lettering in the Digital Age*, a book by Steven Heller and Mirko Ilic, is a wonderful examination and promotion of hand-drawn type, complete with hundreds of inspiring examples from design and advertising. The authors (whose motto is "the hand is mightier than the pixel") cleverly categorize manual lettering into eight creative themes:

- "Scrawl" (raw, splotchy, and untidy)
- "Scratch" (scraped, cut, gouged)
- "Script" (ornate, curlicue, sinuous)
- "Stitch" (sewn, sutured, embroidered)
- "Simulate" (redrawn, fake, copied)
- "Shadow" (dimensional, voluminous, monumental)
- "Suggestive" (metaphorical, symbolic, surreal)
- "Sarcastic" (comical, ironical, satirical)

*Do not confuse this term for manual lettering with a script, digitally "handwritten" typeface, such as Lucida Handwriting.

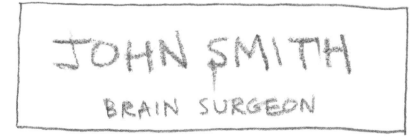

A basic lesson in choice of type: imagine a doctor's sign handwritten in paint, or a fresh eggs sign in a serif font.

Typeface and Typography Websites

Be weary of novelty fonts, pre-stored computer fonts, and amateurish typography websites. Choice of type is subjective, but here are some well-designed, generally well-respected typefaces.

Sans-Serif	Semi- or Slab-Serif	Serifs
Helvetica	Bodoni	Garamond
Univers	Rockwell	Janson MT
Scala Sans	Clarendon	Minion
Futura	Agfa Rotis Semi	Caslon
Interstate		Century Schoolbook

Type = Concept/Execution

Sometimes the type itself plays a central role within the idea and execution of a print or TV ad: it's not just there to communicate the words of a headline, body copy, or super. (Note: TV has the added use of animation, too.) Type as concept/execution often produces an incredibly simple, clever ad because the idea is right there in the text. One of the first examples I ever saw was twenty years ago (and I still remember it) in an *Interview* magazine article on the actor Christopher Walken. The black-and-white photo was of Walken standing by a pedestrian crossing in Manhattan. The title simply read: CHRISTOPHER WALKEN, except the words "stop" and "walk" were in a red and green. (Genius)

The examples in the following ads demonstrate this ability even as simple, hand-drawn roughs.

• •

Exercise: famous people are like brands. We get a feeling as soon as we hear their name: a definite, unique picture. Think of ten famous people (dead or alive), and pick a typeface that expresses each persona. Restrictions: black, roman (upright) type only; UPPERCASE, lower case, or upper and lower.

• •

Optical Type Tweaks

When using left (or right) justified text, a standard text box will position type exactly rather than optically. Because not all letters are the same shape (for left justified, some *begin* with a vertical, e.g., caps B, D, and H, some are horizontal, e.g., T, I, and

Z, some are diagonal, e.g., A, X, and Y, some are rounded, e.g., C, G, and O, and some are randomly curved, e.g., J and S.) This can be uneasy on the eye (especially with larger text-like headlines). As a result, the first letter in each line (or the last letter if right justified) may have to be moved left or right to align optically, depending on which letters are stacked.

Of course, if each type of letter is stacked, no adjustments will have to be made. They are already perfectly left justified. For example:

B…
D…
H…

or

C…
G…
O…

However, it's more than likely to be a mixture of shapes like:

T…
L…
O…

(In this example, none of the letters are vertical, optically speaking, and will need a slight left/right adjusting. This is obviously easier to show in an animated presentation than in a book.)

Note: some tweaking may also be required with centered type, especially with beginning/ending letters with "extra" punctuation (e.g., ",—: ;).

Photography or Illustration?

If your concept contains a visual, you need to decide whether the visual(s) would work better as a photograph, an illustration, or a combination of the two. Most print advertising uses photography, although illustration is becoming increasingly popular. (As is the TV equivalent of illustration—animation.)

Your decision must be based primarily on the idea (not what looks interesting or trendy). In general, pure photography is used when the visual has to feel "real," whereas illustration is relatively abstract and surreal. The chances are, most of your work will require photography rather than illustration. But don't rule out illustration. It may not be as real, but it can still be as dark or humorous.

H_2O
H_2O
H_2O

(TREAT WATER WITH RESPECT THIS CHRISTMAS)

ingle ells,
ingle ells.

The holidays aren't the same without J&B

When you're old you can become cold without even noticing it.
Often without so much as a shiver.

You simply slow down.

Soon you can't be bothered to make yourself
a proper meal. A slice of toast will do.
And why build up the fire? You feel all right.
You don't notice your body getting colder.

And you slow down.

The next thing you don't notice is your
mind slowing down. Did you order the
coal? You can't remember. Never mind.

Now you've really slowed down.

You feel drowsy. Even the effort
of going to bed seems too much.
You just nod off in the chair.
It doesn't seem to
matter any mor

The old can die from the cold without even noticing it.

PLAYSOCCER
American Youth Soccer Organization

Sizing of type = concept/
execution. **Client:** *Asian Pals of
the Planet.* **Agency:** *Batey Ads,
Singapore.* **Creatives:** *Andrew
Clarke, Scott Lambert, Antony
Redman, Mark Ringer.*

Removal of type = concept/
execution. **Client:** *Paddington/
J&B.* **Agency:** *Roy Grace.*
Creatives: *Chris Graves, Craig
Demeter.*

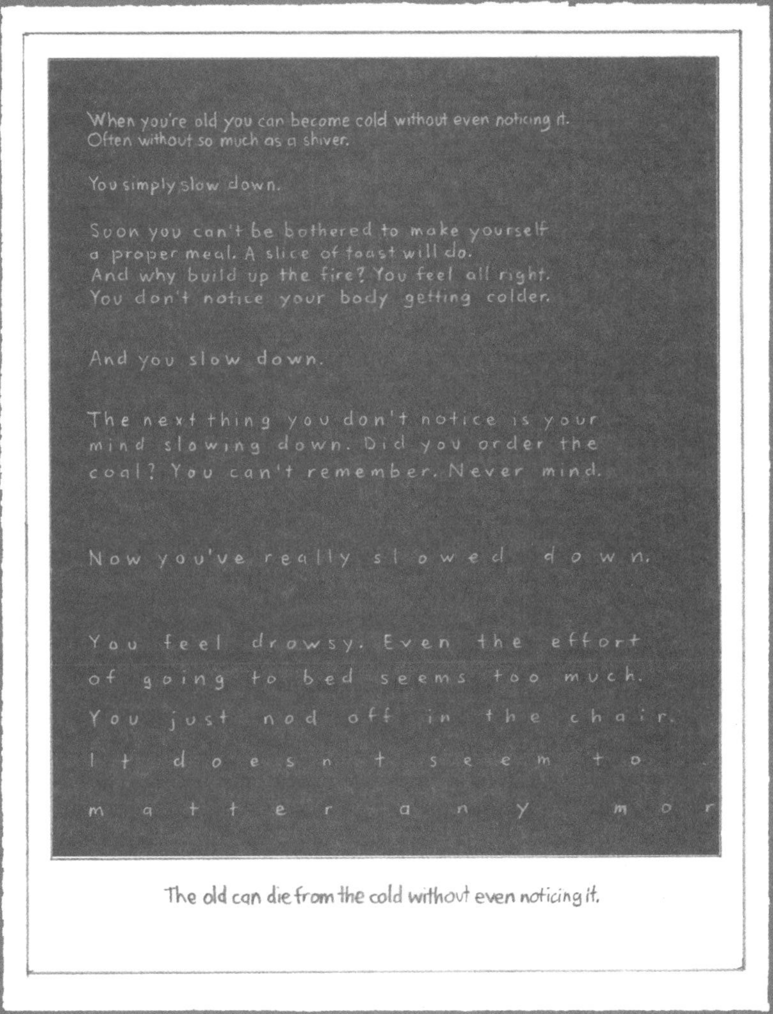

Simple letterspacing of type
communicates the effect of cold
weather on old people. **Client:**
Health Education Council.
Agency: *Saatchi & Saatchi,
London.* **Creatives:** *Paul Arden,
John McGrath.*

Even a car bumper sticker can be
typographically inspiring. **Client:**
*AYSO/The American Youth Soccer
Organization.*

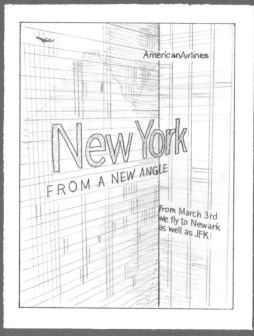

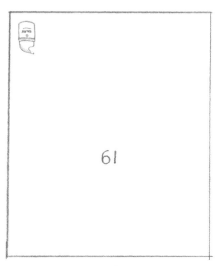

Get to Pro tennis in during tournament. ready see Penn balls action today's

MOM

61

Type, from a different angle.
Client: *American Airlines.*
Agency: *DDB, London.*

Positioning of type = concept/execution. **Client:** *Penn.*
Creatives: *Mike Gibbs, John Seymour-Anderson.*

Turn each ad upside down and the type reveals the message.
Client: *Oil of Olay.* **Agency:** *Saatchi & Saatchi, Australia.*
Creatives: *Jay Benjamin, Andy Dilallo.*

Once you decide between photography and illustration (or for TV, live action and animation), you have to decide on the *style* that best suits your idea. There are dozens of styles and genres for both.

The award-winning campaign for Wannabe Patrick Cox (see page 139) is an example where photography would have been less suited, making the idea of suicidal animals too real and literal. The final ads used hand-drawn cartoons that reflected the comic tone perfectly, whereas using photography would have made the ads less charming and humorous, and more "charity ad." (Conversely, a charity ad showing an illustration of a dead bird killed by an oil spill is likely to be less shocking and appropriate than a photograph.) Other notable uses of illustration are the VW Polo ads "Protective Behaviour" (page 29) and "Martial Arts" (page 87), plus Tampax "Embarrassed" (page 222), both opting for hand drawings throughout their respective campaigns.

"Tear," the VW ad commemorating the life of the Grateful Dead's Jerry Garcia would not have the same integrity or charm as a photographed image (with a "photoshopped" tear).

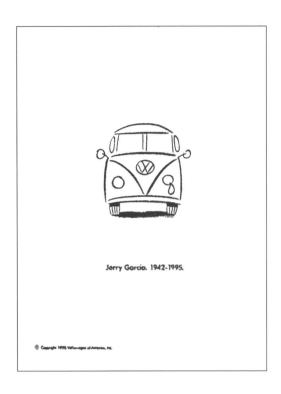

Jerry Garcia. 1942-1995.

© Copyright 1995 Volkswagen of America, Inc.

The use of illustration is tonally appropriate for this idea. Photography would be too contrived, and without the same charm and integrity. (The color version has a lovely light blue tear.) *Client: Volkswagen.* *Agency: Arnold Advertising, Boston.* *Creatives: Alan Pafenbach, Lance Jensen.* *Illustrator: Carla Siboldi.*

Stock Imagery vs. DIY

Once you have decided on whether the visual in your ad (campaign) is a photo or an illustration, you have three ways to create it in finished form, based on your rough layout. In *increasing* order of time and effort:

1. Find the exact, complete visual (stock library, magazines, product brochures, etc.)

2. Shoot or draw the exact, complete visual (camera, or by hand/Illustrator)

3. Re-create the visual with a combination of available images (using Photoshop and/or Illustrator)

Option 1 is the ideal solution in terms of time and effort, providing you've found exactly what you want (or at least an element you can use). Stock photography and illustration has improved a lot in recent years. (The number of cheesy, contrived stock images such as men in suits running a hurdles race, briefcase in hand, is thankfully declining.) These visuals (often laughably self-titled as "concepts") may work fine for wacky greetings cards or 1980s annual reports, but they are not meant for original ad campaigns (unless perhaps you're using them as a spoof).

A high-resolution stock image may look professional, but don't go for a "close enough," substitute visual (it could make a big difference to the concept and execution of your ad). Finally, search beyond stock imagery books and websites: there are literally hundreds of product and lifestyle magazines and free company brochures with excellent photography, all ready to be scanned.

If you can't find the exact visual "in stock" you may have to try Option 2—shoot or draw/illustrate. Digital cameras are a must-have for busy ad students. But be warned. Sometimes you can really tell if someone has used a digital camera—the colors look unnatural and sludgy in artificial light, and close-ups can look blurry. The ad ends up looking "studenty" rather than professional. So try to shoot under a natural light source (e.g., next to a window in average daylight), experiment and hold the camera as still as possible (a tripod is ideal). Of course you also have Photoshop to help you with brightness, contrast, color, and sharpness issues.

Here are some basic tips on DIY photo shoots:

- When setting up your composition, capture the idea. Keep it clean and simple (don't overcrowd the shot with unnecessary objects or people).

- Unless you have access to an airy studio or proper lighting equipment, shoot individual objects in natural light (see paragraph above).

- Make sure you at least cover your original rough composition with the same cropping and framing. (Then try other compositions, angles, cropping, and framing. You may discover something better!)

- Digital photos are virtually free, so take as many versions as you can while you still have everything "set up" at the location.

- Shoot slightly "wide." You can always crop in tight later, and if you shoot too close up you'll have nowhere to go if you choose to widen the shot later.

- Find the right location. Too many students take photos in and around their campuses or living quarters. Even when they try to hide it, it still looks obvious. This screams "student portfolio!" So unless your idea requires such a location, travel around to find a more suitable one.

- Don't DIY unless you have to. Best of all, get someone who has really studied photography and has the equipment to help you.

Finally, you have Option 3. If it's a really difficult image to find, shoot or draw, you might have to re-create the visual with a combination of available images. This translates to many hours in Photoshop. Do the best you can. A good creative director should be able to appreciate that the production values may be too much for one student (vs. an agency's full access to any professional illustrator, photographer, etc.) (See also Agency of One, page 251.)

Stock Imagery Websites
If you don't have access to the original stock books/CDs, the next best thing is the web. Here are some websites worth trying:

- gettyimages.com (Big. Owns many smaller image libraries. Highly recommended)

- agefotostock.com
- istockphoto.com
- photoalto.us
- shutterstock.com
- bbcmotiongallery.com (moving image only)

The Grid System
All good graphic design, in its most fundamental state, is based on a "grid." Including this book. You cannot learn how to use a grid system effectively from reading a few paragraphs on the subject. It comes from studying foundation graphic design, and from years of professional experience in designing printed material for 2-D (and perhaps 3-D) applications. The bible on the subject is *Grid Systems in Graphic Design* by Josef Müller Brockmann (the godfather of the grid). For now, here is an overview.

The origins of the grid system can be dated back to typography of the 1920s and 1930s. But it was the second half of the 1940s that brought the first examples of printed material designed with the aid of a grid. A grid evolved due to a need for the greatest possible order and economy of space on the printed page.

A grid, in essence, is a mathematical formula. It is a set of units divided across a space or page and functions as the underlying structure to establish maximum order and alignment. The grid used for print is not dissimilar from those used by architects and engineers in a set of plans for a building. When a grid is used properly, it will become the most fundamental underlying structure of any successful design.

- Less elements = more freedom (need for grid is reduced)

- More elements = less freedom (need for grid is increased)

In other words, a clean and simple layout usually has fewer elements, whereas a complex composition or layered layout has a greater number (see "Look," page 266).

Information presented with clear, logically positioned typography, illustrations, and photos will not only be read more quickly and easily, but the content will be better understood and retained in the viewer's memory. This isn't an opinion, it's a scientifically proven fact, and one that both ad and graphic designers should always try to remember.

Many designers are ignorant of the grid system as a means of establishing order and alignment.

Can I break the grid? Yes, advertising and graphic designers have produced award-winning work by breaking grids. But you need to use a grid in order to break it.

Both students and professionals are often guilty of not knowing how to best employ a grid and use it properly. Anyone willing to take the necessary time and trouble to learn how to use this simple system of units to structure the page will find that they are better equipped to solve any design problem effectively and efficiently. The end results will always be more functional, rational, and ascetically pleasing. This is partly because each element is aligning with one (or more) other element.

Begin with a Classic Layout

Steve Dunn advises young art directors to "Spend all your available time writing the ad, then even the most basic art direction will work."

What most people consider to be the "classic" print advertising layout is otherwise known as the VW layout, created by Helmut Krone at DDB, New York around 1960, itself an evolution of a classic three-column Ogilvy layout. Originally intended for single-page press ad, it can be adapted to a spread.

It's a clean, simple, and logical layout, and a template for many other later campaigns. It has a definite most-less-least hierarchy (outlined earlier in the Print chapter). It's comprised of a dominant visual above a centered headline below, with body copy below that (three columns for single page, four or more for a double), and logo near the bottom right.

Begin with this layout. Learn the constraints of its rigid consistencies, and appreciate its possibilities. Then experiment around it (see also How to Do a Volkswagen Ad, page 226).

General Layout Considerations

These are space, balance, mood, tone, rhythm, pitch, weight, texture, and type.

Keep it Consistent?

As outlined in The Campaign chapter, the key is to have executions that are "*the same—yet different.*" By "executions," I mean the three or more ads that make up a campaign. Each one mustn't be too similar conceptually, or too alike! In other words, there must be *elements* of consistency that make them part of a bigger campaign thought.

(VISUAL)

Centered headline.

Body copy in three columns   Body copy in three columns   Body copy in three columns
Body copy in three columns   Body copy in three columns   Body copy in three columns
Body copy in three columns   Body copy in three columns   Body copy in three columns
Body copy in three columns   Body copy in three columns   Body copy in [LOGO]

The same is true when it comes to the final art direction and production (the other form of "execution"). In other words, you don't want three ads to be *or* look the same. Neither do you want three disparate, unconnected ads—conceptually or visually. So, what things stay the same, and what things can change? That's entirely up to you, the art director. Just make sure there's some visual connection in there, usually a combination of a consistent typeface, color palette, and positioning of the elements (headline, visual, copy, logo). And unless there's a logical reason for having the third ad's logo or headline in a different position from the other two (e.g., better balance with the third visual), keep it the same.

Begin with a classic, VW layout. Then experiment around it.

The *sizing* of the four elements tends to be the most consistent aspect. For example, a logo looks strange at three different sizes, and there's no logic behind it. Whereas if the headlines within a campaign are set at different sizes, it's probably because they vary in length. Changing the point sizes merely keeps the proportion with the surrounding white space consistent. Again, there's a logical reason for it. (Note: even the headline-only *Economist* posters, with their rigid visual consistency, follow this pattern. The headlines are so dominant in terms of hierarchy that there's no question of the conceptual distinctions.)

Once you've made certain decisions about consistency, stick to them. Now matter how explicit or implicit your grid system is, use the layout "guides" wherever possible to *align* the elements of consistency between each ad, and check all the sizing and positioning. Any discrepancy will look like a mistake rather than deliberate, and immediately distract the eye of a creative director (see also Questions Every Art Director Should Ask Themselves For Each Layout, page 265).

The Layout Twist

As demonstrated in the Basic Tools chapter, the opposite tool applies to all areas of concept. It can also apply to execution, art direction, and layouts. Tim Delaney's creative partner, art director Steve Dunn recommends:

"Logos usually go lower right, so put them top left. Product shots are usually small, make them big. Instead of headlines being more prominent than the body copy, do the opposite. It's perverse, but I'm constantly surprised how many times it works."

Again, as long as there is some logic (a "method to your madness"), an implicit grid system, and a level of consistency, each ad will feel like part of a campaign: an overall vision.

(Again) Don't Do Ads

In terms of concept, an ad doesn't have to *feel* like an ad. The same is true of execution and art direction: an ad doesn't have to *look* like an ad (see Begin with a Classic Layout, page 261). Even a small thing can make an ad look different, and therefore stand out.

Trust Your Instincts

Let's go back to one of the first diagrams in this book: a simple drawing that showed how creativity is split between learning the tools, and learning to use your intuition and instincts (in addition to talent and tenacity). The latter is especially true of art direction and execution, which is perhaps more subjective and infinite than concept. If something doesn't feel right, change it. If it does, don't. Trust your instincts, your subjective opinions, and your personal tastes, some of which you are born with, and some you acquire with age and experience.

Compare and Contrast Your Layouts

A lot of time and effort goes into the final computer execution of a print ad or campaign. It's a long process with lots of decision-making along the way. One mistake that students make is to keep working on (and changing) the same, one page layout. But what happens when end up working on a layout for hours and then deciding you don't like it? Or maybe you prefer an earlier, overwritten version. Or re-create it and then change your mind back again. In short, you end up going around in circles.

However, to make the process and final decision easier, stick to this discipline: *one version = one page = one layout* (or three pages for each campaign). But don't save each version as separate files or documents, which can be slow and confusing. In programs like Quark, designed for desktop publishing, a simple "step and repeat" command (or equivalent) will duplicate an entire "page" for you, as many times as you wish. One for each "version." This simple tool shows you how the layouts have *evolved* (something you couldn't see by constantly revising the same single layout). It quickly and easily allows you to consider, compare, and contrast any variations in position, size, color, typeface, cropping, and framing, etc. This also saves time (especially on the things you may not want to change, e.g., the position of the tagline, body copy, or logo). Once you have chosen a layout you like, then you can work, rework, and tweak the imagery, type, and any other imported elements in Photoshop or Illustrator if desired (see Which Software?, page 264).

Note: from a teaching standpoint, it's difficult to assess how much time and effort a student has really spent on a "final" layout (and how many things he or she tried) if there's only one version/page/layout to look at. The student may have spent five hours or five minutes on it, whereas with multiple versions of layouts there's some stronger evidence of the effort involved (see Creative Process Report, page 267).

Color Palette

Two things that make someone a good dresser are: finding clothes that suit them, and finding colors that go well together. The same is true when it comes to art directing an ad campaign. What colors suit the brand personality? What colors go well together, while also complementing the look or feel of the product? What colors reflect the idea and tone of the ad? The task is to find a color palette, or combination of two or more colors. A good place to start is by examining a traditional color wheel, in which the opposing pairs of colors are visual complements.

Many products have strong visual branding simply by owning, and sticking to, a specific color or color palette. Maybe your brand could do the same, just as each country or competitive sports team "owns" a particular color/palette.

Kodak = yellow
UPS = chocolate brown

Sometimes the product logo or part of its distinctive packaging determines the visual branding of a campaign:

The Economist = red and white
Tiffany = light green
The Financial Times = light pink

At other times the entire product or product name is a color, making the choice of color palette obvious.

Orange = bright orange and white
Amex Blue = blue(s)

Note: one of the most common mistakes a student makes when choosing color for a final layout is poor contrast of tone. As a general rule, when you use two colors together (i.e., foreground against background), and particularly when using type/text, be sure that there is enough contrast between the two. Otherwise the ad will be difficult to read, especially when the type is small. The two colors can be similar (e.g., navy and light blue), or a tint (e.g., 100% blue and 50% blue) as long as there's enough contrast and it's legible.

When it comes to contrast of tone, the results depend on the actual colors you've chosen, but as a general rule:

Light tone + light tone = least legible
Mid tone + mid tone = least legible
Dark tone + dark tone = least legible

Light tone + mid tone = more legible
Mid tone + dark tone = more legible

Light tone + dark tone = most legible

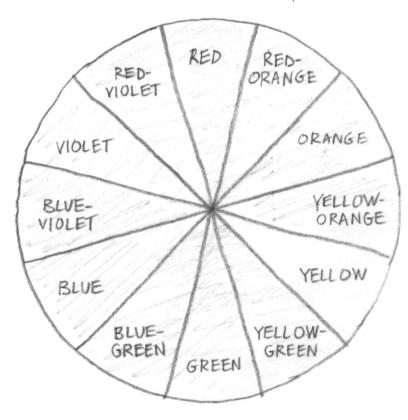

The color wheel: opposing colors act as good visual complements.

If your design requires a third shade, an extreme one like white or black may work best (again, especially for smaller type). Conversely, there may be parts of your layout where you want less contrast (e.g., two background colors). Play around with it.

Colors

Before selecting a color palette, consider two things:

- For which media will your design be produced? (print, TV, online, multimedia?)
- At what scale will your design be produced? (small scale print, e.g., magazines/ newspapers; large-scale print, e.g., billboards; fixed formats, e.g., TV, online)

Depending on your answers, there are unique color and resolution requirements that need to be met.

Print

Most printers (i.e., print-production houses) still prefer artwork to be supplied to them in CMYK mode. However, some forms of digital printing automatically convert artwork supplied in RGB mode to CMYK. In these cases, files will automatically be calibrated to match (approximately) what you see on screen. There are numerous variables depending on the size of the final print and the type of printer being used. Consult with your printer to make sure artwork is produced in the correct format, scale, and color mode for optimal output. Whenever possible, always ask to see a "proof" before a final print is made. It will allow you to make minor adjustments, such as optimizing color, before final prints are produced.

TV

Although RGB is a fixed color constraint for all TV applications, TV formats are unique to different parts of the world. The three primary TV formats are PAL, NTSC, and SECAM. However, since there are other formats in use around the world, it would be best to consult a post-production source before setting up any digital files.

Terms and Definitions

- **CMYK** (Cyan, Magenta, Yellow, Black)
- **RGB** (Red, Green, Blue)
- **PMS** (Pantone Matching System) U = Uncoated/matte, C = Coated/gloss
- **PAL** (Phase Alternating Line)

- **NTSC** (National Television System Committee)
- **SECAM** (Séquentiel couleur à mémoire, French for "Sequential Color with Memory")

Online

There are fixed constraints for all online applications. Designs will need to be in RGB mode and produced at 72 dpi regardless of content. Dimensions of artwork/content will normally be predetermined. If they are not, consult with whomever will be uploading the final visual material online.

Which Software?

Although software applications are converging, and several applications are capable of performing multiple tasks that overlap design disciplines, designers still rely on more than one application. There are certain programs that have tools and unique capabilities for specialized tasks. The "family" of Adobe System products has been produced to promote crossover between applications. However, if you stick to using file formats that can be read universally across programs you shouldn't have any trouble opening files in most applications, regardless of producer, as along as you are working within the same platform.

- **Photoshop***: Raster (image) based program. Best to use for image manipulation.
- **Illustrator***: Vector-based drawing program. Primary use—drawing and graphic layouts with limited copy. (Freehand is equivalent)
- **InDesign***: Desktop publishing program. Used for type setting, long and short copy, layouts, etc. (QuarkXPress is equivalent)
- **Acrobat***: Universally accepted standard application for pdf (Portable Document Format) files.
- **After Effects***: Digital motion graphic and compositing software. Used in film and post-production.
- **Freehand:** Vector-based drawing program. Used for vector drawing and graphic layouts with limited copy. (Adobe Illustrator is equivalent)
- **Flash:** Used for animations, multimedia, online applications such as web

applications, games, and movies, and content for mobile phones and other embedded devices.

- **Final Cut Pro:** Non-liner editing system. Used for multimedia/film editing purposes. Able to edit many digital formats. (Apple's iMovie is recommended for beginners)
- **HTML (HyperText Markup Language):** Predominant markup language for web pages. Provides a means of describing the structure of text-based information in a document by denoting certain text as headings, paragraphs, lists, etc., to supplement that text with interactive forms, embedded images, and other objects.

* All produced by Adobe

Common File Types

- **jpeg (or jpg):** Commonly used method of compression for photographic images. JPEG stands for Joint Photographic Experts Group, the name of the committee that created the standard.
- **tiff:** File format for storing images, including photographs and vector (line) art. Tiff is a popular format for high-color depth images.
- **pdf (Portable Document Format):** Universally accepted standard file format for document exchange. Pdf files encapsulate a complete description of a 2-D document (and, with Acrobat 3-D, embedded 3-D documents) which include the text, fonts, images, and 2-D vector graphics that compose the document. In simple terms, a pdf is like taking a snapshot of a document.
- **indd:** File extension for documents created in InDesign.
- **qxd:** File extension for documents created in QuarkXPress.
- **ai:** File extension for documents created in Illustrator.
- **psd:** File extension for documents created in Photoshop.
- **doc:** File extension for documents created in Microsoft Word.
- **fhd:** File extension for documents created in Freehand.
- **swf:** File extension for documents traditionally called "Flash movies" or "Flash games."

- **flv:** File extension for Flash video files.
- **fla:** File extension used for the basic Flash document file.
- **mov:** File extension for QuickTime movies.

Print Sizes and Ratios

Make sure your layouts are the correct dimensions/size/ratio for press and posters (see page 59 for a comprehensive table).

Keep it Real

Artists have used their hands since time began. Knowing how to use your hands is a big part of being an art director. And that includes when and how to use a computer.

Computers and software applications have made design and production a lot easier in countless ways. But sometimes a bit of back to basics artistic ingenuity can still produce the best, fastest results. For example, a student wanted to create a torn paper effect across part of her ad. She spent hours in Photoshop trying to *re*-create it, only to realize later that simply ripping a real page and scanning it in would have produced the perfect tear.

Another student wanted to create a cropped visual of a scrabble board with numerous words spelt out in traditional wooden letters. Rather than photograph the board, or scan each word and board separately, he simply stuck down all the words in place with some tack and then scanned the entire thing. It looked perfect, right down to the authentic grain in the wood and the details in the board (difficult to photograph), plus the drop shadows (time consuming for even a Photoshop whizz).

Cutting and Mounting

Learn how to use a scalpel knife and spray mount. You may be required to trim and mount your own work for student competitions, as well as future client presentations. If it looks sloppy, it says you don't care about your work—so why should anyone else?

Practice is all it takes. Basic scalpel tips include: check the blade for sharpness, use a proper cutting mat, and always cut vertically toward you.

Questions Every Art Director Should Ask Themselves for Each Layout

There are an infinite number of compositional opportunities for each layout. This can be overwhelming, but doesn't have to be. Layouts are simply about asking the right questions.

1. History

Research the brand's previous ads. Are there any layout decisions and brand attributes (visual and typographical choices) that should be kept, or is this a chance to design something totally different and new? Brand consistency is more relevant to agencies than students, and to graphic designers than ad designers. Note: brand consistency differs from consistency within a campaign, as outlined in Keep it Consistent?, page 261.

2. Hierarchy (Most-Less-Least)

How do you want someone to read your ad? What's the order of importance, and therefore the size and impact of: visual/headline/body copy/tagline/logo. The order, size, and impact should reflect the *tone* of the idea/message.

3. Search

Look around for visual references that may help to communicate your idea, e.g., an unusual type, or color palette. These references can come from anywhere: record/cd covers, photographers, comics, movie titles, graffiti—anything that has not been used in an ad, and remains relevant to your product and idea. When you look at something, ask yourself: "Can I use this for an ad?"

4. "Look"

Will the overall layout have a minimal, "clean" look, or a layered, "collage" look? Or somewhere in between? *Clean* refers to fewer visual elements, solid colors, etc. *Collage* refers to a greater number of elements, usually more colorful and/or textural, combined, and layered like a traditional collage (see opposite). For this, find any interesting (and relevant) material, textures, artifacts, objects, and documents to use as part of the layout. Whether you give a layout a clean, collage, or combo look, *make it look interesting.* (For example, if your idea is to show all the many teams that a famous sportsman has played for over the years, instead of just listing the teams in type, add visual interest by displaying each of his player "cards.") But remember, the most interesting ad is the one that starts with an interesting concept.

5. Branding

Are you giving enough thought to visual branding? Are you missing a useful trick that will make it clear which *brand* you are advertising? Perhaps you could use the typeface of the product/service, the colors of the logo, or an element of the packaging,

etc. (You can spot a "white out of red" *Economist* ad well before you're close enough to read it.) Be aware of the competitions' branding (see Color Palette, page 263).

6. Logo

What size? What version? Should I use a black on white version, or vice versa? Is a logo best, or would a simpler version be better (e.g., a Nike "tick" only). Is there a more interesting visual that complements or replaces the product logo (e.g., a police badge for the NYPD). Brandsoftheworld.com have a comprehensive supply of many famous, pixel-free logos—otherwise scan in a printed example from an ad, brochure or packaging, or re-create in Illustrator.

7. Format

The format dictates the layout and art direction (as a student, you have the freedom to decide on the format). Which format works best? Billboard, or landscape/double-page spread, or single page? And get the size/proportions exact.

8. Visual

If you have a visual(s) is it a photo or an illustration? Which style or genre? Stock imagery or self-produced? Black-and-white or color? Original form or altered in some way (e.g., brightness/contrast, levels, colors, saturation, filter effects, layers, etc.)? How should I crop it? How much of the layout is the visual? (see Hierarchy, above).

9. Typeface (for Headline, Body Copy, and Tag)

Serif or sans serif? Which face? How many faces? (Less is usually more.) How many styles and weights? Original form, altered, or self-produced? What justification? Is the typeface aesthetically pleasing? Is it appropriate for the brand personality, concept tone of voice, audience, and layout? Legibly designed? Flexible? Readable in terms of the total design (setting, sizing, and page positioning)?

10. Color Palette

How many colors? Do they go well together? Do they go with the other elements of the layout? Is it relevant/appropriate? (Don't forget to try shades of the same color, e.g., 70% black with 30% black.)

11. Tone

The *visual* tone of the layout should match the ad's *written* tone of voice. For example, is the tone loud, urgent, direct, and bold? Or is it quiet, thoughtful,

A textural, collage, layered look adds to the authenticity of the message, and the realness of the nursing profession. (Headline: Could you help someone get rid of all the cockroaches on this baby?) *Client:* Department of Health/COI. *Agency:* Saatchi & Saatchi, London. *Creatives:* Colin Jones, John Messum, Mike McKenna.

subtle, and soft? The choice of "look," branding, visual(s), type, and color palette (above) all contribute toward the tone.

12. The Final Test

Does the final ad (concept and execution) have immediate impact? Will the ad be remembered? Will the product be remembered (i.e., branding)? Is the final ad relevant and appropriate for the brand/target?

Note: experiment, and trust your instincts. Ask the above questions first, and if it leads to an unexpected, different, better, or radical solution that still works, go for it!

Concept to Execution: Creative Process Report

A creative process report (CPR) is basically a collection, in chronological order, of all the work that has gone into a particular ad campaign. It reports the progress that has been made, like an A–Z of an ad, from first thoughts (beginning) to final computer layout (end). The more things you try out, the more you get out of it.

A CPR's contents might include the following:
- Strategy statement/creative brief
- Original notes, sketches, thumbnails, and layouts
- Larger, hand-drawn layouts
- Examples of at least three alternative typefaces
- Examples of different colors/color palettes
- Reference material (visual or otherwise)
- Scanned or photographed material
- Demonstration/experimentation of computer layouts, i.e., each stage of layout development and decision making
- Final color computer print layouts (three or more executions)
- Conclusion (minimum 200 words) explaining the reason behind each art direction/graphic design decision, e.g., the final choice of print media, logo, font/s, color/s, visual/s, tagline, "visual tone reflecting written tone" of campaign idea.

· ·

Exercise: next time you create an ad, save and compile everything (from concept to final execution) into what I call a "Creative Process Report." It's a good way for teachers to assess and grade a completed project.

· ·

Even as roughs, this print
campaign shows an effortless
combination of design,
illustration, photography,
and typography. *Client:
Waterstone's.* *Agency: BDDP
GGT, London.* *Creatives: Paul
Belford, Nigel Roberts.*

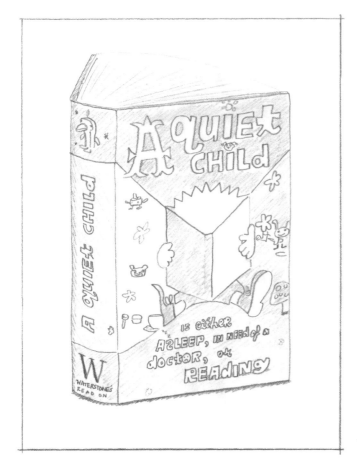

The Power of Execution

If I had to choose one print campaign that
perfectly combines every aspect of execution
(design, illustration, photography, typography)
with a great strategy and concept, it would be
the Waterstone's booksellers campaign by Paul
Belford and Nigel Roberts of BDDP GGT (which
surprisingly, in my opinion, missed out on D&AD
Gold). The sum of these parts is greater than the
whole: the product is unquestionably the hero,
front, and center.

....

Exercise: give an aging ad a face lift. Find a
headline and visual print ad that has a great
concept, but looks dated. (Hint: go through
some 1980s awards annuals.) Now re-art
direct the ad, changing the layout, hierarchy,
type, color palette, etc., as necessary. (If the
visual is from a specific photo shoot, either
Photoshop/Illustrate a new visual, or insert
a similar stock image.) To help you, look at
the two Rolls-Royce "Electric Clock" ads on
page 134.

....

14

Presenting and Selling Your Work

Creating great concepts is half of the battle; getting them made is the second half. It starts with knowing how to present and ultimately sell your ads. If you're a student, this will probably mean presenting in front of the instructor and your classmates, as if they were the creative director or the client.

Even if you have potentially the greatest campaign ever written, poor presentation skills can "unsell" it. Or as Tom Monahan says:

"If your ideas are compromised too deeply too often, maybe it's not the quality of the ideas or the execution; maybe it's a lack of ability to have others see the brilliance of the idea."

Whether you're a natural sales person or not, there are many additional tips and tools you can use to help sell your work. Some of these apply to selling in general, and some are specific to advertising. The secret to presenting is simple: the more you do it, the better you get.

Speak Up
Rule number one. Not everyone is born to be an actor, but everyone is physically able to speak up if they have to. (No one has ever mumbled "fire!")

When people are being presented to, they don't want to have to do anything except listen. *Trying* to listen requires extra effort and distracts people from the focal point of your presentation—the work.

Keep Eye Contact
The oldest tip for job interviews. Don't forget, you're selling yourself as much as your work. Also, eyes are a good indicator of what a client is feeling.

Believe in Your Work
If you don't have conviction in your work, how is anyone else going to? When you sound unsure, it will sow the seed of doubt in other people.

Be Ready for Criticism
The truth is, because every ad is subjective, *any* ad can be criticized. You have to prepare yourself for what those criticisms may be, and try to answer your critics calmly and professionally. If you have enough conviction in what you say, you'll be amazed at your powers of persuasion. Don't take it personally. Clients like to make comments—it's part of their job, and their right. "Choose your battles wisely," as they say. Be objective and look at the big picture. It's better to agree to a small change (that has little impact on your idea) than sacrifice a huge one. In the latter case, creating a new, alternative idea that everyone likes is probably a better option.

Passion vs. Hype
It's one thing to be passionate about your ideas, and it's another to be over confident. Hype sets up a level of expectation that can be hard to live up to.

Never start by saying something like, "You're going to love this work…!" Ideas are subjective and taste is very personal. There is no way you can know with 100% certainty what someone will or will not like. So don't assume anything. What's more, people (especially creative directors and clients) like to feel like they have made the decision themselves, based on their "impeccable" taste. Selling is about minimizing the things a client won't like, and maximizing the things they will like.

Presenting to Your Boss
Your boss could be a senior copywriter/art director, group creative head/director, or executive creative director. Your goal is to ensure that a creative person at each level in your agency approves your work before the client presentation.

Every creative director is different. Some will want you to do a full presentation, some prefer a short introduction, and some like you to leave the work on their desk, or as an email or fax (with no chance to defend it).

Be aware if and when your boss presents *their* work and your work to the client without you. It's rare that they will want your work to go through, and his or her work to bomb. That's why you must at least offer to go to the meeting.

Presenting to an Account Person

You can't expect another person (such as an account handler) to understand your idea in the same way that you do. So don't expect he or she to present the work the same way, unless you brief them carefully. Even though account people are experienced presenters, make suggestions. A good account person will ask you lots of questions in order to understand the strategy, idea, script, headline, visual, body copy as well as you do. Equally, a creative person will not understand the client as well as an account person. Creatives should be aware of any particular beliefs or prejudices the client has, which may not have been mentioned in the creative brief.

Some account people are alarmists, ever quick to double guess what his or her client will like. These people want an easy sell: they don't want to upset the client, and they don't want to tarnish the agency. Although understandable, this can be dangerous (to the point where your idea never even gets to the client). A confident, gifted account person, on the other hand, will have the attitude that if they believe in the idea, they'll be able to sell it.

Presenting to the Client

The most important, "slickest" presentation is the one made to a client. Depending on the way an agency works, you may find yourself presenting the creative work to the client, in place of the creative director or an account person doing so. Often the presentation is divided into sections and speakers, e.g., general client/agency stuff, the strategy, and finally the creative work. Some agencies and clients really like creative teams to present the work (the theory being that no one understands an idea better than its creator), while others prefer an account person who has a closer relationship with the client, keeping "those sensitive, unpredictable creatives" away.

Present to the Decision Maker

Presenting to the client is the biggest challenge, mostly because it's rarely one person who represents the client. The more people involved in the decision making process (including within an agency), the more opinions there will be.

Some people are picky and pedantic, only focusing on the negative, while others see the bigger picture. The larger the client, the more layers of management you have to contend with. Ideally, you will be presenting to the top person *in person* (not over the phone or via fax or email). If you can't, be sure that whomever you present to understands the idea and feels able to present it to their boss in the same way. (Unfortunately, you have no control over exactly what will be said at their subsequent internal client meeting.)

Most clients have their own prescribed checklist of what constitutes a good ad. Common client beliefs and prejudices include "awards don't sell brands," "testimonials always work," and "the video should work without the audio." Plus each individual on the client side has his or her own personal boxes to tick, and bosses to please, etc. Unfortunately it's human nature to make comments and suggest changes, no matter how small or insignificant. It justifies a person's position and job, and gives them a sense of purpose and power. Making a change puts their mark on the project. Others may feel that if there are no changes they must have missed something. (Alfred Hitchcock was renowned for making a tiny, unnecessary lighting change prior to each scene. His long-time lighting man dealt with this problem by deliberately misaligning something to allow Hitchcock to make his change.) Whatever a client's motives, if it means doing something crafty in return, go for it.

Accentuate the Positive, Eliminate the Negative

There are some useful tools that you can use *prior* to showing the work to maximize the chances of a positive reaction (reaching and even surpassing expectations), and minimize the chances of a negative one (reducing nasty surprises). Or as the old Mercer and Arlen song goes, "Accentuate the positive, eliminate the negative, latch on to the affirmative, don't mess with Mister In-Between."

This is achieved by shifting the client's expectations in your favor. If you sense that there are elements in your campaign or executional idea that will raise a client's red flag, argue your reasons beforehand, at the creative rationale stage. This will lower their expectations and minimize any negative surprises. Similarly, if there are things that the client is expecting and you don't feel will work, make your case early. This will eliminate any false expectations. For example, if the client wants an ad that shows their comprehensive product range, argue that it will overload the consumer and cloud the message. If they don't agree at first, at least you've prepared them. Once they see the result (which matches their expectations), they will be more likely to see your point and change their mind.

In terms of positives, make a note of the things that the client has set as a mandatory (that you also agree with). This could be their sacred tagline, or a particular type of music. Go overboard: "We agree with you 100% with the importance of using…" Make it sound more important than it really is. If possible, raise their expectation and match it. This will help to outweigh the negatives even more.

The stuff in the middle (the "Mister In-Between") are the trivial points. If the general consensus is indifference, don't sweat over it and move on.

Walk Them Through it: The Nod Factor

You don't just stand up and show them the ads. As part of the introduction, walk the client through the creative rationale, i.e., the gap (or bridge) between the creative brief/strategy and the creative work. The level to which they agree and understand the rationale depends largely on "the nod factor." Other than eye and facial expressions, nodding is the clearest, most natural sign that someone is in agreement: it's body language for "a positive reaction." Therefore, it's very important to keep people nodding right up until pulling out the work.

But how do you keep them nodding once they see the work? Assuming you've done a good job shifting their expectations in your favor, the rest comes down to *how* you present the work. If the client is already halfway sold (and half expecting what the work will be), presenting the work will be that much easier.

Showing the Work

The introduction and creative rationale is over. Now it's time to show the work. Here are some simple tips for carefully presenting campaigns.

1. Explain the campaign idea succinctly. Then (if applicable) say, "This idea is summed up by the following tagline…" Then show a board (or screen) with the new tagline clearly printed or displayed. Note: if the nod factor is clearly high at this point, continue by showing the ads (you have them half sold now). But if the nodding is low, you may want to have a few alternative taglines prepared, but only use these as a last resort, because it can look like a lack conviction on your part. You can keep the tagline(s) on display if you wish—this will help the client grasp the relationship between the idea and the executions.

2. With a print campaign, show, read, and explain each execution separately. If you display all three at once people's eyes (and minds) will wander: you'll lose them at the most crucial point. Swap each ad for the next one (only keep the current ad on display to avoid any wandering). For TV storyboards, show and swap one board/key frame at a time.

3. Display all the work together.

4. Conclude by briefly explaining your views about the work, and why you believe it works.

5. Ask the client for their feedback, and discuss.

The Mysterious Prop

The "mysterious prop" (MP) is something that is brought to a presentation to tease and intrigue the client: an object* that will be used later when you present the work. Play it cool and draw them in by letting the prop just sit there. If they like or engage with it, you've already got their interest, which means you're closer to selling the idea.

To demonstrate the effectiveness of the MP, let's use a courtroom scenario, with the jury acting as the visually challenged client. What would be the most powerful way for a lawyer to demonstrate a fatal stabbing: describing the murder weapon, *or* actually reenacting the murder scene with the bloody, ten-inch knife?

So, use anything you think will act as a carrot to help convince the "jury" and sell your work, whether it relates to the overall campaign idea, or specific executions. Keep the number of props to a minimum, and make sure the prop doesn't give too much away, in which case use the prop at the ideal moment only. (Immediately before the Silk Cut tobacco client was shown the ads, the agency's simple, long-running campaign idea of "purple silk being cut" was sold to them by using two props: a pair of scissors and a piece of silk fabric.)

*Don't forget, a prop can be a person as well as an object. Borrow someone from the office whose credentials or skills would be perfect to help dramatize your idea.

A UK agency created a humorous TV campaign for a pimple (a.k.a. spot, zit) cream in the late 1980s. Each ad featured a young woman (yet to use the cream) socializing with a bucket on her head (to dramatize the feeling one has when covered in spots—you don't want anyone to see them!) This concept was not an easy sell, especially to a large, conservative pharmaceutical company. So (allegedly), when the agency first presented the idea to the client, they brought a bucket with them and actually placed it on the client's head. This brought the meeting and the idea to life, and gave the client a closer understanding of their target audience. Most importantly, the client felt that they were involved in the idea.

Key Cards
Key cards (as they are sometimes called) are pieces of card with key points/reminders written on them to jog your memory and help steer the presentation. These cards are especially effective during long presentations, and are a good balance between a stiff, fully scripted presentation, and a less structured, improvised one.

These key points can easily be incorporated into a PowerPoint presentation, or other forms of projections, etc. But as we've all experienced, these presentations can be long and overwhelming to read, so remember to use *key* points only.

TV and Radio Scripts
TV and radio scripts are as big, powerful, exciting (and expensive) as advertising gets, so don't just read them out loud, *bring them to life*. For many clients, even the so-called advertising and marketing managers, meeting with their agency is the most exciting part of their jobs, so give them something to tell their colleagues about.

Rehearse every script or storyboard. Decide who is reading the action part, the dialogue, and the voice over for each ad. Reading and presenting scripts is slower than watching a real commercial, so one read through for each ad is probably enough for people to absorb the idea.

When showing a final TV ad or rough cut to a client, set it up so it plays three times in a row, with one-second pauses in between. This allows the client to take everything in before making comments and giving feedback, while minimizing any knee-jerk reactions.

••

Exercise: pick out two different TV scripts from an awards annual (i.e., for two different products). Imagine that you've written the scripts and you have to present each one to the client. Put together an exciting presentation for each commercial.

••

Interactive
Depending on the client's preferences, the type of idea and application, the project time limit, plus which "round" of presentation it is, interactive work can either be storyboarded or animated digitally.

Know Your Limits
Don't present in a way that is over ambitious, especially if you get embarrassed easily. Use *action* rather than *acting*.

Adcepts and Mood Boards
An "adcept" is not quite an ad, not quite a concept. It's usually a pre-produced image or series of images that conveys a general idea, attitude, approach, or direction that an ad campaign will duly take. If it's for TV, it could be a piece of film footage, or a particular person that an agency plans to use for the campaign. To save time and effort in the long run, an agency can "sell in" the adcept first, before the next, more time-consuming stage begins: to create the actual ad campaign. And if the adcept is not approved, less time and effort has been wasted.

"Mood boards" are similar to adcepts, and tend to be a larger collection of stock images and clippings to help convey the overall mood, look, or tone of an ad, plus even the type of consumer they are looking to target.

Whether showing adcepts or mood boards, the key is to explain to a client that these are not final ads or even ad concepts, but general ideas and impressions. Otherwise they may like—and want to use—what they think is an actual ad. Conversely, unless the client is briefed before the presentation, they may be expecting to see an ad concept rather than an adcept.

But with the increasing demands put upon agencies to produce super-quick turnaround campaigns, adcepts are being used less frequently for the initial creative presentation. Equally, with the "aid" of technology, initial concepts are becoming slowly replaced by finished-looking ads, often compiled from cost-effective stock imagery, which are immediately sold and produced "as is" when a commissioned photo shoot or illustration may have been more effective.

The Safer the Work, the Easier the Sell

This is particularly true when it comes to client presentations (hopefully you'll never work in an agency that advocates safe work). Put another way, the braver the work, the harder it is to sell. Great work scares people, especially clients. And most agencies are scared of losing clients. That's partly why so many ads are safe and predictable. Clients spend a lot of money at the risk of losing a lot if the advertising fails. But when a client is educated by the agency about the mutual goals that only creative advertising can bring (to build brands, make money, and win awards), the more they will understand and appreciate ground-breaking work.

Sell it Yourself

Remember, as a student, your work is purely spec (short for "speculative"). The concept and execution should be great, but the bigger challenge exists in the real world, working on real briefs: selling the work and getting it produced.

However, if you have an idea in your book that you feel could (and should) run, contact the client yourself. You have nothing to lose. Some clients will have an exclusive contract with an agency already, but some won't (governments, public services, and charities are usually open to using many agencies).

Plus, small clients may not use an agency, but could easily afford an independent freelancer.

Again, present the work within a context that the client can relate to. Explain why you think the idea is perfect for the brand, how it will raise awareness, and make (or raise) money for them. Telling clients that the idea will win advertising awards is excluding, rather than including, them. They have to feel like it's theirs too.

Finally, in terms of payment, don't give them any work until you've agreed on a price, if any (most charities expect pro bono, non-paying work, unless you're on the staff pay roll). If they agree to pay you, get a record of the price in an email.

••

Exercise: take a stand-up comedy class/ workshop. Sign up by yourself or with a student group. (This is part of the curriculum at Chicago Ad School.)

••

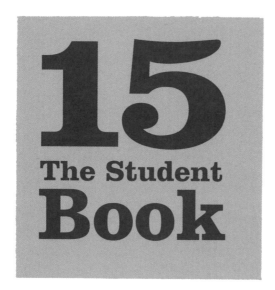

15 The Student Book

The Book

In some respects, a student book is the most important book a person wanting a career in advertising will ever produce, partly because it's his/her first, and also because it's the one that will (hopefully) launch their career.

There are three main areas that combine to make a great student book, most of which also applies to a professional book:

1. The Work

The *quality* of your work is the most important part of your book. Next is the *quantity*. Creative directors (and alike) seem to have less and less time and patience when it comes to viewing portfolios, which is why student books are getting briefer and briefer. There was a time when around 15 projects was the norm. Nowadays, you should aim to have a maximum of 8–10 projects, made up of:

- 3–4 print campaigns (9–12 pieces)
- 2–3 interactive campaigns (include a web or mobile site, a mobile app, standard and/or rich media banners, and social media ideas)✱
- 1 campaign (3 pieces) with body copy (copywriters should aim for at least 2 campaigns)
- 1 or 2 one-offs (1–2 pieces)
- 1 TV or radio spot (1 piece)✱✱
- 1 multimedia/integrated campaign (up to 10 pieces), e.g., print, ambient, direct mail, website, mobile app or site, social media ideas

✱Interactive ideas such as banners should be storyboarded for your book and digitally animated for your website.

✱✱TV ideas for the US ad industry should be presented as a "finished" spot, not long-winded storyboards.

(Sadly, the quantity of pieces required for a typical portfolio will probably continue to fall.)

2. Self-Promotion Pieces

These include a consistent design (including typography and color palette) of the following:

Personal logo: as a freelance art director or copywriter, your name is your brand. Therefore a "word form" logo is usually the most appropriate choice (i.e., your full name in a well-designed typeface). But there's nothing stopping you from designing a "letter form" logo (i.e., your initials), or a "picture form" logo (based on your name or job title), or even a combination of logo forms.

Your logo should work throughout your self-promotion package. So before applying it to each piece, make sure that it's flexible by testing its legibility in black and white, and in large and small format.

Résumés (CVs): the content of a typical junior art director/copywriter résumé is "name and title," "contact details," "education," "work experience," "awards" (student and industry), "computer/typing skills," "interests" (optional).

The length and size should be no more than a single letter page, 8.5" by 11" (A4). This makes it quick to review, eliminates the need for stapling, and reduces the risk of missing pages.

The layout should be simple and legible. The key (as with designing any print ad), is to decide on, and then address, the hierarchy of information. In other words, use a grid, and vary the type size and weight as necessary.

Business cards: the design of your business card should be consistent with your entire portfolio—inside and out. Use a constant typeface(s), layout, color palette, etc. Remember, you are a brand, so design your book as if it were a multimedia campaign. It makes it (and you) look more professional.

Leave behinds: these are perfect snap-shot reminders left after inundated recruiters have seen your work. 3–6 pieces per leave behind is typical, made up of campaigns and one-shots. Try to keep these to a maximum area of a single page of 8.5 by 11" (A4), or less if customized.

Pdfs of your work (1 letter page or more): these act as quick and easy "leave aheads," sent out before contacting/following up busy creative directors. Individual JPEGs are also useful for tailoring what you want to send, depending on what the agency is looking for.

Websites/URLs: these are a mandatory requirement for freelancers as well as full-size agencies. Make them interesting, but easy to navigate. The benefits are obvious—it's a lot simpler, quicker, and cheaper to send and view a web link than a printed, hard copy portfolio of work. But for print ads, there will always be times when people will want to see the work in its original, physical form, so make sure you have a hard copy of everything.

3. Portfolio Presentation

How your work is *packaged* and *laid out* says a lot about you. Things to consider are:

- **Format:** hard-copy print, showreel, digital files, and web/URL. Aim to have all four available to view.
- **Type of portfolio case:** traditional plastic case with/without sleeves, mounted pieces, metal box, custom made, etc. Buy a professional-looking case that can take a lot of abuse. Shop around for something well made *and* well priced.
- **Size/number of portfolios:** typically one standard book, plus some returnable/ non-returnable mini books for your top agency choices. The student book (and the work inside) is generally getting smaller and fewer. Just make sure your print work is not so small that you can't read the words!
- **Order of your work:** start and end with your best work (and ideally, boost the center with something good, too).

Alternate/break up the following:

> **Tone,** e.g., serious, humorous, straight, serious, humorous…
>
> **Art direction styles,** e.g., all type, all visual; headline and visual; color photography, black and white, illustration

Type of products/services, e.g., luxury service, disposable good, mainstream product, specialist dot com, non-profit service…

Never Stop…

Remember Voltaire's famous line (later adopted by legendary ad man Bill Bernbach) "good is the enemy of great."

The golden rule when it comes to your portfolio (or "book") is *never stop working on it.*

Any book should be constantly moving forward and evolving, but without getting too full. When choosing the best executions for a campaign you have to be a tough editor. The same is true when choosing the best campaigns for your book. So to prevent an overcrowded portfolio, and to keep it evolving, apply the busy nightclub rule of "one in, one out." In other words, each time you add a new campaign, take out your (now) worst one. But only put in something new if it's better than the weakest campaign in your current book. Conversely, don't fill up your book for the sake of it. Quality beats quantity, so it's better to have four strong campaigns than four strong ones and one weak one. The weak one will only bring down your book.

Keep evolving your book if only for your own mental state. A creative person needs to be *creating*; a tired book full of old ads can drag you down. And it can look like you've run out of ideas. Plus, when presenting your book, you need to show your enthusiasm. Of course, some people never get bored of talking about their old work. Personally, I do: unless it's something that I'm particularly proud of. Usually people enjoy presenting their recent, fresh projects the most. This also shows others that you are always striving to create new, great work, rather than "riding off" the old stuff.

Fresh Strategies

• Look for a different proposition/benefit. See what kind of advertising the competition is doing and then do something different. Ask yourself: "Can the product be positioned in a different way?"

• Challenge perceptions and tone of voice. For example, most campaigns that encourage people to make a will are usually serious, threatening, or bleak. Why not try something more light hearted or humorous?

• Establish a new market for the brand. HHCL, London used strategic thinking to shift the Pot Noodles target away from manual workers and housewives to students and the general youth market.

• Try taking the most obvious proposition and advertise it with a radical idea. There are lots of brands around that have sound, clear propositions that simply haven't been exploited. For example, "Brillo is the most abrasive cleaner" is a very straightforward benefit. Don't avoid it. It's often the dull, boring, and obvious propositions that need the best ideas.

• Be aware that tackling products or services clearly based on common "superlative" benefits (such as the fastest, toughest, strongest, longest-lasting, etc.) are often viewed as easy brands to advertise.

• Think beyond the page or the TV screen. Perhaps your whole strategy is based on a new form of ambient media (see the Ambient chapter).

Assignments

To show your creative breadth, you must aim to demonstrate a cross section of work in terms of tone, art direction, and types of products. It's all about "filling in the gaps." You don't want to have two or more things that are the same, because one will merely cancel out the other.

The more unique your selection of products/services is, the more unique your book is, and the more unique you are. (I know your can't have levels of uniqueness—one is either unique or not—but you get the point.)

If you're a student, don't keep relying on assignments from your teachers. Get into the habit of finding your own products and services. Look around you, go online, and explore supermarkets and high streets. Create your own original briefs. You also have the luxury of working backwards. In other words, you can have a great idea first, and then fit a strategy and product around it. An agency is always limited by the accounts it has, or the accounts it pitches for. The freedom you possess is largely why many believe that the work in a student book should be better than the best work out there.

However, *don't* waste time on the following types of products (easy, clichéd, "studenty," gimmicky, or obscure):

• Condoms
• Post-It Notes®
• Highlighter pens
• Dating companies
• Holocaust museums and other hard-core charities
• Weird, techie gadgets
• Executive toys
• The Bible…

Don't launch new, unknown products in your book either. There are plenty of familiar products and services around. There are also established brands that are not advertised at all.

Avoid brands that have famous, award-winning advertising already. Your work will always be compared to it: unless, of course, yours is better. There are plenty of brands out there that could do with great, unexpected advertising. And conversely, don't try to advertise things that don't need advertising.

Do spend time on these types of products (generic, hard or boring…but impressive):

• Airlines
• Banks
• Cars
• Car dealers
• Beer
• Fast-food chains
• Tampons
• Bread
• Gas stations
• Newspapers
• Fashion
• Medical
• Insurance companies
• Telecommunications providers
• A voting campaign…

plus more specific briefs (see opposite) such as:

• Department store sales
• Financial deals, e.g., 0% finance, low mortgage rates
• Other deals, e.g., 2-for-1, free sunroof

As a general rule, one great campaign for a bank is worth five great Post-it™ Note campaigns. And as always, don't waste time working up a poor concept (unless you really want to practise your computer skills).

Moving home.
Exciting.
Moving home insurance.
Unexciting.
We'll give you a 20% discount online.*
Exciting-ish?

TESCO | Every Little helps

Openly having fun with a boring subject. *Client: Tesco.* *Agency: Lowe, London.* *Creatives: Jason Lawes, Sam Cartmell.*

PAY HALF NOW AND NOTHING LATER.

A range of five fitted kitchens with every unit at half price.

This furniture ad spoof is a different way of saying the usual "Save 50%" or "50% off." *Client: Texas Home Care.* *Agency: Leagas Delaney, London.* *Creatives: Gary Marshall, Paul Marshall.*

Go Full Circle

For maximum "book clout," try to expand your idea into more than print media. A fully *integrated*, 360° campaign shows an agency that you can THINK BIG (see the Integrated chapter). And in reality, many accounts are won as a result of pitching a big, integrated campaign.

Product and Service Categories

Your student book should reflect the expectations of the best agency work in the industry, including the types of products and services that are commonly advertised by these agencies. The Cannes International Advertising Festival is the largest advertising awards. Below is their official list of competition categories for press advertising. If you get stuck finding new products and services for your student book, start by referring to this comprehensive list, and then research the brands within each section. (Again, avoid those particular categories and/or brands that are easy to create ideas for.)

Savoury Foods

Meats, fish, seafood, soups, delicatessen, fruits and vegetables, rice, pasta, pizza, sauces, mayonnaise, vinegar, oils, spices, herbs, pre-cooked and prepared meals, baby foods and baby milk, cream, butter, cheese, eggs, milk, margarine and spreads.

Sweet Foods

Chocolate, candy, chewing gum, potato crisps, snacks, nuts and dried fruit, sweet and savory bars, cakes, biscuits, crackers, sugar, jam, honey, peanut butter, syrup, bread, crispbread, flour, baking ingredients, breakfast cereals, yoghurt and yoghurt drinks, desserts, ice cream, flavored milk.

Alcoholic Drinks

Beer (including non-alcoholic beer), cider, lager, alcopops, wine, champagne, fortified wines, spirits.

Non-Alcoholic Drinks

Coffee, tea, chocolate and malt drinks, still and carbonated drinks, fruit and vegetable juices, mineral waters.

Household

Detergents, cleaning products, shoe polish, air fresheners, insecticides, foil, cling film and food packaging, light bulbs, batteries (not car batteries), paint, varnish and wood protectors, adhesives.

Home Appliances and Furnishings

House and garden furniture, washing machines, dryers, dishwashers, fridges, freezers, cookers, microwaves, kitchen utensils, appliances and crockery, glassware, bed and table linen, baths, showers and toilets, home decorating and building products, wall and floor coverings, windows and doors, heaters, air conditioners, lamps, clocks, home security products, smoke detectors, tools, garden tools, machinery and products.

Cosmetics and Beauty

Make-up, skin and nail care products, perfumes, eau de toilette and aftershaves, deodorants and body sprays, shampoos and conditioners, hairspray, gel, mousse, dyes, soap, shower and bath products, sun block and tanning products.

Toiletries and OTC Pharmacy

OTC medicines and tablets, vitamins and herbal remedies, diet supplements and products, insect repellents, adhesive plasters, skin remedies, anti-hair loss lotions, condoms, pregnancy tests, other pharmaceutical products, hairbrushes, combs, wigs, toothpastes, toothbrushes, mouthwashes, toilet paper, tampons and sanitary towels, tissues, diapers, razors and shaving products, hair removal products.

Clothing, Footwear, and Accessories

Day, evening and nightwear, underwear, tights and stockings, footwear, sportswear, clothing fabrics and sewing materials, jewelry, watches, luggage, handbags, fashion and designer sunglasses and spectacle frames.

Miscellaneous

Pet food and pet care products, gifts and greetings cards, pens and personal stationery, tobacco and associated products.

Cars

Including jeeps and 4-wheel drives.

Other Vehicles, Auto Products, and Services

Pick-up trucks, vans, lorries, motorbikes, tires, spare parts, accessories including in-car hi-fi, gas/petrol stations, petrol, oil, breakdown and servicing companies, car dealers and car finance and leasing.

Home Electronics and Audio Visual

Televisions, video players, blank audio and video tapes, cameras, video cameras, film, hi-fi, personal stereos, CD players and minidiscs, iPods, home computers, DVD players, personal phone equipment including mobile phones and pagers.

Retail Stores

Department and specialist stores including Ikea, store cards, supermarkets, DIY stores, drugstores, opticians, hairdressers, beauty salons, laundry service, estate agents, photo-processors, TV, video and other rental stores, mail-order companies and catalogues.

Restaurants and Fast Food Outlets

Travel, Transport, and Tourism

Airlines, train and bus companies, ferry and cruise lines, travel agencies, tourist boards, hotels, resorts, city and country promotion, car hire, travel passes.

Entertainment and Leisure

Leisure and theme parks, gyms, health and diet clubs, sporting events, music festivals, orchestras and instruments, exhibitions and shows, nightclubs, bars, museums, art galleries, cinemas and theatres, sports equipment, bicycles, boats and caravans, toys, board games, computer games, PlayStation, Xbox, Game Boy, etc., lotteries, gambling, golf and country clubs.

Publications and Media

Newspapers, magazines, books, records, CDs, cassettes, DVDs, TV and radio stations, networks and programs, encyclopedias and correspondence courses.

Banking, Investment, and Insurance

Banks, building societies, credit cards, current and savings accounts, mortgages and loans, investment companies, personal, health and building insurance, car insurance, pension and retirement plans, buildings development and road construction, real estate investment.

Business Equipment and Services

Business computers and software, photocopiers, fax machines, business phone equipment, office furniture and stationery, courier services, employment agencies, office cleaning services.

Advertising and Media

Advertising agencies, production companies, use of advertising, advertising effectiveness, website design, awards competitions.

Other Business to Business

Advertising that normally appears in trade magazines, e.g., agricultural, industrial and aviation advertising.

Healthcare and Prescription Drugs

Private healthcare and clinics, optical, medical and dental services, prescription drugs, hospital and dental equipment, psychiatrists, sex therapists, plastic surgeons, etc., contact lenses, hearing aids.

Commercial Public Services

Telecommunications services, internet service providers, yellow pages, directories, postal services, electricity, gas, power and water companies, private schools and colleges.

Corporate Image

Non-product based company image, competition and event sponsorship, Christmas messages, company mergers, flotations and relocation, TV program sponsorship.

Public Health and Safety

Anti-smoking, anti-drugs, anti-drink driving, road safety, health, hygiene, Aids awareness.

Public Awareness Messages

Political and religious messages, unions, associations, environmental awareness, government and forces recruitment, state education, racial, ethnic and disability awareness, sex equality.

Fundraising and Appeals

Charities, funds, volunteers, Red Cross, blood and organ donation.

....

Exercise: **create a new book in a week**[*] **(hand-drawn ads). Preferably as a team, produce seven print campaigns, from which the best five are selected. Note to instructors/teachers: work with a reputable agency to create the briefs and critique the final work. As an incentive for the students, offer a placement/internship to the team with the best portfolio.**

....

[*]Allow two weeks for non-portfolio schools (i.e., where students are expected to take non-ad classes).

The Job Pitch

Job Title

You have to decide whether you are pitching yourself as a copywriter/art director (with a preference for copy), or an art director/copywriter (with a preference for art direction).

During the first five years or so put "Junior…" (or nothing at all) in front of one of the above titles on your self-promotional pieces. *Never* put "creative director," unless you have truly been the creative director of an account and/or team(s).

Job Contract

There are two basic types of contract, "temp" and "perm" (temporary and permanent). Temporary jobs are also known as "freelance," and vary from a few hours of work to a few months (and possibly longer). A permanent position is also known as "full time." A third type of contract is "part time," which is usually permanent, sometimes temporary. Some positions are even called "temp to perm," meaning that if they like you they *may* offer you a full-time job. (But don't count on this, because it may be cheaper for them to keep hiring freelancers without having to pay extra health benefits, etc.)

Where to Pitch

The different types of agencies are below the line, or above the line, or full service/multimedia/through the line. "Below the line" means they deal with direct response and related media; "above the line" focuses on the traditional non-direct media of print, TV, and radio; and "through the line" provides both above and below, including interactive media. Find out how each company describes itself: advertising agency, design firm, ad/design hybrid, advertising and marketing company, etc. Whatever the type of agency, be sure to view the quality of their website (and, of course, their creative work) before you approach them.

Size of Agency

Size depends on the number of employees, the accounts, and the billings. Even though no two agencies are the same, size largely determines the culture of the agency (e.g., what the people are like, how good their creative work is, how they treat their employees, etc.) Note that smaller agencies aren't necessarily less "political." For as someone once said, "politics is a room with three people."

Location

As advertising continues on its global path, it's harder to spot an ad from a particular country, state, or city. So before you start determining where you would be willing to move to, research the type of work undertaken by agencies in each location (current awards books, ad publications, and websites are a good place to start). Better yet, ask someone who has had firsthand experience. You may be surprised what you discover—in a good and bad way.

How to Pitch

- **"Cold calling" via email, phone call, mailers:** this is a necessary evil when looking for most jobs. It requires lots of energy and a thick skin. It's very much a "law of averages" game, so keep trying. Look in awards books. Send a simple email to someone whose work you admire.

- **Follow ups:** don't be afraid to hassle prospective employers (within reason). Ad folk are very busy people and usually need chasing up and reminding.

- **Personal contacts (family, friends, etc.):** connections go a long, long way in advertising. Often the reason that there are so few job vacancies advertised is because someone has recommended and hired their friend or cousin before the job has even been advertised!

- **HR departments and creative recruiters:** these are common in the US (especially in the larger agencies), and less so in Europe. The theory is, a creative recruiter in the Human Resources department can "weed out" the bad books, and pass on the good ones to creative directors/teams. This division of labor saves time and effort for the agency, but can be very frustrating for job hunters because creative recruiters constantly have to double guess what the creative director may be currently looking for. And as we all know, advertising is very subjective. Therefore, if there is a way to avoid the HR department altogether, do it. (But be careful, these people often have a lot of power at the agency.)

- **Creative directors, creative teams, and creative individuals:** if you can get to see anyone at an agency with your book, try to see the top creative person—the executive creative director. Next is a group creative director/head, then a senior creative team, etc. If these people like your book, they can always pass it onto the ECD. If you see an individual "creative," make sure he/she is the right half (depending on whether you are a copywriter or an art director).

- **Headhunters and employment agencies:** like agencies, there are good headhunters and employment agencies, and there are not so good ones. Recommendations are usually the best thing. Above all, find one who truly understands the *creative* side of advertising, and one who specializes in your level of experience (some deal exclusively with seniors, some with only juniors, etc.) If none of them are getting your book out, go to another headhunter. They may make you feel that you are legally bound to them, but you are not. The bottom line is…you need work! Finally, if you're a freelancer, don't tell a headhunter where you are/have been working unless you really have to. If you do, don't be surprised to find a pile of competing books in reception the next day! So if a headhunter ever asks where you're working, just say it's a pitch and you've been told not to divulge any information.

Dropping Off Your Portfolio

If someone requests to see a "physical book," be sure to tell them when you'd like it back. Otherwise people will end up sitting on it for weeks (sometimes literally!) To prevent things getting lost, make sure it's in a sturdy, closable, clearly labeled case.

"Creative" Mailers and Stunts

Only attempt these if you have a great idea. In general, creative directors/recruiters find them annoying or contrived—but there's always the exception. A well-designed leave-behind/ahead or mini-book (in snail-mail or email/pdf format) can be a good enough opener for setting up an interview, etc.

Basic Book "Dos" and "Don'ts"

- **Do** have "macced up," finished-looking ads that show clear communication and good use of typography and visual branding across a range of products and services.

- **Do** make sure the size and/or proportion of your posters and press ads are exact.

- **Do** put your name and contact details clearly on the cover, showreel, etc.

- **Do** send a brief thank you note after each interview (preferably a handwritten one, or otherwise an email).

- **Don't** EVER have pixilated images (photos, illustrations, or logos).

- **Don't** present spreads on two pages with sleeve holes/binder rings down the middle of the ad.

- **Don't** always do ads that look like typical ads.

Dealing with Subjective Feedback

In advertising, everyone has an opinion. Some people may hate your campaign/book, and some may love it. Both views are valid. In fact, vague indifference is probably less useful to you. To find the general consensus about your work, keep showing it to people you respect in the industry. Listen, and then decide which advice you agree with—and then act upon it. You'll know when your book is good when *most people like most of your book.* (Or when every piece of work has won a One Show Gold. Note: some headhunters like to cheat beforehand by looking at your résumé/cv to see which ads have won awards.)

Internships and Placements

Some schools believe that a good portfolio is all you need to land your first job. But unfortunately it's no guarantee. People don't just hire books. They hire people…*hungry* people. Therefore, I believe it can't hurt to pursue internships actively during your time at college. In fact, I've found that the students who are the first to get a "proper" advertising job after they graduate are usually the ones with at least one or two internships already under their belts. Note: some schools assign internships for "worthy" students during the academic year.

The Benefits of Internships

- Boosts your résumé/cv and increases your chances of future employment
- Gives you real world experience (how the ad business works, what the people are like, etc.)
- Early indication of whether advertising is "right for you"
- Early indication of whether the creative department is "right for you"
- Relatively easy to find (compared to full paying, permanent positions)

General Tips

- Start interning as early as possible (i.e., your first year at college)
- Contact all types of agency. (Start with large, established agencies that have popular, organized internship programs. Then try award-winning agencies of all sizes. Finally, contact small obscure agencies.)
- Find out exactly whom you should contact within each agency.
- Start by sending your résumé/cv and telling them who you are, what and where you're studying, the classes you've taken, and why you want to intern there, etc.
- Find out if you need to send samples of print work (how many, and in what format).
- Find out if your school already has an internship department.
- Some schools will transfer placements into college "credits."
- Intern at different types of agencies. (For examples, see Where to Pitch, page 280.)
- Not all internships are the same (so don't be put off by a bad one).
- To avoid surprises, find out if and what they pay, or if they'll cover travel expenses.
- Don't stay for more than a few weeks, especially on their intern "salary."
- Mix up your résumé with other part-time or holiday jobs (the more unusual the better).
- Once you're there, work harder than anyone else in the creative department!

Note: in the US, "work experience" includes all employment positions and job history, whereas in the UK, "work experience" only applies to internships and placements.

Student Awards

Because of the highly competitive nature of job hunting within the ad industry, I believe that ad schools should encourage their students to enter awards. It boosts a student's confidence, his or her résumé, and the school's reputation. Again, some instructors argue that time is better spent on getting the best book. A good point, but unfortunately not everyone in the business can recognize good work, and they need to see awards as "proof" of talent. Competitions of any type usually recognize the best work. If not, put it in your book anyway. Win or lose, a national (and sometimes international) competition lets students know what the standard is outside their classroom. Plus it's also good practice for working to a strict deadline.

There are lots of student competitions and awards out there, but only enter the best, most recognized ones. These are:

Assigned Brief

One Show College Competition
British D&AD Global Student Awards
AAF's National Student Advertising Competition

Portfolio Work

CMYK magazine *
Graphis New Talent Annual
Lürzer's International Archive
Student ADDY Awards (Local, District, National) *
Art Director's Club of New York

*Entrants predominantly from US schools

Even as a finalist, your work will be printed in these publications for the world to see. Entry fees vary, and some competitions include prize money. (Some advice to instructors: give a competition brief(s) as a graded assignment to all your students, not a non-graded or optional one. And not to your "best" student either [others will often surprise you]. This will increase the quantity—and therefore quality—of work, while highlighting any common, repeat solutions which will be dismissed at the judging too, wasting time, effort, and money. It's a lottery at the best of times, so only submit student work that is fresh and unexpected. And finally, if the school can't pay for their entry fees, try to include it in their course fees. If not, team them up and send the work via a reliable courier company as one package to split costs and save them money.)

Read and Research

Start collecting the names of the agencies and individuals behind any particular ads you like, and make sure to tell them when you contact them. Flattery usually works wonders.

Keep reading industry publications and websites to follow what's happening (who's won or lost an account, etc.)

US Job Websites

These are five of the larger/better ones (some of which include international job listings), but there are many more, including job and internship lists on individual agency sites:

creativehotlist.com
hotjobs.com
craigslist.com
nytimes.com
krop.com

Magazines (country of origin)
Creativity (US)
Adweek (US)
Advertising Age (US)
CMYK (US)
Shots (UK)
Boards (Canada)
Creative Review (UK)
Campaign (UK)
Print (US)

Awards Annuals and Showreels

One Show
Art Directors Club (of New York)
British D&AD
D&AD Student Annual
Cannes International Advertising Festival
Communication Arts—Advertising
Communication Arts—Design
Communication Arts—Interactive
Clios
Archive (Lürzer's International Archive)
AIGA
Campaign Press (end March)

Campaign Posters (mid October)
Graphis
EFFIEs

Related Websites

aaaa.org
adage.com
adcglobal.org
adcritic.com (Creativity)
adforum.com
adfreak.com (part of Adweek)
adrants.com
adsoftheworld.com
adweek.com
aiga.org
bannerblog.com.au
bestadsontv.com
boardsmag.com
brandsoftheworld.com (downloadable logos)
campaignlive.com
canneslions.com
clioawards.com
cmykmag.com
commarts.com
dandad.co.uk
designeducation.ca
effie.org
graphis.com
ihaveanidea.org
logotypes.ru (downloadable logos)
mad.co.uk (Creative Review)
oneclub.org
printmag.com
shots.net

Again, Aim High

I said it at the beginning of this book and I'll say it again: in terms of the quality of your student work, aim high. In fact, aim higher than high. If you virtually want to guarantee getting a job within the creative department of one of the top agencies out there, aim to have work that's even better than the best award-winning work out there. The fact that you don't have to answer to any clients, or deal with agency politics and egos gives you the extra advantage you need to pull it off.

Good luck…

16
Conclusion

I conclude by borrowing someone else's words: Tom Monahan's "40 things," which first appeared in the 40th anniversary edition of *Communication Arts* in 1999. The technology references may need updating, but the overall message and sentiment remain timeless.

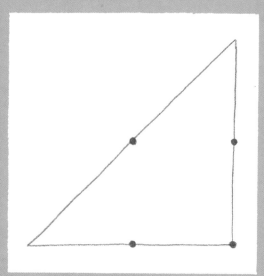

The Four-Dot Test
(see page 14).

40 things that are not concepts

Great film
Finishing on the coast
Photoshop®
A corner office
A huge budget
An amazing photograph
The 60-second version
A killer track
Digital composite
Just like Goodby
Celebrity talent
A gold pencil
A terrific take
Wonderful lighting
An extra camera
A long, impressive job title
A new G3
The version that never ran
Your pet pet-store account
A great spec ad
A custom font
A smaller logo
A fantastic illustration
Claymation®
Pro bono
QuarkXPress®
The 67-second version
Being on the Super Bowl
A title house
Copy fitting
A killer headline
Tasty design
Proprietary music
The director's cut
Wide borders on the proofs
An 18th color
A name director
The bar at the Sunset Marquis
Remix number 34
Shooting in New Zealand

40 things that haven't been concepts, not once, in the past 40 years

Great film
Finishing on the coast
Photoshop®
A corner office
A huge budget
An amazing photograph
The 60-second version
A killer track
Digital composite
Just like Goodby
Celebrity talent
A gold pencil
A terrific take
Wonderful lighting
An extra camera
A long, impressive job title
A new G3
The version that never ran
Your pet pet-store account
A great spec ad
A custom font
A smaller logo
A fantastic illustration
Claymation®
Pro bono
QuarkXPress®
The 67-second version
Being on the Super Bowl
A title house
Copy fitting
A killer headline
Tasty design
Proprietary music
The director's cut
Wide borders on the proofs
An 18th color
A name director
The bar at the Sunset Marquis
Remix number 34
Shooting in New Zealand

40 things to bring a great concept to life, maybe

Great film
Finishing on the coast
Photoshop®
A corner office
A huge budget
An amazing photograph
The 60-second version
A killer track
Digital composite
Just like Goodby
Celebrity talent
A gold pencil
A terrific take
Wonderful lighting
An extra camera
A long, impressive job title
A new G3
The version that never ran
Your pet pet-store account
A great spec ad
A custom font
A smaller logo
A fantastic illustration
Claymation®
Pro bono
QuarkXPress®
The 67-second version
Being on the Super Bowl
A title house
Copy fitting
A killer headline
Tasty design
Proprietary music
The director's cut
Wide borders on the proofs
An 18th color
A name director
The bar at the Sunset Marquis
Remix number 34
Shooting in New Zealand

40 things that can get in the way of a concept, if you're not careful

Great film
Finishing on the coast
Photoshop®
A corner office
A huge budget
An amazing photograph
The 60-second version
A killer track
Digital composite
Just like Goodby
Celebrity talent
A gold pencil
A terrific take
Wonderful lighting
An extra camera
A long, impressive job title
A new G3
The version that never ran
Your pet pet-store account
A great spec ad
A custom font
A smaller logo
A fantastic illustration
Claymation®
Pro bono
QuarkXPress®
The 67-second version
Being on the Super Bowl
A title house
Copy fitting
A killer headline
Tasty design
Proprietary music
The director's cut
Wide borders on the proofs
An 18th color
A name director
The bar at the Sunset Marquis
Remix number 34
Shooting in New Zealand

40 things that won't turn a bad concept into a great concept

Great film
Finishing on the coast
Photoshop®
A corner office
A huge budget
An amazing photograph
The 60-second version
A killer track
Digital composite
Just like Goodby
Celebrity talent
A gold pencil
A terrific take
Wonderful lighting
An extra camera
A long, impressive job title
A new G3
The version that never ran
Your pet pet-store account
A great spec ad
A custom font
A smaller logo
A fantastic illustration
Claymation®
Pro bono
QuarkXPress®
The 67-second version
Being on the Super Bowl
A title house
Copy fitting
A killer headline
Tasty design
Proprietary music
The director's cut
Wide borders on the proofs
An 18th color
A name director
The bar at the Sunset Marquis
Remix number 34
Shooting in New Zealand

40 things that creatives get excited about when the core concept sucks

Great film
Finishing on the coast
Photoshop®
A corner office
A huge budget
An amazing photograph
The 60-second version
A killer track
Digital composite
Just like Goodby
Celebrity talent
A gold pencil
A terrific take
Wonderful lighting
An extra camera
A long, impressive job title
A new G3
The version that never ran
Your pet pet-store account
A great spec ad
A custom font
A smaller logo
A fantastic illustration
Claymation®
Pro bono
QuarkXPress®
The 67-second version
Being on the Super Bowl
A title house
Copy fitting
A killer headline
Tasty design
Proprietary music
The director's cut
Wide borders on the proofs
An 18th color
A name director
The bar at the Sunset Marquis
Remix number 34
Shooting in New Zealand

40 things that creatives work really hard on even when they didn't work hard on the core concept

Great film
Finishing on the coast
Photoshop®
A corner office
A huge budget
An amazing photograph
The 60-second version
A killer track
Digital composite
Just like Goodby
Celebrity talent
A gold pencil
A terrific take
Wonderful lighting
An extra camera
A long, impressive job title
A new G3
The version that never ran
Your pet pet-store account
A great spec ad
A custom font
A smaller logo
A fantastic illustration
Claymation®
Pro bono
QuarkXPress®
The 67-second version
Being on the Super Bowl
A title house
Copy fitting
A killer headline
Tasty design
Proprietary music
The director's cut
Wide borders on the proofs
An 18th color
A name director
The bar at the Sunset Marquis
Remix number 34
Shooting in New Zealand

40 things that usually cost a whole lot more than a great concept

Great film
Finishing on the coast
Photoshop®
A corner office
A huge budget
An amazing photograph
The 60-second version
A killer track
Digital composite
Just like Goodby
Celebrity talent
A gold pencil
A terrific take
Wonderful lighting
An extra camera
A long, impressive job title
A new G3
The version that never ran
Your pet pet-store account
A great spec ad
A custom font
A smaller logo
A fantastic illustration
Claymation®
Pro bono
QuarkXPress®
The 67-second version
Being on the Super Bowl
A title house
Copy fitting
A killer headline
Tasty design
Proprietary music
The director's cut
Wide borders on the proofs
An 18th color
A name director
The bar at the Sunset Marquis
Remix number 34
Shooting in New Zealand

40 things that, if done well, can make sure a great concept gets what it deserves

Great film
Finishing on the coast
Photoshop®
A corner office
A huge budget
An amazing photograph
The 60-second version
A killer track
Digital composite
Just like Goodby
Celebrity talent
A gold pencil
A terrific take
Wonderful lighting
An extra camera
A long, impressive job title
A new G3
The version that never ran
Your pet pet-store account
A great spec ad
A custom font
A smaller logo
A fantastic illustration
Claymation®
Pro bono
QuarkXPress®
The 67-second version
Being on the Super Bowl
A title house
Copy fitting
A killer headline
Tasty design
Proprietary music
The director's cut
Wide borders on the proofs
An 18th color
A name director
The bar at the Sunset Marquis
Remix number 34
Shooting in New Zealand

40 things that the really great advertising creative people of the past 40 years did not build their careers on

Great film
Finishing on the coast
Photoshop®
A corner office
A huge budget
An amazing photograph
The 60-second version
A killer track
Digital composite
Just like Goodby
Celebrity talent
A gold pencil
A terrific take
Wonderful lighting
An extra camera
A long, impressive job title
A new G3
The version that never ran
Your pet pet-store account
A great spec ad
A custom font
A smaller logo
A fantastic illustration
Claymation®
Pro bono
QuarkXPress®
The 67-second version
Being on the Super Bowl
A title house
Copy fitting
A killer headline
Tasty design
Proprietary music
The director's cut
Wide borders on the proofs
An 18th color
A name director
The bar at the Sunset Marquis
Remix number 34
Shooting in New Zealand

Glossary

1-in-10 tool Also known as the law of averages (the more ideas you have, the greater the chance of having a good one).

Above the line The traditional non-direct advertising of print, TV, and radio. See *below the line* and *through the line*.

Account person In advertising this means a person who handles and manages an account (piece of business); an intermediary between the agency and the client. Also called a Project Manager.

Ad Abbreviation for advert or advertisement; a general way to describe an execution. Note: within the industry, ad or advertisement is preferred over advert, which consumers use.

Adcept Not quite an ad, not quite a concept. It's usually a pre-produced image or series of images that conveys a general idea, attitude, approach, or direction that an ad campaign will duly take. See *mood boards*.

Alliteration The occurrence of the same letter or sound at the beginning of several words in succession, e.g., sing a song of sixpence.

Alternative headline A headline that doesn't follow the standard format of a prose-like sentence, e.g., two or more sentences, a list of words, table of information, facts, and figures, a series of questions and answers, letters, numbers, etc.

Ambient media A non-traditional form of media that uses unusual, alternative techniques or places to deliver its message (ambient literally means, "surrounding"). It either uses traditional media in an innovative and interesting way, or it's creating a new media. Also known as under the radar, alternative, unconventional or non-traditional media. See *guerrilla*.

Analogy and visual metaphor Both use one thing to represent another. An analogy is a partial likeness between two things that are often compared to help explain something, e.g., the human heart and a pump. Similarly, a metaphor is the application of a word or phrase to somebody or something that is not meant literally, but is used to make a comparison, e.g., "my boss is a snake." In visual terms, both can include the use of symbols to represent something, e.g., red = anger, dog = loyal. Not to be confused with *visual simile* (see below).

Banner There are two main types of banner. The first is merely a "flag waiver" that provides a quick link to another "landing" site or application, while the second is more interactive in nature.

Below the line Advertising that usually focuses on direct mail/response. See *through the line*.

Binary briefing A method of focused strategic planning that is based on the binary system of 0s or 1s, e.g., a product's advertising can either try to increase its brand share or increase the whole market, but it can't do both.

Blog A portmanteau of "web log," this is a website where entries are usually displayed in reverse chronological order. "Blog" can also be used as a verb, meaning to maintain or add content to a blog. Many amateur blogs have blossomed into powerful, highly influential message boards, attracting the interest of brands.

Book (1) An artist or designer's portfolio. (2) A prestigious advertising awards annual.

Borrowed interest A category of testimonial advertising where a client uses someone or something that is already famous to sell its product or service. Unless there's a relevant reason for such an endorsement, the idea will tend to lack substance; it is merely "borrowing the interest" of that someone or something.

Brand A term that tells you a product is not like anyone else's; it has its own identity. This identity goes beyond rational product differentiation and beyond how a product is advertised or promoted. Because it transcends the physical properties of a product/service, it is sometimes called the product's DNA. A brand can be made up of one or more sub-brands.

Brand loyalty The trusting relationship that a consumer has toward a brand: why he/she chooses one brand over another. It has the potential to last a lifetime, even generations.

Branding (1) A look, feel, and tone that reflects a particular brand. (2) The process of executing, creating (or re-creating) a brand. Note: "visual branding" is just one element of the branding process.

Call to action A line (or more) that tells the reader/viewer/listener the action to take to find out more information, make a donation, etc. This usually consists of a simple telephone number and/or a website address.

Campaign A series of ads that make up a concept/idea, i.e., an idea that has more than one execution—typically three or more. Campaigns are big ideas. Each execution within a campaign should be expressed in the same yet different way. Note: people often incorrectly refer to an ad "execution" as an ad "campaign."

CD-ROMs (Compact Disc Read-Only Memory) A compact disc that contains data accessible by a computer.

Classic layout The print layout otherwise known as the VW layout created by Helmut Krone at DDB around 1960, itself an evolution of a classic three-column Ogilvy layout. Originally intended for single-page press ad, it can be adapted to a spread.

Cliché A hackneyed phrase or idea. Also applies to use of images and visuals.

Client The company, organization or individual for whom an ad is produced.

CMYK The color system used in print production, short for Cyan, Magenta, Yellow, and blacK. Each color is made up of three different percentages of these colors. See *RGB*.

Color palette The choice of color(s) for a design. Many products have strong visual branding simply by owning, and sticking to, a specific color or color palette.

Competition The product's competitors within the marketplace.

Competitive advertising An ad or campaign that directly compares its product to one or more other products in the market. Can be implied or explicit. Also known as comparative advertising.

Concept This leads from the strategy and refers to the thought or argument that is being communicated within a campaign. Sometimes called a campaign thought.

Consecutive (sequential) ads These ads work as a set and can be any identical size, but are usually quarter page or half page ads. Not just "a campaign in a row/in one go," the idea only works if two (or more) ads are read consecutively, one after the other in sequence, often with a twist or product reveal in the final ad.

Contrast and contradiction This is a when a headline is contrasting or contradicting the visual, thereby creating tension and surprise. It's the opposite of headline repeating visual (see below).

Contrasting pair A sentence that uses opposites, e.g., Argos's "Famous names at unheard of prices," Friends of the Earth's "Think globally, act locally." The contrasting pair is a type of "headline twist" (examined in the Print chapter), in that the first part (word or phrase) sends the reader in one direction, and then suddenly sends him/her the opposite way. It's this disarming nature that gives it power.

Copy The words in an ad. Short copy (or short form) is basically headlines, subheads, and taglines. Long copy is the body copy/text, or any design copy of considerable length.

Creative (1) The general term meaning showing use of imagination. (2) A person working in a creative department of an agency. (3) The creative work.

Creative process The order in which advertising is conceived, i.e., strategy, concept, campaign (execution).

Cropping and framing The way in which an art director lays out and visualizes an ad. The "answers" depend on the framing (i.e., the positioning) of the visual, and where and how far to crop (or zoom); a form of "reductionism."

Cut back The technique used in TV and radio where the ad "cuts back" to the action that was interrupted by an end voice over or super, and usually for no longer than a second.

Demonstration ad An approach that focuses solely on ways to show the product benefit explicitly via a "demonstration." A new, clever way to demonstrate the product benefit can actually be the most engaging, direct form of communication. It shows just how good the product is. (Note: do not confuse these ads with the cheesy "product demonstration" infomercials that show obscure or useless inventions.)

Direct visual A visual that relates directly to the headline in some way. Direct visuals are arguably more important than indirect ones because without either the headline or the direct visual, the ad wouldn't make sense. They are also more common than indirect visuals. See *indirect visual*.

Don't tell, show This is the age-old argument for using pictures instead of words. See *theater of the mind*.

Don't write, borrow Sometimes borrowing a piece of writing (as long as it's relevant) can be more effective than creating a new, "scripted" piece. Can be applied to any media.

Double meaning A headline or tagline that has two meanings. These are significantly cleverer and less contrived than rhyming and sound-alike puns because they find and use words that have the same spelling for both meanings, e.g., Labour isn't working.

Double proposition Two benefits in one, e.g., great taste and less filling. To be avoided unless the client demands it, or it's the only logical strategy.

Exaggeration This tool produces an ad that exaggerates the product benefit, but is based on a truth.

Execution An individual ad, usually derived from a campaign idea. Note: execution can also mean the way something is laid out (print ad) or "shot" (TV). Hence, "poor execution" means a bad or sloppy-looking ad.

File type The type of computer file, defined by various suffixes, e.g., .jpg, .pdf.

Generic product A product or service that does not appear to have a Unique Selling Proposition—and therefore is the same as at least one competitor. Also known as a parity product.

Gerunds Words ending in "ing." Too many gerunds make sentences sound complex and unexciting.

Grid Set of units divided across a space or page that functions as the underlying structure to establish maximum order and alignment. The grid used for print is not dissimilar from those used by architects and engineers in a set of plans for a building.

Grid system The thinking (a mathematical formula in essence) that creates a particular grid.

Guerrilla A dramatic form of ambient or alternative media, often involving people, stunts or props. Also known as, or part of, guerilla marketing or guerilla tactics.

Hand-drawn layouts Concepts or layouts produced by pen or pencil (as opposed to computer). Also known as thumbnails, tissues, scamps, loose/tight roughs or comps, depending on the size and/or level of finish.

Headline introducing visual A headline that introduces or "sets up" the visual; the idea or punch line of the ad is "revealed" by the visual. The unexpected is what creates the tension between the two elements.

Headline repeating visual When part of the headline (or the entire headline) is repeating what the visual is already communicating. This is one of the most common mistakes made by beginner advertising students, although there are rare cases when it's needed. Also known as a "see spot run" or "see Janet running" ad.

Headline twist A common technique used by comedians and screenwriters, but can be applied to ads—humorous or serious. It basically starts off by leading the reader/listener's brain in one direction, and then suddenly pulling it back with an unexpected ending, or "twist."

Hierarchy The maximum number of elements in a single print ad is six: headline, sub-headline, visual(s), body copy, tagline, and logo. Hierarchy is order of importance (or "hierarchy") of each element, expressed through the art direction (i.e., the sizing and positioning) of these elements. Also known as most-less-least.

Idea see *concept*

Indirect visual A visual that relates indirectly to the headline in some way, but is often just an art direction piece or a background visual(s) that helps to give the ad a certain look, mood or feeling. See *direct visual*.

Integrated When an idea is translated into more than one form of communication or media (be it advertising, design, or both). It's not just a big idea that translates within one creative area, it's a big idea realized across many areas. Also known as: multimedia, multiple media, mixed media, 360º branding, through the line, innovative marketing (e.g., ambient), and cross channel.

Interactive Media that covers any advertising/design that has been created using digital technology (not to be confused with digital radio, digital TV, etc.) in which the communication demands some form of immediate or ongoing response. Although mostly web based, the term can also include interactive/innovative methods such as ambient media and other guerrilla tactics. Also known as "digital" or "new media."

Interruptive methods Web advertising that interrupts the consumer from their usual activities, e.g., banners, pop ups, over the page animation.

Interstitials An unsolicited page of advertisement on the internet that briefly precedes a selected page.

Invisible thread An imaginary "thread" that helps a piece of body copy flow seamlessly, from line to line, paragraph to paragraph, as if an invisible thread is joining everything up.

Kill your babies A phrase that reminds creatives to get rid of ideas that they like, but aren't working.

KISS Acronym for Keep It Simple, Stupid. The golden rule when it comes to ad concepts.

Legitimate and illegitimate Legitimate forms of online include search-engine advertising, desktop advertising, online advertising directories, advertising networks and opt-in email advertising. The illegitimate side includes spamming (the digital equivalent of "junk [direct] mail").

Linking words/phrases Also known as "transitions," these bridge thoughts and help to make copy flow from one sentence or paragraph to the next, e.g., so, however, in fact.

List of three A common technique used in copy when it appears that two words, facts, phrases, or sentences are too few, and four too many. The third element can give a sentence rhythm, balance, and closure. Also known as "the magic three." See *visual threes*.

Logos There are three basic types of logo: letter form, word form, and picture form. Some are literal, others are more abstract. Also known as "identities" or "marks."

Mandatories (inclusions/exclusions) A list of what should be included or excluded from the advertising executions, usually written at the end of a creative brief.

Marketing The process involved in putting a product or service on the market; it is sometimes defined by the "marketing mix," which is made up of four components called the "4 Ps": product, price, place, and promotion.

Media The term used to describe either a group of mediums (TV, print, radio, etc.) or a single medium (albeit grammatically incorrect). Usually divided into traditional and non-traditional, or offline and online, or analogue and digital.

Mood boards Similar to adepts, except these tend to be a larger collection of stock images and clippings to help convey the overall mood, look, or tone of an ad, plus even the type of consumer they are looking to target. See *adept*.

Mnemonic A "memory aid" that helps people to remember your product or campaign. These can be visual, audio, or both.

Multiple visuals Using a multitude of visuals makes the punch line less immediate. Conversely, the idea might work better with a number of similar visuals to help get the point across.

Mysterious prop An object (or similar) that is brought to a presentation to tease and intrigue the client immediately and will be used later when presenting the work.

New media (1) Digital or interactive media. (2) Any media (digital or analogue) that has not been previously created or defined.

Nod factor The physical response that best communicates to a presenter that the audience (client) is agreeing with the idea.

"One frame" goal A method that forces a creative to keep a TV idea simple; to aim for as close to one frame (two or three is good, too), or at least be in a position to capture the basic idea in a single frame, as if it were a poster, even if the final ad uses more frames to improve the story telling. This is another form of reductionism.

One-shot An execution that is not part of a campaign. One-shots are smaller, solitary, limited ideas that cannot be developed into a campaign (sometimes called a "one-off" ad).

Opposite tool The technique of turning everything (strategies, ideas, headlines, visuals, taglines, art direction) on its head to create something different.

Overnight test The process of stepping away from an idea and coming back to it later with a fresh pair of eyes.

Parity product A product of equal status with one or more competitor. Also known as a generic product.

Pixilation This occurs when the resolution (number of pixels/dots per inch) is not high enough for the size the image is being printed or displayed at, creating a low-quality, "blocky" looking image. For the screen (e.g., the internet), 72 dpi is sufficient, whereas printed work usually requires a minimum of 300 dpi.

PMS (Pantone Matching System) A universal color system used in all forms of design. (Note: U = Uncoated/matte, C = Coated/gloss.)

Post-production The period when the director, editor, and creative team sit down at a post-production "house" to watch, discuss, compile, and edit a commercial.

Posters Billboards and other outdoor posters, transport posters (bus/train shelter ads, exterior bus-side ads, interior posters/subway cards, platform/cross-track posters), scrolling/changing posters (triptych billboards/posters, illuminated sites), vehicle wraps, giant/supersite posters, building posters, and other special builds.

Pre-production meetings (PPM) The meetings before a shoot to go over script, director's storyboard, cast, wardrobe, location, etc. The first meeting is usually between the director and producer and the creative team and agency producer. Then the client is informed about the decisions (and may even request another PPM including themselves and an agency account/project manager).

Press magazine and newspaper ads. (Note: in design, the term "print" can also include collateral material, direct mail, brochures, annual reports, etc.)

Print Print advertising. In this book, it refers to both posters and press ads, but is sometimes used to define poster advertising only.

Problem to solve A particular marketing problem that exists within the business/advertising objective of a strategy statement.

Product/service The client's product or service that is being advertised. Often "product" is used to mean either product or service. It could be due to the way the product is being used, targeted, packaged, distributed, or even advertised.

Proposition Also known as promise, or benefit. See *single-minded proposition*.

Proster A relatively new term that neatly defines the hybrid of a press/poster ad, reflecting the recent trend in visual-led press ads with little or no copy.

Punctuation Used in moderation, it can add richness and texture to body copy, e.g., colon, semi colon, brackets (parenthesis), "quotes," dot, dot, dot…

Push it A popular phrase among creative directors and college instructors. It basically means to tweak, rework, and improve your idea (or headline, visual, copy etc.)

Reductionism The practice of reducing the elements of an ad to the point where the communication still works. Also known as "fat-free advertising."

RGB The color system used in TV or digital production, short for Red, Green, and Blue. Each color is made up of three different percentages of these colors. See *CMYK*.

ROSE REFS An anagram to help summarize the process of writing body copy: Research, Organize, Shape, Edit, Rewrite, Edit, Finesse, Speak.

Same ad three times The syndrome of making the executions within a campaign not distinctive enough. Defining exactly what makes a SATT campaign is not always easy.

Self-promotion The promotion materials produced by an individual or agency to get more work. For an ad student, this includes a résumé (CV), website (URL), and a leave behind.

Single-minded proposition (SMP) The single benefit that the product/service is proposing to/ promising the consumer. Also known as promise or benefit. Do not confuse with USP (see below).

SLIP IT A corny but useful acronym. An ad should try to do at least one of the following: make you smile or laugh, inform, provoke, involve and/or make you think.

Sound effects (SFX) In a commercial this can refer to any non-speaking sound, including a continuous segment of original music (or a cover version), or a composed, commissioned track. It could also be non-music, such as natural sounds that relate to the action or the background/ environment. The term "under and throughout" is often used to describe a sound that carries on "throughout" the commercial and "under" any voice overs and other sound effects.

Spot A single TV ad, either part of a campaign, or a one-shot.

Stock imagery Photography or illustration that is pre-produced rather than specially created for a specific brief or project.

Strategy The overall marketing or selling approach. It is the thinking behind the concept/idea. The strategy (or strategic thought) can come from a proposition/benefit of the product or service, or perhaps the choice of target group/market. It should have an element of distinction (small or large) from the competitions' strategies. All strategies should be written in the form of a strategy statement, or "creative brief." As a result, a strategy is a progression from (and a reflection of) the strategy statement.

Sub-headline (subhead) A line that works directly from/follows the headline, either to complete or explain the idea, or to add some other useful information (in the same way that the first line of body copy might do).

Super A TV term that refers to a piece of text/type that is "superimposed" onto the screen; also known as "title."

Support points The list of points or facts (usually between one and five) that back up the previously defined proposition. A campaign thought can often come from expanding on a specific support point.

Supposition The section of a strategy statement that outlines a relevant product and market background.

Symbol A type of visual metaphor, whereby one thing represents another (basic examples include red = anger, dog = loyal, cheetah = speed). Symbols are a form of shorthand—a good, graphic way to simplify an idea, especially in print.

"Tacked on" product A generic idea that could be for a number of products, i.e., the product is "tacked on" to the ad.

Tagline (or tag) A sentence that expresses the campaign thought. Sometimes it refers to the proposition/ benefit. Often the tag, idea, and proposition are interlinked. It's the last thing you read when viewing an ad. A great tag has an "invisible" equals sign (=) before it; it's the summation of the communication. A working tag can be used until a final version is created. Also known as strapline (UK), theme line, endline, payoff, or slogan.

Target Abbreviation for target group, target market, or target audience. In other words, who the advertising is aimed at. Usually the more you can define the audience, the more effective the advertising will be.

Teaser campaign A series of ads that aim to tease the consumer gradually, the intrigue growing with each execution. The final stage is the "big reveal"—the time when the last piece(s) of the "jigsaw" are added.

Testimonials Advertising that uses a famous or non-famous consumer(s) to favorably report their experiences with the product or service.

Theater of the mind The way in which radio can use imagination more than any other medium (both in terms of the writer, and the listener).

It creates what's known as a "theater of the mind," or "pictures in the mind."

Through the line Multimedia, i.e., both above and below the line advertising, including interactive media. Such agencies often refer to themselves as "full service."

Time length The lengths (in seconds) of a TV or radio script/commercial. Abbreviated to 30" or :30.

Tone of voice The tone in which an ad or campaign is written in (often reflected in the visual tone of the art direction); often dictated by the product's target group, and/or by the product itself, and must be kept consistent throughout a campaign.

Topping and tailing This is when a TV ad works in two sections or halves (of any length), usually broadcast close together during the same ad break— one toward the beginning (top) and one toward the end (tail). Hence "topping and tailing."

Traditional advertising Typically, the media of print, TV, and radio. See *above the line*.

Truisms These are simply life's truths. Sometimes called human truths, these are "facts of life" rather than hard, statistical facts and figures (although those can also be useful when writing ads). Truisms can be used to advertise and sell a product/service successfully because they are: (i) simple, and (ii) hard to argue with.

Type A general term for letters and lettering (letter, word, and sentence displays). From the Greek word "typos," which means "letterform." A typeface is a specific design of an alphabet (e.g., Baskerville, Bodoni, Futura, Times Roman). *See the Execution chapter for a list of typographic terms.*

Unique selling proposition (USP) Those rare products that have a benefit or promise none of its competitors can claim, or have yet claimed. Do not confuse with single-minded proposition (SMP).

Variety proposition Products/ services that have a "something for everyone" benefit. Initially un-singleminded, there are ways to tackle it.

Vignette A brief scene from a movie or a play. A commercial has to tell a "story" in a much shorter space of time, so a vignette (or series of vignettes) is a common and useful technique. Can cover any period in time: minutes, weeks, years, or centuries that would otherwise take too long to show.

Viral effect The digital version of "word of mouth." The web's influence makes it easier to pass on links and files; any online advertising can ultimately become viral (contagious) media. In effect, it's free advertising.

Viral films and viral commercials Two forms of video produced specifically for web viewing, and differentiated by their relative time lengths. Also known as "webisodes."

Visual simile When one thing looks similar to something else (in print advertising when a visual/object looks like something related to the proposition or the product itself). The "likeness" is usually a result of the way an object is cropped, or due to a specific angle or point of view that creates a similar shape or appearance.

Visualization The art of seeing things, often in a fresh or unique way.

Visual threes The visual equivalent to the "list of three" tool is used in copy—two or four visuals look too symmetrical and unnatural, and five becomes too much.

Visual twist A clever spin on an idea or image, sometimes as a result of using the opposite tool. Different from a visual pun.

Visual twos (double visuals) The use of two visuals, as in the case of a "before and after" ad (or a "without the product/with the product"). In this case, you don't need three visuals because the second visual acts as the punch line.

Voice over (VO or V/O) A TV and radio term, it's the "unseen" person's voice that can be heard over the other sound effects, etc. It can be the voice of someone in the commercial, or a third person. MVO = male voice over; FVO = female voice over.

Websites and microsites Websites refer to the main website for a brand. Microsites (or mini sites) refer to sites that are specific to a single message or campaign and therefore separate from the main website.

White space The deliberate negative space in an ad that surrounds a headline and/or visual. The amount will directly affect how the ad is read, plus its tone.

Word puns A play on words, the most contrived being the rhyming pun (e.g., pranks for the memories) and the sound-alike pun (e.g., Czech it out).

Bibliography

Books

Aitchison, Jim, *Cutting Edge Advertising*, Singapore, 2004

The Art Directors Club, Inc., *Mad Ave: Award-Winning Advertising of the 20th Century*, New York, 2000

Burtenshaw, Ken, Mahon, Nik, and Barfoot, Caroline, *The Fundamentals of Creative Advertising*, London, 2006

Craig, James, *Basic Typography: A Design Manual*, New York, 1990

Day, Barry, *100 Greatest Advertisements*, London, 1978

The Design and Art Directors Association of the United Kingdom 1995, *The Copy Book: How 32 of the World's Best Advertising Writers Write Their Advertising*, London, 2000

The Design and Art Directors Association of the United Kingdom 1996, *The Art Direction Book: How 28 of the World's Best Creatives Art Direct Their Advertising*, London, 1996

Dobrow, Larry, *When Advertising Tried Harder*, New York, 1984

Felton, George, *Advertising: Concept and Copy*, New York, 2006

Ford, Rob and Wiedemann, Julius (eds), *Guidelines for Online Success*, London and Los Angeles, 2008

Ford, Rob and Wiedemann, Julius (eds), *The Internet Case Study Book*, Los Angeles, 2010

Heller, Steven, and Ilic, Mirko, *Handwritten: Expressive Lettering in the Digital Age*, New York, 2004

Himpe, Tom, *Advertising Next: 150 Winning Campaigns for the New Communications Age*, London and San Francisco, 2008

Iezzi, Teressa, *The Idea Writers: Copywriting in a New Media and Marketing Era*, New York, 2010

Jewler, A. Jerome, and Drewniany, Bonnie L., *Creative Strategy in Advertising*, USA, 2005

Johnson, Michael, *Problem Solved: A Primer in Design and Communication*, New York, 2002

Monahan, Tom, *The Do-It-Yourself Lobotomy: Open Your Mind to Greater Creative Thinking*, New York, 2002

Müller-Brockmann, Josef, *Grid Systems in Graphic Design*, Switzerland, 1996.

Myerson, Jeremy, and Vickers, Graham, *Rewind: Forty Years of Design and Advertising*, London and New York, 2002

Olins, Wally, *On Brand*, London, 2004

Pricken, Mario, *Creative Advertising: Ideas and Techniques from the World's Best Campaigns*, London, 2002

The Radio Advertising Bureau, *The Radio Advertising Hall of Fame*, London, 2000

Robinson, Mark, *100 Greatest TV Ads*, London, 2000

Sullivan, Luke, *Hey Whipple, Squeeze This: A Guide To Creating Great Ads*, Hoboken, New Jersey, 2003

Williams, Eliza, *This is Advertising*, London, 2010

Magazines, Journals, and Books

Campaign, *Campaign Hall of Fame: The 100 Best British Ads of the Century*, London, 1999

Cosmopulos, Stavros, *Make the Layouts Rough and the Ideas Fancy*, 1983

The One Club, *One. A Magazine: Best of the Past Ten Years*, vol. 7, issue 4, New York, Spring 2004

The One Club, *One. A Magazine: 2007 One Show*, vol. 11, issue 1, New York, Summer 2007

Articles

Cannes International Advertising Festival, *2007 Awards Categories*, 2006, www.canneslions.com

Carter, Earl, "The Spearhead of Branding," *AdSlogans*, 2001, www.adslogans.co.uk

Communication Arts, "Integrated Campaigns," *Communication Arts Advertising Annual*, vol. 47, no. 7, December 2005

Copyopolis, "How to Write an Amazing Website," *Create Magazine*, March–April 2007

Cullingham, Tony, "Binary Briefing," 1995–96 (unpublished)

Cullingham, Tony, "Radio: Communication Characteristics," 1995–96 (unpublished)

Cullingham, Tony, "Six Copywriting Rules," 1995–96 (unpublished)

D&AD, *2007 Awards Categories*, London, 2006, www.dandad.org

Green, Harriet, "The End of the End Line," *Campaign*, London, June 12 1998

Hudder, Tom, "Critique," *CMYK*, no. 27, p. 19, Fall 2004

Jaffe, Joseph, "The History of the Banner," *i-Intelligence*, November 2004

Marcantonio, Alfredo, "How I Write My Copy," 1995–96 (unpublished)

Monahan, Tom, "40 Things," Communication Arts, *Communication Arts Advertising Annual*, vol. 41, no. 1, March–April 1999

Rosenthal, Steven, and Vitale, Frank, "The New iRake," *Jest*, vol. 2, issue 6, pp. 32–33, 2003

Williams, Eliza, "Writing Returns," *Creative Review*, March 2006

Index

Names and Topics

Notes

· ·

ALTOIDS is a registered trademark of Callard & Bowser. This trademark is being used with their kind permission.

MATCHBOX and associated trademarks and trade dress are owned by, and used under license from Mattel, Inc. © 2008 Mattel, Inc. All Rights Reserved. Mattel makes no representation as to the authenticity of the materials obtained herein. The author assumes full responsibility for facts and information about Mattel contained in this book. All opinions expressed are those of the author and not of Mattel, Inc.

The MCDONALD'S ads in this book are used with the permission of McDonald's Restaurants Limited.

PEDIGREE®, DOGS RULE® and other insignia are trademarks of Mars, Incorporated and its affiliates. These trademarks are used with permission. © Mars, Inc. 2008